ROME
& SOUTHERN ITALY
GUIDE

BE A TRAVELER - NOT A TOURIST!

DISCARD

**OPEN ROAD TRAVEL GUIDES SHOW YOU
HOW TO BE A TRAVELER – NOT A TOURIST!**

Whether you're going abroad or planning a trip in the United States, take Open Road along on your journey. Our books have been praised by **Travel & Leisure**, **The Los Angeles Times**, **Newsday**, **Booklist**, **US News & World Report**, **Endless Vacation**, **American Bookseller**, **Coast to Coast**, and many other magazines and newspapers!

Don't just see the world – experience it with Open Road!

ABOUT THE AUTHOR

Having spent more than eight years living in Italy roaming through the country, Douglas E. Morris is the author of Open Road's berst-selling *Italy Guide* and this second edition of *Rome & Southern Italy Guide*. Published in a wide variety of media, Mr. Morris gives you the most accurate, up-to-date, and comprehensive information.

ACKNOWLEDGMENTS

Many people assisted considerably in the development of this book, but I wish to extend my special thanks to Heddi Goodrich for her unique insight into the heart of Naples. My parents, Don and Denise, and my brother Dan were invaluable for their support, information, suggestions, and numerous leads. Special thanks for Alain DeCock's editorial and creative assistance. I am exteremly indebted to Anamaria Porcaro for her intimate knowledge of Rome, as well as Theresa Luis and the MMI class of '76 for their thoughtful insights. And most of all this book is better for the invaluable suggestions and feedback offered by our many readers, including Jack Sawinski, Pamela A. Motta, Hugh L. Curtin, and Senator Paul Simon. Keep your e-mails coming to *Roma79@aol.com*.

BE A TRAVELER, NOT A TOURIST - WITH OPEN ROAD TRAVEL GUIDES!

Open Road Publishing has guide books to exciting, fun destinations on four continents. As veteran travelers, our goal is to bring you the best travel guides available anywhere!

No small task, but here's what we offer:

• All Open Road travel guides are written by authors with a distinct, opinionated point of view – not some sterile committee or team of writers. Our authors are experts in the areas covered and are polished writers.

• Our guides are geared to people who want to make their own travel choices. We'll show you how to discover the real destination – not just see some place from a tour bus window.

• We're strong on the basics, but we also provide terrific choices for those looking to get off the beaten path and *experience* the country or city – not just *see* it or pass through it.

• We give you the best, but we also tell you about the worst and what to avoid. Nobody should waste their time and money on their hard-earned vacation because of bad or inadequate travel advice.

• Our guides assume nothing. We tell you everything you need to know to have the trip of a lifetime – presented in a fun, literate, no-nonsense style.

• And, above all, we welcome your input, ideas, and suggestions to help us put out the best travel guides possible.

ROME
& SOUTHERN ITALY
GUIDE

BE A TRAVELER - NOT A TOURIST!

DOUGLAS MORRIS

OPEN ROAD PUBLISHING

OPEN ROAD PUBLISHING
We offer travel guides to American and foreign locales. Our books tell it like it is, often with an opinionated edge, and our experienced authors always give you all the information you need to have the trip of a lifetime. Write for your free catalog of all our titles.
**Catalog Department, Open Road Publishing
P.O. Box 284, Cold Spring Harbor, NY 11724**

2nd Edition

Text Copyright ©1999 by Doug Morris
Maps Copyright ©1999 by Doug Morris
- All Rights Reserved -

Library of Congress Catalog Card No. 97-66334
ISBN 1-883323-85-1

Front cover photo and top back cover photo Copyright©1998 by Donald Nausbaum, Caribphoto, Toronto, Canada. Bottom back cover photo Copyright©1998 by James Knudsen.

The author has made every effort to be as accurate as possible, but neither the author nor the publisher assume responsibility for the services provided by any business listed in this guide; for any errors or omissions; or any loss, damage, or disruptions in your travels for any reason.

TABLE OF CONTENTS

1. INTRODUCTION   11

2. EXCITING ROME & SOUTHERN ITALY! - OVERVIEW   12

3. ROMAN ITINERARIES   18

4. LAND & PEOPLE   24
Land   24
People   26
Useful Phrases   28

5. A SHORT HISTORY   32

6. PLANNING YOUR TRIP   49
Before You Go   49
   Climate & Weather   49
   What to Pack   50
   Public Holidays   50
   Making Airline Reservations   51
   Passport Regulations   52
   Vaccinations   52
   Travel Insurance   53
   Customs Regulations   53
Getting to Italy   53
   Flying to Italy   53
   Discount Travel Agents   54
   Courier Flights   55
   Diplomatic & Consular Offices in Italy   56
Accommodations   56
   Hotels – What to Expect   56
   Hotel Rating System   57
   Renting Villas & Apartments   58

7. ARRIVALS & DEPARTURES   61
By Air   61
Getting To & From the Airports in Rome   63

8. GETTING AROUND ROME & SOUTHERN ITALY   64
Getting Around Rome   64
Getting Around Southern Italy & Sicily   71

9. BASIC INFORMATION   79

10. FOOD & WINE   87
Food   87
Wine   90
Order Like a Native: Reading an Italian Menu   91

11. BEST PLACES TO STAY IN ROME & SOUTHERN ITALY   94

12. WHERE TO STAY   100
Near Termini Station   101
Trevi Founation/Via Veneto area   109
Piazza di Spagna area   114
Piazza Navona & Campo dei Fiori area   116
Piazza del Popolo to the Pantheon   120

13. WHERE TO STAY   126
Roman Cuisine   126
Trastevere   131
Trevi Founation/Via Veneto area   134
Piazza di Spagna area   137
Piazza Navona & Campo dei Fiori area   139
Piazza del Popolo to the Pantheon   140
Outside of Town   143

14. SEEING THE SIGHTS   145
Ancient Rome   146
    The Imperial Forums   146
    The Colosseum   150
    Arch of Constantine   151
    The Roman Forum, Palatine Hill, & Nearby Sights   151

    Baths of Caracalla   156
    Baths of Diocletian   156
    Campidoglio   157
    Circus Maximus   157
    Catacombs   158
    Altar & Mausoleum of Augustus   158
    Pyramid of Gaius Cestius   158
    Ponte Milvio   159
    Aurelian Wall   159
    Column of Marcus Aurelius   160
    Temple of Hadrian   160
Christian Rome   160
    Castel Sant'Angelo   160
    Saint Peter's   161
    Vatican City   163
Piazzas, Fountains, Monuments, Palazzi & Gardens   164
    Piazza Navona   164
    Piazza di Spagna   165
    Campo dei Fiori   165
    Trevi Fountain   165
    Pantheon   166
    The Borghese Gardens   167
    Vittorio Emanuele II Monument   168
    Isola Tiberina   168
    Ponte Fabricio   168
    Palazzo Barberini   168
    Palazzo Farnese   169
Roman Neighborhoods   169
    Piazza del Popolo   169
    Via Veneto   170
    Via Appia Antica   170
    Trastevere   170
    Jewish Ghetto   171
    Gianicolo   171
Churches   172
    Saint Paul's Outside The Walls   172
    Santa Maria Sopra Minerva   173
    San Pietro in Vicolo   173
    Santa Maria Maggiore   174
    San Giovanni in Laterano   174
    San Clemente   175
    Santa Cecilia in Trastevere   175
    Santa Maria in Trastevere   176

Museums   176
   Capitoline Museum   176
   National Museum – Museo delle Terme   177
   Galleria Borghese   178
   Museum of Villa Giulia   178
   Vatican Museums   179
   Museo della Civilita Romana   182
Walking Tour of Michelangelo's Rome   183
Literary Rome   187

15. NIGHTLIFE   189

16. SHOPPING   196

17. CULTURE & ARTS   209

18. SPORTS & RECREATION   217

19. PRACTICAL INFORMATION   221

20. EXCURSIONS FROM ROME   229
Tivoli Gardens   229
Castel Gandolpho   231
Frascati   232
Lago di Bracciano   238
Cervetri   239
Ostia Antica & Lido di Ostia   240
Rural Retreats Around Rome   244

21. NAPLES & THE AMALFI COAST   247
Naples   247
   Pompeii & Herculaneum   265
Capri   268
Procida   276
Ischia   278
The Amalfi Coast   283
   Positano 283 • Amalfi 287 • Ravello 291 • Salerno 292

22. SOUTHERN ITAY & SICILY   295
Southern Italy   293
   Bari   295
   Barletta   306

Trani   309
   Lecce   311
   Acaia Castle   316
   Gallipoli   317
   Otranto   320
Sicily   323
   Palermo   333
   Trapani   346
   Erice   351
   Agrigento   354
   Siracusa   360
   Mount Etna   368
   Taormina   369
   Isole Eolie   377
      Lipari 378 • Vulcano 381 • Stromboli 382 • Salina 383 • Panarea 384 • Filucidi 384 • Alicudi 385

INDEX   386

MAPS

Note: Rome maps A, B, and C include hotels, restaurants, and sights.

Italy & Neighbors   15
Italy   25
Train Departure Board   77
Rome (Map A)   104-105
Rome (Map B)   118-119
Rome (Map C)   122-123
Rome's Metro   147
Rome (Map D – Sights only)
   152-153
Tivoli   229
Frascati   233
Naples   251
Capri   271
Procida   276
Ischia   280
Bay of Naples & Amalfi Coast
   285

Positano   286
Amalfi   289
Salerno   293
Bari   299
Barletta   307
Trani   309
Lecce   313
Gallipoli   319
Sicily   325
Palermo   335
Trapani   348
Erice   351
Agrigento   355
Siracusa   361
Taormina   371
Isole Eolie   377

SIDEBARS

Italy's Four Seasons 50
Local Festival Days &
   Their Patron Saints 51
Registration by Tourists 52
Home Exchange 60
Improvements for the Year 2000 65
Towed Car? 66
Moped Caution & Rates 67
How to Buy a Metro Ticket 71
EUROSTAR Style 75
Boarding The Right Train 78
US & Canadian Exchange Rates 80
Air Mail Prices 82
Weights & Measures 86
Glossary of Italian Eateries 88
Italian Wines by Region 90
List of Hotels by Map 103
The Ten Best Hotels In Rome 108
Stay in a Convent – For Less 125
Where to Get Your Wine to
   Take Home 129
List of Restaurants by Map 130
Rome's Ten Best Restaurants 134
Ten Must-See Sights in Rome 146
List of Sights by Map 149

Really Seeing the Sights 151
Proper Attire, Please! 161
Free Tours of St. Peter's 162
Rome's Beautification Program 187
When in Rome, Do as the Irish Do! 193
Get Your Tax Rebate on
   Purchases 197
Italian Soccer Attire 201
Italian Deparment Stores 202
Shopping Streets 203
Classy Consignment Shop 204
Alimentari 208
Opera Addresses & Phone
   Numbers 213
Shakespeare's Italy 216
Consider Frascati! 234
Be Alert – Be Aware 248
Napoli Ponta Aperta – Open
Open Door Naples 259
Bari's Santa Claus 296
Stop Over in Bari 297
Car Rental in Sicily 330
It's a Beautiful Night in the
   Valley of the Temples 357

1. INTRODUCTION

If you're looking for great fun, serious relaxation, unparalleled artwork, dazzling museums, ancient civilizations, and world-class accommodations, then Rome is the place for you! Plus, in my humble opinion, Italian food is arguably the best in the world. And don't forget the great wine.

There is so much to see and do that a trip to Rome can be overwhelming. But with this Open Road guide, your days and nights in Italy will be filled with exciting possibilities. I've given you lots of options to tailor the perfect vacation to your particular needs.

If you're looking for that perfect hotel, I've reviewed a huge number of excellent possibilities for you to choose from in every price range. When you get hungry, I've prepared a wide selection of terrific restaurants, with lots of detail about the different regional cuisines and wines from all over Italy. You won't want for things to do and sights to see: imperial Roman ruins, awe-inspiring medieval and Renaissance museums, incredible churches and monuments (including the many wonders of Vatican City), fun and varied neigborhoods to wander about and enjoy a relaxing cappucino, and all manner of piazzas, palazzi, fountains, and gardens – all part of the wonderful tapestry of life that is modern Rome!

And if you have more time, I've also included several chapters worth of terrific excursions, including a number of hill towns and beaches not far from Rome, and a few destinations further afield: the Amalfi Coast; the ancient towns of Pompeii and Herculaneum, preserved through the ages through the volcanic lava flow from nearby Mt. Vesuvius; and extensive coverage of Naples, the isle of Capri, the Amalfi Coast, Southern Italy and Sicily, a beautiful region filled with sleepy fishing hamlets and port cities, old churches, ancient ruins, and undiscovered but (of course) great hotels and restaurants.

So read on, and have the trip of a lifetime in Rome & Southern Italy!

2. EXCITING ROME & SOUTHERN ITALY! - OVERVIEW

ROME & CENTRAL ITALY

Central Italy extends north of Rome, but for the purposes of this book I've included it in this region. Although only a small part of the area is composed of lowlands, central Italy plays an important role in farming and in some branches of industry, specifically wine growing. **Rome** is the main tourist city in Central Italy with great museums, beautiful churches, and great sights to see. Even if you're a seasoned Italy traveler you should make a point of visiting Rome to refresh your memory of the historical beauty of Italy.

Looking for a respite from Rome? **Frascati**, a quaint hill town just outside of Rome, may be the answer. Every year they have a bacchanalian wine festival celebrating the pressing of the local wine. If you're in Rome during September you have to visit, since Frascati is only a 30 minute train ride away. And if you come any other time of year and want to stay in a small, peaceful, medieval hill town, with wonderful views over the surrounding countryside (vineyards), wonderful little wine bars, plenty of great restaurants, and a quaint ambiance that will be remembered forever, Frascati is the place for you.

Besides Frascati, I've also icluded some other Rome area excursions, plus some further afield, such as **Pompeii** and **Herculaneum**, those ancient cities smothered but preserved by the lava and ash of the local volcano; **Naples** and the **Amalfi Coast**; and the quaint fishing towns and villages of **Southern Italy**.

SOUTHERN ITALY & SICILY

Southern Italy is generally considered to be everything south of Rome. There are few lowlands in the area, and only two have importance in farming. One is the lowland surrounding **Naples**, and the other is the lowland of **Apulia**, the segment of the east coast that includes the heel of the Italian boot.

Naples is a vast port city that boasts one of the best museums in Italy. It is a vibrant city, as are all ports, and can be a little dicey at times, if you're out late at night in the wrong place; but if you look beyond its reputation as being less than meets the eye, and look into its heart, Naples is a fun city to visit. In its old section it has the ambiance of a large medieval city with its tiny streets and shops of artisans practicing crafts you would never believe still exist outside of factories. You can find violin makers, doll makers, cabinet makers and similar craftsmen hidden down the side streets and on the second stories of Naple's **centro storico**.

Naples is the perfect stopping-over point on your way to the quaint islands of **Capri**, **Ischia** or **Procida** in the bay of the city; and is the perfect transit stop for visits to **Pompeii** and **Herculaneum**, those ancient cities smothered but preserved by the lava and ash of the local volcano. These two ancient Roman cities have to be visited if you are a student of history. If sunning and funning is more your speed, the towns along the **Amalfi Coast** are a summer vacation paradise. Beautifully set on the hills overlooking the sea, these little towns offer stunning vistas and all types of summer recreation.

Farther south in Italy you can find the resting place of **Santa Claus**. Saint Nicholas is buried in the Church of San Nicola deep in the old town of **Bari**. Down in the heel of Italy's boot is the virtually untouristed **Lecce**, which boasts an array of 17th century Baroque architecture. Besides viewing Lecce's architecture, the city is the perfect jumping-off point to explore the **Salentine peninsula**, which is dotted with medieval fortresses and castles. Exploring the base of Italy's heel is like going back in time, but it is an adventure not to be undertaken except by the most experienced travelers. Southern Italy can sometimes be dangerous if you venture off the beaten coastline and into the hills.

Sicily is a historian's dream. Here you'll find the most complete Greek ruins outside of Greece, located just below the town of **Agrigento**. You can also find ancient medieval hill towns like **Erice**, located 80 km west of Palermo, complete with walls, fortress and even a temple dedicated to Venus. Sicily is also a summer sportsman's paradise, since it has many resorts and is naturally surrounded by water.

THE ETERNAL CITY: THE BEST OF ROME!

Rome has so many options that it's easy to neglect seeing a certain sight, or taking the time to go to a specific restaurant, or making an effort to visit a particular spot late in the evening to enjoy the ambiance and charm. Even though I've itemized the best places to stay, eat, and see while you're here, if you only have a little time, you have to go to the places listed below while in Rome.

Even if you are the furthest thing from being religious, make the effort to see **St. Peter's** and the **Vatican Museum**. This will take the better part of a day if you do a proper tour. No church is more magnificent and no museum is more complete. All others in Rome and the rest of Italy will pale in comparison.

That night, make sure you get to the **Trastevere** district and sample the atmosphere of **La Canonica**, a converted chapel and now a restaurant that also has many tables spilling out along the street. Reserve a spot inside since this may be your last chance to have a meal in a quaint converted chapel. Try their *Spaghetti alla Carbonara* (with a light cream sauce, covered with ham, peas, and grated parmesan cheese) for primo and for your main course sample the light fish dish, *Sogliala alla Griglia* (grilled Sole). Then sojourn to one of the cafés in the **Piazza Santa Maria in Trastevere**, grab a drink, and savor the evening.

During another day it is imperative that you visit **Piazza Navona** and grab an ice cream at one of the cafés, and either lounge on their terraces or take it with you and sit on the edge of one of the fountains. The best vantage point is on Bernini's magnificent **Fontana Dei Quattro Fiumi** (Fountain of Four Rivers). The four figures supporting the large obelisk (a Bernini trademark) represent the Danube, the Ganges, the Nile, and the Plata Rivers. Notice the figure representing the Nile. It is shielding its eyes from the facade of the church facing it, **Santa Agnese in Agone**, which was designed by Bernini's rival at the time, Borromini. An ancient artistic quarrel comes to life everyday in Piazza Navona.

From there, only a few blocks away is the quaint little **Campo dei Fiori** where you'll find one of Rome's best fruit and vegetable markets every day until 1:00pm, except Sunday. Make sure you get here to shop or just to enjoy the atmosphere of a boisterous Roman market.

Here is where you should also enjoy at least one meal, at **La Carbonara** in the square. Even though the name would lead you to believe that the best dish to get is the *Spaghetti alla Carbonara*, I believe you haven't been to Rome if you neglect to sample their exquisite *Spaghetti alla Vongole Verace* (with a spicy oil, garlic, and clam sauce). If you want to sit outside, you should wait until about 2:00pm, after the debris from the outdoor market has been swept up from the piazza. Other dishes you should

EXCITING ROME & SOUTHERN ITALY! – OVERVIEW 15

ITALY AND NEIGHBORS

sample are the *penne all'arrabiatta* (literally means angry pasta; it's tubular pasta made with a spicy garlic, oil, and tomato-based sauce), the *tortellini alla panna* (cheese or meat filled pasta in a thick cream sauce), and any *abbacchio* (lamb) or *maiale alla griglia* (grilled pork).

In the evening, don't miss the **Trevi Fountain**, all lit up and surrounded by locals and tourists strumming on guitars and drinking wine. It's definitely a party atmosphere. Come here with friends or arrive and meet new ones. For one of your evening meals, there's a place somewhat close by a little past the **Spanish Steps**. If you're here in Spring, stop for a minute and admire the floral display covering the steps.

Then move onto **La Capriciossa** where you can sit in a peaceful little piazza just off the Via del Corso, Rome's main shopping street, while you enjoy your meal. They are known for making excellent pizza (only in the evening) as well as preparing perfect Roman pasta dishes and exquisite meat plates. If you haven't already sampled the *penne all'arabiatta*, do so here, and try the succulent *abbacchio arrosto* (roast lamb), another staple of the Roman diet. And to finish the meal, order a *Sambucca con tre mosce* (literally translated, it means a sweet liquor with three flies, but it actually uses three coffee beans). Remember to bite into the beans as you have the sweet liquor in your mouth. The combination of tastes is exquisite.

There is obviously much more to do in Rome than this, but if you only have a little time, make sure you get to the places mentioned above. Then you can say you were truly Roman for a short while.

EXPERIENCE HISTORY

Home to the ancient world's most powerful empire, Italy is awash in history. Daily life revolves around ruins thousands of years old. Modern buildings incorporate ancient structures into their walls. Medieval streets snake through most Italian cities. In Italy you can see the tapestry of history woven directly in front of you. Museums abound with ancient artifacts, beautiful paintings, and stunning sculpture.

You can easily spend an entire trip roaming through museums – or for that matter inside the beautiful churches where you'll see some of the most exquisite paintings and sculptures anywhere on earth!

A FEAST FOR THE EYES!

Even though you could spend an entire trip inside museums or churches, if you decided to do so you would miss out on what makes Italy such a wonderful vacation: its natural beauty, charm, and ambiance. Being in Italy is like walking through a fairy tale. The old winding streets, twisting around the quaint refurbished buildings, leading to a tiny piazza centered with a sparkling fountain all seems like something out of a dream. And you'll find a similar scene in virtually every city you visit in Italy.

FOOD & WINE

But a feast for the eyes is not all you'll get. Italy has, arguably (pipe down, you Francophiles!), the best food you'll find anywhere in the world. In most cases it's simple food, but with a bountiful taste. Take, for example, a Roman favorite: *abbacchio arrosto*. This is a succulent lamb dish slowly cooked over an open flame until perfectly prepared. It is usually accompanied by *patate arrosto*, roast potatoes cooked with rosemary, olive oil, and salt that makes my mouth water just thinking about them.

And since Italy is surrounded on almost all sides by water you can sample any flavor of seafood imaginable. Usually caught the same day,

EXCITING ROME & SOUTHERN ITALY! - OVERVIEW 17

especially in the small towns along the sea, the seafood in Italy will have you coming back for more.

And don't forget the pasta. You'll find all shapes and sizes covered with sauces of every description and variety. Regions are known for certain pasta dishes and when there you have to sample them all. The area around Bologna is known for the production of the best ham in the world, *Prosciutto di Parma*, which is fed from the scraps of the magnificent cheese they make in the same region, *Parmiggiano Reggiano*. Both of these foods feature prominently in *spaghetti alla bolognese* – smother mine with the locally made parmesan cheese, *Parmiggiano Reggiano*!

To wash down all these savory dishes you need look no further than the local wine list. Italian wines may not be as full-bodied as French or California wines, but they have an intimate, down to earth, simple taste. Order from the wine list or be adventurous and get a carafe of the house wine, which is usually delicious, and more often than not comes from the local vineyards you saw outside the city as you arrived.

SPORTING ACTIVITIES

If you've noticed your waistband stretching a little from all the wonderful food and wine you've been enjoying, have no fear – Italy has plenty of activities for you to shave off some of those unwanted pounds. Not far from Rome and the towns in Southern Italy are wonderfully clear water and beaches all along the **Mediterranean Sea** and the **Adriatic Sea**.

You can go waterskiing, snorkeling, skin diving, sailing or just lie on the beach and sunbathe. Many vacation beaches are topless today, an unheard of activity ten years ago, so you'll be treated to an added adventure either trying it or enjoying it.

There are also a number of top-level golf courses not far from Rome, plenty of tennis courts, horseback riding in the country, fishing in lakes and sailing in the seas.

3. ROMAN ITINERARIES

If you only have a short period of time in **Rome** and you want to fill it up with the best sights, restaurants, hotels, cafes at which to lounge, and pubs from which you can crawl back to your bed, all you have to do is follow the itineraries listed below. The hotels, sights, and restaurants mentioned are all described in more detail in the Rome chapter. Simply refer to this chapter to more fully plan your Roman adventure.

The places listed in these itineraries are among my favorites in Rome, but there were plenty of close calls! So follow my advice if you wish, or plow through my chapter on Rome and find the perfect itinerary for you.

THE PERFECT THREE DAYS
Day One
This is going to be a somewhat slow day since you'll have just arrived and will be slightly jet lagged.
- Arrive on direct flight to Rome's Leonardo da Vinci airport at 8:00am.
- Take a cab to the **Hotel Locarno** near **Piazza del Popolo**, shower and unpack.
- Stop at the cafe next to the excellent restaurant **Dal Bolognese** in the Piazza del Popolo and grab a cappuccino, cafe, or espresso to get you going.
- Take the second road on your left, the **Via del Babuino** to the **Spanish Steps**.
- Get your picture taken while you lean over and grab a drink from the fountain in front of the steps.
- Walk to the top of the steps for the magnificent view over the city
- It should be about lunch time now, so walk back down the steps, cross the street, and take a left into the third street at the edge of the piazza, **Via delle Croce**. Follow this to the end, find an outside seat at the superb local restaurant **Osteria del Tempo Perso**, at Via del'Oca 43. Try any of their exquisite Roman pasta specialties – *arrabiata*, *amatriciana*, or *vongole verace* – or the ever so succulent *tagliatelle ai funghi porcini*.

ROMAN ITINERARIES 19

- After lunch it should be about nap time. But remember to only take a 2-3 hour nap, wake up right away, take a shower and get out again – otherwise you'll sleep until 10:00pm and be wide awake because jet-lag will have set in.
- Now it's time to explore the streets around the **Piazza di Spagna**, **Via della Croce**, **Via del Corso**, **Via dei Condotti** and admire all the different shops.
- After shopping/exploring, take a small walk (or short cab ride) to **Piazza Navona**.
- Stop at **Le Tre Scalini** and sample some of the world famous Italian *gelato* (ice cream). If you sit at the tables outside the cost will double or triple.
- If some liquid refreshment is more your style, exit the Piazza Navona on the other side, cross the **Via Vittorio Emanuele**, visit the **Campo dei Fiori** (where they have a superb market in the mornings which we'll get to in a few days) and stop in at the **Drunken Ship** for some Guiness, Harp, or Kilkenny. Enjoy the lovely English speaking female bartenders. and have a few ales for me.
- From here you are within striking distance of **Trastevere**, the place for Roman nightlife, on the other side the river. Cross the pedestrian bridge **Ponte Sisto** and make your way to **Piazza Santa Maria** in Trastevere.
- If it's too early for dinner (7:30pm or 8:00pm is the beginning time) stop at one of the outdoor cafes and replenish your fluids.
- For dinner stop at **La Canonica** just outside of the piazza. Here you should also try one of the typical Roman pasta specialties, *arrabiata, amatriciana*, or *vongole verace*; as well as some *sogliola alla griglia* (grilled sole) for seconds.
- After dinner, if you're not too tired, let's go to the **Trevi Fountain**. It is beautiful lit up at night. To do so walk down the long road leading to the Piazza, **Via della Lungaretta**, to the large main road **Viale Trastevere**. From here catch a cab to Piazza Colonna, near the fountain. The sidestreets leading up to the fountain are usually packed and the cab wouldn't be able to move through the crowds anyway. Go across the big road, Via del Corso and take Via di Sabini to the fountain.

Day Two
- Today is museum day. Start off at the best in the city, the **Vatican Museum** and the **Sistine Chapel**. This should take you all morning.
- Instead of a long sit-down meal, stop at one of the cafes around the museum and St. Peter's and order a light snack. My suggestion is getting a *Medallione*, a grilled ham and cheese concoction that is tasty

and filling. You don't order at the counter, you first pay for your order with the cashier (order your drink at the same time), then bring the receipt up to the counter and tell the bartender what you'll have. A good tip to leave is about L500.
- After your meal, let's explore **St. Peter's**. Remember to dress appropriately (see *Seeing the Sights* chapter). Walk up or take an elevator to the top to get a great view over St. Peter's Square.
- Once done here, which should be late afternoon, let's stop at **Castel St. Angelo** and explore the ancient armaments museum and fortifications of the fortress that protected the Vatican in the past.
- Now it's time to go home for a 2-3 hour nap, if you need it.
- Dinner tonight is at the nearby **La Buca di Ripetta**, on Via di Ripetta, where you should try either the *Lasagna al Forno, Saltimbocca alla Romana,* or the *Ossobuco di Vitello.*
- After dinner, if you missed the **Trevi Fountain** last night, go there tonight. It's about a 20 minute walk (if you're staying at the Locarno), or a short cab ride away.
- If not, you must return to the **Piazza Navona** to soak up the ambiance there at night with its fountains lit up. Either bring your own bottle of wine and sit at one of the benches or grab a table at one of the cafes and enjoy a beautiful Roman evening.

Day Three
- Time to explore some serious ruins. On the way, stop at the market in the **Piazza Venezia**.
- From here make your way down **Via dei Foro Imperiali** to the entrance to the Forum on the right hand side. Up ahead you'll see the **Colosseum**, our next destination.
- View the Colosseum.
- Lunch. Time to hail a cab and go back up the Via dei Foro Imperiali, to Piazza Venezia, then on to **Gino ai Funari** on Via dei Funari. This is a small local place in the Jewish Ghetto that makes the Roman pasta specialties perfectly (*carbonara, amatriciana, vongole verace, and arrabiata*). Or you can try the *conniglio alla cacciatore* (rabbit hunter style made with brandy tomatoes and spices). It is superb.
- After lunch, before we go back up the Via di Teatro Marcello to go to the second best museum in Rome – the Campidoglio – since it's so close by, let's pay a visit to the **Isola Tiberina**.
- After a quick exploration of this island, let's get to the **Campidoglio**. Remember to find *La Buca della Verita*. This should take most of the afternoon.
- When completed, make your way to the **Pantheon** (or back to the hotel if you're tired) and sit at one of the outside cafes and savor the sight

ROMAN ITINERARIES

of one of Rome's oldest buildings in a quaint medieval square. If it is super hot, sit by the pillars at the entrance of the Pantheon since it is always wonderfully cool there.
- Back to the hotel to freshen up for your meal this evening at **La Carbonara** in **Campo dei Fiori**. Remember you were here on Day One at the Drunken Ship? They make the best *spaghetti alla vongole verace* I've ever had.
- You can stay in Campo dei Fiori for the whole evening and take in the sights and sounds of one of Rome's most popular nighttime piazzas. Most evenings they have live bands playing. You've already been to Navona, Santa Maria in Trastevere, and Trevi, the other three great piazzas where you can get a true taste of Roman nightlife.

THE PERFECT FOUR DAYS

Follow the above itinerary for the first three days, and add Day Four immediately below.

Day Four
- Time to go to church (you don't have to pray if you that's not your thing). To get to these churches you're going to need to take the metro and buses or rely on Roman taxis. Our first stop is **Saint Paul's Outside the Walls**. Get your picture taken in the middle courtyard with one of the trees in the background. When you next return to Rome, do the same thing and trace how long it has been by how far the tree has grown. My family has been doing that for over 40 years now.
- From here cab it back into town to **Santa Maria Sopra Minerva**.
- Next is **Santa Maria Maggiore** near the train station.
- On to **San Pietro in Vincoli** close to the Colosseum.
- Located between the Colosseum and San Giovanni in Laterano is our next stop, **Church of San Clemente**
- Our next church is the cathedral of Rome, which isn't St. Peter's, it is **San Giovanni in Laterano**.
- Time to get ourselves to Trastevere for a late lunch, and **Sabatini's** is the perfect choice. Here we can sit in their large outdoor terrace on the Piazza and enjoy a fine meal.
- Most people don't come to Trastevere to look at churches. They come for the more bacchanalian aspects of the area. But we religious types have first come to see **Santa Maria in Trastevere** in the same piazza as Sabatini's, then the **Church of Santa Cecilia in Trastevere**.
- Since you've been traveling all over town, let's return to the hotel for brief siesta, since everything is closed anyway, or stop off at **Babbington's Tea Room** near the Spanish Steps for a "cuppa."

22 ROME & SOUTHERN ITALY GUIDE

- When the stores re-open, let's do some antique shopping on the nearby streets of **Via del Babuino** and the **Via Margutta**, Rome's best for antiques.
- If you want to buy a book, stop into the **Lion Bookshop** at Via del Babuino 181.
- For dinner try the ever popular **Otello Alla Concordia** at nearby Via Della Croce 81, where you can get some of the most succulent *abbacchio alla griglia* anywhere in Rome.
- For an after-dinner vino, sample **Antica Bottigleria Placidi**, a great wine bar on the same street.

THE PERFECT SEVEN DAYS

Follow the above itinerary for the first four days, then add Days Five through Seven immediately below.

Day Five

- If you don't feel as if you are able to truly appreciate some of the activities listed above, by all means return and enjoy them today, but before you run off and do that we're all starting together by waking up early and going back to the **Campo dei Fiori** to see how different it is in the mornings. Here you'll find one of Rome's best food and flower markets. Don't miss it.
- For lunch, return back into the city and find this great place located between Piazza Navona and the Spanish Steps, Orso "80" at Via dell'Orso. Here they make great *spaghetti alla carbonara* as well as the *abbacchio alla griglia*.
- Now the fun begins. We're going to a terrific town – **Frascati**. If we are lucky and it's September, we may stumble into their wine festival (and definitely stumble out).
- To get to Frascati, go to the train station, buy a ticket, go to track 27, board the small local train (takes 35 minutes and costs L6,500), and enjoy the scenery along the way.
- Enjoy the views, exploring the winding medieval streets and the relative peace and quiet compared to Rome. Don't forget to search out some of the little wine stores. My favorite is **Cantina Via Campania**.
- For dinner, let's give the wild and raucous **Pergatolo** at Via del Castello 20 a try. If you're into something more sedate, **Zaraza** at Viale Regina Margherita 21 should be your choice.
- Once dinner is done, make your way back to Rome.
- After arriving at the train station, let's go to a nearby Irish pub, **The Fiddler's Elbow** on Via dell'Olmata, that serves up fine ales, an authentic atmosphere, English conversation, and a fun evening to end an adventurous day.

ROMAN ITINERARIES 23

Day Six
- Let's start off the day at the nearby **Mercato de Stampe**, at Piazza Fontanella, which is open from 9:00am–6:00pm Monday through Saturday. Here you can find maps, stamps, books, almost anything on the intellectual side.
- When done here, take a cab or stroll the short distance to the **Piazza Barberini** at the base of the **Via Veneto**.
- First we'll stop in the **Palazzo Barberini**, located on the Via Quattro Fontane that leads up the hill from the Piazza. This palazzo is the home of the **National Portrait Gallery**.
- After soaking up the art, walk back almost to the piazza to a small street named Via degli Avignonesi. At the end of it you'll find a great little local place, **Trattoria Da Olimpico**. Stop here for lunch.
- Once lunch is over go back up the street to the piazza, and start up Via Veneto, the street that embodies the good life – *La Dolce Vita*. Halfway up you'll pass by the **American Embassy** on the right hand side. Stop at one of the cafes for refreshment.
- At the top of the steps, go through the massive gate, cross the street and enter the beautiful park, **Villa Borghese**. Let's take a leisurely stroll through the gardens to the **Galleria Borghese** that has portraits, paintings, and sculptures galore.
- Follow the roads to the other entrance to the park and back to the hotel
- Dinner tonight is at **Dal Bolognese** in the Piazza del Popolo. Try their *fritto misto*, a fried mix of veggies, cheese, and meat.
- End the evening by going to the top of the **Spanish Steps** for a view over the city at night.

Day Seven
- Assuming today is a Sunday, you must visit the **Porta Portese** market that lines the Tevere every Sunday. Starting at the **Ponte Sublico**, you'll find all sorts of interesting antiques and junk here. A must visit if you're in Rome on a Sunday.
- After the market, and since it is Sunday and everything is closed (that's right, no museums, hardly any shops, etc.) except restaurants, it's time to return to the restaurant you liked best that you tried before. I always do this wherever I travel. It ensures that one of my last meals is going be great, and it makes me feel somewhat like I belong. Go to one with an outside terrace like **La Carbonara** in Campo dei Fiori.
- Return to your hotel and pack, and afterwards go for a stroll around your new neighborhood.
- End your stroll at the top of the **Spanish Steps** again. Tonight we're going to the terrace restaurant in the **Villa Hassler** for a scenic and romantic last dinner in Rome. Try their specialty *abbacchio al forno*.

4. LAND & PEOPLE

LAND

From the top of the boot to the toe, Italy is a little more than 675 miles (1,090 kilometers) long. The widest part, in the north, measures about 355 miles (570 kilometers) from east to west. The rest of the peninsula varies in width from 100 to 150 miles (160 to 240 kilometers). The peninsula of Italy has a total area of about 116,000 square miles (300,400 square kilometers).

A mountainous country, Italy is dominated by two large mountain systems – the **Alps** in the north and the **Apennines** throughout the peninsula. The Alps, which are the highest mountains in Europe, extend in a great curve from the northwestern coast of Italy to the point where they merge with Austria and Slovenia in the east. Just west of the port city of Genoa, the **Maritime Alps** are the beginning of the chain. Despite mighty peaks and steep-sided valleys, the Alps are pierced by modern engineering marvels of mountain passes that have always allowed commerce between Italy and its northern neighbors to flow freely. These highway and railroad tunnels provide year-round access through the mountains.

The Apennine mountain system is an eastern continuation of the Maritime Alps. It forms a long curve that makes up the backbone of the Italian peninsula. The Apennines extend across Italy in the north, follow the east coast across the central region, then turn toward the west coast, and, interrupted by the narrow Strait of Messina, continue into Sicily.

There are numerous smaller mountains in Italy, many of volcanic ancestry, and thankfully many extinct. The two active volcanoes, **Mount Vesuvius** near Naples and **Mount Etna** in Sicily, are the only active volcanoes on the European continent. Maybe that has something to do with the heated Italian temperament?

LAND & PEOPLE 25

PEOPLE

The Italian people are considered to be one of the most homogeneous, in language and religion, of all the European populations. The only significant minority group live in the region called **Trentino-Alto Adige**. These Alpine valleys of the north once made up part of the Austrian province of Tyrol, and the several hundred thousand German-speaking residents still refer to their homeland as South Tyrol. The region was incorporated into Italy after World War I, and both Italian and German are official languages in this region. Obviously, the people of the region have developed their own sense of identity – part of, but separate from, the rest of Italy.

One much smaller minority also lives in northern Italy. This group, the **Valdotains**, dwells in the region called **Valle d'Aosta** in the northwestern corner of the country, and also has two official languages, Italian and French.

About 95 percent of the Italian people speak Italian, while members of the two aforementioned groups make up the other 5%. For more than seven centuries the standard form of the language has been the one spoken in Tuscany, the region of central Italy centered around Florence. However, there are many dialects, some of which are difficult even for Italians to understand. Two of these principal dialects, those of Sicily and Sardinia, sound like a foreign language to most Italians. If you have lived in Italy for a while, it is easy to pick the different accents and dialects and pinpoint where someone is from.

But all this is just about where they live and how they speak. What are the Italians like?

Shakespeare was enamored with Italians and things Italian, as is evidenced by many of his plays taking place in Italy. And when he wrote "All the world's a stage," he definitely had Italy in mind. Filled with stunningly beautiful architecture and ancient ruins, Italy's physical landscape is a perfect backdrop for the play of Italian life. In Italy everyone is an actor, dramatically emphasizing a point with their hands, facial expressions leaving no doubt about what is being discussed and voices rising or falling based on what the scene requires.

Play in the Piazza

Italians are some of the most animated people in the world and watching them is more than half the fun of going to Italy. These people relish living and are unafraid to express themselves. There is a tense, dramatic, exciting directness about Italians which is refreshing to foreigners accustomed to Anglo-Saxon self-control. In Italy they find that combination of sensuality, love and sincerity that is so lacking in their own lives.

In every piazza, on every street, there is some act being played. Whether it's two neighbors quarreling, vendors extolling the virtues of their wares, a group of older ladies chatting across the street as they lean out their windows, lovers whispering, hands caressing each other as they walk, a man checking his reflection in the mirror primping for all to see, there is something about the daily street scenes all over Italy that make this country seem more alive, more animated than the rest. And Italians love to watch these everyday scenes unfold.

Seats are strategically placed in cafés to catch all that occurs. And it is easy, even for the uninitiated, to see what is transpiring a distance away because Italians are so expressive. On the faces of Italians it is easy to read joy, sorrow, hope, anger, lust, desire, relief, boredom, despair, adoration and disappointment as easily as if they were spoken aloud. When Italians visit Northern Europe, England, or America they seem lost since they seldom know what is going on, as everyone is so expressionless.

Fashion & Art

Italians love fashion. The Italians are some of the best dressed people in the world, and they love to prance around like peacocks displaying their finery. 'Style over substance' is an adage that well describes Italians; but they live it with such flair that it can be forgiven – because that also adds to the scenes that unfold around you. The beauty of the people is unparalleled.

And Italians love art. If you ask an Italian to take your photograph expect to be posed and re-posed for at least five minutes. All Italians imagine themselves to be Federico Fellini, the famous film producer. They want to get the light just right, the shading perfect and the framing ideal. But you'll get a great picture.

They also love architecture. What happened in the United States where beautiful buildings were destroyed all over the country to erect parking lots would never happen in Italy, where you'll never see garish strip malls or ugly suburban sprawl. The McDonalds' in Italy do not stand out the way they do in America with the golden arches glowing the location for all to see. The store signs have been blended to the architecture of the building in which they are located. A balance has been found between commercialism and aesthetic appeal that has been forgotten in America.

Their love for style over substance is why Italians have always excelled in activities where appearance is paramount, like architecture, decorating, landscaping, fireworks, opera, industrial design, graphic design, fashion and cinema. That's why warfare has never been Italy's forté. Even during the Renaissance, battles were mere window dressing. Well paid *condottieri* headed beautifully appointed companies of men, resplendent in their finest silks, carrying colorful flags bearing the emblem of the families who were paying them. Martial music was played, songs were sung, and bloodcurdling cries were bellowed. There were limited casualties, and when blood was shed it was usually by accident. "Armies" would pursue each other back and forth for weeks in a pageantry of color and celebration until a settlement was decided by negotiation, not bloodshed. This may seem to be a ludicrous form of warfare, but it is a brilliant expression of life.

Religion & Family

In all, it is easy to say that Italians are fun. They will "live while they have life to live, and love while they have love to give." But they are also seriously religious. As the center of Roman Catholicism, Italy is a shining example of Christian piety, even though many of the saints they worship are only decorated pagan gods dating back to the pre-Christian era. The Pope is revered as if he truly is sitting on the right hand of God. Virtually every holiday in Italy has some religious undertones and the people perform the necessary rites and rituals associated with those holidays with vigor and enthusiasm.

Christmas is a prime example of religion's effect. In Italy it is not as garish and commercial an activity as it is in America. Religion takes precedence over purchase. Having a lavish dinner with family and friends is more important than going into debt to show people you love them through product purchases. Most decorations are of religious figures, not the commercial icons like Santa Claus and Rudolph.

Religion may guide the people, but the family is paramount. In a society where legal authority is weak, the law is resented and resisted (estimates place the number of people that actually pay income tax at around 20%) and the safety and welfare of each person is mainly due to the strength of the family. Family gatherings are common. Knowing your third cousins is not rare. And many family members live and die all in the same small neighborhoods where they were born, even in the large cities of Florence, Venice, Naples and Rome. Family traditions are maintained, strengthened and passed on. The young interact, learn from and respect their elders. The family is the core of Italian society. It is strong and durable, and from it grows a healthy sense of community.

USEFUL PHRASES
General
- Excuse me, but ....   *Mi scusi, ma ....*

    (This is a good introduction to virtually any and all inquiries listed below. It is a polite way of introducing your questions.)
- Thank you   *Grazie*

LAND & PEOPLE

- Please   *Per favore*
- If you are in trouble, yell "Help" – *Aiuto* (eyeyootoh)
- If you are looking for something, a restaurant, a hotel, a museum, simply ask "where is ..."
- Where is the restaurant (name of restaurant) *Dov'é il ristorante* _____?
- Where is the hotel (name of hotel)   *Dov'é l'hotel* _____?
- Where is the museum (name of museum)   *Dov'é il museo* _____?

    Note: *(Dov'é* is pronounced "Dove [as in the past tense of dive] -ay")

Travel-Trains

- Where is track number ...   *Dov'é binnario ...*

1	*uno*	11	*undici*
2	*due*	12	*dodici*
3	*tre*	13	*tredici*
4	*quatro*	14	*quatordici*
5	*cinque*	15	*quindici*
6	*sei*	16	*sédici*
7	*sette*	17	*diciassette*
8	*otto*	18	*diciotto*
9	*nove*	19	*dicianove*
10	*dieci*	20	*venti*

- Is this the train for Florence Roma?   *E questo il treno per Firenze Roma?*
- When does the train leave?   *Quando partira il treno?*
- When is the next train for Naples/Milan?   *Quando e il prossimo treno per Napoli/Milano?*

Travel-Cars

- Where is the next gas station?   *Dov'é la prossima stazione di benzina?*
- I would like some oil for my car. *Voglio un po di olio per il mio automobile.*
- Can you change my oil?   *Puo fare un cambio dell'olio per me?*
- I need a new oil filter   *Voglio un nuovo filtro dell'olio.*

Travel-Public Transport

- Where is the (name of station) metro station? *Dov'é la stazione di Metro* _____?
- Where can I buy a Metro ticket?   *Dov'é posso prendere un biglietto per il Metro?*
- How much is the ticket?   *Quanto costa il biglietto?*
- Where is the bus stop for bus number ___. *Dov'é la fermata per il bus numero ___?*
- Excuse me, but I want to get off.   *Mi scusi, ma voglio scendere.*
- Where can I catch a taxi?   *Dov'é posso prendere un tassi?*

Purchasing

    The following you can usually get at a drug store *(Farmacia)*:
- Where can I get...?   *Dov'é posso prendere ...?*

toothpaste	*dentifricio*
a razor	*un rasoio*
some deodorant	*un po di deodorante*
a comb	*un pettine*
rubbers	*dei profilattici*
a toothbrush	*un spazzolino*
some aspirin	*un po di aspirina*

The following you can usually get at a *Tabacchaio*:

stamps	*francobolli*
a newspaper	*un giornale*
a pen	*una penna*
envelopes	*buste per lettere*
some postcards	*dei cartoline*

The following you can usually get at an *Alimentari*.

some mustard	*un po di senape*
some mayonnaise	*un po di maionese*
tomatoes	*tomaté*
olive oil	*olio d'oliva*

• I would like ...	*Voglio ...*
1/4 of a pound of this salami	*un etto di questo salami*
1/2 of a pound of *Milanese* salami	*due etti di salami milanese*
3/4 of a pound of this cheese	*tre etti di questo formaggio*
a small piece of mozzarella	*un piccolo pezzo di mozzarella*
a portion of that cheese	*una porzione di quel' formaggio*
a slice of ham.	*una fetta* (or *una trancia*) *di prosciutto*
one roll	*un panino*
two/three/four rolls.	*due/tre/quatro panini*

• How much for the toothpaste, razor, etc? *Quante costa per il dentifrico, il rasoio, etc.*
• How much for this? *Quante costa per questo?*
• Excuse me, but where I can find a ...? *Mi scusi, ma dov'é un ... ?*

pharmacy	*Farmacia*
tobacconist	*Tabacchaio*
food store	*Alimentari*
bakery	*Panificio*

Communications
• Where is the post office? *Dov'é l'ufficio postale?*
• Where is a post box? *Dov'é una buca delle lettere*

LAND & PEOPLE 31

- Where is a public telephone? *Dov'é una cabina telefonica?*
- May I use this telephone? *Posso usare questo telefono?*

Hotel
- How much is a double for one night/two nights?
Quanto costa una doppia for una notte/due notte?
- How much is a single for one night/two nights?
Quanto costa una singola per una notte/due notte?
- Where is the Exit/Entrance? *Dov'é l'uscita/l'ingresso?*
- What time is breakfast? *A che ora e primo colazione?*
- Can I get another....for the room? *Posso prender un altro ... per la camera?*

blanket	*coperta*
pillow	*cuscino*
bed	*letto*

Miscellaneous
- Where is the bathroom? *Dov'é il cabinetto?*
- What time is it? *Che oré sono?*
- Sorry, I don't speak Italian. *Mi scusi, ma non parlo italiano.*
- Where can I get a ticket for ...? *Dov'é posso prendere un biglietto per ...?*

a soccer game	*una partita di calcio*
a basketball game	*una partita di pallacanestro*
the theater	*il teatro*
the opera	*l'opera*

- You are truly beautiful. *Tu sei veramente bella* (spoken to a woman)

  Tu sei veramente bello (spoken to a man)

- Can I buy you a drink? *Posso comprarti una bevanda?*
- Do you speak any English? *Parli un po d'Inglese?*
- Do you want to go for a walk with me? *Voi andare a una passeggiata con me?*
- Is there anyplace to go dancing nearby? *Ch'é un posto per ballare vicino?*

5. A SHORT HISTORY

A short history of the peninsula of Italy is a contradiction in terms. So much has occurred in this narrow strip of land which has affected the direction of the entire Western world that it is virtually impossible to succinctly describe its history in a brief outline. We've had the Etruscans, Romans, Greeks, 'Barbarian' hordes, Holy Roman Emperors, the Papacy (although not the whole time – the seat of the Catholic Church was moved to Avignon, France from 1305 until 1377), painters, sculptors, the Renaissance, Crusaders, Muslim invaders, French marauders, Spanish conquistadors, Fascists, American soldiers, Red Brigades, and much more.

What follows is a brief outline of the major events on the Italian peninsula, concentrating mainly on the Roman Empire, since we will cover the Renaissance in Chapter 10. I don't claim to be an historian, only a mere *scrittore di guidi di viaggio*, so please accept this brief historical background for your travel enjoyment.

ETRUSCANS

Long before Rome was even a glimmer in Romulus' and Remus' eye (legend had it that these two were raised by a she-wolf and eventually became the founders of Rome), Italy was the home of a people with an already advanced civilization – the **Etruscans**. This powerful and prosperous society almost vanished from recorded history because not only were they conquered by Rome but also devastated by marauding **Gauls**. At such times, it is assumed that most of their written history was destroyed, and little remains today.

Because of this, and the fact that the language of the inscriptions on their monuments has been only partially deciphered, archaeologists have gained most of their knowledge of the Etruscans from studying the remains of their city walls, houses, monuments, and tombs.

From their research, archaeologists believe that the Etruscans were a seafaring people from Asia Minor, and that as early as 1000 BCE (Before the Common Era) they had settled in Italy in the region that is today **Tuscany** and **Lazio** (basically from Rome's Tiber River north almost to Florence's Arno River). Their rule eventually embraced a large part of western Italy, including Rome.

As a seafaring people, the Etruscans controlled the commerce of the Tyrrhenian Sea on their western border. After losing control of Rome, they strengthened their naval power through an alliance with Carthage against Greece. In 474 BCE, their fleet was destroyed by the Greeks of Syracuse. This left them vulnerable not only to Rome, but the Gauls from the north. The Gauls overran the country from the north, and the Etruscans' strong southern fortress of Veii fell to Rome after a ten-year siege (396 BCE). As was the Roman way, the Etruscans were absorbed into their society, and eventually Rome adopted many of their advanced arts, their customs, and their institutions.

THE ETRUSCAN KINGS OF EARLY ROME

When Greece was reaching the height of its prosperity, Rome was growing in strength. Rome didn't have any plan for its ascension to world domination, it just seemed to evolve. There were plenty of set-backs along the way, but everything fell into place at the right time.

The early Romans kept no written records, and their history is so mixed with fables and myths that historians have difficulty distinguishing truth from fiction. The old legends say that **Romulus** founded the city in 753 BCE when the settlements on the seven hills were united. This date is probably too late for the actual founding of the city. As is the case with many emerging societies, their founders are mythical figures, as was Romulus, but there is some evidence that the kings who followed him actually existed.

Shortly before 600 BCE, Rome was conquered by several Etruscan princes. The Etruscans were benevolent conquerors (except for Tarquinius Superbus) and set about improving the Roman lifestyles to match their own.

The first Etruscan king, **Tarquinius Priscus**, drained the city's marshes, improved the **Forum**, which was the commercial and political center of the town, and also founded a temple to Jupiter. He protected Rome by carrying on wars with neighboring peoples.

Under **Servius Tullius**, the second Etruscan king, a treaty was made with the Latin cities which acknowledged Rome as the head of all **Latium**. This was the beginning of the concept of Rome as the center of the universe. At the same time he enlarged the city and built a wall around all seven hills, parts of which still stand today.

The last of the Etruscan kings of Rome, **Tarquinius Superbus**, was a tyrant who oppressed the people and scorned the Roman religions. His activities started the fires of rebellion that would eventually unseat the Etruscans from Rome.

Even with this oppression, the Etruscans built Rome into the center of all Latium. Impressive public works were constructed, like the huge sewer **Cloaca Maxima**, which is still in use. Trade also expanded and prospered, and by the end of the 6th century BCE Rome had become the largest and richest city in Italy.

THE NATIVE ROMAN POPULATION REVOLTS

But in spite of all this progress and development, the old Latin aristocracy wanted their power back. **Junius Brutus** led a successful revolt around 509 BCE, which expelled the Etruscans from the city. That was when the people of Rome made themselves a **republic**.

The Etruscans tried and failed many times to regain control of the city. Rome's successful thwarting of the Etruscans allowed the young republic to begin its long history of almost constant warfare and conquest. At the time, it was only a tiny city-state, much like the city-states that were flourishing at the same time in Greece, with a population of roughly 150,000. Who would have thought that this small republic would eventually rule the known world?

ROME'S EARLY REPUBLIC

In the beginnings of early Rome, the **patricians** (Rome's aristocracy) controlled the government and ruled the **plebes** or **plebeians** (Common People). Because they were shut out from the government, the plebeians were politically and economically oppressed by their wealthy fellow citizens. The internal history of the republic for the next three centuries is mainly a story of how the plebeians wrested reform after reform from the patricians and gained more and more control over their existence and the eventual direction of Roman politics.

What forced the plebes to seek their freedom was the shackle of the patrician's oppression. The wealthy patricians continued to expand their land holdings, taking the best property and increasing their herds until they monopolized the public pasture. They also continued the practice of lending money at ruinous interest to the small proprietors, eventually reducing the plebes to abject slavery when they could not pay.

At the same time, the population of Rome was increasing too fast for the land and their primitive farming methods could not support it. Also the burden of constant warfare fell most heavily on the plebeians, who had to leave their little farms to fight the state's battles. This didn't allow them to provide for their families or even begin to pay off their debts they incurred to start farming the land.

To right these wrongs the plebeians went on what today would be called a general strike. In 494 BCE, they marched out of Rome in a body and threatened to make a new city. At the fear of losing its large labor force, the patricians agreed to cancel all debts and to release people who were in prison for debt. By 350 BCE, the plebes gained the ability to participate fully in the Republic's government.

While these important changes were taking place at home, the little city-state had been gradually extending its power. Compelled at first to fight for its very existence against its powerful neighbors (mainly the Etruscans, Aequians, and Volscians), Rome gradually fought its way to the leadership of the Italian peoples. This dependence on military strength helped pave the way for Rome's conquest of the world.

THE GAULS SACK ROME

Rome's progress in leadership of all of the Latin tribes received a temporary setback in 390 BCE, when marauding Gauls advanced through the heart of Italy. They decimated the farmland as they went and captured and burned Rome. After a stand-off, with Romans slowly taking their city back, the Gauls accepted a heavy ransom to depart promptly and returned to the valley of the Po.

Although Rome had been burned, the Etruscans had suffered far worse in the invasion and were so weakened that Rome was able to seize their southern possessions. In another century, Rome conquered their whole territory.

ROMAN CONQUEST OF ITALY

Meanwhile the **Latin League** had grown to dislike the growing power and arrogance of their ally and attempted to break away from its control; but Rome won the two year long war that followed (340-338 BCE). As a warning, some towns were reduced to being vassals of the new state, while others were given full Roman citizenship and others partial citizenship.

Another strong foe in central Italy still remained to be reckoned with: the **Samnites**, who were also of Italic stock. The truce that was made when the Latin League was feuding was broken a few years later (326 BCE), and a wild-fought struggle ensued, with a variety of interruptions, until the decisive battle of **Sentinum** (295 BCE), which made Rome supreme over all central and northern Italy.

Southern Italy, still occupied by a disunited group of Greek city-states, still remained independent. Alarmed at the spread of Roman power, the Greek cities appealed to **Pyrrhus**, king of Epirus in Greece who inflicted two telling defeats on the Roman army. He then crossed to Sicily to aid the Greek cities there in eliminating Carthaginian rule. This was a classic example of spreading your forces too thin over an extended battlefield. Encouraged by the arrival of a Carthaginian fleet to combat the Greeks, Rome renewed its struggle for the Greek city-states in southern Italy, and in 275 BCE defeated Pyrrhus in the battle of **Beneventum** and a new phrase was born: a Pyhrric victory, where you win the war but at excessive cost. Eventually, one by one the Greek cities were taken, and just like that Rome was ruler of all Italy.

KEEPING THE CONQUERED LANDS HAPPY

Rome gradually welded the lands conquered into a single nation, contented and unified. Rome could have exploited the conquered cities of Italy for its own interests, but instead made them partners in the empire's future success.

Rome granted many of them the privileges of Roman citizenship, in full or in part. As it had done for the Latin cities, they gave them the status of allies or partners. These new conquests were allowed to govern themselves, had the right to trade freely with and intermarry with Roman citizens, which would also make the non-Roman a citizen. These newly conquered people did not, however, have the right to vote.

Rome also set about establishing colonies of its citizens, who still retained their full civil rights, all over Italy. Almost one sixth of all Italy was annexed and distributed among these colonizing Roman citizens. By encouraging this colonization, a common interest in the welfare of Rome spread throughout the Italian peninsula.

THE PUNIC WARS

These centuries of warfare had developed Rome into a nation of soldiers. Its only remaining rival in the western Mediterranean was the Phoenician colony of **Carthage**, the established sea power of the time. Rome obviously was the chief land power. At the time Carthage had a policy of sinking any trading vessel of any other city that dared to bid for a share of the rich commerce of the Mediterranean region. Rome could not abide by these restrictions, so a series of **Punic Wars** for Mediterranean supremacy began in 264 BCE.

The courage and endurance of Rome were tested to the utmost in this long and disastrous series of wars. After the battle of **Zama** (202 BCE), Carthage was reduced to the position of a vassal state. In 146 BCE, during the **Third Punic War**, because Carthage was again beginning to flex its military and economic might, Rome once more savagely attacked its defeated rival and razed the city.

WINNING WORLD MASTERY

Now Rome was well on its way to world domination. Emboldened with this sudden rise to power, the new generation of Roman statesmen ignored the just policies of their successful predecessors. Most of the conquered lands were administered by governors (**proconsuls**), and citizens were given little chance to become full Roman citizens. These governors ruled like czars, and through the enormous taxes levied on the local populations, tried to amass in their one year of office enough wealth to last them a lifetime.

These taxes also enriched the greedy collectors (**publicans**), who purchased the privilege of collecting the taxes. Incredible amounts of gold, jewelry, and money in the form of taxes poured into Rome from all over the world, and the ancient simplicity of Roman life gave way to luxury and pomp. Morals were undermined, and vice and corruption flourished. (For an example of the debauchery that ensued, try and get a copy of the movie *Caligula* – not a movie for family viewing, but it will give you an insight into what happened to Rome during this time of expansion.

The suddenly enriched official bureaucrats acquired estates by buying up the small farms of the peasants. Even if they kept their land the peasants were too poor to compete with the hordes of slaves who worked the great plantations. Because of this the streets of the capital grew clogged with ruined farmers, along with discharged soldiers and the poor from all over Italy. These people lived on state and private charity, as well as on bribes that were given by political candidates to vote for them in the next election.

THE END OF THE ROMAN REPUBLIC

Once again a conflict began to brew between the aristocracy (formerly the Patricians) and the vast oppressed poor citizens (formerly the Plebes). Men tried to step forward and right the wrongs that were occurring, but each man who did ended up assassinated for his efforts.

To try and maintain a semblance of order a law was forcibly passed that transferred supreme power from the people to the **Senate**. The aristocrats, who became Senators, however, were too corrupt and feeble to hold power, and so the Roman Republic came to an end.

Two brilliant statesmen, **Gaius Julius Caesar** and his great-nephew **Augustus** (**Octavian**), helped save Rome by scrapping the old republican framework and remolded the tottering structure into an empire. All power was gradually concentrated in the hands of a single ruler, who was backed by the might of the Roman Legions.

TWO CENTURIES OF PEACE & PROSPERITY

With the establishment of the Empire, two centuries of profound peace developed, only broken by small frontier warfare. In the provinces men held power responsibly, possibly because they feared the omnipotent wrath of the emperor, and in Rome literature and civilization flourished. Increasingly the Mediterranean came to resemble one great nation, with paved roads leading from the south of Italy into what are now France and Germany. Even today fragments of Roman roads and ruins still exist in Britain, aqueducts and bridges can be seen in France, Roman wells are still used in the Egyptian oases of the Sahara Desert, and Roman amphitheaters can be visited in the heart of Tunisia.

Roman citizenship was extended to all free men throughout the Empire, and Roman law was administered in every court. The **Roman Peace** (*Pax Romana*) extended over the civilized world. But signs of decay were everywhere.

The pursuit of a good time once again obsessed the people of Rome. The rich amused themselves by giving splendid feasts. The poor had their circuses where free bread was distributed (you've heard of bread and circuses?). Slave labor had degraded the once sturdy peasantry to the status of serfs or beggars, and the middle class, which once had been the backbone of the nation, had almost disappeared. A welfare mentality overcame the population. The Roman governors again began to concentrate on sucking the provinces dry instead of keeping abreast of the economic and political climate.

THE FALL OF THE ROMAN EMPIRE

The strength and discipline of the Roman Empire were being sapped by political decay, economic troubles, and decadent living. At this time, German 'barbarians,' who were a violent people led by warrior chiefs living on the fringes of the empire, began to attack the edges of the empire in the 4th century CE (Common Era). They defeated unprepared Roman garrison after garrison. These **Goths**, **Vandals** (so that's where the phrase comes from!), **Lombards**, **Franks**, **Angles**, **Saxons**, and other tribes sacked and pillaged the decadent and crumbling empire. With the fall of the Western Roman Empire in CE 476, this was the beginning of the medieval period called the **Dark Ages**. They were so called because these 'barbarians' let Roman civilization collapse along with its artistic and engineering achievements.

What the 'barbarians' did bring with them, however, that helped shape the future of Western civilization, was their belief that the individual was important, more so than the state. In contrast, the Romans believed in the rule of the state over the people – in despotism. The 'barbarians' gave us a rudimentary form of personal rights, including more respect for women, government by the people for the people, and a system of law represented by the people being governed. Kings and chiefs were elected by tribal councils, which also served as courts of law. In essence, they brought with them the beginnings of democracy. So, in 20-20 hindsight, who was civilized and which was barbaric?

AFTER THE ROMAN EMPIRE

In CE 330, when the Roman emperor **Constantine** moved the capital to **Constinantinople** (today's Istanbul in Turkey), the Western Roman Empire decayed and was overrun by waves of 'barbarians.' Rival governors fought over fragments of Italian territory.

Even **Charlemagne**, who had conquered the Lombard rulers and had himself crowned emperor of the **Holy Roman Empire** in CE 800, could not stop the disintegration of everything the Roman Empire had built. The Holy Roman Empire was a union between the Papacy and Charlemagne in which management of the empire was shared.

But Charlemagne's Holy Roman Empire fell apart after his death, only to be refounded by the Saxon **Otto I** in 962 CE, bringing Italy into a close alliance with Germany. The Holy Roman Empire ruled over the lands north of Rome into Austria and Germany until 1806. During that time, the Holy Roman Empire took on many shapes, sizes, and rulers. It included at different times France, Germany, Luxembourg, the north of Italy (because the Muslims, and then the Normans had taken control of Italy south of Naples), Austria, Switzerland, and more. It had rulers from the Saxon Line, Franconian Line, Hohenstaufen Line, Luxembourg Line, and the Hapsburg Line. It may have been constantly in flux but it did last over 1,000 years.

While the Holy Roman Empire expanded and contracted, it eventually contracted itself outside of Italy, leaving government to warring city states. Florence, Venice, Milan, and the Papacy became the strongest of the contending powers. They came to dominate the countryside while feudalism declined. They drew their riches from the produce of their fertile river valleys and from profits generated in commerce between the Orient and Europe. This trade flowed in by way of Venice (and eventually) Genoa, and passed through other northern cities on its way across the Alps.

THE ITALIAN RENAISSANCE

Under the patronage of the Papacy and of the increasingly prosperous princes of the city-states, such as the **Medici** of Florence, the scholars, writers, and artists created the masterpieces of literature, art, and science that made the **Italian Renaissance** one of the most influential movements in history. In this period many splendid churches, palaces, and public buildings were built that still inspire awe in Italians and visitors alike. At the same, these beautiful cities, such as Florence, Pisa, Venice, and Milan, were filled with social strife and political unrest.

PAWN OF STRONG NATIONS

While Italy was torn by struggles between the local rulers and the Papacy, strong nations developed elsewhere in Europe, and the Italy of separate city-states became an area of conquest for the powers struggling for European supremacy. French and Spanish rivalry over Italy began in 1494. **Charles VIII of France** valiantly fought his way through the peninsula to Naples, but by 1544 **Charles I of Spain** had defeated the French three times and had become ruler of Sicily, Naples, and Milan.

For centuries the states of Italy remained mere pawns in other nations' games of power. The city-states passed from one to another of Europe's rulers through war, marriage, death, or treaty. The **Papacy** was, however, usually strong enough to protect its temporal power over the areas in central Italy known as the **States of the Church**, or **Papal States**. The tiny republic of **San Marino** in the northeastern Appenines has remained through the centuries as a relic from this period. Although its 24 square miles are entirely surrounded by Italian soil, it is legally independent of Italy and claims to be the oldest state in Europe.

SPANISH & AUSTRIAN RULE

For some 150 years (1559-1713), Spain was the dominant power in Italy. Then the **Treaty of Utrecht** (1713) ended the **War of the Spanish Succession** and established the Austrian Hapsburgs in place of the Spanish as Italy's paramount power.

As time went by the Spanish began to feel slighted by the amount of land that had been ceded to Austria, so they sought to take back their former possessions. In 1734 **Don Carlos**, son of Philip V of Spain, conquered Naples and Sicily, and ruled the area as **Charles III of Naples**.

During this time, in the 18th century, enormous wealth was held by the few while the masses lived in squalor and ignorance. This disparity was especially noticeable in Italy, where the feudal system lingered on. The peasants were without rights or defenders. They lived in hovels and caves, and as a result crime rates were shocking despite harsh laws and punishments.

Ideas of reform coming from other nations found some response among the intellectuals and the middle class, and the concepts of liberty and equality stirring in France gained many Italian supporters. Many

Italians were so blinded with the concepts that they offered assistance to a foreigner, **Napoleon Bonaparte**, as he began his conquest of Italy in the 1790s. As time went by the Italians realized their mistake, and hungered to be free of the yolk of French imperialism.

But even when Napoleon was defeated, most Italian states went back to their former sovereigns. For example, Venezia (Venice) was re-absorbed into Austrian rule, and Naples and Sicily were re-absorbed into Spanish rule. Italy was still a pawn in European politics.

MOVEMENT FOR POLITICAL UNITY

Eventually hatred of foreign rule mounted. With it grew the **Risorgimento**, or movement for political unity. Such secret societies as the Carbonari (charcoal burners, the name given from their use of charcoal burners' huts for meeting places), plotted against the Austrians, but the **Carbonari Revolts** were crushed in 1821 and again in 1831 by Austrian troops.

Then the idealistic republican leader, **Giuseppe Mazzini**, organized his revolutionary society, **Young Italy**, and called upon **Charles Albert**, king of Sardinia-Piedmont and a member of the ancient House of Savoy, to head a movement to liberate Italy. By early 1848, revolts had broken out in many regions, and constitutions had been granted to Naples, Piedmont, and Tuscany. When Mazzini drove out the pope and set up a short-lived republic in Rome the French came to the pope's aid, while Austria quelled the revolt in the north. Eventually Charles Albert abdicated his rule in Sardinia-Piedmont in favor of his son **Victor Emmanuel II**.

Under the able leadership of the shrewd diplomat **Count Camillo di Cavour**, the minister of Victor Emmanuel, Sardinia-Piedmont grew strong in resources and in alliances. Cavour had learned that, genuine as was Italian patriotic fervor, Italy would never be unified without help from abroad.

Therefore he cleverly won an alliance with **Napoleon III** of France, and in the spring of 1859 Austria was goaded into declaring war against Sardinia-Piedmont and France. Austria was defeated, and Italy claimed the lands of Lombardy for a united Italy, but the Austrian's allowed France to retain Venezia.

Cavour and Victor Emmanuel lobbied the peoples of Tuscany, Modena, Parma, and Emilia who eventually voted to cast out their princes and join Sardinia-Piedmont. Napoleon III consented to such an arrangement, but only if Savoy and Nice voted to join France. (Politics is too complicated. I'll stick to travel writing).

GARIBALDI TO THE RESCUE

The second step toward a united Italy came the next year, when the famous soldier of fortune **Giuseppe Garibaldi** and his thousand red-shirted volunteers stormed the island of Sicily and the rest of the Kingdom of Naples on the mainland. The people everywhere hailed him as a liberator, and the hated Bourbon king was driven out.

Victor Emmanuel II was proclaimed king of Italy in February 1861, but now only the Papal States and Venezia remained to be joined to the new Italian nation. Venezia was gained in 1866, after Austria was defeated by Prussia in alliance with Italy. The Papal States were now the only ones outside the Italian kingdom, besides San Marino. San Marino was small and isolated, but since they were then about the size the current region of Lazio and not just the small little walled-in city they are today, the lack of that territory was a very real handicap to Italy.

VATICAN CAPTURED - KINGDOM OF ITALY UNITED

But since French troops still guarded the pope's sovereignty, Victor Emmanuel, being the apt pupil of Cavour (who had died in 1861), did not want to attack the French and perhaps undo all that had been accomplished. Then, miraculously in 1870, the **Franco-Prussian War** forced France to withdraw its soldiers from Rome, at which time Italian forces immediately marched in.

Pope Pius IX, in his infinite wisdom and understanding, excommunicated the invaders and withdrew behind the walls of the Vatican. There he and his successors remained 'voluntary prisoners' until the **Concordat of 1929**, or **Lateran Treaty**, between Italy and the Holy See, which recognized the temporal power of the pope as sovereign ruler over Vatican City (all 108.7 acres of it, or about 1/6 of a square mile!). Then, as many would argue now, the Vatican was afraid of adapting to a modern world, and wanted the status quo to remain.

MODERN ITALY - THE BEGINNING

Staggering under a load of debt and heavy taxation, giant steps needed to still be taken for Italy to survive. Leaders of the various regions, always trying to gain an edge, were in constant disagreement – even in active conflict. At the same time citizens, used to the ultimate control of despotic rule, found it difficult to adopt the ways of parliamentary government. As a result, riots and other forms of civil disorder were the rule in the latter half of the 19th century.

Despite all of these problems, in the typical Italian fashion of functioning despite complete political chaos, an army and navy were developed; railroads, ports, and schools were constructed; and a merchant marine was developed. At the same time, manufacturing started to flourish.

But then, in 1900, **King Umberto I** (son of Victor Emmanuel II) was assassinated, and his son, **Victor Emmanuel III**, rose to the throne. Meanwhile, trying to relive the glory days of the Roman Empire, Italian government officials were attempting to gain territory in Africa for colonial expansion. Eventually on Africa's east coast they obtained two colonies, **Eritrea** and **Italian Somaliland**, and on the north coast of Africa they won **Tripoli** after a war with Turkey (1911-12).

Although having joined with Germany and Austria in the **Triple Alliance** in 1882, in the early 1900s Italy began to befriend France and England. With Austria's invasion of Serbia in 1914, after the assassination of Archduke Ferdinand of Austria, Italy declared its neutrality despite being Austria's ally. In April 1915, Italy signed a secret treaty with the **Allies** (Russia, France, and England), and the next month it stated that it had withdrawn from the Triple Alliance. On May 23, 1915, the king declared war on Austria.

When World War I ended in 1918, the old Austro-Hungarian Empire was broken up. Italy was granted territory formerly under Austrian rule, including "unredeemed Italy" of the Trentino in the north and the peninsula of Istria at the head of the Adriatic.

MUSSOLINI & FASCISM

The massive depression after World War I brought strikes and riots, which were fomented by anarchists, socialists, and Communists. The government of Victor Emmanuel III seemed powerless to stop bands of former servicemen lawlessly roaming the country. In these bands, **Benito Mussolini** saw his opportunity. With his gift of oratory he soon molded this rabble into enthusiastic, organized groups in many communities all over Italy, armed them, and set them to preserving the order that they had destroyed. These bands formed the nucleus of his black-shirted **Fascist** party, whose emblem was the *fasces*, the bundle of rods that had symbolized the authority of the Roman Empire.

The party grew rapidly because Mussolini promised everything to everybody. On Oct. 28, 1922, the **Blackshirts**, meeting in Naples, were strong enough, well enough prepared, and willing to march on Rome and seize the government. The king, fearing civil war and his own life, refused to proclaim martial law, forced the premier to resign, and asked Mussolini to form a government.

Within a few years Mussolini, *Il Duce* (The Leader), had reorganized the government so that the people had no voice at all. Mussolini first abolished all parties except his own Fascist party, and took from the

Chamber of Deputies the power to consider any laws not proposed by him. The king remained as a figurehead because he was revered by the people and had the support of many wealthy and important families. In 1939, he replaced the Chamber of Deputies with the Chamber of Fasces and Corporations, composed of all his henchmen. No semblance of popular rule remained. Mussolini even took control of the provinces and cities by naming the prefects of the provinces and the mayors of the cities.

All opposition was crushed by intimidation or violence. Suspected critics of the regime were sentenced to prison by special courts or were terrorized, tortured, or murdered by Blackshirt thugs. News was censored and public meetings could not be held without the government's permission. The new Fascist state was based on the doctrine that the welfare of the state is all-important and that the individual exists only for the state, owes everything to it, and has no right to protection against it. It was a return to the despotism of the later Roman Empire.

A RETURN TO THE ROMAN EMPIRE?

Mussolini, like other Italian leaders before him, longed to create a new Roman empire and to bring back Italy's lost glory. So, in 1935, with his large army and recently expanded navy, he attacked and conquered the weak, backward, and poorly defended African country of Ethiopia.

In October 1936, at Mussolini's invitation, the **Rome-Berlin Axis** was formed between Italy and Nazi Germany to oppose the power of France and England. Strangely enough, at this time Mussolini was considered the stronger ally of the two. Through its military and economic support of Spain, this alliance between Rome and Berlin helped Franco achieve victory in the Spanish Civil War. (Spain was also the training ground for Germany's shock troops that would eventually march through Poland in a matter of days.) In April 1939, Italy invaded Albania, and at that time Italy and Germany became formal military allies.

But when Germany's program of aggression plunged it into war with England and France on September 3, 1939, Italy at first adopted the position of a non-belligerent. But on June 10, 1940, Italian forces attacked southeastern France in an invasion coordinated with German forces in the north. But they had only gotten involved when it was obvious that France was no longer a threat.

DEFEAT IN WORLD WAR II

Italy, however, lacked the military power, resources, and national spirit for fighting a large-scale war. Within six months, Italian armies met defeat in Greece and North Africa. (A running joke during World War II was that Italian tanks had only one gear: reverse.) Italy then humbly accepted the military assistance of Germany. This soon grew into economic dependence, and Italy was forced to let Germany occupy it and control its home affairs, and Mussolini became a German puppet.

After the Allies invaded and won all Italian territory in North Africa as well as Sicily in July 1943, public unrest forced Mussolini to resign. He was arrested and held under guard. The constitutional monarchy was restored, with Marshal Pietro Badoglio as premier.

The Allies invaded Italy's mainland from Sicily on Sept. 3, 1943, and after what some considered to be a token resistance (the soldiers buried beneath the graves of Anzio might beg to differ), Italy surrendered unconditionally that same day, and on October 13 declared war on Germany. Meanwhile, Mussolini had been freed by German paratroopers and had fled into German-held north Italy, where he established a "Republican Fascist State."

The entire length of the mountainous north became a bitter battleground, but eventually enemy forces surrendered their hold on northern Italy on April 29, 1945. Mussolini and his wife were subsequently captured by partisans, hung, shot, and for good measure, beaten until he was unrecognizable.

The end of the war found Italy with a large part of its industry and agriculture shattered. During its occupation, the Germans had almost stripped Italy's industry bare by commandeering supplies. Italian factories, roads, docks, and entire villages were ruined by the Allied bombing raids and during the invasion. To make things worse, as the Germans retreated they had wrecked whatever industries and transportation remained.

Even with the Allies contributing substantial quantities of food, clothing, and other supplies, the people were cold, hungry, and jobless. After the war, the United Nations Relief and Rehabilitation Administration gave more aid to Italy than to any other country. Reconstruction lagged, however, because of internal political turmoil, such turmoil becoming something of a theme in postwar Italian politics.

POSTWAR POLITICAL CHANGES

During the battle for Italy its people were politically restless, and so a variety of parties representing many political views, from the extreme left to the far right, had been born. The more liberal parties demanded an end to the monarchy, but backed by the Allies, Victor Emmanuel III retained his sovereignty until the liberation of Rome in 1944.

On May 9, 1946, Victor Emmanuel III formally abdicated in favor of his son, who reigned for less than one month as **Umberto II**, because on June 2, 1946, the Italian people voted to found a republic. They also elected deputies to a Constituent Assembly to draft a new constitution.

Finally on February 10, 1947, the peace treaty between Italy and the Allies was ready to be signed. The treaty stripped Italy of its African 'empire' of Libya, Italian Somaliland, and Eritrea. The pact also ceded the Dodecanese Islands to Greece, internationalized Trieste, made minor boundary changes with France, and gave about 3,000 square miles to Yugoslavia, including most of the Istrian peninsula.

Italy had to pay $360 million in reparations, and was also forced to restore independence to Ethiopia and Albania. One lone gain was that **south Tyrol**, which Austria had been forced to cede after World War I, remained with Italy, and eventually, in 1954, **Trieste** was given to Italy by agreement with Yugoslavia.

On January 1, 1948, Italy's newly formed constitution became effective. It banned the Fascist party (unfortunately, there are today plenty of political parties in Italy that go by another name but informally call themselves *Fascisti*) and the monarchy. Freedom of religion was guaranteed, but Catholicism remained the state religion.

But a constitution alone cannot recreate a country. Italian leaders had the double task of creating a stable parliamentary system of government while at the same time restoring the economy. (They still haven't solved the first problem.) The main economic hindrance was the poverty-stricken south contributing little to the improving economy of the north. As a result there were many riots and moments of intense civil unrest.

LAND REFORM

The south was so poor because much of central and southern Italy, Sicily, and Sardinia were among the last aristocratic European strongholds of large-scale landowners. The estates of these landowners covered many thousands of acres and employed only small numbers of laborers, mostly at harvest time. These landless peasants, who had no work during much of the year, lived in nearby villages and small towns and barely made ends meet all year. These citizens either stayed peaceful, contributed to civil unrest, or emigrated to find better employment and living conditions.

In the early 1950s, the Italian parliament passed special land reform laws that divided large private estates into small farms and distributed them to the peasants. The new owners were given substantial government support for their first years on the land, and the previous owners received cash compensation. Thousands of new small farms were created in this way during the 1950s, and farm production, as a result of the land reform and other measures, rose quickly.

The Italian government not only invested large sums of money in land reform but at the same time also started to develop the southern infrastructure to help the farmers. New roads were built to help carry produce to market, and new irrigation systems, needed during the long, dry summers, were constructed. Warehouses and cold storage facilities for farm products were provided, and the government also helped to introduce new crops.

Flower growers in The Netherlands began to send seeds to southern Italy, where they could start growing early while the fields of Holland might still be covered with snow. In spring, Italian growers would ship the young plants back north for final growth. As a result of these changes, farming in central and especially southern Italy began to bounce back.

CHAOS MIXED WITH STABILITY

Even with the south's new-found prosperity, Italy's economic development was mainly due to spectacular gains in industrial production in the north. Then during the mid-1960s, Italy began to suffer from severe inflation. A government austerity program to combat this trend produced a decline in profits and a lag in investments. To add insult to injury, devastating floods – the worst in 700 years – hit the country in 1966, ravaging one third of the land and causing losses of more than $1.5 billion. To make matters even worse, some of the priceless art treasures of Florence were irreparably damaged when the flood waters poured through that city.

In 1971 Italy had its largest economic recession since the country's post-World War II recovery. Strikes affected nearly every sector of the economy as Italian workers demanded social reforms. The problems of inflation, unemployment, lack of housing, and unfavorable balance of payments continued in the 1970s. Nevertheless, the economy showed resiliency for the five-year period ending in 1976 with an increase in gross domestic production.

When Italy was about to pull out of its economic problems, political terrorism escalated, culminating in March 1978, when **Aldo Moro**, leader of the Christian Democratic party and former premier, was abducted in Rome by the **Red Brigades**, an extreme left-wing terrorist group. During the two months that Moro was held, Rome was like an armed camp, with military roadblocks everywhere. Eventually Moro was found murdered and left in the trunk of his car two months later.

In 1980, in Italy's worst natural disaster in more than 70 years, an earthquake killed more than 3,000 persons in the Naples area. As if things could only get worse, in May 1981 a Turkish political dissident tried to kill Pope John Paul II in St. Peter's Square. Also in 1981, a corruption scandal involving hundreds of public servants who were allegedly members of a secret society erupted and brought down the government.

Then for the first time in the 35-year history of the Italian republic, a non-Christian Democratic premier was elected. However, the Christian Democrats regained their power in November 1982, and socialist **Bettino Craxi** served as premier from 1983 to 1987, the longest term of any Italian leader since World War II.

Economic conditions in the early 1980s were affected by growing recession and rising inflation. The Vatican Bank and the Banco Ambrosiano of Milan, Italy's biggest private banking group, were involved in a major banking scandal that forced the liquidation of Banco Ambrosiano in 1982. Two natural disasters, an earthquake and a landslide, caused widespread damage in the regions of Perugia and Ancona in late 1982.

In 1989, another bank became involved in a scandal when it was revealed that an American branch of the Banca Nazionale del Lavoro had loaned billions of dollars to Iraq. Then severe drought occurred throughout Italy in the winter of 1989 and in Venice some canals were unusable because water levels had dropped so low. And still, in the late 1990s, the Italian government is under intense investigation for rampant corruption including officials taking bribes from members of the Mafia.

Despite all of this, the Italian economy continues to improve, to the point where it is one of the more successful in Europe. Throughout all of this chaos, Italy perseveres. It's almost as if without a reasonable amount of disorder, Italy could not survive.

Most recently, a separatist political party has emerged. The **Northern League** is attempting to create the 'federal republic of Padania' in the industrial north of Italy. Founded in 1984, the party is now gaining support and popularity because northern Italians pay a disproportionate share of the country's taxes – which they say goes to support the impoverished south and keep the government bloated in Rome. The idea of splitting Italy in two is not so far fetched, when you realize that only in the last century has the peninsula been one unified country. There have always been glaring differences in culture between south and central Italy and their northern cousins. And to emphasize this point in the last local elections, the Northern League won over 10% of the vote.

6. PLANNING YOUR TRIP

BEFORE YOU GO

CLIMATE & WEATHER

The climate in Italy is as varied as the country itself, but it never seems to get too harsh. Any time is a good time to travel to Italy. Most of the country has a Mediterranean type of climate, meaning cool, rainy winters and hot, dry summers.

The summers are mild in the north, but winters in the north tend to be colder because these regions are in or near the Alps. The Alps protects the rest of Italy from cold northern winds. Because Italy is a peninsula and thus surrounded by water, the entire country tends to be calm and mild except for the south and Sicily. These regions are very hot in the summer, and in the winter, wetter than normal. Winter temperatures along and near the coasts of southern Italy seldom drop to freezing in winter, and summer temperatures often reach 90°F (32°C) or higher.

Winter is the rainy season, when stream beds that remain empty during much of the year fill to overflowing and flash floods are common.

When to Go

With this in mind, anytime is good time to travel to Italy. The climate doesn't vary greatly making Italy a pleasant trip any time of year. Then again I'm biased – I spent eight wonderful years in Italy and I think it's fantastic all year. The busiest tourist season is from May to October, leaving Spring and Autumn as the choice times to have Italy all to yourself.

The sidebar below offers you a breakdown by season of the best regions to visit during those times:

> ### ITALY'S FOUR SEASONS
>
> **Spring** – Italy has an early spring. The best places to visit are Florence, around Naples and Sorrento, Sicily, and Rome.
>
> **Summer** – Summer can be a little hot at times, so to cool you down there are plenty of beach resorts along most of Italy's coast, especially in Liguria on the Italian Riviera. But the best place to go is the mountains of Tuscany or the northern regions of Lombardia, Piemonte, or Trentino Alto-Adige. This is not to say that Rome or Venice would not be pleasant, just crowded with tourists and relatively warm.
>
> **Autumn** – This is a pleasant time to visit Rome and other major cities, since they are less crowded and much cooler.
>
> **Winter** – Time for winter sports. You can find ski centers in the Alps as well as the central Apennines near Florence and Rome. Also at this time, the southern regions and Sicily are at their best.

WHAT TO PACK

One suitcase and a carry-on should suffice for your average week to ten day trip. Besides, there are countless clothing stores from which you can buy yourself any needed item. Also it's advised to pack light so you can move your belongings with ease. In conjunction, you can always find a local *Tintoria* (dry cleaner) to clean any dirty clothes for you, if your hotel does not supply such a service. If you want to do it yourself, it's best to look for a *Lavanderia* instead, your basic coin operated Laundromat.

Remember to pack all your personal cosmetic items that you've grown used to using, since, more than likely, they're not available in Italian stores. The Italian culture just hasn't seemed to grasp the necessity of having 400 types of toothpaste, or 200 types of tampons.

Also important to remember, especially if you're traveling in the winter time, is an umbrella, a raincoat, and water-proof shoes. You never know when the rain will fall in the winter.

PUBLIC HOLIDAYS

Offices and shops in Italy are closed on the dates below. So prepare for the eventuality of having virtually everything closed and stock up on picnic snacks, soda, whatever, because in most cities and towns there is no such thing as a 24 hour a day 7-11. The Italians take their free time seriously. To them the concept of having something open 24 hours a day is, well, a little crazy.

- **January 1**, New Year's Day
- **January 6**, Epiphany

PLANNING YOUR TRIP

- **April 25**, Liberation Day (1945)
- **Easter Monday**
- **May 1**, Labor Day
- **August 15**, *Ferragosto* and Assumption of the Blessed Virgin (climax of Italian family holiday season. Hardly anything stays open in the big cities through the month of August)
- **November 1**, All Saints Day
- **December 8**, Immaculate Conception
- **December 25/26**, Christmas

Listed below are some dates that may be considered public holidays in different areas of Italy, so prepare for them too:
- **Ascension**
- **Corpus Christi**
- **June 2**, Proclamation of Republic (celebrated on the following Saturday)
- **November 4**, National Unity Day (celebrated on following Saturday)

LOCAL FESTIVAL DAYS & THEIR PATRON SAINTS

Town	Date	Patron Saint
Rome	June 29	Sts. Peter and Paul
Palermo	July 15	Santa Rosalia
Naples	Sept. 19	St. Gennaro
Cagliari	Oct. 30	St. Saturnino
Bari	Dec. 6	St. Nicola

MAKING AIRLINE RESERVATIONS

Since airfares can vary so widely it is advised to contact a reputable travel agent and stay abreast of all promotional fares advertised in the newspapers. Once you're ticketed getting there is a breeze. Just hop on the plane and 6-8 hours later you're there. Italy's two main international airports are Rome's **Fiumicino** (also known as **Leonardo da Vinci**) and Milan's **Malpensa**, which handle all incoming flights from North America, Australia, and the United Kingdom.

There are other, smaller regional airports in Bologna, Pisa and Venice that accept flights from all over Europe as well as the Untied Kingdom, but not from North America or Australia. So, if you are only visiting the fairy tale city of Venice and want to fly almost directly there, contact your travel agent and make sure they get you on an airline, most likely British Air, that will allow for a transfer in London and a connection to Venice.

Fares are highest during the peak summer months (June through mid-September) and lowest from November through March (except during peak Christmas travel time). You can get the best fares by booking far in advance. This will also assure you a seat. Getting a non-stop flight to Italy at the last minute is simply an impossibility during the high season. If you are concerned about having to change your schedule at the last minute, and do not want to book far in advance, look into some special **travel insurance** that will cover the cost of your ticket under such circumstances. Check with your travel agent about details and pricing since these, like ticket prices, change almost on a daily basis.

PASSPORT REGULATIONS

A visa is not required for US or Canadian citizens, or members of the European Economic Community, who are holding a valid passport, unless s/he expects to stay in Italy longer than 90 days and/or study or seek employment. While in Italy, you can apply for a longer stay at any police station for an extension of an additional 90 days. You will be asked to prove that you're not seeking such an extension for study or employment, and that you have adequate means of support. Usually permission is granted almost immediately.

VACCINATIONS

No vaccinations are required to enter Italy, or for that matter, to re-enter the U.S., Canada, or any other European country. But some people are starting to think it may be wise, especially for Hepatitis A. One of those people is Donna Shipley, B.S.N, R.N. and President of Smart Travel, an international health service organization. She says, "Even though the perception is that Italy is safe and clean, it is still not like North America. In other words it is better to be safe than sorry. Prevention makes sense." For information about vaccinations contact:
• **Smart Travel**, *Tel. 800/730-3170.*

REGISTRATION BY TOURISTS

This is usually taken care of within three days by the management of your hotel. If you are staying with friends or in a private home, you must register in person at the nearest police station within that three day period. Rome has a special police information office to assist tourists, and they have interpreters available: Tel. 461-950 or 486-609.

TRAVEL INSURANCE

This is the most frequently forgotten precaution in travel. Just like other insurance, this is for 'just in case' scenarios. The beauty of travel insurance is that it covers a wide variety of occurrences, such as trip cancellation or interruption, trip delay/missed connection, itinerary change, accident medical expense, sickness medical expense, baggage and baggage delay, and medical evacuation/repatriation. And to get all that for a week long trip will only cost you $25. You'll spend more than that on the cab ride from the airport when you arrive.

For travel insurance look in your local yellow pages or contact this organization below:
• **Travelex**, *Tel. 800/228-9792*

CUSTOMS REGULATIONS

Duty free entry is allowed for personal effects that will not be sold, given away, or traded while in Italy: clothing, books, camping and household equipment, fishing tackle, one pair of skis, two tennis racquets, portable typewriter (I suppose they mean a portable computer now), record player with 10 records, tape recorder or Dictaphone, baby carriage, two still cameras with 10 rolls of film for each, one movie camera with 10 rolls of film (I suppose they mean 10 cassette tapes now), binoculars, personal jewelry, portable radio set (may be subject to small license fee), 400 cigarettes, and a quantity of cigars or pipe tobacco not to exceed 500 grams (1.1 lbs), two bottles of wine and one bottle of liquor, 4.4 lbs of coffee, 6.6 lbs of sugar, and 2.2 lbs of cocoa.

This is Italy's official list, but they are very flexible with personal items. As well they should be, since technology is changing so rapidly that items not listed last year could be a personal item for most people this year (i.e. Sony Watchmans, portable video games, etc.).

(GETTING TO ITALY)

FLYING TO ITALY

Alitalia is Italy's national airline. As you probably know, most international carriers have amazing service, pristine environments, serve exquisite food and overall are a joy to travel – but to be honest Alitalia is not one of them. If you're up for the adventure of the chaos of Italy's system (take their frequent lack of a government, for example) at 30,000 feet, try flying Alitalia. As another example of Alitalia's disorganization, they are the only major airline in the U.S. without their own toll-free number. Despite their problems Alitalia does have the most frequent direct flights from North America to Italy.

Airlines
   Below is a list of some other major carriers and their flights to Italy:
- **Air Canada**, *Tel. 800/776-3000; www.aircanada.com.* Flights from Canada to London or Paris, then connections on another carrier to Rome or Milan.
- **American Airlines**, *Tel. 800/433-7300; www.americanair.com.* Direct flights from Chicago to Milan.
- **British Airways**, *Tel. 800/247-9297; www.british-airways.com.* Connections through London's Heathrow to Rome, Milan, Bologna or Venice.
- **Delta**, *Tel. 800/221-1212; www.delta-air.com.* Direct flights from New York to Rome or Milan.
- **United**, *Tel. 800/538-2929; www.ual.com.* Direct flights from Washington Dulles to Milan.
- **US Airways**, *Tel. 800/622-1015; www.ual.com.* Direct flights from Philadelphia to Rome.
- **Northwest**, *Tel. 800/2245-2525; www.nwa.com.* Flights to Amsterdam connecting to KLM and onto Rome or Milan.
- **TWA**, *Tel. 800/221-2000; www.twa.com.* Direct flights from New York's JFK to Rome or Milan.

DISCOUNT TRAVEL AGENTS

   The best way to find a travel agency for your travel to Italy is by looking in your local yellow pages. But if you want to get the same flights for less, the two numbers below are for organizations that consistently offer the lowest fares available.
- **Fly Cheap**, *Tel. 800/FLY-CHEAP*
- **Fare Deals, Ltd.**, *Tel. 800/347-7006*

   In conjunction, also featured are some on-line travel booking services that offer great fares. On-line travel searching can be cumbersome, since there is a registration process for each of the listings below, and each are different in their approach to the reservation and booking process. In essence, what you learn from these services is what your travel agent goes through when they work with reservation systems like Apollo, Worldspan and System One. Also, if you shop here to find out what prices and availability are and then book your flights the regular way, from the airline or a live travel agent, these on-line service do not like that. Some will even terminate your registration if you shop too frequently without buying.
   With that said, here are your web sites:
- **Internet Travel Network**, *www.itn.net*

- **Preview Travel**, *www.previewtravel.com*
- **Expedia**, *www.expedia.com*
- **Travelocity**, *www.travelocity.com*

COURIER FLIGHTS

Acting as an air courier – whereby you accompany shipments sent by air in your cargo space in return for discounted airfare – can be one of the least expensive ways to fly. It can also be a little restrictive and inconvenient. But if you want to travel to Italy, at almost half the regular cost, being a courier is for you.

The hassles are (1) that in most cases you have to get to the courier company's offices before your flight, (2) most flights only originate from one city and that may not be the one where you are, (3) since you usually check in later than all other flyers you may not get your choice of seating, (4) you can only use a carry-on since your cargo space is being allocated for the shipment you are accompanying, (5) your length of stay is usually only 7-10 days – no longer, and (6) courier flights don't do companion flights, which means you fly alone.

But contrary to the common impression, as a courier you usually do not even see the goods being transported and you don't need to check them through customs. Also you are not legally responsible for the shipment's contents – that's the courier company's responsibility – according to industry sources and US Customs.

All of that aside, if you are interested in saving a large chunk of change, give these services a try:
- **Halbart Express**, *Tel. 718/656-8189*
- **Now Voyager**, *Tel. 212/431-1616. Fee of $50*
- **Discount Travel International**, *Tel. 212/362-8113*
- **Airhitch**, *Tel. 212/864-2000; www.airhitch.org.* Air hitching is the least expensive but they are also the most restrictive. You really need to be very flexible, i.e. can travel at the drop of a hat.

For more information about courier flights, listed below are some books you can buy or organizations you can contact:
- **"Insiders Guide to Air Courier Bargains"** *by Kelly Monaghan. Tel. 212/569-1081*
- **The Intrepid Traveler**, *Tel. 212/569-1081; www.intrepidtraveler.com. Company is owned by Monaghan.*
- **International Association of Air Travel Couriers**, *Tel. 561/582-8320, www.courier.org.*
- **"A Simple Guide to Courier Travel"**, *Tel. 800/344-9375*

DIPLOMATIC & CONSULAR OFFICES IN ITALY

These are the places you'll need to contact if you lose your passport or have some unfortunate brush with the law. If such situations occur, remember that the employees of these offices are merely your government's representatives in a foreign country. They are not God. They cannot do everything in the blink of an eye, but they will do their best to remedy any unfortunate situation in which you may find yourself.

Embassies
- **US**, *Via Veneto 119A, 00187 Roma, Tel. 06/46741*
- **Canada**, *Via GB de Rossi, 00161 Roma, Tel. 06/445-981*
- **Ireland**, *Largo del Nazereno, 00187 Roma, Tel. 06/678-25-41*
- **South Africa**, *Via Tanaro 14, 00187 Roma, Tel. 06/841-97-94*
- **United Kingdom**, *Via XX Settembre 80A, 00187 Roma, Tel. 06/475 5441 and 475 5551*
- **Australia**, *Via Alessandro 215, 00187 Roma, Tel. 06/852-721*
- **New Zealand**, *Via Zara 28, 00187 Roma, Tel. 06/440-2928 or 440-40-35*

US Consulates
- *Piazza della Repubblica, 80122 Napoli, Tel. 081/583-8111*
- *Via Vaccarini 1, 90143 Palermo, Tel. 091/ 343-546*

Canadian Consulates
- *Delegation du Quebec, Via XX Settembre 4, 00187 Roma, Tel. 06/488-4183*

UK Consulates
- *Via San Lucifero 87. 09100 Cagliari, Tel. 070/66 27 55*
- *Via Francesco Crispi 122. 08122 Napoli, Tel. 081/20 92 27, 63 33 20 and 68 24 82*
- *Via Marchese di Villabianca 9, 90143 Palermo, Tel. 091/33 64-66*

ACCOMMODATIONS

HOTELS - WHAT TO EXPECT

Don't be surprised by the excessive hotel taxes, additional charges, and requests for payment for extras, such as air conditioning. Sometimes these taxes/service charges are included in room rates; check upon arrival. Remember to save receipts from hotels and car rentals, as 15% to 20% of the value-added taxes (VAT) on these services may be refunded if you are a non-resident. For more information, call **I.T.S. Fabry**, *Tel. 803/*

PLANNING YOUR TRIP 57

720-8646 or see Chapter 9, *Shopping*, Tax-Free Shopping section.

The Italian Government tourist agency rates all of the hotels in Italy with a star basis, so we will continue their system. A five star deluxe hotel (*****) is the best, a one-star hotel (*) is the least desirable and usually the least expensive too. The term *Pensione* is in the process of being phased out, and is being replaced by hotels with a designation of one-star (*), two-stars (**), or three stars (***).

Hotel Prices

The prices that are listed sometimes include a range, for example L100,000-150,000 (the L in front of the number stands for *lire*). The first number in the range indicates what the price is during the off-season, the second price is the going rate during high season. If there is no range, then the hotel doesn't raise its rate for the off-season.

The high season is generally April through September, with Christmas and New Year's week thrown in. Also, the high season for the ski areas will be winter, not summer, so it is important to inquire up front about what the rates will be.

HOTEL RATING SYSTEM

The star rating system that the Italian Tourist Board officially uses has little to do with the prices of the hotels, but more to do with the amenities you will find there. The prices for each category will vary according to the locale, so if it's a big city, a four star will be super-expensive; if it's a small town, it will be priced like a three star in a big city.

In the ambiguous way of the Italians, nothing is ever as it seems, which means that even the amenities will be different for each star category depending on whether you are in a big city or a smaller town. But basically the list below is what the ratings mean by star category:

*****Five star, deluxe hotel**: Professional service, great restaurant, perfectly immaculate large rooms and bathrooms with air conditioning, satellite TV, mini-bar, room service, laundry service, and every convenience you could imagine to make you feel like a king or queen. Bathrooms in every room.

****Four star hotel**: professional service, most probably they have a restaurant, clean rooms not so large, air conditioning, TV-maybe satellite, mini-bar, room service, laundry service and maybe a few more North American-like amenities. Bathrooms in every room.

***Three star hotel**: a little less professional service, most probably do not have room service, should have air conditioning, TV and mini bar, but the rooms are mostly small as are their bathrooms. Some rooms may not have bathrooms.

Two star hotel: Usually a family run place, some not so clean as higher rated hotels. Mostly you'll only find a telephone in the room, and you'll be lucky to get air conditioning. About 50% of the rooms have either a shower/bath or water closet and sometimes not both together. Hardly any amenities, just a place to lay your head.

*One star hotel: Here you usually get a small room with a bed, sometimes you have to share the rooms with other travelers. The bathroom is usually in the hall. No air conditioning, no telephone in the room, just a room with bed. These are what used to be the low-end *pensiones*. Definitely for budget travelers.

RENTING VILLAS & APARTMENTS

One of the best ways to spend a vacation in Italy is in a rented villa in the country or in an apartment in the center of town. It makes you feel as if you actually are living in Italy and not just passing through. Staying in "your own place" gives your trip that little extra sense of belonging.

The best way to find a place of your own in Italy is to contact one of the agencies listed below that specialize in the rental of villas and apartments in Italy:

- **At Home Abroad, Inc.**, *405 East 58th Street, New York, NY 10022. Tel. 212/421-9165, Fax 212/752-1591*
- **Astra Maccioni Kohane** (CUENDET), *10 Columbus Circle, Suite 1220, New York, NY 10019. Tel. 212/765-3924, Fax 212/262-0011*
- **B&D De Vogue International, Inc.**, *250 S. Beverly Drive, Suite 203, Beverly Hills CA. Tel. 310/247 8612, 800/438-4748, Fax 310/247-9460*
- **Better Homes and Travel**, *30 East 33rd Street, New York, NY 10016. Tel. 212/689 6608, Fax 212/679-5072*
- **CIT Tours Corp.**, *342 Madison Ave #207, New York, NY 10173. Tel. 212/697-2100, 800/248-8687, Fax 212/697-1394*
- **Columbus Travel**, *507 Columbus Avenue, San Francisco, CA 94153. Tel. 415/3952322, Fax 415/3984674*
- **Destination Italia, Inc.** (Excluive U.S. Representative for Cuendet & Cie spa). *165 Chestnut Street, Allendale, NJ 07401. Tel. 201/327-2333, Fax 201/825-2664*
- **Europa-let, Inc.** *92 N. Main Street or P.O. Box 3537, Ashland, OR 97520. Tel. 503/482-5806, 800/4624486, Fax 503/482-0660*
- **European Connection**, *4 Mineola Avenue, Roslyn Heights, NY 11577. Tel. 516/625-1800, 800/345 4679, Fax 516/625-1138*
- **Four Star Living, Inc.**, *640 Fifth Avenue, New York, NY 10019. Tel. 212/518 3690, Fax 914/677-5528*
- **Heaven on Hearth**, *44 Kittyhawk, Pittsford, NY 14534. Tel. 716/381-7625, Fax 716/381-9784*
- **Hidden Treasure of Italy**, *934 Elmwood, Wilmettw IL 60091. Tel. 708/*

853-1313. Fax 708/853-1340
- **Hideaways International**, P.O. Box 1270, Littleton, MA 01460. Tel. 508/486-8955, 800/8434433, Fax 508/486-8525
- **Home Tours International**, 1170 Broadway, New York, NY 10001, Tel. 212/6894851, Outside New York 1-800-367-4668
- **Interhome Inc.**, 124 Little Falls Road, Fairfield, NJ 07004. Tel. 201/882-6864, Fax 201/8051 742
- **International Home Rentals**, P.O. Box 329, Middleburg, VA 22117. Tel. 703/687-3161, 800/221-9001, Fax 703/687-3352
- **InternationalServices**, P.O. Box 118, Mendham, NJ 07945. Tel. 201/545-9114, Fax; 201/543-9159
- **Invitation to Tuscany**, 94 Winthrop Street, Augusta, ME 04330. Tel. 207/622-0743
- **Italian Rentals**, 3801 Ingomar Street, N.W., Washington, D.C. 20015. Tel. 202/244-5345, Fax 202/362-0520
- **Italian Villa Rentals**, P.O. Box 1145, Bellevue, Washington 98009. Tel 206/827-3964, Telex: 3794026, Fax 206/827-2323
- **Italy Farm Holidays**, 547 Martling Avenue, Tarrytown, NY 10591. Tel. 914/631-7880, Fax 914/631-8831
- **LNT Associates**, Inc., P.O. Box 219, Warren, Ml 48090. Tel. 313/739-2266, 800/582 4832, Fax 313/739-3312
- **Overseas Connection**, 31 North Harbor Drive, Sag Harbor, NY 11963. Tel. 516/725-9308, Fax 516/725-5825
- **Palazzo Antellesi**, 175 West 92nd Street #1GE, New York NY 10025. Tel. 212/932-3480, Fax 212/932-9039
- **The Parker Company**, 319 Lynnway, Lynn MA 01901. Tel. 617/596-8282, Fax 617/596-3125
- **Prestige Villas**, P.O.BOx 1046, Southport, CT 06490. Tel. 203/254-1302. Outside Connecticut 800/336-0080, Fax 203/254-7261
- **Rent a Home International, Inc.**, 7200 34th Avenue. N.W.. Seattle, WA 98117. Tel. 206/789-9377, 800/488-RENT, Fax 206/789-9379, Telex 40597
- **Rentals In Italy**, Suzanne T. Pidduck (CUENDET), 1742 Calle Corva, Camarillo, CA 93010. Tel. 805/987-5278, 800/726-6702, Fax 805/987-5278
- **Rent-A-Vacation Everywhere, Inc.** (RAVE), 585 Park Avenue, Rochester, NY 14607. Tel. 716/256-0760, Fax 716/256-2676
- **Unusual Villa Rentals**, Tel. 804/288-2823. Fax 804/342-9016. Email johng@unusualvillarentals.com. www.unusualvillarentals.com
- **Vacanze In Italia**, P.O. Box 297, Falls Village, CT 06031. Tel. 413/528-6610, 800/533-5405, Fax 413/528-6222

- **Villas and Apartments Abroad, Ltd.**, *420 Madison Avenue. New York, NY 10017. Tel. 212/759-1025. 800/433-3021 (nationwide), 800/433-3020 (NY)*
- **Villas International,** *605 Market Street, Suite 610, San Francisco, CA 94105. Tel. 415/281-0910, 800/221-2260, Fax 415/281-0919*

YOUTH HOSTELS

Youth Hostels (*ostelli per la gioventu*) provide reasonably priced accommodations, specifically for younger travelers. A membership card is needed that is associated with the youth hostel's organization, i.e. a student ID card. Advanced booking is a must during the high season since these low priced accommodations fill up fast. Hundreds of youth hostels are located all over Italy. Contact the Tourist Information office when you arrive in the city to locate them.

HOME EXCHANGE

*A less expensive way to have "a home of your own" in Italy is to join a **home swapping club**. These clubs have reputable members all over the world. All you'd need to do is coordinate travel plans with a family in a location you'd like to stay in Italy, and exchange houses. Think of how much money you'd save. The best one that we know is* **Home Link***, PO Box, Key West FL 33041, Tel. 305/294-3720, Tel. 800/638-3841, Fax 305/294-1448.*

7. ARRIVALS & DEPARTURES

BY AIR

Most travelers will arrive at **Rome's Fiumicino (Leonardo da Vinci) Airport** that handles most incoming flights from North America, Australia, and the United Kingdom. If you are arriving from other points in Europe you may arrive at Rome's **Ciampino** airport.

Rome's Fiumicino has a dedicated **train** to whisk you directly to the central train station (**Termini**). To get to the train at the airport simply follow the signs (**Treno**) right after you get through customs. After you leave the arrivals building you'll see the train station about fifty feet in front of you across the street and up a ramp. The trip costs L12,000 and takes 30 minutes. The trains leave every half hour starting at 7:38am and the last train is at 10:08pm. The trains are air conditioned. Then when you arrive at the **Termini** train station you can get a taxi from the taxi stand outside in front of the station to get to your hotel. Or you can hop on the Metro, or a take city bus to get close to your hotel.

If you want to spend the equivalent of a night in a hotel on a **taxi** ride from the airport directly to your hotel, by all means do so. This choice can sometimes take longer depending on the traffic situation in and around the airport. Your best bet is to take the train to Termini station and catch a cab there. When returning to the airport, the same is true about the trains: they run every half an hour departures starting at 6:52am and ending at 9:22pm.

There is also a **Metropolitana** service from the airport to **Stazione Tiburtina** stopping at the following stations: Ponte Galleria, Muratella, Magliana, Trastevere, Ostiense, and Tuscolana. Departures are every 20 minutes from 6:00 am to 10:00 pm. The trip takes about 45 minutes, and trains are air conditioned.

If you are renting a car, you will get explicit directions from your rental company. See the *Renting a Car* section in the next chapter for

62 ROME & SOUTHERN ITALY GUIDE

more complete information. If they neglect to give you directions, get on the large road – **SS 201** – leading away from the airport to the **GRA** *(Grande Raccordo Anulare)*, which is Rome's beltway and is commonly known as the **Anulare**, going north. Get off at **SS 1** (**Via Aurelia**) and follow this road all the way into town.

If you arrive at Rome's **Ciampino**, there are dedicated airport buses that leave for the **Anagnina Metro Station** every half an hour. They take 15 minutes to get into town. Taking a **taxi** from here also costs an arm and a leg but not nearly as much as from Fiumicino, since this airport is closer to Rome. If you rent a car, simply take **Via Appia** all the way into town. For the scenic view get on the **Via Appia Antica** a kilometer or so after passing the **GRA**.

By Car

To get into Rome you will have to either get on or pass by the **GRA** *(Grande Raccordo Anulare)* which is Rome's beltway and is commonly known as the **Anulare**. If arriving from the north you will be using **Via Cassia** (which can get congested), **Via Flaminia**, **Via Salaria** or the fastest route, the **A1** *(Autostrada del Sole)*, which will dump you onto the GRA.

If arriving from the south, the fastest route is the **A2**, also referred to as the *Autostrada del Sole*. A more scenic route is along the **Via Appia**.

Sample trip lengths on the main roads:
- **Florence**: 3 1/2 hours
- **Venice**: 6 1/2 hours
- **Naples**: 3 hours
- **Bari**: 13 hours

By Train

When arriving by train, you will be let off at Rome's **Termini** station. From here you can catch a **taxi** at the row of cabs outside the front entrance, walk down to the **Metro** and catch a train close to your destination, or hop on one of the **buses** in the main square (Piazza Cinquecento) just in front of the station.

Termini is a zoo. Packed with people from all over the world, queuing up to buy tickets, trying to cut in line to get information, and in some cases looking for unprotected belongings. Don't leave your bags unattended in any train station in Italy. The Tourist information office is located near the train tracks *(Tel. 06/487-1270)*. You can get a good map here and make a hotel reservation. The railway information office faces the front entrance along with the taxis and buses. If you're planning a trip, you should come here to find out when your train will be leaving. All attendants speak enough English to get by.

ARRIVALS & DEPARTURES

Sample trip lengths and costs for direct *(diretto)* trains:
- **Florence**: 2 1/2 hours, L35,000
- **Venice**: 5 hours, L56,000
- **Naples**: 2 hours, L25,000
- **Bari**: 12 hours, L70,000

GETTING TO & FROM THE AIRPORTS IN ROME

The Italian transportation system is the complete opposite of their airline: on-time, goes everywhere, and is clean and comfortable.

Rome has a dedicated train to whisk you directly to the central train station, where you can get a taxi to your hotel (doing it this way will be much less expensive than taking a taxi straight from the airport and just about as convenient). From the train station, you can also hop on the Metro or a city bus to take you near your hotel.

When you are departing the country remember to have at least L15,000 on hand to pay the airport tax.

Rome Fiumicino (Leonardo da Vinci) Airport
- **Direct Link** – A new train service is now available from the airport directly to **Stazione Termini** (Rome's Central Railway Station). The trip costs L18,000 one way and takes 30 minutes. There are trains every half hour. They start at 7:38am and end at 10:08pm. The trains are air-conditioned. Returning to the airport the trains are also every half hour but start at 6:52am and end at 9:22pm.
  Note: You can pick up a schedule for the train when you buy your tickets. This will help you plan for your departure.
- **Metropolitan Link** – Train service from the Airport to **Stazione Tiburtina** stopping at the following stations: Ponte Galleria, Muratella, Magliana, Trastevere, Ostiense, and Tuscolana. Departures are every 20 minutes from 6:00 am to 10:00 pm. Trip takes about 45 minutes. Trains are air-conditioned.

Rome Ciampino Airport
Dedicated airport buses can be caught outside of the **Agnina Underground Station**. Time to airport: 15-25 minutes, depending on traffic.

8. GETTING AROUND ROME & SOUTHERN ITALY

GETTING AROUND ROME
BY CAR
Are you nuts? Unless you are from Boston and used to aggressive driving tactics, driving a car to get around Rome is a crazy idea, considering that the public transportation system is so good and that virtually everything is within walking distance. Now if you want to rent a car for a day trip at the beach at Lido di Ostia or another excursion, that's another story. But even in those circumstances, you can still get to those destinations and most others by train from Stazione Termini.

So think twice about renting a car, because Italian drivers are like nothing you've ever seen. And if you do rent a car, beware to those automobiles with a big letter "P" taped to the rear windows or trunks. It stands for *Principinate di Patente Fresche*, meaning a newly licensed driver. They are the worst. Also beware of the cars with the words *Scuola Guida* (Driving School) on them.

And if you rent a car you'll need to buy gas, besides being expensive, sometimes it can be inconvenient. There are some unmanned stations in Italy whose pumps only take crisp L10,000 bills. Remember to carry some at all times.

Renting a Car
Cars can be rented at **Fiumicino** or **Ciampino airports**, booked in advance by a travel agent, or rented at many offices in the city, especially at the train station **Termini**. Try the following places:
- **Avis**, *Main Office, Piazza Esquino, Tel. 06/478-001 or 478-011. Open Monday through Friday 9:00am-1:30pm and 2:30pm-6:00pm. Their office at Termini Station is open Monday-Saturday 7:00am-8:00pm, and Sundays*

> ### IMPROVEMENTS FOR THE YEAR 2000
> *Rome is busy scrubbing itself clean from years of smog and soot; the monuments haven't gleamed like this since they were first built. The city has also started using some of the new red buses, complete with air conditioning and much more comfortable seating that will be out in force for the year 2000 celebrations. On top of cleaning all their monuments, adding new buses, introducing the fast and efficient EUROSTAR train service, creating covered waiting areas for taxis and buses at the train station, Romans are making everything much more efficient and intuitive for travelers, from signs describing train schedules and layouts to Metro ticket dispensers. Other cities, like Florence, Siena, Perugia and others, are feverishly going through the same cleansing and organizing to accommodate the massive influx of pilgrims and tourists expected for 2000. Rome and all of Italy have never looked better. This is the time to visit.*

from 8:00am-11:00pm (Tel. 06/470-1219). Their office at Fiumicino is open every day from 7:30am-11:00pm (Tel. 06/601-551).
- **Budget Rent A Car**, *Main Office, Via Ludovisi. Tel. 06/482-0966 or 482-0927. Open Monday through Friday 9:00am-1:30pm and 2:30pm-6:00pm. The office at Fiumicino airport is open Monday-Saturday 7:00am-8:00pm, and Sundays from 8:00am-11:00pm (Tel. 06/6501-0347 or 06/652-9133). The office at Ciampino holds the same hours (Tel. 06/7934-0137).*
- **Hertz**, *Main Office is on the Via Veneto #156. The phone number is 06/321-6831 or 06/321-6834. It's conveniently located in the underground garage that can be accessed from either the Piazza di Spagna Metro stop or the Via Veneto. In and of itself it's something that should be seen and walked through while you're in Rome. The office is open Monday - Saturday 7:00am-8:00pm and Sunday 8:00am-1:00pm. The office number at Termini station is 06/474-6405; at Fiumicino it's 06/602-448; at Ciampino it's 06/7934-0095.*

The fees usually include the costs for towing, minor repairs, and basic insurance, but you should ask. Also most firms require a deposit equal to the daily cost of the rental, which is usually between L200,000 and L300,000. The minimum age usually is 21 and you must have had a drivers license for at least a year. Rules and regulations will vary according to company. Standard industry business practices haven't hit Italy yet.

> **TOWED CAR?**
>
> *If your car happens to have been towed, it means you parked in an illegal spot. To find out where your car is call* **Vigili Urbani***, Tel. 06/67691, and give them the registration number, make of car and place where it was removed. They will tell you where your car has been placed, but you can only pick up your car after you have paid your fine at Via della Consolazione 4. Take your receipt with you when you retrieve your car. On Sundays the office to pay your fine is closed, but the towers are still working – so don't park illegally on Sundays.*

BY MOPED

If you are looking for a new experience, a different way to see Rome (or any city in Italy), try renting a moped. Walking, riding a bicycle, driving a car, taking the bus, or riding in a taxi cannot come close to the exhilaration of riding a moped.

A moped gives you freedom. A moped gives you the ability to go from one corner of Rome to another, quickly. Riding a moped makes you feel in tune with the flow of the city. With no plan, no sequence, no itinerary, no boundaries, you can go from the tourist areas to a part of Rome tourists rarely see. You can find monuments and markets in Rome you would never have seen if not on a moped. It makes you feel a part of the city, and this familiarity gives you the confidence to widen your explorations.

Now that I've built it up, think hard about renting a moped. As with cars, a moped is even more dangerous since you have nothing to protect you. Only if you feel extremely confident about your motorcycle driving abilities should you even contemplate renting a moped. This isn't the Bahamas where everyone's polite. The Romans will just as soon run you over as make way for you.

Personally, I find a moped to be the most fun way to get around Rome. They're inexpensive, quick, easy to maneuver, and practical since parking is virtually impossible for a car. But, granted, I have had my accidents. Once, as I was speeding between cars who were stopped at a light, a pedestrian walked in front of me and POW, next thing you know I'm wrapped around a pole. And then there was the time a public bus decided that he had the right of way in a circle and casually knocked me down. Anyway, only if you're *un po pazzo* or very brave should you attempt to rent a moped.

GETTING AROUND ROME & SOUTHERN ITALY 67

> ### MOPED CAUTION & RATES
>
> *If you cannot ride a bicycle, please do not rent a moped. The concept is the same, one vehicle just goes a little faster. Also, start off renting a 50 cc (**cinquanta**), not a 125 cc (**cento venti cinque**). With more than twice the engine capacity, the 125 cc is a big difference, and in the traffic of Rome it's best to start slow. But if you insist on riding two to a moped, then a 125 cc is necessary. It's the law. (Not that any Italians abide by it). Also you need to be at least sixteen years old to rent a moped, but you don't need a motorcycle license. Just hop on, and ride away... but don't let Mom and Dad know about it.*
>
> *A sizable deposit (around L200,000+) is required for each moped. The deposit will increase based on the size of moped you want to rent. Your deposit can be cash in any currency, travelers checks, or on a credit card. This is standard procedure for all rental companies. Do not worry, you'll get your money back. Daily rates are between L50,000 and L80,000. Renting for a more extended period can be a better bargain. Rates should be prominently posted.*

Renting a Moped
- **Bici e Baci**, *Via Principe Amadeo 2B, Tel. 06/474-5389. Open 8:00am-7:00pm. All credit cards accepted.*
- **Scooters for Rent**, *Via Della Purificazione 66, Tel. 488-5685. Open 9:00am-7:30pm, seven days a week.* A centrally located moped rental, just off the Piazza Barberini. After the steep climb up this street, you will definitely want a moped. This is a small, quaint little rental outfit that, to the best of my knowledge, were the first to start renting mopeds to tourists many years ago. The people here are fun, helpful, and friendly.
- **I Bike Rome di Cortessi Ferruccio**, *Viale Galappatoio, near Via Veneto. Tel. 06/322-5240. Open Monday-Saturday 9:00am-1:00pm and 4:00pm-8:00pm, and Sundays 9:00am-8:00pm.* They rent from the same underground parking garage (connecting the Piazza di Spagna Metro Stop and the Via Veneto) as does Hertz. Maybe that's why you get a 50% discount with a Hertz card.
- **St. Peter's Moto**, *Via di Porto Castello 43, Tel. 06/687-5719. Open Monday-Saturday 9:00am - 1:30pm and 3:30pm-9:30pm.*
- **Scoot-A-Long**, *Via Cavour 302, Tel. 06/678-0206. Open Monday-Saturday 9:00am-7:00pm, Sunday 10:00am-2:00pm and 4:00pm-7:00pm.*
- **Scooter Center**, *Via in Lucina 13/14. Tel. 06/687-6455. Open daily 9:00am-7:30pm. Credit cards accepted. One day L80,000. Three days L200,000.*

BY BICYCLE

Bicycles make getting from one spot in Rome to another quicker and easier, but if you haven't been on one in awhile, trying to re-learn on the streets of Rome is not a good idea. And don't even think about having children younger than 14 try and ride around Rome unattended. Not only could they get lost very easily, but the traffic laws are so different they may not be able to adapt very well.

I've seen older teenagers fare very well, especially around the Trevi Fountain, Spanish Steps area. Letting your kids do this gives them a sense of freedom, but reinforce to them how careful they have to be.

Renting a Bike

Each place listed above that rent mopeds also rent bicycles on a daily or hourly basis. The cost for an entire day varies from place to place, and year to year, but the latest price is L25,000 per day and L8,000 per hour, except at the one below, which is only L20,000 a day and L5,000 per hour.
- **Bici e Baci**, *Via Principe Amadeo 2B, Tel. 06/474-5389.* Run by a beautiful and animated Italian *signorina* with bubbling brown eyes who insisted I refer to her as *Laura delle Biciclette* (Laura of the Bicycles). Her effervescence is in the name of her business *(Bici e Baci)* which means "Bikes and Kisses." Her rates (for the bicycles) are L5,000 for an hour and L20,000 for a day. She now also rents, cars, vans, and trucks through Italyrent and motor scooters on her own.

BY TAXI

Taxis are the best, and also the most expensive, way to get around Rome. They are everywhere so flagging one down is not a problem. But since they are so expensive I wouldn't rely on them as your main form of transportation. Use them as a last resort, when you start to get tired from walking. Also have a map handy when a cabby is taking you somewhere. Since they are on a meter, they sometimes decide to take you on a little longer journey than necessary. And also watch out for the fly-by-night operators who don't have a licensed meter. They will really rip you off.

The going rate as of publication was L3,500 for the first 2/3 of a kilometer or the first minute (which usually comes first during the rush hours), then it's L300 every 1/3 of a kilometer or minute. At night you'll also pay a surcharge of L3,000, and Sundays you'll pay L1,000 extra. If you bring bags aboard, say for example after you've been shopping, you'll be charged L500 extra for each bag.

Besides having to flag down a cab, there are strategically placed **cab stands** all over the city. The ones that will benefit you as a tourist the most are probably the ones in Piazza del Popolo, Piazza della Repubblica, Piazza Venezia, and at Piazza Sonino just across the bridge in Trastevere.

GETTING AROUND ROME & SOUTHERN ITALY 69

Rome also has several radio taxi cooperatives: **La Capitale** *(Tel. 4994)*, **Roma Sud** *(Tel. 6645)*, **Roma** *(Tel. 3570)*, **Cosmos** *(Tel. 88177)* and **RadioTaxi Tevere** *(Tel. 4157)*. Be warned that when you call for a taxi the cab's meter starts running when it is summoned, not when it arrives to pick you up.

BY BUS

At each bus stop, called **fermata**, there are signs that list all the buses that stop there. These signs also give the streets that the buses will follow along their route so you can check your map to see if this is the bus for you. Also, on the side of the bus are listed highlights of the route for your convenience. Nighttime routes (since many of them stop at midnight) are indicated by black spaces on newer signs, and are placed at the bottom of the older signs. (Italians just aren't as compulsive as we are about changing everything at once. They seem to ween the population into everything more slowly.) In conjunction the times listed on the signs indicate when the bus will pass the *fermata* you're at during the night so you can plan accordingly.

Riding the bus during rush hour is like becoming a sardine, complete with the odor, so try to avoid the rush hours of 8:00am to 9:00am, 12:30pm to 1:30pm, 3:30 to 4:30pm, and 7:30pr.1 to 8:30pm. Yes, they have an added rush hour in the middle of the day because of their siesta time in the afternoon.

The bus fare costs L1,500 and lasts for 75 minutes, during which time you can transfer to any other bus, but you can only ride the Metro once. Despite the convenience and extent of the Roman bus system, which helped me get anywhere I wanted to go in Rome for a long time, since the advent of the Metro I recommend taking the underground transport as it is easier, quicker, less crowded, and more understandable.

Never board the metro or a bus without a ticket, which can be bought at any ATAC/CO.TRA.L booth or kiosk and at tobacco shops, newstands and vending machines. Then once on board remember to stamp the ticket at the rear stamp machine. If you do not have a ticket <u>and</u> stamp it with the date and time, and an inspector catches you, you face and instantaneous L50,000 fine. For more information, *call ATAC at 06/4695-4444 or CO.TRA.L. at 06/5912-5551.*

ATAC Bus Tours & Bus 119

If you are a hardy soul, take the no-frills *Giro di Roma* tour offered by **ATAC**, the intra-city bus company *(Tel. 06/469-51)*. This three hour circuit of the city leaves from the information booth in the middle of the **Piazza Cinquecento** in front of the train station daily at 3pm and at 2:30pm on Saturday, Sundays and holidays. For your L15,000 fee they give you a free map and a semi-guided tour in a kind of half-Italian half-English monologue that lets you see many parts of the city for cheap.

If you really want to be a native, the **regular bus #119** takes you to some of Rome's classic sights. It starts in the Piazza Augusto Imperatore and takes you by the Pantheon, Piazza Colonna, Via del Tritone, Piazza di Spagna, and the Piazza del Popolo. This is a regular bus route, and I know it doesn't sound too exciting, but it takes you through the heart of old Rome and is an inexpensive alternative to a guided bus tour (only L1,000).

You can buy these 1 hour bus tickets and other longer versions at all *tabacchi* in the city. They are indicated by the large "T" sign in the front of their stores.

Bus Passes

If you are staying in Rome for an extended period of time and need to use the buses frequently since your hotel or destinations are not on a Metro line, you can buy one of the following bus tickets:
- **Weekly Ticket** *(Biglietto Settimanale)*: *L24,000*
- **Monthly Pass** *(Bonamente Mensile)*: *L50,000*

Lost & Found

If you misplace something on a bus, you can report the item missing at the main office, Via Volturno 65 (near the train station). But nine times out of ten ... I don't think you'll get it back, especially if it is an expensive item.

BY METRO

The Roman *Metropolitana* (**Metro**) has two lines (Linea A and Linea B) that intersect in the basement of Termini station. You'll find these and all other stations marked with a prominent white "M" inside a red square up on a sign outside. **Linea A** is probably the most used by the tourists since it starts at Ottaviano, near St. Peter's, and has Piazza del Popolo, Piazza di Spagna, Piazza Barberini, and Piazza della Repubblica as stops. **Linea B** comes in a close second since it takes you to the Colosseum, the Circus Maximus, and the Piramide (which really isn't the greatest sight in the world, but I always return since my family members have been getting their picture taken in front of the Piramide since the 1950's).

Buses used to be the way to get around Rome, quickly, efficiently, and inexpensively, but now that convenience is joined by the Metro. But beware, the Metro can get quite crowded around the Stazione Termini and during rush hours. Sardine-like is the best way to describe it. Besides the crush of humanity, the rides can be very pleasant. But, always be on the look out for pickpockets. There are signs (in Italian) in the Metro and

GETTING AROUND ROME & SOUTHERN ITALY

on buses warning people about pickpockets, so be prepared. The best way to do that is to put your wallet in your front pants pocket.

The Metro runs from 5:30am to 11:30pm.

HOW TO BUY A METRO TICKET

Walk down the steps into the subterranean caverns of the Roman Metro, then buy the ticket at the ever-present ticket booths or vending machines in any station. To get to the trains you stamp the ticket in an ugly bright orange machine. The stamp received from these hideous looking devices marks the start of your 75 minutes. When you get back on the system just stamp your ticket again. Simple.

*If it's late at night, the ticket booths are usually closed so you'll have to use one of the ever-present vending machines in all stations. Simply have L1,500 ready, or close to it in bills or coins. Then a touch tone screen awaits your commands. Press the upper left image on the screen to indicate to the machine you want a 75 minute ticket. Then insert your bills or coins as indicated (the machines do not like **Gettone**, the coins that used to be used exclusively for the telephones, and which are about the same size as a L200 coin), and presto your ticket and change (if any) will appear.*

Lost & Found

If you misplace something on the metro, you can report the item missing at the office at the main station, Servizio Movimento delle Ferrovie dello Stato, *Tel. 06/4669, ext. 7682.* But you probably won't get it back, especially if it is an expensive item.

Take the Metro to the Beach!

If you're interested in going to the beach or visiting the ruins at Ostia Antica, take the Linea B Metro to the Magliana stop and transfer to the train that will take you there. You'll have to pay a new fare, since the Metro and the train systems are different animals.

GETTING AROUND SOUTHERN ITALY & SICILY

Italy is connected by extensive highway systems, a superb train system, a series of regional airports, and naturally, since Italy is virtually surrounded by water and has a number of islands, a complete shipping service involving ferries, hydrofoils, and liners. Your mode of transportation will depend on how long you're staying in Italy and where you are going.

If you have plenty of time on your hands, there will be no need to fly throughout Italy, and travel by train and car will suffice. If you are going to rural, off-the-beaten path locations, you'll need a car, because even if the train did go to where you're going, the *Locale* would take forever since it stops at every town on its tracks.

BY AIR

You can fly between many Italian destinations quite easily. If you are on business, using air travel makes sense to fly from Milan to Rome, but not if you are a tourist. You could enjoy a relaxing three hour train ride in the morning to Florence, spend a day shopping and sightseeing, then get on another three hour train ride to Rome and get there in time for dinner. And the entire cost would only be around $40, a lot less than if you had flown.

But if you insist on flying, here is a list of towns that have airports that receive service from the larger venues in Rome and Milan: Alghero, Ancona, Bari, Bologna, Brindisi, Cagliari, Catania, Firenze, Genoa, Lamezia Terme, Lampedusa, Napoli, Olbia, Pantelleria, Pescara, Pisa, Reggio Calabria, Torino, Trapani, Trieste, Venice, Verona.

BY BICYCLE

You may think that riding a bicycle among Italian drivers would be ludicrous, but they are actually very respectful and courteous of bicyclists. Cycling is a national sport in Italy, so your reception in Italy will be more as a hero than a villain, as you can all too often be viewed in North America. And if you get tired, one benefit of the Italian train system is that some trains have bicycle cars to accommodate travelers such as us. So if you get to one location and feel like you want a breather, or to make better time, you can hop on trains to your next destination.

Another way to bike around Italy is with an organized tour group. One such wonderful organization is Ciclismo Classico. They offer magnificent tours all over Italy, from Sardinia to Tuscany, to Venice and beyond. Their guides are completely knowledgeable and professional and speak impeccable English. And with Ciclismo you stay at fine hotels, eat fantastic food, meet wonderful people, and interact with locals – all while seeing Italy up close and personal on a bicycle. I find this to be a truly authentic way to appreciate and experience Italy.

To get more information, contact **Ciclismo Classico**: *13 Marathon Street, Arlington MA 02174; Tel. 800/866-7314 or 781/646-3377, Fax 617/641-1512. E-mail: info@ciclismoclassico.com. Web Page: www.ciclismoclassico.com.*

BY BUS

Most long distance travel is done by train, but the regional bus systems can be beneficial for inter-city trips to smaller towns, and the Pullman buses can be perfect for a very long trip. If you're not a rental car person, and you simply have to get to that beautiful little medieval hill town you saw from the train window, the only way you're going to get there is by regional bus. Also, if you're going from Florence to Bari to catch the ferry to Greece, it is more convenient to catch a direct bus since you won't have to stop in the Rome or Naples train station to pick up other passengers.

Conveniently, most bus stations are next door to or near the train station in towns and cities. The Italian transportation system is something to be admired and hopefully replicated since they make it so convenient. And comfortable too. Most long range buses are equipped with bathrooms and some have televisions on them (not that you'd understand what was on). The regional inter-town buses are a little less comfortable but still palatial compared to the same type of bus in Central America.

I suggest sticking to the trains, unless the trains don't go where you want to go, which is about everywhere, then take the bus.

BY CAR

The world's first automobile expressways were built in northern Italy during the 1920s. Today, Italy and Germany have the most extensive networks of fast, limited-access highways in Europe. Motorists can drive without encountering traffic lights or crossroads – stopping only for border crossings, rest, or fuel – from Belgium, Holland, France, or Germany across the Alps all the way to Sicily. Two highway tunnels through the Alps, under the Great St. Bernard Pass and through Mont Blanc, enable motor vehicles to travel between Italy and the rest of Europe regardless of weather. The expressways, called *Autostradas*, are superhighways and toll roads. They connect all major Italian cities and have contributed to the tremendous increase in tourist travel.

Driving is the perfect way to see the entire variety of Italy's towns, villages, seascapes, landscapes, and monuments. The Italian drivers may be a little *pazzo* (crazy), but if you drive confidently you should be fine. Still, be alert on Italy's roadways.

Driver's Licenses

US, British, and Canadian driving licenses are valid in Italy, but only when accompanied by a translation. This translation is obtainable from **AAA**, the offices of the **Touring Club Italiano** in Italy, at the offices for the **Italian Government Tourist Office**, and at the Italian frontier.

Even if your native driver's license is accepted, it is strongly recommended that you apply for and receive an 'International Drivers Permit,' which you can get from the Italian Government Tourist Offices listed below.

- **Touring Club Italiano**, *Via Marsala 8, 00185, Roma. Tel. (06) 49 98 99*
- **Italian Government Tourist Office** – in the US: *500 N Michigan Ave, Chicago, IL 60611, Tel. 312/644-0990; 630 Fifth Ave, Suite 1565, New York, NY 10111, Tel. 212/245-4822, Fax 212/586-9249; 360 Post Street, Suite 801, San Francisco CA 94109, Tel. 415/392-6206;* in Canada: *Store 56, Plaza 3, 3 Place Ville Marie, Montreal, Quebec, Tel. 514/866 7667.*

Car Rental

In all major cities there are a variety of car rental locations, and even such American stalwarts as Avis and Hertz (see each city's individual section for specifics). All you need to do to rent a car is contact the agency in question, or have the management of your hotel do it for you. Remember to have had your driver's license translated prior to your arrival (see above). From your car rental place, you will be able to pick up detailed maps of the area in which you want to drive.

Driving through the back roads of Italy can offer you some of the best sights of secluded little hill towns, clear mountain lakes, snow capped mountains and more; but it can also be one of the most expensive items on you trip, not only because of the exorbitant cost of the rental itself, but the cost of $6 or more per gallon of gas. There are ways to keep the cost down, the best of which is making the best use of you car. Don't rent it for your entire trip, allowing it to sit in a garage when you are in a big city and you're getting around on bus, metro, or taxi.

Use a rental car to travel through the isolated hills and valleys in between the big cities and drop off the car once you arrive. Compared to the cost of the rental, drop-off charges are minimal. And of course, make sure you have unlimited mileage, otherwise the cost will creep up by the kilometer. Beside the beauty you'll encounter, and the expense you'll incur, be aware of the possible danger you'll also be putting yourself into. Unless you are from Boston and are used to aggressive driving tactics, driving a car to get around Italy should be avoided. The country's train system is so superb that if you're only going to the major cities and towns you won't need a car. So think twice about renting a car. Italian drivers are like nothing you've ever seen.

BY TRAIN

The Italian railroad system, which is owned by the government, provides convenient transportation throughout the country. Ferries link the principal islands with the mainland, and those that travel between southernmost Italy and Sicily carry trains as well as cars, trucks, and people.

The railroad system is most extensive in the north, but main lines run along both coasts, and other routes cross the peninsula in several places.

GETTING AROUND ROME & SOUTHERN ITALY

The **Simplon Tunnel**, one of the world's longest railroad tunnels, connects Italy and Switzerland. Other rail lines follow routes across the Alps between Italy and France, Austria, and Slovenia.

> ### EUROSTAR STYLE
> *A feather in the cap of the Italian rail system is the **EUROSTAR** **trains**. These are very comfortable, luxurious and fast. Travel between Rome and Florence (and Venice and Florence) has been reduced to less than two hours each way. The seats on these trains are large and accommodating, in both first and second class. In first class they serve you a snack with free beverage service, and offer you headphones that you can keep. A truly wonderful way to travel. So if you are going by train and want to enjoy luxury on the rails, try the EUROSTAR. Price is L110,000 each way.*

Taking the train is one of the best ways to travel throughout Italy, and they go almost every place you'd like to visit. The efficiency of the railway system in Italy is directly attributed to Mussolini. You may have heard the saying, "He may not have done much else, but he got the trains to arrive on time." Always remember to stamp your ticket before boarding the train. Otherwise you will incur an automatic fine of L40,000. The machines to stamp your ticket with the time and date are at the front of every track platform.

Types of Train Tickets

There are two different levels of seating on most every train in Italy: **first class** and **second class**. The difference in price is usually only a few dollars, but the difference in convenience is astounding. First class ticket holders can make reservations in advance, while second class ticket seating is on a first come first serve basis.

In conjunction, the seating quality is light-years apart. An example of the price difference between first class and second when traveling between Rome and Florence is $35 for first class, $22 for second class.

Ticket Discounts

The Italian Railway System offers a variety of discounts on its tickets. Listed below are some that may fit into your travel plans:

- **Silver Card for Senior Citizens**: Available to all people 60 years and older. It allows for a 30% reduction on all first class and second class tickets. Must be purchased in Italy. A one year pass costs L10,000; A two year pass costs L18,000; a permanent pass costs L24,000.

- **Green Card for Youth Travel**: Available to all persons from 12 to 26 years of age. It allows for a 30% reduction on all first and second class tickets. Must be purchased in Italy. A one year pass costs L10,000; a two year pass costs L18,000.
- **Italy Flexi Railcards**: There are many rules and regulations associated with these cards, but they do not hinder the bearer in any way. Example of some rules: cannot be sold to permanent residents of Italy, card is not transferable, card must be validated at any Italian State Railway station's ticket office before travel can commence, validation slip must be kept separate from card (kind of like the validation slip for travelers checks), and lost or stolen cards can not be refunded or replaced unless bearer has validation slip. Rules, rules, rules. Here are the prices for the Flexi Railcards:

	1st Class	2nd Class
4 days of travel within 9 days of validity	$170	$116
8 days of travel within 21 days of validity	$250	$164
12 days of travel within 30 days of validity	$314	$210

- **Italian Unlimited Rail Pass** or the "BTLC Italian Tourist Ticket:" all travel and any type of train is unlimited and free, except for the special **TR450** trains where a supplemental fee will be required. The time period begins on the first day of its use. Here are the prices for the Unlimited Rail Pass:

Validity	1st Class	2nd Class
8 days	$226	$152
15 days	$284	$190
21 days	$330	$220
30 days	$396	$264

Types of Trains
- **IC-Intercity**: Both first and second class seating is available with most first class compartments air-conditioned. Dining cars are also available.
- **EC-Eurocity**: These are the trains that are used in international rail service.
- **EXPR-Expresso**: Ordinary express trains usually carry first and second class passengers. No supplemental fare and reservations are necessary, but I recommend you make them.. Food and drink service is available. These are the trains to take. Hardly any stops at all. Kind of like the MetroLiner Service on Amtrak between Washington DC and New York.

GETTING AROUND ROME & SOUTHERN ITALY 77

- **DIR-Diretto**: Semi-express trains that make plenty of stops. They often have second class seating only. During off-peak hours they are not crowded, but at peak hours they're sardine-city.
- **Locale**: These trains stop everywhere on their route and take forever, but to get to rural locations these are the only options.

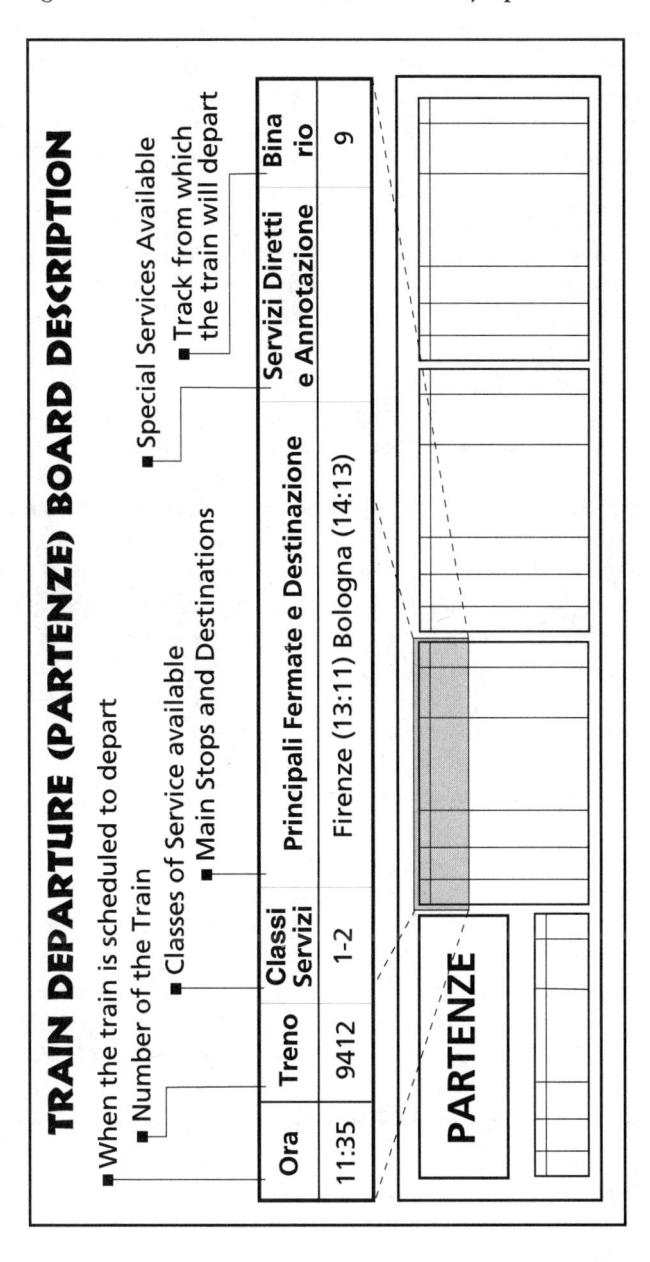

TRAIN DEPARTURE (PARTENZE) BOARD DESCRIPTION

- When the train is scheduled to depart
  - Number of the Train
    - Classes of Service available
      - Main Stops and Destinations
- Special Services Available
  - Track from which the train will depart

Ora	Treno	Classi Servizi	Principali Fermate e Destinazione	Servizi Diretti e Annotazione	Binario
11:35	9412	1-2	Firenze (13:11) Bologna (14:13)		9

PARTENZE

BOARDING THE RIGHT TRAIN

When taking the trains to any location in Italy, such as Pisa or Lucca, the ultimate destination of the train you're taking may not be the one to which you are going. To get to Pisa, sometimes you have to take a train whose ultimate destination is Livorno. Ask the information desk in the train station when your train is leaving, then try one of two things (or both) to make sure you're boarding the proper train:

1. Consult one of the large glass-enclosed schedules (see graphic below) located in the information offices and usually by the tracks that normally have a crowd hovering around, gesturing wildly and speaking in tongues (at least it sometimes seems that way). Match your intended departure time with the time printed on the sheet. Then check directly to the right of the time to see the list of all the destinations for the train. If the name of your destination is listed, you're golden. Next write down the ultimate destination of the train so you can check the main board at the station that lists **partenze** (trains leaving) to see which **binnario** (track) you should board.

2. If that still doesn't assuage your concerns, ask someone waiting at the track or inside the train if it is going to your destination. Ask at least two people, since I've had he experience of asking workers going home at night saying "No," since for forty years they haven't bothered to pay attention to where their train actually stops. Anyway, to politely ask in Italian whether the train is going to your destination say **"Scusa, ma questo treno va a Lucca?"** (Excuse me but does this train go to Lucca?) Obviously substitute the underlined city name for the destination to which you wish to go. This question is asked countless times by many people, including Italians, who shockingly enough are actually riding the train for the first time.

Finally, if you're standing on the platform waiting for the train to come and you suddenly see all the Italians moving away en masse, that usually means that the public address announcer just declared a track change. Ask one of the departing Italians "Has the track for the train to Lucca changed?" **(E cambiato il binnario per il treno per Lucca?)** If s/he says yes (si), either get the number and go there or simply follow them, and as you pass the board that lists the trains leaving, you'll see the change already officially noted.

9. BASIC INFORMATION

BUSINESS HOURS

Store hours are usually Monday through Friday, 9:00am to 1:00pm, 3:30/4:00pm to 7:30/8:00pm, and Saturday 9:00am to 1:00pm. Most stores are closed on Sunday and on national holidays. Don't expect to find any 24-hour convenience stores just around the corner. If you want some soda in your room after a long day of touring you need to plan ahead.

Also, you must plan on most stores not being open from 1:00pm to 4:00pm. This is the Italian siesta time. Don't expect to get a lot done except find a nice restaurant and enjoy a pleasant afternoon.

BANKING HOURS

Banks in Italy are open Monday through Friday, 8:35am to 1:35pm and from 3:00pm to 4:00pm, and are closed all day Saturday and Sunday and on national holidays. In some cities the afternoon open hour may not even exist. Even if the bank is closed, most travelers checks can be exchanged for Italian currency at most hotels and shops and at the many foreign exchange offices in railway stations and at airports.

CURRENCY

The current rate of exchange is **US $1= £1,730 lire** and this is reflected in the cost of restaurants, hotels, bars, etc. The Canadian Dollar to the lira is Can$1 =1,380 lire.

You cannot bring in any currency that totals more than 20 million lire (approximately $11,500) without declaring it at the customs office. This is also the same amount of money that can be legally exported from Italy without declaring it.

If you arrive in Sicily without Italian currency, the airports have banks and monetary exchange offices *(Ufficio di Cambio)*. Remember to keep your receipts from your monetary exchanges, because at some banks, when you want to change lire back to your native currency, you will need to show proof that you first exchanged your currency for Italian currency.

The monetary unit in Italy is the **lira** (leer-ah), the plural is **lire** (leer-ay). Notes are issued for 1,000, 2,000, 5,000, 10,000, 50,000, and 100,000 lire. Coins come in 50, 100, 200 and 500 lira denominations.

US & CANADIAN EXCHANGE RATES
US DOLLAR/ITALIAN LIRE EXCHANGE RATES
US$1 = £1,730 lire

Lire	100	500	1,000	5,000	10,000
US Dollars	6¢	29¢	58¢	$2.89	$5.78

US Dollars	$5	$10	$20	$50	$100
Lire	8,650	17,300	34,600	86,500	173,000

CANADIAN DOLLAR/ITALIAN LIRE EXCHANGE RATES
CDN$1 = £1,380 lire

Lire	100	500	1,000	5,000	10,000
Canadian Dollars	7¢	36¢	73¢	$3.62	$7.25

Canadian Dollars	$5	$10	$20	$50	$100
Lire	6,900	13,800	27,600	69,000	138,000

Note: The currency situation vis-a-vis the US and Canadian dollar is constantly floating. Please check the paper or a bank for the current rates of exchange.

ELECTRICITY

The standard electric current in Italy is 220v, but check with your hotel before you plug in an appliance to find out what the current is, because it's not always 220v! If you want to use your blow dryer, electric razor, radio, or plug in your laptop you are going to need an adapter to adapt your appliance from a two prong to a three prong insert. These can be found at most hardware stores. Also check before you leave to see if your appliance automatically changes the voltage from 110v to 220v. If it doesn't, you will need to purchase a converter.

If you can't find these devices at your hardware store, you can order them from the **Franzus Company**, *Murtha Industrial Park, PO Box, 142, Beacon Falls, CT 06403, Tel. 203/723-6664, Fax 203/723-6666*. They also have a free brochure *Foreign Electricity Is No Deep Dark Secret* that can be mailed or faxed to you.

EXPRESS COURIERS

In Italy, contact **DHL**, *Tel. 167-345345* (a toll free number in Italy) to arrange pickup of your package or documents. Someone's at this number 24 hours a day, 7 days a week. They have over 160 service centers in Italy.

HEALTH CONCERNS

A wonderful "just in case..." option is Personal Physicians Worldwide. This organization can provide you with a list of physicians and hospitals at your destination. If you have a medical condition that may need treatment, or you just want to be safe, they can help. Your personal medical history will be confidentially reviewed by the Medical Director, Dr. David Abramson. He will then contact designated, qualified physicians at your destination to see if they will agree to be available and to care for you, if the need arises, while you are in their location. This is a great service since you never know where you'll be when you need the care of a competent doctor. To find out more information, contact:

- **Personal Physicians Worldwide**, *Tel. 888-657-8114, Fax 301/718-7725. You can e-mail Myra Altschuler, Director, at myra@personalphysicians.com, or Dr. David Abramson, Medical Director at doctors@personalphysicians.com. Their web site home page is http://www.personalphysicians.com.*

NEWSPAPERS & MAGAZINES

At most newsstands in Italy you can find the world renowned *International Herald Tribune,* which is published jointly by The Washington Post and The New York Times and printed in Bologna. You may also be able to find a condensed version of *USA Today*. Besides these two, you can also find newspapers from all over the world at almost any newsstand.

If you want an insight into what may be going on in the English language community of the city you are visiting, simply stop into the local English-language bookstore. They usually have a community newsletter that will fill you in on upcoming events.

PETS

If you're bringing your precious pooch (unfortunately your dog will have to be on a leash and wear a muzzle in public in Italy) or kitty into Italy with you, you must have a veterinarian's certificate stating that your pet has been vaccinated against rabies between 20 days and 11 months before entry into Italy, and that your pet is in overall good health. The certificate must contain the breed, age, sex, and color of your pet and your name and address. This certificate will be valid only for 30 days. The specific forms that the vet needs to fill out are available at all Italian diplomatic and consular offices.

Parrots, parakeets, rabbits, and hares are also subject to health certification by a vet, and will also be examined further upon entry into Italy. Also Customs officials may require a health examination of your pet if you have just come from a tropical region or that they suspect the pet to be ill. All this means that they can do whatever they want whenever they want, so it might be wise to leave your pet at home.

POSTAL SERVICE

Stamps can be purchased at any post office and tobacco shop. If you send a letter airmail with insufficient postage it will not be returned to sender, but will be sent surface mail, which could take months. So try and mail your letters from a post office and have them check the postage for you. Post offices are open from 8:30am to 2:00pm Monday through Friday. On Saturdays and the last day of every month most close at 12 noon; on Sundays they are closed.

AIR MAIL PRICES

Postcards to US and Canada	1100 lire
Letter (up to 20 grams)	1250 lire
Each additional 20 grams	400 lire
Aerograms for all countries	850 lire

SAFETY

Italian cities are definitely much safer than any equivalent American city. You can walk most anywhere without fear of harm, but that doesn't mean you shouldn't play it safe. Listed below are some simple rules to follow to ensure that nothing bad occurs:

- At night, make sure the streets you are strolling along have plenty of other people. Like I said, most cities are safe, but it doesn't hurt to be cautious.
- Always have your knapsack or purse flung over the shoulder that is not directly next to the road. Why? There have been cases of Italians on motor bikes snatching purses off old ladies and in some cases dragging them a few blocks.
- Better yet, have your companion walk on the street side, while you walk on the inside of the sidewalk with the knapsack or purse.
- Better still is to buy one of those tummy wallets that goes under your shirt so no one can even be tempted to purse-snatch you.

That's really all you should need, but always follow basic common sense. If you feel threatened, scared, or alone, retrace your steps back to a place where there are other people.

STAYING OUT OF TROUBLE

Staying out of trouble is paramount, because in Italy you are guilty until proven innocent, unlike in the states where it's the other way around. And most importantly, if arrested you are not simply placed in a holding cell. The Italian officials take you directly to a maximum security prison and lock you up.

And that's where you'll stay for as long as it takes your traveling partners to figure out where you are, bribe your case to top of the local judge's pile, and have your case heard. That whole process can sometimes take months.

So if you like your drinks strong and your nights long, remember to keep your temper in check. And don't even think about smuggling any banned substance into the country, or God forbid, buying something illicit when you're in Italy. If you are approached to buy some hashish or something else, say politely, *No Grazie* (no thank you) and walk away.

TAXIS

Taxi service is widely available in all major cities in Italy, and a little less so in smaller cities such as Pisa or Lucca, and almost non-existent in remote towns and villages. Rates are comparable to those charged in your basic American city. Generally taxis locate themselves in special taxi stands located at railway stations and main parts of the city, but many are out cruising the streets for fares. At these taxi stands are usually telephones that you can call directly from your hotel, but remember, in Italy, if called, the meter starts at the point of origin, so you'll be paying the cabby to come pick you up.

Fares will vary from city to city, but basically when you get in the cab there will be a fixed starting charge, approximately 2,800 to 6,400 lire, and a cost per kilometer, approximately 1,000 to 1,250 lire. Some extra charges may come into play, like the **nighttime supplement** (between 10:00pm and 6:00am), a **Sunday and public holiday supplement**, as well as a **per item luggage charge**. All of these vary from city to city.

There is fierce taxi-cab competition in Italy. Some private citizens dress up their cars to look like cabs, so only take the yellow, metered cabs.

TELEPHONES & FAX
Calling Italy

When you call or fax Italy from the US using the numbers in this book, remember to discard the leading zero in the city code. For example, when calling Rome, whose city code is 06, discard the zero (0) when dialing. So you'd first dial the international prefix, 011, then the country code, 39, then the city code for Rome without the leading zero, 6, then the number you wish to reach.

The reason the leading zero is included in this guide is that Italy has recently required that every call made *within the country* has to include the complete city prefix. At the same time, in some countries you need to use all the digits of the city code, including the leading zero, when dialing Italy.

Long Distance Calling
When you phone from your hotel room, you may incur an exhorbitant cost, so the best bet is to find a quiet public phone from which to call. Some phones in Italy only use **phone cards** (which you can buy at tobacco shops for L5,000/10,000/or 15,000) but most use a combination of cards and coins. You will usually only need to use L200 when you make a long distance phone connection so a phone card may be a little extensive. But if you don't want to keep change on you, buy a phone card. It can even be a great souvenir.

AT&T – *Tel. 172-1011* (a toll free number in Italy) to gain access to an AT&T operator (or English language prompts) for efficient service. You can bill your AT&T calling card, local phone company card, or call direct.

Canada Direct – *Tel. 172-1001* (a toll free number in Italy) and you will be connected to the Canadian telephone network with access to a bi-lingual operator. You can bill your *Calling Card, Call Me*™ service, your *Hello!* Phone Pass or call collect.

MCI – *Tel. 172-1022* (a toll free number in Italy) for MCI's World Phone and use your MCI credit card or call collect. All done through English speaking MCI operators.

Sprint – *Tel. 172-1877* (a toll free number in Italy) for access to an English speaking Sprint operator that can charge your phone card or make your call collect.

Modem or Fax Usage
To connect you modem or fax to the wall you will need an adapter. These too can be bought from a hardware store or from the Franzus Company (see above under Electricity). Many hotels in Italy are starting to use the American standard phone plug, so this may not be a concern. When making your reservations, inquire about the type of plugs in use to insure you can communicate with home without a problem.

TIME

Italy is **six hours ahead of Eastern Standard Time** in North America, so if it's noon is New York it's 6:00pm in Rome. Daylight savings time goes into effect each year in Italy usually from the end of March to the end of September.

BASIC INFORMATION 85

TIPPING
Hotels
A service charge of 15-18% is usually added to your hotel bill, but it is customary to leave a little something else. The following figures are simply guidelines. Based on the service rendered you can increase or decrease these figures. In many cases people do not tip at all and that also is acceptable:
- **Chambermaid**: 1,000 lire per day
- **Concierge**: 3,000 lire per day; additional tip necessary for additional services
- **Bellhop or Porter**: 1,500 lire per bag
- **Doorman** (for hailing or calling you a cab): 1,000 lire
- **Room Service Waiter**: 1,000 lire minimum and a little more depending on the amount ordered

Restaurants
A service charge of around 15% is usually automatically added to all restaurant bills. But if you felt the service was good, it is customary to leave between 5-10% more for the waiter. Also, it is not a requirement that you receive an official receipt, so if you need one please ask.

In cafes and bars, if the bill does not already include a gratuity (and most will so be sure to check) a 15% tip is expected even if you don't eat a meal. Two hundred lire is normal if you're standing at the counter drinking a soda, cappuccino, etc. If you have an alcoholic beverage, something to eat, etc. at the counter, the tip should be 500 lire or more.

Theater Ushers
Yep – they get 1,000 lire or more if the theater is very high class.

Taxis
Give the cabby 10% of the fare, otherwise they just might drive away leaving you without your luggage. (Just kidding).

Sightseeing Guide & Driver
Give 2,000 lire minimum per person for half day tours, and 2,500 minimum per person for full day tours.

Service Station Attendant
Give 1,000 lire or more for extra service like cleaning your windshield, or giving you directions while also filling up your tank.

WEIGHTS & MEASURES

You guessed it, Italy uses the metric system, where everything is a factor ten. This system of measurement is the simplest and easiest; even England converted their entire country some years ago. The only country in the world to still use an antiquated system of measurement, is, you guessed it, our United States. Canada's now about half metric, half American, but that's because they're America's largest trading partner, so they have to know what we do.

The table below gives you a list of weights and measures with approximate values.

WEIGHTS & MEASURES

Weights

Italy	14 grams		Etto		Kilo
US	1/2 oz		1/4 lb		2lb 2oz

Liquid Measure

Italy	Litro
US	1.065 quart

Distance Measure

Italy	Centimeter		Meter		Kilometer
US	2/5 inch		39 inches		3/5 mile

YELLOW PAGES

There is now an **English Yellow Pages** (EYP) in Italy. It is the annual telephone directory of English-speaking professionals, organizations, services and commercial activities in Rome, Florence, Milan, Naples, Genoa and Bologna. The EYP is a well-known resource and reference source among the international community in Italy, from which one can easily find numbers for airlines and embassies, English-speaking doctors and dentists, international schools and organizations, hotels, moving companies, real estate agents, accountants, attorneys, consultants, plumbers, electricians, mechanics and much more. Listings are complete with address including zip code, phone and fax numbers, e-mail and web sites.

You can find copies at embassies, international organizations (FAO, IFAD, WWF, etc.) schools & universities, social and professional associations, English-language churches, foreign press offices, local events within the expat community and various businesses that deal directly with an international clientele. It is on sale at most international bookstores. This is a great resource for any resident or visitor to Italy.

10. FOOD & WINE

FOOD

Most Italian food is cooked with fresh ingredients making their dishes healthy and satisfying. There are many restaurants in Italy of international renown, but you shouldn't limit yourself only to the upper echelon. In most cases you can find as good a meal at a fraction the cost at any *trattoria*. Also, many of the upper echelon restaurants you read about are only in business because they cater to the tourist trade. Their food is good, but the atmosphere is a little hokey.

The traditional Italian meal consists of an *antipasto* (appetizer) and/or soup, and/or pasta and is called **primo**, a main course **secondo** (usually meat or fish), with separately ordered side dishes of *contorni* (vegetables) or *insalata* (salad) which come either *verdi* (green) or *mista* (mixed), then **dolci** (dessert), which can be cheese, fruit, or *gelato* (ice-cream). After which you then order your coffee and/or after dinner drink.

Note: Pasta is never served as an accompanying side dish with a secondo. In Italy, it is always served as a separate course. It is time to forget everything you thought you knew about "Italian" food that was learned at some run-of-the-mill restaurant chain.

As you will notice in each regional chapter, I feature those restaurants that are the top of the line, and usually off the well worn tourist path.

Most North Americans think that there is one type of Italian food, and that's usually spaghetti and meatballs. As a result they don't know what they are missing. Region by region Italy's food has adapted itself to the culture of the people and land. In Florence you have some of the best steaks in the world, in the south the tomato-based pastas and pizzas are exquisite; in Genoa you can't miss the pesto sauce (usually garlic and basil); and don't forget the seafood all along the coast.

Listed below is a selection of the main regional specialties that you should try. In each regional section, I have itemized for you some of the best places to find these and other dishes.

- **Piemonte** – *fonduta (cheese with eggs and truffles)*, *agnolotti* (cheese stuffed pasta), and chocolates and toffees

GLOSSARY OF ITALIAN EATERIES

Bar – Not the bar we have back home. This place serves espresso, cappuccino, rolls, small sandwiches, as well as sodas and alcoholic beverages. It is normal to stand at the counter or sit at a table when one is available. You have to try the **Medallione**, a grilled ham and cheese sandwich available at most bars. A little 'pick-me-up' in the morning is **Café Corretto**, coffee 'corrected' with the addition of **grappa** (Italian brandy) or Cognac.

Gelateria – These establishments offer **gelato** - ice cream - usually produced on the premises. Italian gelato is softer than American but very sweet and rich.

Osteria – Small tavern-like eatery that serves local wine usually in liter bottles as well as simple food and sandwiches

Panineria – A small sandwich bar with a wider variety than at a regular Italian bar, where a quick meal can be gotten. One thing to remember is that Italians rarely use condiments on their sandwiches. If you want mustard or such you need to ask for it.

Pasticceria – Small pasty shops that sell cookies, cakes, pastries, etc. Carry-out only.

Pizzeria – A casual restaurant specializing in pizza, but they also serve other dishes. Most have their famous brick ovens almost directly in the seating area so you can watch the pizza being prepared. There are many featured excellent pizzerias in this book.

Pizza Rustica – Common in central Italy. These are huge cooked rectangular pizzas displayed behind glass. This pizza has a thicker crust and more ingredients than in a regular Pizzeria. You can request as much as you want, since they usually charge by the weight, not the slice. Carry-out only.

Rosticceria – A small eatery where they make excellent inexpensive roast chickens and other meats, as well as grilled and roasted vegetables, mainly potatoes. Sometimes they have baked pasta. Carry-out only.

Trattoria – A less formal restaurant with many local specialties.

Ristorante – A more formal eating establishment, but even most of these are quite informal at times.

Tavola Calda – Cafeteria-style food served buffet style. They feature a variety of hot and cold dishes. Seating is available. Great places for a quick lunch.

- **Lombardia** – *risotto all milanese* (rice with saffron), *minestrone* (stock and vegetable soup), *ossobuco alla milanese* (knuckle of pork dish), *robiola, gorgonzola, stracchino, Bel Paese* (a variety of cheeses)

FOOD & WINE

- **Veneto** – *risi e bisi* (soup with rice and peas), *polenta* (corn meal dish) *zuppa di pesce* (fish soup), *scampi* (shrimp or prawns)
- **Liguria** – *minestrone* (stock and vegetable soup), *pasta al pesto* (pasta with an aromatic garlic basil sauce), *torta Pasqualina* (Easter pie filled with spinach, artichokes, and cheese)
- **Emilia Romagna** – *lasagna verde* (lasagna made with spinach), *cappelletti alla bolognese* (small hats pasta covered with a tomato meat sauce), *scallope* (scallops) *Parmigiano Reggiano* (cheese) and a variety of salamis
- **Toscana** – *bistecca all Fiorentina* (large T-bone steaks grilled), *arista* (roast pork), *cacciucco* (fish soup)
- **Lazio** – *abbacchio arrosto* (roast lamb), *porcetta* (roast pork), and pastas, including *penne all'arrabiata* (literally translated it means angry pasta; a spicy hot, garlic-laden, tomato dish; should not be missed) and *Tortellini all Panna* (meat or cheese pasta in a heavy cream sauce)
- **Campania** – *spaghetti alla vongole verace* (with a spicy garlic oil sauce.), Fantastic pizzas because of their wonderful cheeses (*mozzarella, provola, caciocavallo*)
- **Sicilia** – fresh fruits, pastries like *cannoli alla Siciliana*; c*aponata di melanzane* (eggplant dish), and seafood

RESTAURANT LISTINGS IN THIS BOOK

Here's a sample listing you'll find in this book in each of our *Where to Eat* sections. The number preceding the name of the restaurant tells you where to find it on the accompanying city or town map:

"**3. LA LEPANTO**, *Via Carlo Alberto 135, Tel. 079/979-116. Closed Mondays in the winter. All credit cards accepted. Dinner for two L140,000.*

A fine place with a quaint terrace located in the heart of the old city, but the preparation of dishes is haphazard. Sometimes it's great, other times so-so. Maybe it's because they try to do too much. The menu is extensive and seems to have everything that surf and turf could offer. I've always been pleased with the *i polpi tiepido con le patate* (roasted octopus in an oil and garlic sauce with roasted potatoes) and the *spaghetti con gamberi e melanzane* (with shrimp and eggplant). For antipasto, try the exquisite *antipasto misto di pesce spada affumicato* (smoked swordfish) or the *insalata mista* (mixed salad) with fresh vegetables from the region."

The restaurant listings indicate which credit cards are accepted by using the following phrases:
- **Credit cards accepted** = American Express and/or Visa or Mastercard
- **All Credit cards accepted** = Everything imaginable is accepted, even cards you've never heard of
- **No credit card accepted** = Only cash or travelers checks (if a listing is left without an indication, that means that no credit cards are accepted.)

Each list will also give a ballpark price for a dinner for two in Italian lire. For example: "Dinner for two L80,000." With the exchange rate at roughly $1=L1,600, for this example the dollar price would be $50 for the meal. This price includes a *primo* and *secondo* per person and a bottle of house wine with the meal. In most cases you will get by with one course. Thus the actual price you will pay will be less than indicated.

WINE

Italy is also famous for its wines. The experts say the reds are not robust enough, and the whites are too light, but since I'm not an expert, I love them, one and all. Most importantly, to get a good bottle of wine, you don't have to spend a fortune. You can find some excellent wines straight out of vats in small wine stores in every city in Italy.

ITALIAN WINES BY REGION

Piemonte – **Barolo** *(red, dry)*, **Barbera** *(red, dry)*, and **Asti Spumanti** *(sweet sparkling wine)*

Lombardia – **Riesling** *(white, dry)*, **Frecciarossa** *(rose wines)*

Trentino-Alto Adige – **Riesling** *(white, dry)*, **Santa Maddalena** *(red, semi-dry)*, **Cabernet** *(red, dry)*

Veneto – **Soave** *(white, dry)*, **Valpolicella** *(red, dry or semi-sweet)*

Liguria – **Cinqueterre** *(named after a section of Liguria you must visit. Cinqueterre is five small ocean side towns inaccessible by car or train, you have to walk. They're simply gorgeous.)*

Emilia Romagna – **Lambrusco** *(red, semi-sparkling, several kinds going from dry to sweet)*, **Sangiovese** *(red, dry)*, **Albano** *(white, dry or semi-sweet)*

Tuscany – **Chianti** *(red, dry; look for the Chianti Classico. They're the ones with a black rooster on the neck of the bottle)*

Marche – **Verdicchio** *(white, dry)*

Umbria/Lazio – **Orvieto** *(white, dry)*, **Frascati** *(white, dry or semi-sweet)*, **Est Est Est** *(white, slightly sweet)*

Abruzzi – **Montepulciano** *(red, dry)*

Sardinia – **Cannonau** *(red, dry to semi-sweet)*

Sicily – **Etna** *(red and white, wide variety)*, **Marsala** *(white, dry or sweet)*

Campania, Apulia, Calabria, Basilicata – **Ischia** *(red and white, several varieties)*, **San Severo** *(red, dry)*

FOOD & WINE

As you read each regional chapter, you notice I mention quite a few. This is because I had to have something to go with our picnic lunches during siesta time. Also, at any restaurant, all you'll need to order is the house wine to have a satisfying and excellent wine. (*Vino di casa*: House Wine. *Roso*: Red. *Biancho*: White).

But if you're a connoisseur, or simply want to try a wine for which a certain Italian region is known, in the sidebar above you'll find a selected list of wines and their regions (if you like red wine, try the **Chianti**, and if it's white you prefer, try **Verdicchio**).

ORDER LIKE A NATIVE: READING AN ITALIAN MENU

Here are a few choice words to assist you when you're ordering from a menu while in Italy. Usually, the waiter should be able to assist you, but if not, this will make your dining more pleasurable. You wouldn't want to order octopus, rabbit or horse by surprise, would you?

ENGLISH	ITALIAN	ENGLISH	ITALIAN
Menu	*Lista or Carta*	Teaspoon	*Cucchiaino*
Breakfast	*Prima Colazione*	Knife	*Cotello*
Lunch	*Pranzo*	Fork	*Forchetta*
Dinner	*Cena*	Plate	*Piatto*
		Glass	*Bicchiere*
Cover	*Coperto*	Cup	*Tazza*
Spoon	*Cucchiao*	Napkin	*Tovagliolo*

Antipasto

Soup	*Zuppa*	Broth	*Brodo*
Fish Soup	*Zuppa di Pesce*	Vegetable soup	*Minestrone*
Broth with beaten egg	*Stracciatella*		

Pasta

Ravioli with meat stuffing	*Agnolotti*	Egg noodles	*Fettucine*
Large rolls of pasta	*Cannelloni*	Potato-filled, ravioli-like pasta	*Gnocchi*
Thin angel hair pasta	*Capellini*	Thin pasta	*Vermicelli*
Little hat pasta	*Capelletti*	Macaroni-like pasta	*Penne*

Eggs	*Uova*		
soft-boiled	*al guscio*	hard boiled	*sode*
fried	*al piatto*	omelet	*frittata*

Fish	*Pesce*		
Seafood	*Frutti di mare*	Eel	*Anguilla*
Lobster	*Aragosta*	herring	*Aringa*
Squid	*Calamari*	Carp	*Carpa*
Mullet	*Cefalo*	Grouper	*Cernia*
Mussels	*Cozze/Muscoli*	Perch	*Pesce Persico*
Salmon	*Salmone*	Clams	*Vongole*
Octopus	*Polpo*	Bass	*Spigola*
Oysters	*Ostriche*	Mixed fried fish	*Fritto Misto Mare*

Meat	*Carne*		
Spring Lamb	*Abbacchio*	Lamb	*Agnello*
Rabbit	*Coniglio*	Chicken	*Pollo*
Small Pig	*Porcello*	Veal	*Vitello*
Steak	*Bistecca*	Breast	*Petto*
Pork	*Maiale*	Liver	*Fegato*
Cutlet	*Costellata*	Deer	*Cervo*
Wild Pig	*Cinghiale*	Pheasant	*Fagione*
Duck	*Anitra*	Turkey	*Tacchino*

Methods of Cooking			
Roast	*Arrosto*	Boiled	*Bollito*
On the Fire/ Grilled	*Ai Ferri Alla Griglia*	Spit-roasted	*Al Girarrosto*
Rare	*Al Sangue*	Grilled	*Alla Griglia*
Well Done	*Ben Cotto*	Medium Rare	*Mezzo Cotto*

Miscellaneous			
French fries	*Patate Fritte*	Cheese	*Formaggio*
Butter Sauce	*Salsa al burro*	Tomato and Meat Sauce	*Salsa Bolognese*
Tomato Sauce	*Salsa Napoletana*	Garlic	*Aglio*
Oil	*Olio*	Pepper	*Pepe*
Salt	*Sale*	Fruit	*Frutta*
Orange	*Arancia*	Cherries	*Ciliege*
Strawberry	*Fragola*	Lemon	*Limone*
Apple	*Mela*	Melon	*Melone*
Beer	*Birra*	Mineral Water	*Aqua Minerale*

Orange Soda	*Aranciata*	7-Up Like	*Gassatta*
Lemon Soda	*Limonata*	Juice (of)	*Succo (di)*
Wine	*Vino*		
Red	*Roso*	White	*Bianco*
House wine	*Vino di Casa*	Dry	*Secco*
Slightly Sweet	*Amabile*	Sweet	*Dolce*
Local Wine	*Vino del Paese*	Liter	*Litro*
Half Liter	*Mezzo Litro*	Quarter Liter	*Un Quarto*
A Glass	*Un Bicchiere*		

On all menus you'll find the universal cover charge, *pane e coperto* (literally "bread and cover") that changes restaurant to restaurant, and in some cases can be quite expensive. This is above and beyond any tip you decide to leave. There will also be a statement about whether service is included, *servizio incluso*, or not, *servizio non incluso*. If service is included it is usually 15% of the bill. If you felt the service was good, it is customary to leave between 5-10% more for the waiter.

Another feature of most menus are *piatti di giorno* (daily specials) and *prezzo fisso* (fixed price offerings.) The latter can be a good buy if you like the choices.

11. BEST PLACES TO STAY IN ROME & SOUTHERN ITALY

ROME

EDEN, *Via Ludovisi, 49, 00187 Roma. Tel. 06/474-3551. Fax 06/482-1584. 100 rooms all with private bath. Single L420,000-450,000; Double L600,000-750,000, Suites L1,100,000. Continental breakfast is L28,000 extra, buffet breakfast is L43,000. (Metro-Barberini or Spagna)* *****

Located west of Via Veneto in the exclusive Ludovisi section, the Eden has a long tradition of excellent service. Year after year it maintains its top-ranked exclusivity attracting all the cognoscenti (those in the know) to its exquisite accommodations. Declared one of the Leading Hotels of The World, it has an ultra-sophisticated level of service and comes with amenities virtually unmatched anywhere in the world. In a quiet section of Rome, but still in the middle of everything, you are but steps from the famous Via Veneto and Spanish Steps, and the Trevi Fountain is just down the street. Ideally situated for sightseeing.

Some of the amenities of the Eden include the terrace restaurant with a spectacular view over the rooftops of Rome. Guests and locals alike flock to this restaurant, not just because of the view but because of the excellence of Chef Enrico Derflingher. The former personal Chef to the Prince and Princess of Wales, Chef Derfingher makes sure you receive food fit for royalty. And after a sumptuous meal you can work it off in their fully appointed gym, featuring everything from cardiovascular equipment to free weights. If you want to stay in the lap of luxury while in Rome, the Eden is the paradise you've been looking for.

HOTEL BAROCCO, *Piazza Barberini 9 (entrance on Via della Purificazione 4), 00187 Roma. Tel. 06/487-2001/2/3, 487-2005. Fax 06/485-994. 30 rooms all with bath. Single L280,000; Double L380,000. Breakfast included. All credit cards accepted. (Metro-Barberini)* ****

If you're looking for an intimate and elegant four-star experience in Rome and don't want to get lost in the crowd at the Eden, this is the place for you. A small hotel where everyone knows your name, the Barocco has so much charm and character that the best way to describe the hotel is that it is truly romantic.

Each room is furnished differently, but all are well appointed and comfortable. Some have two levels and others come with small terraces; but in each room every decoration and piece of furniture is supremely elegant. For the safety of your valuables each room comes with its own electronic safe. The bathrooms are a little small but do come with every modern amenity including hair dryer and courtesy toiletry kit. In the summer, the abundant buffet breakfast (rolls, croissants, fresh fruit, juice, cheese, salami, yogurt and coffee and tea) is served on the pretty roof terrace. A perfect way to start the day.

When you stay at the Barocco you are also smack dab in the middle of everything in Rome: the Trevi Fountain is virtually right outside your door; the Via Veneto is just around the corner; the Spanish Steps are a short walks away; and the Metro is just across the Piazza Barberini a few meters away A great place to spend an entire vacation, or simply to pamper yourself on the last night of a long one.

HOTEL LOCARNO, *Via della Penna 22, 00186 Rome. Tel. 06/361-0841. Fax 06/321-5249. American Express, Mastercard and Visa accepted. 38 rooms all with bath. Single L130,000-190,000; Double L230,000-280,000; Suite L420,000. Breakfast included. (Metro-Flaminio)* ***

Walking into the Locarno is like going back in time. They have successfully maintained the authentic atmosphere of the 1920s when the hotel opened. Everything about this place resembles the charm, the elegance and the refinement of that bygone era, especially the old but functional elevator around which the marble stairs circle leading up to the Locarno's comfortable rooms. The glassed-in ground floor solarium and elaborately decorated bar area are also reminiscent of this Art Deco ambiance. I was actually surprised not to see the staff dressed in zoot suits or other period garb. In the summer or in good weather the buffet breakfast is served either on the roof garden or in the solarium. Each is a stunning way to start the day.

The rooms are all furnished differently, many with the original pieces that have been around since 1920s. Each is a magnificent display of taste and style. The bathrooms are also diverse; some have only showers and others come only with bath, but all are clean, accommodating and come with hair dryers and a complete courtesy toiletry kit.

Situated between the Piazza del Popolo and the Tiber River, in a nice neighborhood of stores and galleries, this hotel is perfectly located. There are excellent restaurants all around too, like the upscale Da Bolognese or the local Osteria del Tempo Perso, both of which are only about 100 feet away. This means you won't have to wander far for your gastronomic pleasures. The Locarno offers an ideal respite from the hectic pace of Rome.

HOTEL VENEZIA, *Via Varese 18, 00184 Roma. Tel. 06/445-7101. Fax 06/495-7687. Email: Venezia@flashnet.il. American Express, Diners Club, Mastercard and Visa accepted. 61 rooms all with bath. Single L213,000; Double L288,000. Generous buffet breakfast included. (Metro-Termini)* ***

If your schedule demands it or you simply desire to stay near the Stazione Termini, this is the hotel for you. Definitely the best hotel in this area of Rome, and for a three star the prices are rather low and the service very high so you can't go wrong. Supremely professional in their service in a wonderfully accommodating and charming environment, the Hotel Venezia is a charm.

Located on a side street away from all the noise, you would never know that you're a block from the train station. If you're traveling alone ask for one of the single rooms on the fifth floor so you can relax and enjoy the wonderful Roman evenings on their individual balconies. The rest of the rooms are just as nice even without the balconies. Some rooms have showers to cater to North Americans, others have a bath. Each rooms is furnished simply but with comfort in mind.

The hotel caters to travelers like us but its main clientele are business customers and professors visiting nearby Rome University. To accommodate the professional needs of their clientele, The Venezia has an office with computer, printer, copier, and fax machine available for your use.

When you come down for breakfast, don't be surprised to see the buffet spread on a 16th century altar. The continental breakfast has everything you could want including four different types of pate to spread on your rolls or toast. Another interesting sight is the huge 16th century table that dominates the conference room.

Say hello to the charming, beautiful, and ever hospitable owner and operator, Patrizia Diletti, for me when you get there. She has imbued this hotel with a personable sense of style and grace. If you want to do some research on your own, you can check out the hotel from their web page at *http://www.venere.it/home/roma/venezia/venezia.html*.

HOTEL CAMPO DEI FIORI, *Via del Biscione 6, 00186 Roma. Tel. 06/ 687-4886. Fax 06/687-6003. All credit cards accepted. Four singles with shower each L115,000; Nine doubles with shower each L170,000, 14 doubles without shower each L100,000.* ******

Many of the amenities of a three star with the best, I repeat, the best roof terrace in Rome, all at two-star prices. Why? The hotel is on six floors in a sliver of a building but it doesn't have an elevator. This can make walking up to your room a chore after a long day of touring. Also there's no air conditioning, which can be a problem in August. But at any other time this is a the best budget place to stay in Rome.

The rooms are all tastefully decorated and most are comfortably spacious. but since this place is so popular and has only 31 rooms, make sure you book far enough in advance. Remember to request a room with a bath if that is what you want. Also, you may prefer the inside rooms so the noise from the nightly gathering in the piazza below won't seep in and disturb your sleep.

Another of the major pluses about this place is its ideal location. You are only a few blocks away from the Trastevere area and its nightlife; and the best outdoor market in the city, the Campo dei Fiori, is right around the corner where you can buy food supplies for the day and soak up the ambiance and charm it exudes. This piazza also has one of the best restaurants (La Carbonara) in Rome, and one of the wildest bar/pubs (The Drunken Ship). The area is also surrounded with pleasant local fashion shops, greengrocers, bakers, and food stores, which makes staying here feel like you've blended into the community.

You also have the wildest and friendliest staff, to go with the inexpensive prices, and don't forget the terrace to beat all terraces. The best budget hotel in Rome.

POSITANO - AMALFI COAST

HOTEL LE SIRENUSE, *Via Cristoforo Colombo 30, 84071 Positano. Tel. 089/875-066. Fax 089/811-798. 60 rooms all with bath. Single L350,000-450,000. Double L440,000-600,000. Credit cards accepted. Breakfast included. Full board L360,000-555,000.* *********

Definitely the place to stay in Positano – everything about this hotel is beautiful, especially the building itself, a stunning villa from the 17th century. Nothing overly fancy, nothing too ostentatious, just accommodating and comfortable, almost like a home away from home. There is a stunningly beautiful pool with a terrace at your disposal, as well as a sauna, and a small boat to ferry you along the coast. The views from the windows overlooking the coast are picturesque and panoramic.

Their restaurant is one of the best, if not the best, in the city. Expensive, yes, but when the food is combined with the great views from the terrace, the price is irrelevant. All the food they make here is great, but I believe the chef concocts the best *spaghetti alla vongole* (with spicy clam sauce) in Positano.

And the rooms ... they are furnished with antiques but nothing too frilly; and naturally they come with all the necessary amenities like TV, Frigo bar, and air conditioning, making each room accommodatingly comfortable. The bathrooms as you would expect also have every imaginable creature comfort. To top it all off the breakfast buffet is so ample as to dissuade most from lunch. And everything is performed with the utmost care and professional service. If you are staying on the Amalfi Coast, stay here.

CAPRI - SOUTHERN ITALY

LA SCALINATELLA, *Via Tragara 10, 80073 Capri. Tel. 081/837-0633. Fax 081/837-8291. 30 rooms, 2 suites, all with bath. Single L250,000-400,000; Double L320,000-630,000. All credit cards accepted. Closed November to March.* ****

Located on the sea, this intimate hotel offers you all the traditional charm you're looking for when you think of Capri. Stupendous service, stunning panoramic views, excellent food, everything about this place is superb. Run by the same family that operates the Quisisana, but here they can give you much more personal attention, as there are only 30 rooms here compared to 150 at the Quisisana.

The hotel has a relaxing pool around which you can get your meals served. In the restaurant proper you are offered a wonderfully romantic setting with stunning views over the water, which makes for an intimate dining experience. The rooms are stylishly furnished with antiques and are quite sizable and comfortable. But there are two different types of rooms: those with breathtaking views over the water and those overlooking an inner garden. The rooms facing the garden area are much less expensive because you are deprived of the breathtaking views over the water. Make sure you request a sea view. The bathrooms, as expected, come with all modern conveniences, including spa-like water massage bathtubs in ten rooms. The tubs are an ideal setting for a relaxing evening, just the two of you, a candle and a bottle of wine.

This is definitely the most romantic place to stay in Capri.

SICILY - TAORMINA

VILLA DUCALE, *Via Leonardo da Vinci 60, 98039 Taormina. Tel. 0942/28153. Fax 0942/28710. 10 rooms all with bath. Single L140,000-190,000; Double L200,000-250,000. All credit cards accepted. Breakfast included.* ***

What a lovely, lovely, quaint, charming and romantic little hotel. This place has all the character, charm and amenities to be a five star but with only 10 rooms it has to beg to be a rated as a three. There are plenty of four and five star hotels in the area, but this 'bed and breakfast'-like inn beats them all hands down.

The rooms are all furnished in a different fashion from one another, and are filled with Sicilian ceramics, locally made bed frames and have bed covers with the hotel's logo in gold on them. Some have handmade furniture created by local artist Tino Giammona, and all have wonderful terraces with stunning panoramic views. Overlooking the water with Mount Etna in the distance, the view from these terraces is breathtaking. Naturally the rooms comes with TV, air conditioning, Frigo-bar and every other high-end amenity.

The bathrooms are also super-accessorized and tastefully decorated with local ceramic tile from Cattagirone. And the breakfast is absolutely excellent. You can't go wrong with this place. But you need to make reservation in advance. With only ten rooms, they book up quickly.

12. WHERE TO STAY

Hotels in Italy are strictly controlled by a government rating system that categorizes them from "no star" hotels to "four star deluxe" hotels. Each and every hotel must prominently display their official ranking for all visitors to see.

These ratings have little or nothing to do with price. They only indicate what types of facilities are available at each hotel. Also, the stars do not indicate what level of service you will receive, how clean the hotels are, whether management is surly or sweet. Even in hotels with the same rating, the quality of facilities is unequal. The stars only indicate which facilities are available. Listed below is the star ranking (see Chapter 6, *Planning Your Trip*, for more details on accommodations and ratings).

You'll find the stars listed at the end of the italicized basic information section (name of hotel, address, phone, price, cards accepted, etc.) before the review itself begins for each hotel.

*****Five star, deluxe hotel**: Professional service, great restaurant, perfectly immaculate large rooms and bathrooms with air conditioning, satellite TV, mini-bar, room service, laundry service, and every convenience you could imagine to make you feel like a king or queen. Bathrooms in every room.

****Four star hotel**: professional service, most probably they have a restaurant, clean rooms not so large, air conditioning, TV-maybe satellite, mini-bar, room service, laundry service and maybe a few more North American-like amenities. Bathrooms in every room.

***Three star hotel**: a little less professional service, most probably do not have room service, should have air conditioning, TV and mini bar, but the rooms are mostly small as are their bathrooms. Some rooms may not have bathrooms.

Two star hotel: Usually a family run place, some not so clean as higher rated hotels. Mostly you'll only find a telephone in the room, and you'll be lucky to get air conditioning. About 50% of the rooms have

either a shower/bath or water closet and sometimes not both together. Hardly any amenities, just a place to lay your head.
* **One star hotel**: Here you usually get a small room with a bed, sometimes you have to share the rooms with other travelers. The bathroom is usually in the hall. No air conditioning, no telephone in the room, just a room with bed. These are what used to be the low-end pensiones. Definitely for budget travelers.

No Hotel Reservations?

If you get to Rome without a reservation and arrive at the train station, there is a free service located at the end of **track #10** that will get you a room. There is no fee, but you usually do have to pay them for the first night's stay up front. They call ahead and book your room, give you a map, and show you how to get to your badly needed bed. It's a great service for those who like to wing it or arrived in Rome on a whim. Sometimes the lines are long, so be patient.

NEAR TERMINI STATION

1. ALBERGHO IGEA, *Via Principe Amadeo 97, 00184 Roma. Tel. 06/446-6913. Fax 06/446-6911. Mastercard and Visa accepted. 42 rooms, 21 doubles, 21 singles, all with shower and W/C, air conditioning, and TV. Single L50,000-100,000; Double L65,000-130,000;. Breakfast L8,000 per person. (Metro-Termini or Vittorio Emanuele)* **

The rooms are large, clean, and with full bath facilities, air conditioning and TV in each room, it can't be beaten for the price. The lobby is large and spacious, completely covered in white marble making it a pleasant place to relax; and the staff is friendly, knowledgeable, and professional. So why only the two stars and low price? They're still remodeling and to get three stars you need a mini-bar in the room. Also, they're around the train station which has a reputation for being not so hospitable.

Granted there's not much to do around the station, and the restaurants are better almost anywhere else in the city, but if you want a lot of amenities for a low price, stay here.

2. HOTEL ADLER, *Via Modena 5, 00184 Roma. Tel. 06/484-466. Fax 06/488-0940. Mastercard and Visa accepted. 16 rooms, 10 with bath. Single L55,000-95,000; Double L66,000-126,000. Breakfast Included. (Metro-Repubblica)* **

Located near the Via Nazionale, but off on a side street, this hotel offers a good location for shopping as well as sightseeing. The rooms are Spartan but clean, and the staff is wonderfully helpful. Most of them speak more English than the normal tourist does Italian, so you can make yourself understood. They have a person at the desk all night long to let you take care of those late night phone. One good feature is a small terrace overlooking an interior courtyard that is not that pretty but is cool and calming and makes you feel a part of Italian life. Check out some of the other two stars before you stay here, but if need be this place to is a good stay.

3. HOTEL ASTORIA GARDEN & MONTAGNA, *Via Bachelet 8/10, 00187 Roma. Tel. 06/446-9908. Fax 06/445-3329. 30 rooms, 23 with bath. Single L56,000-67,000, Double L97,000-121,000. (Metro-Termini or Castro Pretorio)* **

You cannot beat the prices at this place. A single with a bath for L67,000. Oh, that feels good. This has got to be the best kept secret in Rome in terms of price. But the decor and ambiance are great also. Better than their neighbor Hotel Select that charges through the roof. This place is a little darker, but has more character and their outside enclosed garden doesn't glare out onto an ugly building. This place has loads of old-world charm to spare ... downstairs. But upstairs they have modernized all the rooms, which makes for great comfort.

4. HOTEL BRITANNIA, *Via Napoli 64, 00184 Roma. Tel. 06/488-3153. Fax. 06/488-2343. 32 Rooms all with private baths. Air conditioning. Parking Available. All credit cards accepted. Single L240,000; Double L275,000-330,000. Breakfast included. Children up to ten share parent's room for free. (Metro-Repubblica)* ***

Located just north of the Via Nazionale, on a small side street, this is an efficiently run hotel that offers guests every conceivable attention. The entrance hall spills into the American-style bar area and the breakfast room. The rooms are all modern with different furnishings in each. All are clean and comfortable and come with an safe, satellite TV and mini-bar. The bathrooms are also modern all with hair dryers, sun lamps and courtesy toiletry kits. In the mornings, they have Italian and English language newspapers at your disposal and in the evenings chocolate for your pleasure. The service is supremely courteous and professional. Situated near a Metro stop for easy access to all parts of the city.

5. DIANA, *Via Principe Amadeo 4, 00185. Tel. 475-1541. Fax 06/486-998. 190 rooms all with private baths. All credit cards accepted. Single L90,000-190,000; Double L120,000-270,000. Suites L375,000. Breakfast included. Lunch or Dinner costs an extra L40,000. (Metro-Termini)* ***

Located near Stazione Termini and the opera, this is a comfortable well run three star hotel on the Principe Amadeo, a street in limbo caught between the old and the new. This is definitely an old and elegant hotel. The lobby and common areas are an eclectic mixture of marble floors and columns with subtle lighting and paintings, with two meeting rooms that can hold 30-40 people. And the restaurant is large enough to hold 300 people and the food is quite good. The room sizes vary greatly but the smallest is still very comfortable. The smallest rooms can't fit the mini-

WHERE TO STAY 103

LIST OF HOTELS BY MAP

Map A – see pages 104-105

1. Igea
2. Adler
3. Astoria Garden
4. Brittania
5. Diana
6. Fiorini
7. Flavia
8. Galileo
9. Grand Hotel
10. Giglio dell'Opera
11. Luxor
12. Massimo d'Azeglio
13. Select
14. Venezia
15. Ambasciatori Palace
16. Barocco
17. Bristol
18. Eden
19. Excelsior
20. Flora
21. Fontana
22. Golden
23. Jolly
24. Merano
25. Mecentate Palace
26. Memphis
27. La Residenza
28. Savoy
29. Carriage
30. Doge
31. Hassler
32. Homs
33. Internazionale
34. Manfredi
35. Suisse
36. Scalinata di Spagna
47. Parlamento

Map B – see pages 118-119

37. Hotel Campo dei Fiori
40. Hotel Ponte Sisto
41. Hotel Rinascimento
42. Arenula
43. Hotel Sole

Map C – see pages 122-123

38. Hotel Genio
39. Hotel Portoghesi
44. Albergo Abruzzi
45. Sole Al Pantheon
46. Hotel Margutta
48. Hotel Locarno
49. Albergho Santa Chiara
50. Hotel Valadier

104 ROME & SOUTHERN ITALY GUIDE

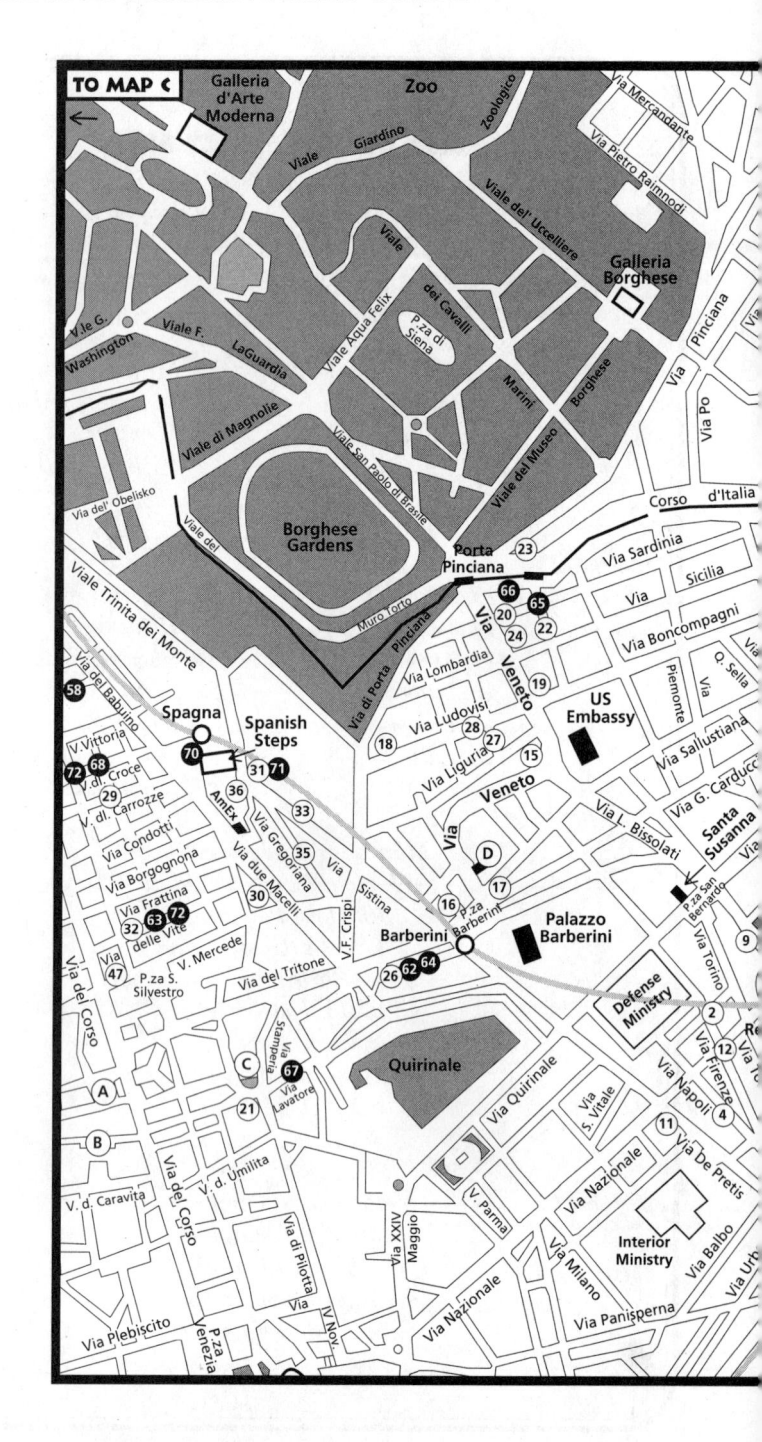

WHERE TO STAY 105

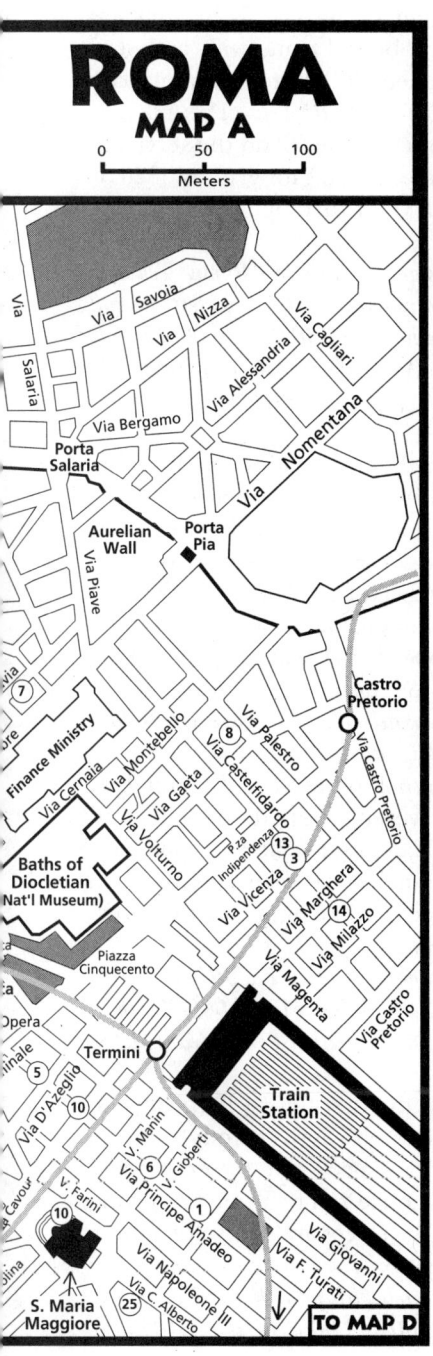

ROMA
MAP A
0   50   100
Meters

SIGHTS
A. Column of Marcus Aurelius
B. Temple of Hadrian
C. Trevi Fountain
D. Santa Maria della Concezione
   (aka Church of Bones)

HOTELS
1. Igea
2. Adler
3. Astoria Garden
4. Brittania
5. Diana
6. Fiorini
7. Flavia
8. Galileo
9. Grand Hotel
10. Giglio dell'Opera
11. Luxor
12. Massimo d'Azeglio
13. Select
14. Venezia
15. Ambasciatori Palace
16. Barocco
17. Bristol
18. Eden
19. Excelsior
20. Flora
21. Fontana
22. Golden
23. Jolly
24. Merano
25. Mecentate Palace
26. Memphis
27. La Residenza
28. Savoy
29. Carriage
30. Doge
31. Hassler
32. Homs
33. Internazionale
34. Manfredi
35. Suisse
36. Scalinata di Spagna
47. Parlamento

RESTAURANTS
58. Le Bistrot
61. Sora Lella
62. Gioia Mia
63. Da Mario
64. Da Olimpico
65. Giovanni
66. Girarrosto Toscano
67. Al Moro
68. Re degli Amici
70. Babington's Tea Rooms
71. Hassler
72. Otello alla Concordia
73. Le Grotte

bars, but still have the satellite TV for your CNN. The bathrooms are nothing special (only 30 have hair dryers) but all come with bath and shower. There is an American style bar open all the time with intimate little glass tables that seem straight out of *La Dolce Vita*. This place is comfortable and cozy, a good value for your money. And the service is exquisitely professional. Also, they have special rates for groups of 20 or more that will make your stay very cheap if you're arranging for a group. You need to call or fax for details.

 6. HOTEL FIORINI, *Via Principe Amadeo 62, 00184 Roma. Tel. 06/488-5065. Fax 06/488-2170. American Express, Diners Club, Mastercard and Visa accepted. 16 rooms, 15 with bath. Single no bath L30,000-70,000; Single L50,000-115,000; Double L60,000-130,000. Add 35% for each extra person. A sumptuous buffet breakfast included with fruits, cheeses, meats, bread, sweet rolls, coffee, and tea. (Metro-Termini)* **

 Even though this hotel is located near the train station and is on the fifth floor, the appeal of this place is not dimmed. The streets it's on is a parade of food, clothing, and shoes stores, as well as outside cafés, bars, and restaurants. After you've taken all you can out of Rome, you can quietly relax in their clean airy rooms, watch a little TV or amble down to their Bar/Breakfast room for a nightcap and a conversation with some other guests. The beautiful proprietor Roberta is charming and friendly.

 7. HOTEL FLAVIA, *Via Flavia 42, 00184 Roma. Tel 06/488-3037. Fax 06/481-9129. No credit cards accepted. 30 rooms all with bath. Single L100,000; Double L130,000; Triple L190,000. (Metro-Repubblica)* **

 Located near the Via Veneto and parallel to the Via XX Settembre, this place would be priced higher if they weren't located on the second floor and the rooms were a little bigger. The entrance area is small, as is the breakfast and guest rooms, but for your money you can't ask for much more. You also get the amenities of a three star like mini-bar, TV, direct dial phones, etc., for the price of a two star.

 8. HOTEL GALILEO, *Via Palestro 33, 00185 Roma. Tel. 06/444-1205/6/7/8. Fax 06/444-1208. Single L80,000-150,000; Double L110,000-220,000. All credit cards accepted. 80 rooms all with bath. Breakfast included. (Metro-Castro Pretorio)* ***

 They have a lovely garden terrace on the first floor where you can have your breakfast or relax at the end of the day. There are four beautiful floors in this hidden treasure. The only drawback is that the entrance is down a driveway that leads to a garage. But once you're inside everything is transformed to cater to all your needs. The prices are so low for a three star, I think, because of the driveway situation.

 9. GRAND HOTEL, *Via Vittorio Emanuele Orlando, 00185 Roma. Tel. 06/4709. Fax 06/474-7307. Single L294,000-442,000; Double L405,000-*

650,000; Suites L1,500,000. Extra bed costs L85,000. Continental or American Breakfast is extra. (Metro-Repubblica) ****

Located between the Piazza della Repubblica and Piazza San Bernardo, near the American speaking church in Rome, Santa Susanna, this top-class luxury hotel has everything you'd ever need. There is a hairdresser service, beauty salons, and saunas. The hotel used to be located in one of the most fashionable quarters but it has long since lost its chic. Nonetheless that doesn't detract from the ambiance of opulence. Rooms and suites are palatial, some with 16 to 17 foot ceilings. You'll feel like a prince or princess too when they serve you afternoon tea downstairs at 5pm. If tea is not your style, there's a relaxing but expensive American-style bar.

10. HOTEL GIGLIO DELL'OPERA, *Via Principe Amadeo 14, 00184 Roma. 62 rooms all with bath. Tel. 06/484-401 or 488-0219. Fax 06/487-1425. Single L60,000-200,000; Double L70,000-270,000. (Metro-Termini)* ***

Close to the opera, this hotel is a favorite with some of the performers and their hangers-on. If you like the chic crowd that always dresses fashionably, this is the place to stay. The rooms are all attractive in a neo-classic style, but not all of them have been renovated but the level of comfort is the same. The only real missing piece in these rooms is the hair dryer in the bathrooms, which all come with courtesy toiletry kit. The lounge area is large and is perfect for artsy types that stay here. Also they have a small and intimate area that serves as a bar in the evenings. You'd better know music to get involved in the conversations. Breakfast is served in a Spartan, white, brightly lit room off the lobby.

11. HOTEL LUXOR, *Via A. De Pretis 104, 00184 Roma. Tel. 06/485-420. Fax 06/481-5571. 27 rooms all with bath. Single L110,000-170,000; Double L150,000-230,000. Breakfast included. All credit cards accepted. (Metro-Repubblica)* ***

This is a quaint hotel off the Via Nazionale that is located in three stories of a building from the last century. The lobby is a little cramped as it's on the entrance way for the stairs. The proprietor and her husband will do almost anything to make you happy. It has all the amenities of a three star hotel and you'll just love the classic "fin de siecle" beds and armoires. Each room is different from the other and all are quite large and accommodating. The bathrooms are comfortably sized with complimentary toiletry kit and hair dryer. There is a very small roof garden for relaxation. Centrally located, on a great shopping street and near a Metro.

12. MASSIMO D'AZEGLIO, *Via Cavour 18, 00184 Roma. Tel. 06/460-646 or 487-0270. Fax 06/482-7386. Toll free in Italy 167/860004. 203 rooms, all with private baths. Single L187,000-285,000; Double L216,000-385,000. (Metro-Termini)* ****

Located near Stazione Termini, this hotel first opened in 1875 and still continues in its old fashioned ways, which give the place its charm.

They have all the modern amenities to be rated a four-star in Italy, but the look and feel of the place is definitely 1950s. The best part is the *Cantina* restaurant downstairs that looks like a wine cellar. There are lots of nooks and crannies in which to get lost. But if you're going to spend the money, stay on the Veneto or another better located place, but do come and visit, especially the restaurant. The rooms are spacious and elegant and the bathrooms are clean and accommodating.

THE TEN BEST HOTELS IN ROME

You'll find plenty of great hotels when in Rome, and I've already given you my top five in Chapter 11, "Best Places to Stay in Rome & Southern Italy, but here are some more of my favorites:

Two star hotels

37. HOTEL CAMPO DEI FIORI, Via del Biscione 6, Four singles with shower each L115,000; Nine Doubles with shower each L170,000, 14 doubles without shower each L100,000.

44. HOTEL MARGUTTA, Via Laurina 34, 24 rooms all with bath. Single or Double L90,000-140,000.

24. HOTEL PENSIONE MERANO, Via Vittorio Veneto 155, 30 rooms 28 with bath. Single without bath L70,000-90,000; Single L95,000-120,000; Double without bath L80,000-100,000; Double L115,000-140,000.

Three star hotels

46. HOTEL LOCARNO, Via della Penna 22, 38 rooms all with bath. Single L130,000-190,000; Double L230,000-280,000; Suite L420,000.

36. HOTEL SCALINATA DI SPAGNA, Piazza Trinita Dei Monte 17, 15 rooms all with baths. Single L150,000-350,000; Double L200,000-420,000.

14. HOTEL VENEZIA, Via Varese 18, 61 rooms all with bath. Single L213,000; Double L288,000.

Four star hotels

16. HOTEL BAROCCO, Piazza Barberini 9 (entrance on Via della Purificazione 4), 28 rooms all with bath. Single L280,000; Double L380,000.

25. MECENTATE PALACE HOTEL, Via Carlo Alberto 3, 62 rooms all with bath. Single L210,000-320,000; Double L270,000-430,000.

Five star hotels

31. VILLA HASSLER, Piazza Trinita Dei Monti 6, 80 rooms all with bath. Single L440,000-470,000; Double L650,000-720,000.

18. EDEN, Via Ludovisi, 49, 100 rooms all with private bath. Single L420,000-450,000; Double L600,000-750,000.

WHERE TO STAY

13. HOTEL SELECT, *Via V. Bachelet 6, 00187 Roma. Tel. 06/6994-1349. Fax 06/6994-1360. American Express, Mastercard and Visa accepted. 19 rooms all with bath. Single L50,000-195,000; Double L70,000-250,000. (Metro-Termini)* ***

Located just off the Piazza Indipendenza this hotel has a pleasant outside garden except for the building it faces. Still, a good place to relax after touring. The lobby lounge and bar are also a good place to lift up your feet for a while. The rooms are made to seem larger with the mirrors strategically placed on the armoires; each room has the necessary amenities for a three star. Quiet and calm, but for your money I'd stay next door at the Hotel Astoria (see above) with the same accommodations (save for the rooms without a bath) for a much lower price. But if this is where you can get in, the staff will make sure you enjoy every minute.

14. HOTEL VENEZIA, *Via Varese 18, 00184 Roma. Tel. 06/445-7101. Fax 06/495-7687. Email: Venezia@flashnet.il. American Express, Diners Club, Mastercard and Visa accepted. 61 rooms all with bath. Single L213,000; Double L288,000. Generous buffet breakfast included. (Metro-Termini)* ***

If you have to or simply desire to stay near the Stazione Termini, this is the place to stay. For a three star the prices are so low and the service so high at this wonderful hotel you can't go wrong. Located on a side street away from all the noise, if you are traveling alone ask for one of the single rooms on the fifth floor so you can relax and enjoy the wonderful Roman evenings on their individual balconies. The rest of the rooms are just as nice even with the balconies. Some rooms have showers to cater to North Americans, others have baths.

The hotel caters to tourists like us, business customers as well as visiting professors (the University is just around the corner); and there's an office with computer, printer, copier, and fax machine for your use. You'll love the 16th century altar that serves as buffet table for breakfast and bar at night, as well as the huge 16th century table that centers their conference room. Say hello to the charming, beautiful, and ever hospitable owner and operator, Patrizia Diletti, for me when you get there. You can check out the hotel from their web page at *http://www.venere.it/home/roma/venezia/venezia.html*.

TREVI FOUNTAIN/VIA VENETO AREA

15. AMBASCIATORI PALACE, *Via Vittorio Veneto 62, 00187 Roma. Tel. 06/47-493. Fax 06/474-3601. 103 rooms and 8 suites, all with private bath. All credit cards accepted. Single L350,000; Double L500,000; Suite L700,000. Buffet breakfast included. (Metro-Barberini)* ****

Virtually in the center of the Via Veneto, this hotel deserves its luxury rating since it has impeccable service, palatial rooms, and a top class restaurant *La Terrazza* to complement its fine ambiance. Your every need can be taken care of here: massage, evening companion, theater reservations, travel arrangements, etc. If you're looking for deluxe treatment at a deluxe price, look no further.

16. HOTEL BAROCCO, *Piazza Barberini 9 (entrance on Via della Purificazione 4), 00187 Roma. Tel. 06/487-2001/2/3, 487-2005. Fax 06/485-994. 30 rooms all with bath. Single L280,000; Double L380,000. Breakfast included. All credit cards accepted. (Metro-Barberini)* ****

If you're looking for an intimate and elegant four-star experience and don't want to get lost in the crowd at the Flora or the Eden, this is the place for you. The entrance hall is decorated with shots of Roman scenes. Each room is different from the other, some with two levels, others with small terraces. Every decoration and piece of furniture is supremely elegant. Each room comes with its own electronic safe. The bathrooms are a little small and come with hair dryer and courtesy toiletry kit. In the summer, breakfast is served on the roof terrace. A great location for an evening's relaxation. Centrally located with the Trevi Fountain, Spanish Steps, Via Veneto all around the corner. A great place to spend an entire vacation, or simply the last night of a long one.

17. BERNINI BRISTOL, *Piazza Barberini 23, 00187 Roma. Tel. 06/488-3051. Fax 06/482-4266. 124 rooms all with private baths. Single L250,000-390,000; Double L570,000-600,000; Suite L1,100,000. Continental Breakfast buffet L25,000. VAT excluded. (Metro-Barberini)* *****

The hotel is located in the Piazza Barberini at the foot of the Via Veneto facing Bernini's Triton Fountain. This is another hotel that deserves its luxury rating. Established in 1870 this hotel still retains the charm and atmosphere of that era. The entrance salon is beautifully appointed with antique furniture and lamps as well as a crystal chandelier. All rooms are elegantly furnished (each in its own style), well lit, and quite large. The bathrooms are large and come with a phone and courtesy toiletry kit. They offer every possible convenience and comfort here and are definitely waiting on that fifth star. The suites on the top floor all have wonderful terraces with splendid views. The restaurant where you are served an abundant breakfast has a panoramic view of the Piazza Barberini. Perfectly located for shopping and sightseeing, you can get to the Spanish Steps and Trevi Fountain in minutes.

18. EDEN, *Via Ludovisi, 49, 00187 Roma. Tel. 06/474-3551. Fax 06/482-1584. 100 rooms all with private bath. Single L420,000-450,000; Double L600,000-750,000, Suites L1,100,000. Continental breakfast is L28,000 extra, buffet breakfast is L43,000. (Metro-Barberini or Spagna)* *****

Located west of Via Veneto in the exclusive Ludovisi section, the Eden is a long-established top-ranked, exclusive hotel. One of the *Leading Hotels of The World*, it has a sophisticated level of service and amenities virtually unmatched the world over. Just off the crowded Via Veneto is an advantage since it makes your stay at the Eden much quieter. The terrace restaurant has a spectacular view of the city and the Villa Borghese. Chef Enrico Derflingher is the former personal Chef to the Prince and Princess of Wales, which means you'll receive food fit for royalty. Also available is a complete gym with everything from cardiovascular equipment to free weights. The Eden is truly a paradise.

19. **EXCELSIOR HOTEL**, *Via Vittorio Veneto 125, 00187 Roma. Tel. 06/4708. Fax. 06/482-6205. All 244 doubles, 38 singles, and 45 suites have private baths. Single L290,000-440,000; Double L410,000-680,000, Suite L1,200,000. An extra bed costs L90,000. Continental breakfast is L27,000 extra and American breakfast is L42,000. (Metro-Barberini or Spagna)* *****

This superb hotel is located on the east side of the Via Veneto not far from the walls that lead to Villa Borghese. All rooms and common areas are done up with ornate moldings and elegant decorations. A truly palatial experience. They have a world renowned restaurant, *La Cuppola*, as well as a piano bar at night. You can do anything and get anything here, even rent the CIGA corporate jet!

20. **FLORA**, *Via Vittorio Veneto 191, 00187 Roma. Tel. 06/489-929. Fax 06/482-0359. All 8 suites and 167 rooms have private baths. All credit cards accepted. Single L270,000; Double L360,000, Suites L600,000. Breakfast included. (Metro-Barberini or Spagna)* ****

Located immediately at the top of the Via Veneto by the old Roman walls, this old-fashioned hotel has first class traditional service. The public rooms are elaborately decorated with antiques, oriental rugs, and soothingly light color schemes reminiscent of the turn of the century. The rooms are immense and some have wonderful views over the walls into the lush greenery of Villa Borghese. Try and request one of those rooms, since Borghese is beautiful at night. The bathrooms have been recently renovate and come with all modern creature comforts. Take it from my friend Jack Sawinski, "This hotel offers everything you could want: location, service, and great rooms."

21. **FONTANA**, *Piazza di Trevi 96, 00187 Roma. Tel. 06/678-6113, 06/679-1056. 24 rooms all with bath. Single L240,000; Double L300,000. All credit cards accepted. (Metro-Barberini)* ***

The location of this hotel is great, but is not secluded or tranquil because it is in the same square as one of Rome's most famous monuments, the Trevi Fountain. You can hear the cascading waters and ever-present crowds far into the night. If you're a heavy sleeper this hotel's location is perfect, but if not try elsewhere. The rooms are sparse but comfortable and since this is a converted monastery, some rooms have been made by joining two monk's cells together. There is also a pleasant roof garden from which you can sip a drink and gaze over the rooftops of Rome.

22. RESIDENCE GOLDEN, *Via Marche 84, 00187 Roma. Tel. 06/482-1659.* 12 of the 13 rooms have private baths. All credit cards accepted. Single without bath L60,000-80,000; Single L90,000-110,000; Double without bath L80,000-100,000; Double L125,000-150,000. *(Metro-Barberini or Spagna)* **

Kind of an upscale pensione since it has air-conditioning, TV, phone, and mini bar in every room. It's located on the first floor of an old house, on a quiet street off of the Via Veneto. The stark white breakfast room that serves you your mini-buffet in the mornings doubles as the bar/lounge in the evenings. All the amenities of a three star, with the location of a one star at the prices of an upscale two star.

23. JOLLY HOTEL, *Corso d'Italia 1, 00198 Roma. Tel. 06/8495. Fax 06/884-1104. Toll free in Italy 167-017703. Toll free in US and NYC 1-800/221-2626. Toll free in NY State 1-800/247-1277.* All 200 rooms have private baths. All credit cards accepted. Single L140,000-340,000; Double L180-425,000. Breakfast an extra L100,000. *(Metro-Barberini or Spagna)* ****

You haven't seen anything like the Jolly. Its ultra-modern, Buck Rogers glass and steel architecture contrasts sharply with the ancient Aurelian wall just across the street. Located just outside of the old Aurelian wall overlooking the Villa Borghese, the Jolly sits in a perfectly serene position. If you like the standards of comfort and efficiency associated with North American hotel chains, and don't mind a rather impersonal modern atmosphere, then this is the hotel for you. The rooms are relatively small but all their amenities make up for it. Try to get a room with a view of the Borghese Gardens, otherwise you'll end up looking at the Aurelian wall and be woken up by the traffic on the Corso D'Italia.

24. HOTEL PENSIONE MERANO, *Via Vittorio Veneto 155, 00198 Roma. Tel. 06/482-1796. Fax 06/482-1810.* American Express, Diners Club, Mastercard and Visa accepted. 30 rooms 28 with bath. Single without bath L70,000-90,000; Single L95,000-120,000; Double without bath L80,000-100,000; Double L115,000-140,000. *(Metro-Barberini or Spagna)* **

Another great find. Perfect location on the Via Veneto at rock bottom prices. The only reason the prices are so low is that you have to ride an elevator up to the third floor of a building to get to the hotel. The entranceway is dark and dingy but the rooms are warm and cozy. Everything is spic and span in the bathrooms, and you don't have to worry about remembering to buy your drinks for the evening. They sell beer, soda, and water. If you want to enjoy Rome inexpensively, this is one of the better places from which to do it.

25. MECENATE PALACE HOTEL, *Via Carlo Alberto 3, 00187 Roma. Tel. 06/4470-2024. Fax 06/446-1354.* All credit cards accepted. 62 rooms all with bath. Single L210,000-320,000; Double L270,000-430,000. Includes breakfast. ****

Attentive service, elegant accommodations, first class dining, and a spectacular view of Rome all adds up to a wonderful stay. This hotel is a study in cozy elegance and is new, having only been opened in 1995. Conveniently located near the train station, it boasts its own roof garden with a view of St. Peter's in the distance and Piazza Santa Maria Maggiore nearby. Fast becoming famous for its exceptional service and beautifully appointed, welcoming rooms, the Mecentate is one of Rome's most sophisticated hotels. And what a great restaurant: the *Terrazza dei Papi* is also becoming famous, not only because of chef Pasquale D'Anria's specialties, but also as a result of the splendid panorama of the city from its rooftop perch.

26. HOTEL MEMPHIS, *Via degli Avignonesi 36-36A, 00187 Roma. Tel 06/485-849. Fax 06/482-8629. 24 rooms all with bath. Single L170,000-260,000; Double L230,000-340,000. Extra bed costs L90,000. Breakfast is L23,000 extra. (Metro-Barberini)* ****

This is a small four star hotel that has begun to develop a reputation worldwide. There are plenty of mirrors everywhere to make the place look bigger. All they did to me was offer me a fright whenever I passed by. It has all the amenities of a four-star and a great location. If you stay here, try the Tube Pub just up the street. Great darts, drinks, and conversation.

27. LA RESIDENZA, *Via Emilia 22/24, 00187 Roma. Tel. 06/488-0789. Fax 06/485-721. Mastercard and Visa accepted. 27 rooms all with bath. Single L130,000; Double L270,000. Full American Buffet breakfast offered. (Metro-Barberini or Spagna)* ***

Wonderfully located just off of the Via Veneto, La Residenza offers well appointed and large rooms, a cozy American-style bar where you can sink into the leather chairs after a few drinks, an intimate roof terrace for those late night escapades, and one of the best buffet breakfasts around. You'll find a few Roman cats strolling around the grounds regally ignoring your presence unless you throw them a scrap of food. The only reason it's not a four star is because its entranceway is a little jumbled looking. Everything inside is perfect.

28. SAVOY, *Via Ludovisi 15, 00187 Roma. Tel. 06/474-141. Fax 06/474-68122. All 135 rooms have private baths. All credit cards accepted. Single L90,000-340,000; Double L100,000-399,000; Suite L650,000. (Metro-Barberini or Spagna)* ****

Located in the upscale Ludovisi section west of Via Veneto, this is a comfortable and well run hotel and features an excellent restaurant, offering both a la carte ordering and a superb buffet for quick dining, and a lively but still relaxing bar downstairs. The service is impeccable as it should be and the decor is elaboratcly expensive. The rooms that face off of the Via Veneto are quiet and comfortable. The location is perfect, especially if you're a spy – the hotel is almost directly across the street from the American Embassy.

PIAZZA DI SPAGNA AREA

29. HOTEL CARRIAGE, *Via delle Carrozze 36, 00187 Roma. Tel. 06/ 679-3312. Fax 06/678-8279. All credit cards accepted. 30 rooms all with bath. Single L215,000-230,000; Double L270,000-295,000; Suite L660,000. Breakfast included. (Metro-Spagna)* ***

Located near the Piazza di Spagna on a pedestrian street, which makes it blissfully quiet, this elegant little hotel is luxuriously furnished with a variety of antiques and has a courteous and professional staff. They have a lovely roof garden terrace from which you can have your breakfast or an evening drink. There's not much of a view, but just being above the street level with the open sky above you has a calming effect. The rooms are not that large but are comfortable and come with every convenience such as TV, mini-bar and phone. The bathrooms are immaculately clean and have hair dryers and courtesy toiletry kit. Request one of the two rooms with tiny balconies that overlook the rooftops. There is also a nice terrace on the top floor – the perfect place for relaxing after a long day and where breakfast is served in the summer. A quaint, comfortable and convenient place to stay.

30. HOTEL DOGE, *Via Due Macelli 106, 00187 Roma. Tel 06/678-0038. Fax 06/679-1633. American Express, Mastercard and Visa accepted. 11 rooms all with bath. Single L90,000-110,000; Double L130,000-150,000. Breakfast extra. (Metro-Spagna)* **

The accommodations here are clean and Spartan as well as comfortable, and you'll notice the prices are pretty good considering this is one block from the Spanish Steps. It's located on the fourth floor of an apartment building that you enter by walking through the entrance/retail show space of a local sports store. The prices are so low because it doesn't have its own entrance. A good value for your money in a prime location. Only 11 rooms, so reserve far in advance.

31. VILLA HASSLER, *Piazza Trinita Dei Monti 6, 00187 Rome. 06/678-2651. Fax 06/678-9991. No credit cards accepted. 80 rooms all with bath. Single L440,000-470,000; Double L650,000-720,000. Continental breakfast L30,000 extra. Buffet breakfast L45,000 extra. (Metro-Spagna)* *****

In many traveler's opinions, this is the best hotel in Rome. And even if it's not, people come here to see each other and be seen. Located at the top of the Spanish Steps, with its own garage, a relaxing courtyard restaurant in the summer, and an excellent (but expensive) roof garden restaurant with the best view of the city. Remember to request one the nicer apartments facing the church belfry and the Spanish Steps. That's the whole point of staying here: the beautiful view. Even if you don't stay here, come to the restaurant, sample the food, and enjoy the superb view.

32. HOTEL HOMS, *Via Delle Vite 71, Tel. 0/679-2976. Fax 06/678-0482. All credit cards accepted. 50 rooms 49 with bath. Single without bath L70,000-80,000; Single L130,000-140,000; Double without bath L140-155,000; Double L210,000-240,000. Breakfast included. (Metro-Spagna)* **

Located on the same street as the great Tuscan restaurant Da Mario and just across from the Anglo-American bookstore, as well as being virtually in between the Trevi Fountain and the Spanish Steps, this hotel has a quaint, pleasant ambiance and decor. Since Via Delle Vite is not well traveled you also escape the traffic noise. The lobby area is dark, but the rooms are light and airy (though small) with simple furnishings. The bathrooms are tiny too but do have complimentary toiletry sets. There is also a wonderful terrace with great views of the rooftops of Rome, which, I believe, is the main reason this place is a little on the pricey side.

33. HOTEL INTERNAZIONALE, *Via Sistina 79, 00187 Roma. Tel. 06/6994-1823. Fax 06/678-4764. All credit cards accepted. 42 rooms all with bath. Single L210,000; Double L295,000; Extra bed L90,000. Buffet breakfast included. (Metro-Spagna or Barberini)* ***

Located just a stone's throw away from the top of the Spanish Steps, you can hardly find a better location at a better price. The building itself is a part of history, having been redone and built upon since the first century BC. The lobby is small and without embellishment, reflecting the time when it was a convent. Once you move into your rooms and the other public areas, the antiques and tasteful decorations abound. The rooms are all different from one another with a wide variety of different decorations and furnishings, all appealing and accommodating. Some have little side rooms; those on the fourth floor have private terraces. The bathrooms have all amenities of a three star including complimentary toiletry kit. The buffet breakfast is extensive and includes meats, cheeses, cereal, croissant, bread, coffee, tea, etc.

34. HOTEL MANFREDI, *Via Margutta 61, 00187 Roma. Tel. 06/320-7676. Fax 06/320-7736. American Express, Mastercard and Visa accepted. 17 rooms all with bath. Single L180,000-200,000; Double L230,000-280,000; Triple L370,000. American style breakfast buffet included. (Metro-Spagna)* ***

This cozy, accommodating hotel is located near the Spanish Steps and has all the charm, service, and amenities of a four-star hotel, but it is on the third floor of a local building so they are a relegated to three star status. They even have VCRs in some rooms as well as movies to rent at the front desk for your convenience. The street they're located on is cute, extremely quiet, and home to some of Rome's best antique stores and art galleries. If you only stay here for the American style buffet breakfast of ham, eggs, cheese, fruit etc., it is worth it.

35. HOTEL PENSIONE SUISSE, *Via Gregoriana 54, 00187 Roma. Tel. 06/678-3649, 06/678-6172. Fax 06/678-1258. No credit cards accepted.*

14 Rooms, only 9 with private baths. Single without bath L50,000-80,000; Single L70,000-95,000; Double without bath L70,000-95,000; Double L80,000-130,000. Breakfast included. (Metro-Spagna) **

Located near the Spanish Steps, this long-running and efficiently run small hotel is on two floors of an old building. It used to be part of two buildings but their lease ran out on one (for those of you that remember her before 1990). The rooms are large, spotlessly clean, and comfortably furnished. There is also a public room in which to relax as well as a breakfast room. The staff is superb, especially the matriarch who is a little hard of hearing but will assist you in any way she can, in four languages.

36. HOTEL SCALINATA DI SPAGNA, *Piazza Trinita Dei Monte 17, Roma. 06/679-3006 and 06/679-0896. Fax 06/684-0598 American Express, Mastercard and Visa accepted. 15 rooms all with baths. Single L150,000-350,000; Double L200,000-420,000; Suite for 5 people L700,000. Breakfast included. (Metro-Spagna)* ***

Just across the Piazza from the Hassler, this used to be a moderately priced, quaint little pensione. But since it received a three star rating its prices have sky-rocketed. Nothing much else has seemed to have changed so the proprietor must be making up for lost time by bringing in all the money he can. The best feature of this hotel is its location at the top of the Spanish Steps and the superb view of the city from the roof terrace. The roof is open in the summer months for breakfast, as well as for your own personal nightcaps for the evening. Having a roof terrace makes this place wonderful and will make your stay in Rome so much more pleasant and intimate.

PIAZZA NAVONA & CAMPO DEI FIORI AREA

37. HOTEL CAMPO DEI FIORI, *Via del Biscione 6, 00186 Roma. Tel. 06/687-4886. Fax 06/687-6003. All credit cards accepted. Four singles with shower each L115,000; Nine Doubles with shower each L170,000, 14 doubles without shower each L100,000.* **

All the amenities of a three star with the best, I repeat, the best roof terrace in Rome, all at two-star prices. Why? The hotel is on six floors in a sliver of a building without an elevator. Also there's no air conditioning, which could be a problem in August. But at any other time this is the place to stay in Rome, bar none, if you're on a budget or not.

You have a great location only a few blocks away from the Trastevere area and its nightlife. Here you are in the perfect location to visit the best outdoor market in the city, the Campo dei Fiori, eat at some of the best restaurants (*La Carbonara* in Campo dei Fiori), a great bar/pub nearby (*The Drunken Ship* in Campo dei Fiori), and the best sights just around the corner. You also have the wildest, craziest, friendliest staff, as well as inexpensive prices, and the terrace to beat all terraces. Breakfast is served in a basement dining area, but you are free to bring it to the roof with you. The only real drawback is that it's not near a Metro line, but plenty of buses do pass this way.

38. HOTEL GENIO, *Via Zanardelli 28, Roma 00186. Tel 06/683-2191, 06/683-3781. Fax 06/6830-7246. American Express, Mastercard, and Visa accepted. 61 rooms all with bath. Single L60,000-198,000; Double L110,000-300,000 An extra bed costs L70,000. A large breakfast buffet is included.* ***

Located almost in the Piazza Navona you get a great location in the Old City of Rome. Most of the guests are from Scandinavia and Germany so you may not rub elbows with any Americans here. The rooms are well appointed with tasteful paintings, Persian rugs, and cream colored wall coverings. The lobby/common areas seem a little worse for the wear but the roof garden terrace has a spectacular view. This is where you'll be served your breakfast in the morning. A great way to wake up, gazing at the Dome of St. Peter's.

39. HOTEL PORTOGHESI, *Via dei Portoghesi 1, 00186 Roma. Tel. 06/686-4231. Fax 06/687-6976. Mastercard and Visa accepted. 27 rooms all with bath. Single L150,000-170,000; Double L230,000-280,000. Suite L260,000-300,000. An extra bed costs L50,000.* ***

Between Piazza Navona and the Mausoleum of Augustus, nestled beside the church of Sant'Antonio, and on a narrow medieval style street, this small hotel's central location is ideal. It may be not be near a Metro line but the restaurants, shops, food stores, small streets, and sights all around it make its location perfect. There are a smattering of antiques all over the hotel to give the place a feeling of old world charm that matches its unique location. The rooms are large and airy but the common areas are a little cramped. Not to worry: there are great restaurants all over the place where you can relax. A great place to stay.

40. HOTEL PONTE SISTO, *64 Via dei Pettinari, 00186 Roma. Tel. 06/686-8843. Fax 06/6830-8822. All credit cards accepted. Single L167,000; Double L208,000. Over 100 rooms all with bath. Breakfast included.* ***

Located close to the walking bridge Ponte Sisto which offers you access to Trastevere, the Renaissance quarter, this is a well situated and finely appointed hotel. The hotel is popular with tour groups because of its size and location, but it is very comfortable, and the rooms and common areas are spacious. I especially love the central outside terrace garden with its fountain and palm trees. The perfect place to relax at the end of hard day. Try to get a room on a higher floor so you can have great views from your window. The staff is superbly professional and are fluent in many languages. Also located very near the Campo dei Fiori.

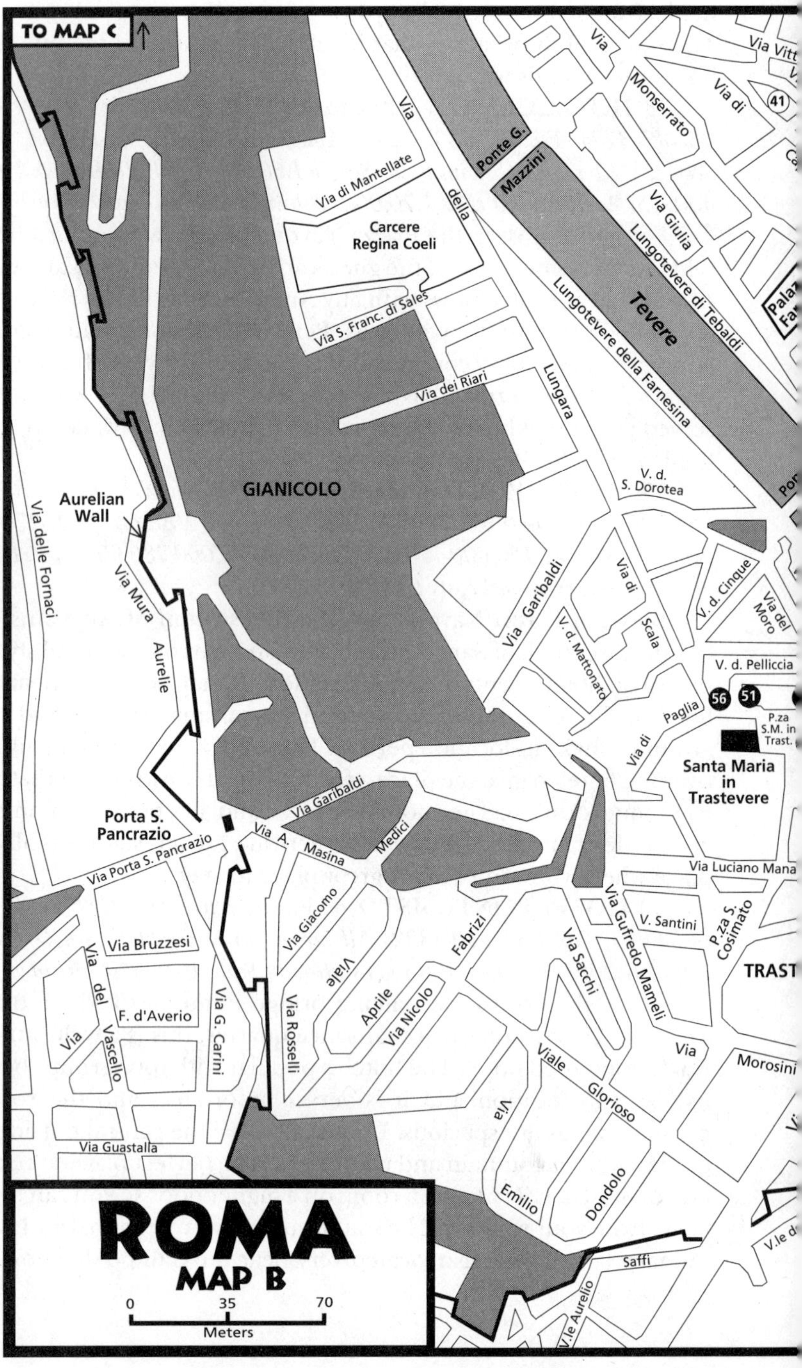
TO MAP C
ROMA
MAP B
0
35
70
Meters
GIANICOLO
Aurelian Wall
Carcere Regina Coeli
Porta S. Pancrazio
Santa Maria in Trastevere
Tevere
Ponte G. Mazzini
Via di Mantellate
Via S. Franc. di Sales
Via dei Riari
Via della Lungara
Lungotevere della Farnesina
Lungotevere di Tebaldi
Via Giulia
Monserrato
Via di
41
V. d. S. Dorotea
Via delle Fornaci
Via Mura Aurelie
Via Garibaldi
V. d. Mattonato
Via di Scala
V. d. Cinque
Via del Moro
V. d. Pelliccia
56
51
P.za S.M. in Trast.
Via di Paglia
Via Porta S. Pancrazio
Via A. Masina
Medici
Via Luciano Mana
V. Santini
P.za S. Cosimato
Via Gufredo Mameli
Via Sacchi
Via Giacomo
Viale Aprile
Fabrizi
Via Nicolo
Via Bruzzesi
Via del Vascello
Via F. d'Averio
Via G. Carini
Via Rosselli
Viale Glorioso
Via Morosini
Via Emilio Dondolo
Via Guastalla
Saffi
V.le Aurelio
TRAST

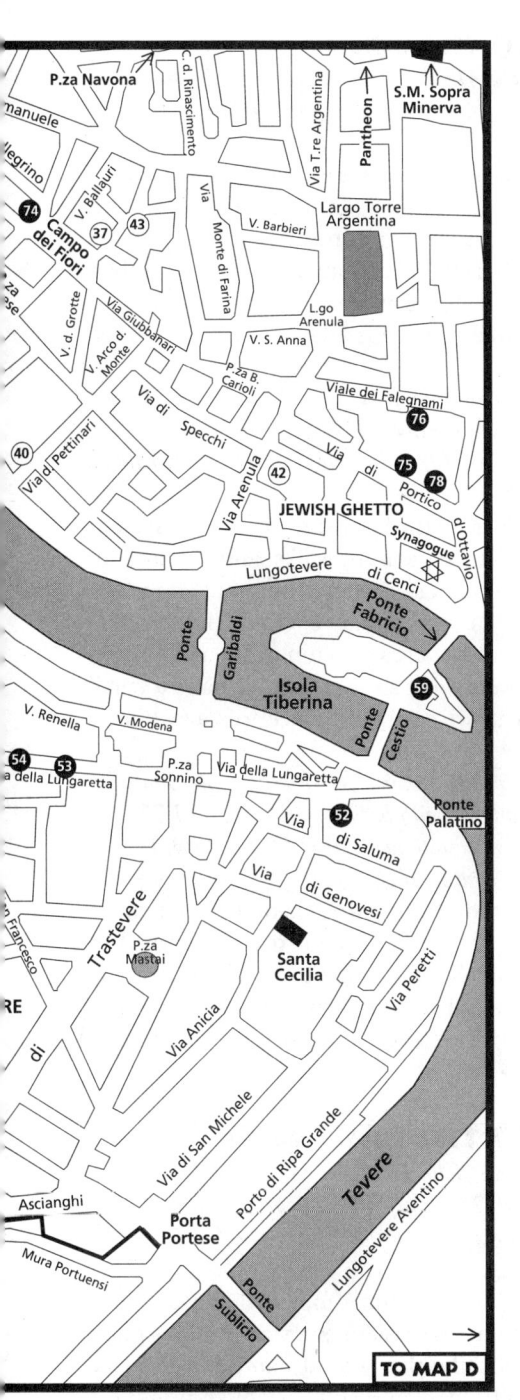

HOTELS
37. Hotel Campo dei Fiori
40. Hotel Ponte Sisto
41. Hotel Rinascimento
42. Arenula
43. Hotel Sole

RESTAURANTS
51. La Canonica
52. Camparone
53. Da Cencia
54. Gino in Trastevere
55. Sabatini I
56. La Tana de Noantri
57. Taverna del Moro
59. Sora Lella
74. La Carbonara
75. Gino ai Funari
76. Hostaria Guilia
78. Vecchia Roma

41. HOTEL RINASCIMENTO, *122 Via Del Pellegrino, 00186, Rome. Tel. 06/687-4813. Fax 06/683-3518. All credit cards accepted. 20 rooms all with bath. Single L135,000. Double L215,000. L72,000 for an extra bed. Breakfast included.* **

Perfectly situated for the sightseer. It's five minutes from the Piazza Navona (where you can get gelato at *Tre Scalini*), Campo dei Fiori (where you can shop for local produce in the mornings), and 10 minutes from the Pantheon and the Vatican (in different directions). There is mostly a German clientele here, but that is changing as we speak. The rooms and bathrooms are clean but a little small. There is a large buffet breakfast served in the mornings.

42. ARENULA, *Via Santa Maria de'Calderari, 47, 00186 Roma. Tel. 06/687-9454. Fax 06/689-6188. 50 rooms, 45 with bath. Single without L100,000; Single L130,000; Double without L130,000; Double L160,000. Breakfast L20,000. All credit cards accepted.* **

On the inside of an old building from the last century, in a quaint area (The Jewish Ghetto) where you can take pleasant walks, and situated on a small street, this is a great two star. There is everything that a modern hotel would have with amazing charm and ambiance. On the first floor is the small entrance, TV lounge, breakfast area and ten of the rooms. On the third floor the rooms come only with shower but all have a small complimentary toiletry set. A great price/quality place to stay while in Rome.

43. SOLE, *Via del Biscione 76, 00186 Roma. Tel. 06/6880-6873 or 687-9446. Fax 06/689-3787. 58 rooms only 24 with bath. Single without L75,000-85,000; Single L95,000-110,000. Double without L100,000-115,000; Double L140,000-160,000. No breakfast. No credit cards.* **

A simple two star in a great location with two relaxing garden areas on the second and third floors. It seems a little run down as you enter, but the rooms are clean and comfortable. Keep a look out for Cleopatra, the resident cat. Ten rooms have TV and only 24 with private bath. Not as nice as the Hotel Campo dei Fiori just up the street, but is still a good place to stay for those on a budget.

PIAZZA DEL POPOLO TO THE PANTHEON

44. ALBERGO ABRUZZI, *Piazza della Rotunda 69, 00186 Roma. Tel. 06/679-2021. No credit cards accepted. 25 rooms on four floors all without bath. 2 bathrooms in every corridor. Single L65,000-83,000; Double L92,000-110,000.* **

Even though you don't have a private bathroom, you do have a great location at a great price. Besides, there is a sink in every room. This place decided not to upgrade its facilities like the Sole al Pantheon did (see below) and is content being a small, clean, and comfortable *pensione* for travelers who like to stay on a budget. There is no common area, but the rooms are large enough to relax in. If not, the piazza in front of the Pantheon is a great place to kick back with a bottle of wine, or if you're more upscale you can sit at a nearby sidewalk café.

45. SOLE AL PANTHEON, *Piazza dell Rotunda 63, 00186 Roma. Tel. 06/78-0441. Fax 06/6994-0689. All credit cards accepted. 62 rooms all with bath. Single L320,000-335,000; Double L440,000-470,000; Suite L530,000-600,000.* ****

This is a place that used to be a small well appointed *pensione* that upgraded its rooms prior to the new "star" ratings and voila: we have a fantastic four-star hotel. The clean white walls and delicate furniture attest to the changes made under new ownership. Most of the furniture is of the neo-classic mold but leaning towards almost modern. Some of the rooms have a view over the Piazza della Rotunda and the Pantheon, which is a beautiful people watching scene, and come with sound-proof windows so it's quiet at night. They have been in business since 1513 so they know how to treat guests. The service is exquisite and everything conforms to the highest standards, making this a well-located fine little four-star hotel. For those with the means, a great place to stay.

46. HOTEL MARGUTTA, *Via Laurina 34, 00186 Roma. Tel. 06/322-3674. Fax 06/320-0395. American Express Diners Club, Mastercard and Visa accepted. 24 rooms all with bath. Single or Double L134,000-140,000. #s 50 and 52 share a terrace and cost L170,000 each. #59 is great and costs L180,000. Breakfast included. (Metro-Spagna or Flaminio)* **

The prices are great since it's a two star, and it has that rating because there is no TV or mini-bar in the room, and no air conditioning which is a must in August. The hotel has been totally renovated and is as modern as can be. There's a relaxing lounge area and the rooms are all spacious and airy (except in August). The bathrooms are micro, especially those with showers. The ones with bathtubs are a little bigger and all come with phone and courtesy toiletry kit. And its location is fantastic, right between the Piazza del Popolo and the Spanish Steps, almost right on the super shopping street Via Del Corso. Who could ask for more? That, coupled with the excellence of the accommodations and the low prices, make this place a definite rare gem of price/quality considerations.

47. HOTEL PARLAMENTO, *Via delle Convertite 5, 00186 Roma. Tel. 06/6992-1000. Fax 06/679-2082. All credit cards accepted. 22 rooms, 19 with bath. Single without L94,000. Single L120,000. Double L160,000. Breakfast included. (Metro-Spagna)* **

They just aded a small (read micro) elevator so you no longer have to climb the entire three flights of stairs to get to this wonderful two star. A homey atmosphere with simply furnished rooms. There is a view of the rooftops of Rome from their tiny terrace, where in the summer you are

122 ROME & SOUTHERN ITALY GUIDE

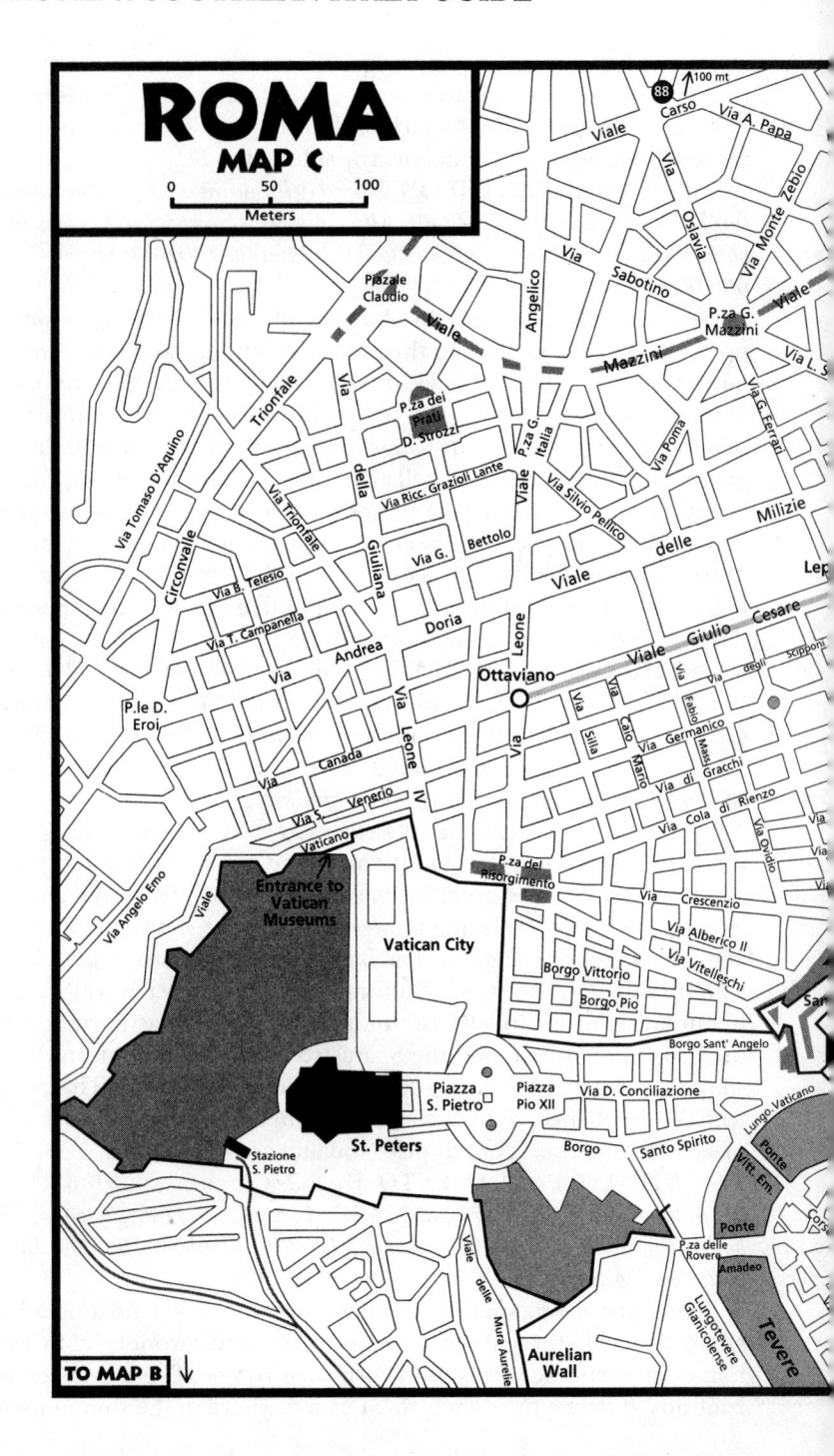

WHERE TO STAY 123

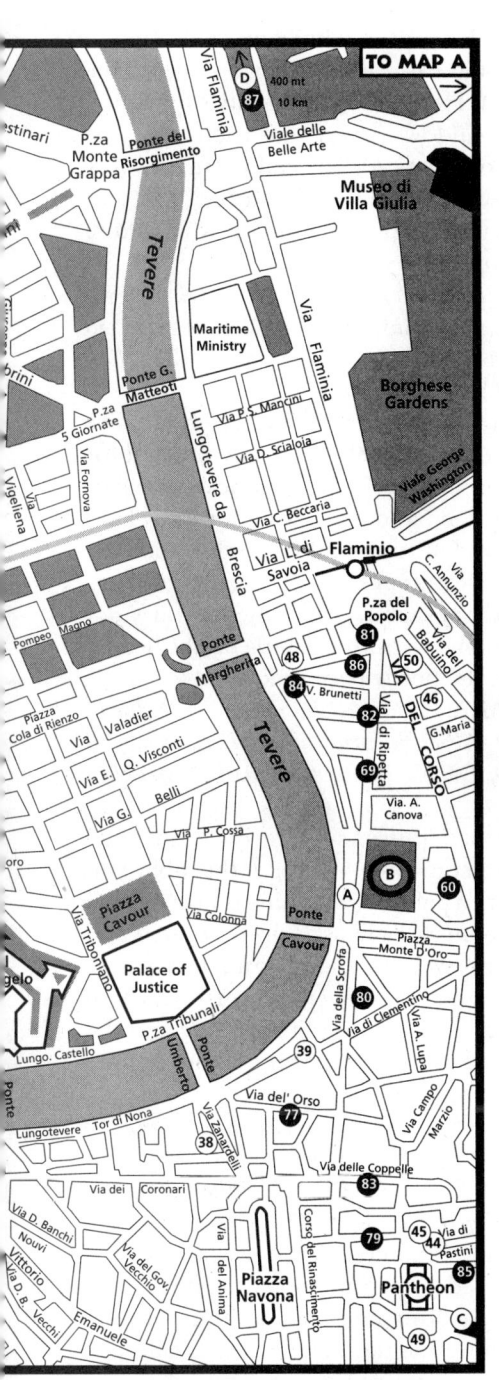

SIGHTS
A. Tomb of Augustus
B. Mausoleum of Augustus
C. Santa Maria Sopra Minerva
D. Ponte Milvio

HOTELS
38. Hotel Genio
39. Hotel Portoghesi
44. Albergo Abruzzi
45. Sole Al Pantheon
46. Hotel Margutta
48. Hotel Locarno
49. Alberghe Santa Chiara
50. Hotel Valadier

RESTAURANTS
60. Pizzeria La Capricciosa
69. Taverna Ripetta
77. Orso "80"
79. Da Alfredo all'Angoletto
80. Alfredo alla Scrofa
81. Dal Bolognese
82. Buca di Ripetta
83. La Nuova Compania
84. La Fontanella
85. La Screstia
86. Osteria al Tempo Perso
87. Il Casale
88. Er Cucurucu

served your breakfast. In a completely renovated building, the common rooms are decorated with panoramic frescoes of Roman scenes. The rooms are all decorated differently and some have antique style furniture, and all have TVs and sound-proof windows (but if your room is on the main road, this is Rome, so noise does seep in). The bathrooms are very new and kept immaculate; some even have a phone. Most of the staff speaks English and are more than willing to help you find what you're looking for. A great price/quality option.

48. HOTEL LOCARNO, *Via della Penna 22, 00186 Rome. Tel. 06/361-0841. Fax 06/321-5249. American Express, Mastercard and Visa accepted. 38 rooms all with bath. Single L130,000-190,000; Double L230,000-280,000; Suite L420,000. Breakfast included. (Metro-Flaminio)* ***

Situated between the Piazza del Popolo and the Tiber River, in a nice neighborhood of stores and galleries, this hotel is perfectly situated for those of you who love to shop. It has a very relaxing American-style bar, spacious common areas, a small garden patio, and a roof terrace where breakfast is served in good weather. On top of all this, the rooms are tastefully decorated: not too many faux antiques here. There are excellent restaurants all around, *Da Bolognese* for example, which means you won't have to wander far for your gastronomic pleasures. A little off the beaten path too, so it offers a respite from the hectic pace of Rome.

49. ALBERGHO SANTA CHIARA, *Via Santa Chiara 21, 00186 Roma. Tel. 06/687-2979. Fax 06/687-3144. All credit cards accepted. 90 rooms all with bath. Single L180,000-242,000; Double L250,000-336,000. Breakfast included.* ***

A three star that should be a four star, this is a supremely elegant hotel in the heart of Rome, near the Pantheon. Once you enter the lobby you feel as if you've been whisked away to a palace. Everything is marble, and the ceilings reach to the sky. The rooms are all tastefully decorated and the ones on the top floors get great breezes, if you don't want to use your air conditioning. You also have some good views over the rooftops. There is also a tranquil inside garden area. The service is impeccable and the breakfast buffet huge. This place is great. If you want four star accommodations for a three star price, stay here.

50. HOTEL VALADIER, *Via della Fontanella 15, 00187 Roma. Tel. 06/361-0592, 361-0559, 361-2344. Fax 06/320-1558. 50 rooms and suites all with bath. Single L270,000-330,000; Double L370,000-450,000, Suite L400,000-600,000. All credit cards accepted. (Metro-Flaminio)* ****

The first word that comes to mind is opulent. There is black marble everywhere, and the effect is doubled by the placement of the many mirrors and shining brass fixtures. But you ain't seen nothing yet. The wood paneling here sparkles, it's so well shined. The rooms are no less ostentatious with lights, mirrors (some on the ceiling ... and yes, even over the beds), and the ever-present marble. The bathrooms are a little small but accommodating and have every amenity. If you want to feel like an oil sheik who has money to burn, spend your stay in Rome here. Ideally located between the Piazza del Popolo and the Spanish Steps, you are in walking distance to many sights and shops.

STAY IN A CONVENT - FOR LESS

The price of a double room in Rome added onto museum fees and meals can dent anyone's wallet. Some of the best and least known places to stay, which can reduce the cost of a stay in Rome, are convents. While you may think that convents would only take women pilgrims as guests, most also welcome single men, married couples, and familes with children. Couples 'living/traveling in sin' are usually not welcome, but some well placed pieces of jewelry can usually fool the best nun. Also, all these places are immaculate (no pun intended) since the nuns take pride in their work.

Suore Teatine, *Salita Monte del Gallo 25, 00165 Roma. Tel. 06/637-4084 or 06/637-4653. Fax 06/3937-9050. L70,000 per person with full board. L60,000 with half board. L50,000 with only breakfast. Not all rooms have private bath. Curfew is 11:00pm.*

Franciscan Sisters of the Atonement, *Via Monte del Gallo 105, 00165 Roma. Tel. 06/630-782. Fax 06/638-6149. L70,000 per person with full board. L60,000 with half board. L45,000 with only breakfast. All rooms have private bath. Curfew is 11:00pm. English spoken. Parking available. Great spacious pine-shaded garden.*

Suore Dorotee, *Via del Gianicolo 4a, 00165 Roma. Tel. 06/6880-3349. Fax 06/6880-3311. L 80,000 full board. L70,000 half board. Some rooms have private baths. Curfew is 11:00pm. Recomended by the Vatican Tourist Information Bureau.*

Pensione Suore Francescane, *Via Nicolo V 35, 00165 Roma. Tel. 06/3936-6531. L55,000 per person with breakfast. No private baths. No curfew. Small but lovely roof graden with views of St. Peter's. English spoken. Great location.*

Domus Aurelia-Suore Orsoline, *Via Aurelia 218, 00165 Roma. Tel. 06/636-784. Fax 06/3937-6480. L95,000 for a double. L65,000 for a single. L120,000 for room with three beds. All rooms with private bath. Breakfast extra. 11:30pm curfew.*

Suore Pallotini, *Viale della Mura Aurelie 7b, 00165 Roma. Tel. 06/635-697. Fax 06/635-699. L55,000 for single with breakfast. L95,000 for double without private bath. L130,000 for double with private bath. 10:00pm curfew for first night. Any night after that they give you a key.*

Fraterna Domus, *Via di Monte Brianzo 62, 00186 Roma. Tel. 06/6880-2727. Fax 06/683-2691. L70,000 per person with full board. L60,000 with half board. L45,000 with breakfast only. Single rooms add L18,000 extra. All rooms with private bath. Curfew is 11:00pm.*

Le Suore Di Lourdes, *Via Sistina 113, 00187 Roma. Tel. 06/474-5324. Fax 06/488-1144. L50,000 per person without bath. L55,000 per person with bath and breakfast. Curfew is 10:30pm.*

13. WHERE TO EAT

Before I guide you to the wonderful restaurants Rome has in store for you, below I've prepared an augmented version of Chapter 10, *Food & Wine*. The maps are in Chapter 12, *Where to Stay*; the list of restaurants by map is on page 130.

ROMAN CUISINE

"Italian Food" is definitely a misnomer, because each region of Italy has its special dishes, and in most cases so do each province and locality. As a rule, Roman cooking is not elegantly refined and is considered a simple cuisine. The food is basic, unpretentious, and enjoyable. Gone are the days of the Roman Empire's lavish banquets.

Authentic Roman dishes today are often based on rudimentary ingredients, such as tomatoes, garlic, hot pepper, and parmesan cheese, and the results are magnificent. Some favorite dishes, like brains, tripe, oxtail, and pig's snout, never seem to find their way onto the plate of squeamish foreigners like myself. Instead we get treated to the omnipresent pasta and grilled meats.

Besides these staples, Romans enjoy the harvest of seafood from the shores just 15 miles from their city, and prepare excellent grilled seafood dishes and the famous *spaghetti alla vongole verace* (spicy clam sauce), as well as other pastas brimming with other fruits from the sea. The Roman countryside provides exquisite fresh greens and vegetables, which arrive daily at their open air markets. Also in never-ending supply are the local cheeses, *pecorino*, made from sheep's milk, and plump *mozzarella* balls, generally made from the milk of water buffaloes.

The Jewish ghetto has made a lasting impression on Roman cuisine. The most memorable dish to come from there is the *carciofo alla giudia*, a small artichoke flattened and fried. What I'm trying to say is that it is very difficult not to eat well in any one of Rome's 5,000-plus restaurants.

In case you didn't know, lunch hour is usually from 12:30pm to 3:00pm, and dinner any where from 7:30pm to 10:00pm, but is usually served at 8:30pm. So enjoy your meal and remember to take your time. Meals are supposed to be savored, not rushed through.

Traditional Roman Fare

You don't have to eat all the traditional courses listed below, but in some restaurants it is considered (bad form) not to. But most Italians accept the difference in our culture, even if they don't understand it, so don't feel embarrassed if all you order is a pasta dish or an entrée with a salad or appetizer.

But if you do want to order the way the Italians do, expect to spend a lot of time over dinner, which traditionally consists of an *antipasto* (appetizer) and/or soup and/or pasta and is called **primo**; a main course is **secondo** (usually meat or fish) with separately ordered side dishes of *contorni* (vegetables) or *insalata* (salad) which come either *verdi* (green) or *mista* (mixed); then **dolci** (dessert), which can be cheese, fruit, or *gelato* (ice-cream). After which you then order your coffee and/or after-dinner drink.

Note: Pasta is never served as an accompanying side dish with a secondo and especially never on the same plate. It is always served as a separate course. It is time to forget everything you thought you knew about "Italian" food that was learned at some run-of-the-mill restaurant chain. In Italy it's time to eat Italian food the proper way!

ANTIPASTO - APPETIZER

- **Bruschetta** – garlic bread brushed with olive oil
- **Antipasto Misto** – Mixed appetizer plate. Differs from restaurant to restaurant
- **Tomate, Mozzarella ed olio** – Tomato and mozzarella slices covered in olive oil with a hint of basil

PRIMO PIATTO - FIRST COURSE

Pasta
- **Spaghetti alla carbonara** – Spaghetti tossed with bacon, garlic, peppers, grated cheese, and a raw beaten egg
- **Bucatini all'amatriciana** –Thin tubes of pasta with red pepper, bacon, and pecorino cheese
- **Pennc all'arrabbiata** – Literally means angry pasta. It is short ribbed pasta tubes with a hot and spicy tomato base, garlic and parsley sauce (this is my favorite, but if your stomach can't handle spicy food, steer clear of this delicacy)
- **Fettucine al burro** – fettucine with butter and parmesan

- **Spaghetti alla puttanesca** – Literally translated it means whore's spaghetti! So named because the ingredients, peppers, tomato, black olives and garlic, are so basic that prostitutes could quickly create a meal between tricks

Zuppa – Soup
- **Stracciatella** – a light egg-drop soup
- **Pasta e ceci** – a filling pasta and chick pea soup
- **Zuppa di telline** – soup made from tiny clams

SECONDO PIATTO - ENTRÉE
Carne – Meat
- **Abbacchio** – Milk-fed baby lamb. Can be grilled (alla Griglia), sautéed in a sauce of rosemary, garlic, onions, tomatoes, and white wine (alla Cacciatore), or roasted (al Forno)
- **Saltimbocca alla Romana** – veal fillets that are covered in sage and prosciutto and cooked in butter and white wine
- **Pollo alla cacciatore** – same dish as the lamb above but replaced with chicken
- **Pollo alla Romana** – Chicken stewed with yellow and red dell peppers
- **Pollo al diavolo** – so called because the chicken is split open and grilled over an open fire and flattened by a weight placed on top of it. I guess it's what Romans think hell would be like.
- **Fritto misto** – a selection of mixed deep-fried meats and seasonal vegetables
- **Lambata di Vitello** – Grilled veal chop
- **Porchetta** – Tender suckling pork roasted with herbs
- **Maile arrosto can patate** – Roasted pork with exquisite roast potatoes

Pesce – Fish
- **Sogliola alla griglia** – Thin sole lightly grilled
- **Ciriole** – Small tender eels dredged from the Tiber

Contorno – Vegetable
- **Carciofi alla giuda** – Jewish-style artichokes, pressed flat and fried. Usually served with an anchovy garlic sauce
- **Peperonata** – Stewed red and yellow bell peppers
- **Patate arrosto** – Roasted potatoes that usually come with a grilled meats but can be ordered separately
- **Insalata Mista** – mixed salad. You have to prepare your own olive oil and vinegar dressing. American's lust for countless types of salad dressings hasn't hit Italy yet

WHERE TO EAT 129

> ### WHERE TO GET WINE TO TAKE HOME
> *The most complete and perfectly located store to buy your duty free wine quota (three liters per person) is **Buccone** (Via di Ripetta 19-20, Tel./Fax 06-361-2154) near the Piazza del Popolo. The walls of these two storefronts are lined from floor to ceiling with bottles from every different region in Italy, as well as other countries. Extensive does not do this place justice. The prices here are comparable with duty free at the airport and you get a much better selection. The prices for Sambuca and Limoncello are better at the airport, but get your wine here.*

Wines

Romans prefer 'local' wines from the **Castelli Romani** area: **Frascati**, **Marino**, **Velletri**, etc. These are soft, well-rounded simple white wines that most anyone can appreciate. They do well in countering the aggressive flavors of the Roman food. In most restaurants you can also get better known wines such as Chianti, Orvieto, Verdicchio, Pinto Grigio, and Barolo, but the best bet if you're not a wine expert is to simply try the *vino da casa* (house wine) of the restaurants you visit. You will find this to be not only less expensive but usually as enjoyable as a more expensive bottle.

The house wine can be ordered in liters *(un litro)*, halves *(mezzo litro)*, or quarters *(quarto do un litro)*.

Sambuca liqueur

You have to try the Sambuca, an anise-flavored after dinner drink, usually served with an odd number of coffee beans (to serve it with an even number is bad luck). It's called *Sambuca con mosce*, Sambuca with flies. If you blur your vision a little they do look a little like flies floating, without the legs of course, in the milky liqueur. When sipping this small drink get one of the beans in your mouth and chew on it. The bitter taste compliments the sweetness of the liqueur perfectly. The best brand of Sambuca is **Molinari**, and the next is **Romana**, which is better known in the States because of the company's aggressive marketing campaign.

Limoncello

The latest after-dinner drink to rage across Italy is Limoncello, a tasty lemon flavored high octane drink that many establishments make on their own. That's right, Limoncello is mostly made prohibition-style. One place that makes some of the best is La Buca di Ripetta. But they'll only serve it to you if they consider you 'worthy' – since it is considered a special drink, lovingly created, and sparingly served.

LIST OF RESTAURANTS BY MAP

Map A – see pages 104-105
58. Le Bistrot
61. Sora Lella
62. Gioia Mia
63. Da Mario
64. Da Olimpico
65. Giovanni
66. Girarrosto Toscano
67. Al Moro
68. Re degli Amici
70. Babington's Tea Rooms
71. Hassler
72. Otello alla Concordia
73. Le Grotte

Map B – see pages 118-119
51. La Canonica
52. Camparone
53. Da Cencia
54. Gino in Trastevere
55. Sabatini I
56. La Tana de Noantri
57. Taverna del Moro
59. Sora Lella
74. La Carbonara
75. Gino ai Funari
76. Hostaria Guilia
78. Vecchia Roma

Map C – see pages 122-123
60. Pizzeria La Capricciosa
69. Taverna Ripetta
77. Orso "80"
79. Da Alfredo all'Angoletto
80. Alfredo alla Scrofa
81. Dal Bolognese
82. Buca di Ripetta
83. La Nuova Compania
84. La Fontanella
85. La Screstia
86. Osteria al Tempo Perso
87. Il Casale
88. Er Cucurucu

WHERE TO EAT 131

TRASTEVERE

This is the perfect place for exploring the way Romans actually live. **Trastevere** literally means "across the river," and this separation has allowed the area to remain virtually untouched by the advances of time. Until recently it was one of the poorest sections of Rome, but now it is starting to become gentrified. These changes have not altered Trastevere's charm. You'll find interesting shops and boutiques, and plenty of excellent restaurants among the small narrow streets and *piazzetta* (small squares). The maze of streets is a fun place to wander and wonder where you're going to end up.

This area offers some of the best dining and casual nightlife in town. Here you can sit in a piazza bar, sipping Sambuca or wine and watch the life of Rome pass before your eyes. To accommodate this type of activity, many stores have begun to stay open later.

51. LA CANONICA, *Vicolo dei Piedi 13, just off of the Piazza Santa Maria in Trastevere. Closed Mondays. Major credit cards accepted. Tel. 06/580-3845. Dinner for two L80,000.*

In the capital of the Catholic world, what better way to dine than in a de-consecrated chapel transformed into one of Rome's most entrancing restaurants. Located across from Rome's only exclusive English language movie theater, *Il Pasquino*, at Vicolo del Piede 13, La Canonica's Baroque facade is delicately covered with vines and flowers. In the summer months tables are set outside (and around the corner into the adjacent street) to enjoy this beautiful display and the warm Rome evenings. The best place to sit is inside; it's always cool and you can soak in the atmosphere of a renovated chapel that now has meats, kegs, and bottles hanging from the ceiling.

The menu is dominated by seafood and pasta. My recommendations: *Spaghetti alla Vongole Verace* (spaghetti with spicy clam sauce of garlic, basil, oil, and hot peppers) or the *Spaghetti alla Carbonara* (spaghetti with a light cream sauce, covered with ham, peas, and grated parmesan cheese). For the main course, try the light fish dish of *Sogliola alla Griglia* (grilled Sole). The *Grigliato Misto di Pesce* (mixed grilled fish) is also good and is sold by the *etto*, which is about a quarter of a pound.

52. CAMPARONE, *Piazza in Piscinula 47. Tel 06/581-6249. Closed Mondays. Credit cards accepted. Dinner for two L75,000.*

This restaurant owns the entire block, starting with the bar/café on the left, this restaurant in the middle, and the pizzeria/birreria on the right. The outside seating at the restaurant is the best pace to enjoy a true Trastevere evening. Their food includes an excellent rendition of *ossobuco alla Romana*. They do it with *fungi* (mushrooms). Mmm, good. They are mainly known for their grilled meats and some of their pastas.

53. DA CENCIA, *Via della Lungaretta 67, 00153 Roma. Tel. 06/581-2670. Credit cards accepted. Closed Sundays and Mondays for lunch. Dinner for two with wine L75,000.*

They have crowded outside seating in a side area under an awning, but it's perfect for people watching. Inside is small but the tables are spaced a little farther apart. Inside is where you'll find all the locals sitting and savoring the restaurant's fine food.

Try any of their pastas for a primo (*arrabbiata, amatriciana, vongole*, etc.). They are all Roman specialties and are made perfectly. Then move onto the *fritto misto mare* (mixed fried fish) and you won't be disappointed.

54. GINO IN TRASTEVERE, *Via Della Lungaretta 85, 00153 Roma. Tel. 06/580-3403. 06/580-6226. Closed Wednesdays. Dinner for two L80,000.*

The spacious and bright interior makes you want to sit outside under their awning on the side or in the front by the main road. Wherever you end up the food will be exceptional. One of the proprietors, Paulo, will greet you at the door and make sure everything is perfect all night long. Since it's popular it tends to get crowded, so get there early (7ish) or late (10ish) otherwise you may be in for a wait. But later is better because then you can watch the parade of people pass by on their way to Piazza Santa Maria.

They have an extensive fish and meat menu: try the *Sogliola alla Griglia* (grilled sole), or the *saltimbocca alla Romana* (veal shanks in sauce and spices) for seconds. Your primo piatto has to be one of their great Roman pasta dishes like *arrabiata* (tomato-based with garlic and peppers), or *vongole verace* (clams in a spicy oil, garlic, and basil sauce). Or if the desire for pizza hits you, it's great here.

55. SABATINI I, *Piazza Santa Maria in Trastevere 13, Tel. 06/581-8307 (outside seating) or 06/581-2026 (inside seating with an entrance on side). Closed Wednesdays, and two weeks in August. But at that time their other restaurant is open. No credit cards accepted. Very expensive. At least L100,000 for two.*

Besides the excellent fish dishes here, you can soak up the Trastevere life-style, especially in summer when outside seating is available. At night the floodlights keep the church at the opposite end of the piazza aglow. Try the *spaghetti cozze* (mussels), *zuppa di pesce*, the *spiedino misto di pesce al forno* (mixed grilled fish), and the grilled sole (*sogliola alla griglia*). If you want to see the fish grilled go to the very back of the restaurant and there they'll be roasting over an open fire, scales and all. (You can watch your meal being de-boned, de-headed and de-tailed). The inside is cozy and comfortable and they have singers walking through the tables serenading the customers, which is nice if you like that sort of thing.

ROME'S TEN BEST RESTAURANTS

You'll find plenty of good restaurants in Rome, but for a truly great meal every time, here is a list of my ten best.

51. LA CANONICA, Vicolo dei Piedi 13, Dinner for two L80,000.

55. SABATINI I, Piazza Santa Maria in Trastevere 13, At least L100,000 for two.

57. TAVERNA DEL MORO, Via del Moro 43, Dinner for two L55,000.

59. SORA LELLA, Via Ponte Quattro Capi 16, Dinner for two L130,000.

72. OTELLO ALLA CONCORDIA, Via Della Croce 81, Dinner for two L80,000

74. LA CARBONARA, Campo dei Fiori 23, Dinner for two L90,000.

82. LA BUCA DI RIPETTA, Via di Ripetta 36, Dinner for two L70,000.

83. LA NUOVA COMPANNINA DA ENRICO E VITTORIO, Piazza delle Coppelle 8, Dinner for two L60,000.

86. OSTERIA DEL TEMPO PERSO, Via dell'Oca 43, Dinner for two L65,000.

88. ER CUCURUCU, Via Capoprati 10, Dinner for two L100,000.

56. LA TANA DE NOANTRI, *Via della Paglia 1-2-3, 00158 Roma. Tel. 06/580-6404 or 06/589-6575. Credit cards accepted. Closed Tuesdays. Dinner for two L75,000.*

Located past Piazza Santa Maria and past the tables laid out for La Canonica, this superb restaurant has rather boring seating inside, but oh so wonderful places outside in the Piazza di San Egidio which they take over at night. You can sit under awnings in the quiet piazza and savor dish after dish of succulently seasoned Roman specialties.

I've had the *pizza con salsiccia* (with sausage) as a primo, then moved onto the *Braccioline di abbacchio* (literally translated it means "little arm of lamb"). My partner had the *Tortellini alla crema di funghi* (meat or cheese stuffed tortellini with cream sauce and mushrooms). Even though we were too full to go on, we lingered over a bottle of white wine then ordered some *spaghetti alla carbonara* to close out the night. It was a real feast in a great atmosphere.

57. TAVERNA DEL MORO, *Via del Moro 43, Tel. 06/580-9165. Closed Mondays. No credit cards accepted. Dinner for two L55,000.*

A great inexpensive place to eat and enjoy an evening in Trastevere after you go pick up a novel at Clair Hammond's Corner Bookstore just up the road. Here you'll find the pizza superb, as well as their pasta's and meats. On Fridays they have Egyptian night in the back complete with belly dancers and more. A fun local place. When in the area, give this small, charming place a try. Their *spaghetti alla carbonara* is as great as is their *alla vongole*.

TREVI FOUNTAIN & VIA VENETO AREA

The **Trevi Fountain** is the place where you toss a coin at Neptune's feet for a guarantee that you will one day return to Rome. It is a powerful 18th century baroque statue that dominates the square it is in. In fact, it seems overbearing for so small a space, especially at night when it is lit up by floodlights.

All around Trevi are shoe stores and small *pizzerie*. Then you have the **Via Veneto**, backdrop for the 1959 film *La Dolce Vita*. It used to be the chic gathering place for international movie stars but now it's simply an expensive place to stay, shop, and eat.

Besides these two places in this section, the area is modern, hectic, and devoid of many real sights. There are exceptions like the **Baths of Diocletian** and the **Economy Bookstore**, the latter selling English-language new and used books, but overall, Trevi and Via Veneto are the places to see in this section.

58. LE BISTROT, *Via dei Greci 5, Tel. 967-97704. Open evenings only from 8:00pm -2:00am. Closed Sundays and three weeks in August. Dinner for two L80,000. (Metro-Spagna)*

If you're interested in trying some good French food during your stay in Italy, give Le Bistrot a try. Even though the name is French, they also have some Italian pasta dishes since the place is owned by an Italian. Furnished in authentic Art Nouveau style. I'm not a big fan of French food, but I found the *soupe a l'oignon* (onion soup) a worthwhile light meal in the early evening.

59. SORA LELLA, *Via di Ponte Quattro Capi 16, Tel. 06/686-1601. Closed Sundays . Dinner for two L130,000. Credit cards accepted.*

A local place magically situated on the Isola Tibertina in the middle of the Tiber River, you'll find great local atmosphere and wonderful food. Family-run for generations, they make real *cucina Romana* (Roman cooking) here. There are only two rooms that can seat maybe 45 people. Try their *gnocchi alla amatriciana* (dumplings in a red pepper, bacon and pecorino cheese sauce) or the *spaghetti al tonno* (with a tuna sauce). For seconds their *abbacchio* (lamb) is some of the best in Rome. It may seem expensive but the food justifies the cost.

60. PIZZERIA LA CAPRICCIOSA, *Largo dei Lombardi 8 just off of the Via Del Corso. Tel.06/6794027 / 6794706. Open lunch and dinner (until 1 am). Closed Tuesdays. No credit cards accepted. Dinner for two L75,000. (Metro-Spagna)*

Don't be fooled by the name. This is no ordinary pizzeria. It is a large, wonderfully authentic Italian restaurant with over 50 tables inside. At night and on weekends, the restaurant expands outside into the Largo dei Lombardi. The best place to dine is outside, because inside the nickname for this place is La Cucaracha. La Capricciosa is in a convenient location directly in the middle of Rome's premier shopping area, Via del Corso. So after an evening of shopping, stop in. But remember to bring cash, because La Capricciosa doesn't like to accept credit cards.

They have a large selection of antipasto with all sorts of prepared vegetables, ham, salami, and mozzarella. Mainly a pasta and pizza restaurant (pizza served only in the evenings), they also serve great meat. and vegetable platters. Their best pizza is gargantuan *Pizza capricciosa*, one with everything, Italian style. They also make all of the Roman pasta staples perfectly: *arrabbiata, amatriciana,* and *vongole*. One pasta dish that was a little different but really good was the *spaghetti al burro con funghi* (with butter and mushrooms). Or try the *mezzo pollo al diavolo* (half chicken cooked over the flames) if you're in the mood for poultry.

61. LA CUPOLA, *in the Hotel Excelsior, at Via Veneto 125, Tel. 06/4708. Credit cards accepted. Open 7 days a week. Dinner for two L100,000. (Metro-Barberini or Spagna)*

This is the restaurant in the Hotel Excelsior where I first had *spaghetti al burro* when I was a kid. It's expensive and the French Empire style decorations are ostentatious, but you can have your basic Roman-style dishes, like *penne all'arrabbiata, amatriciana, or carbonara*, some nouvelle cuisine the chef creates, or anything your little heart desires. If you want to feel like you're part of *La Dolce Vita*, eat here. Otherwise try something else.

62. GIOIA MIA, *Via degli Avignonesi 34. Tel. 06/462-784. Closed Wednesdays. Credit cards accepted. Dinner for two L70,000. (Metro-Barberini)*

A small family-run pizzeria which serves excellent *calzone, bruschetta* (garlic bread made with olive oil), and pizza. They can also make you a *crostino* sandwich that they roast in their oven. Another favorite in this restaurant is their roasted or grilled meats. The *abbacchio* (lamb) is great.

63. DA MARIO, *Via della Vite 55, Tel. 06/678-7381. Closed Sundays and August 5-30. Dinner for two L80,000. (Metro-Spagna)*

You can tell the specialty of this restaurant by the stuffed game birds in the window. Da Mario serves unpretentious Tuscan food. I suggest trying the *ribollita* (thick cabbage soup) and the staple of all Tuscan restaurants, the *Bistecca alla Fiorentina*, which is big enough for two. Try all of this with a bottle of the house wine (excellent Chianti) and you should be able to get a meal for a good price. If you order two dishes apiece you'll match the price listed above.

64. TRATTORIA DA OLIMPICO, *Via degli Avignonesi 37. Credit cards accepted Closed Tuesdays. Dinner for two 60,000. (Metro-Barberini)*

Located just up the road from the Hotel Memphis, this is a great inexpensive place to eat. The street it's on is not well traveled, so they lure people in to sample their succulent dishes by offering great prices. Their *pizza margherita* (tomatoes and cheese) and other pizzas are made the perfect Roman Way. If you only eat the pizza and have a bottle of wine you could get out of here with only a L30,000 meal.

65. GIOVANNI, *Via Marche 64, Tel. 06/482-1834. Closed Saturdays and the entire month of August. Credit cards accepted. Dinner for two L150,000. (Metro-Barberini)*

Close to the hustle and bustle of the Via Veneto is this good restaurant with an Adriatic flair. The owners are from Ancona and they serve fresh fish brought in from there. The soups in their restaurant are also very good, so if you've had your fill of pasta, come here and try the seafood and soups. I really like the *Calamaretti ai ferri* (small shrimp cooked over and open flame). The house white, from the Verdicchio region is quite good.

66. GIRARROSTO TOSCANO, *Via Campania 29, Tel. 06/493-759. Closed Wednesdays. No credit cards accepted. Dinner for two L120,000. (Metro-Barberini)*

Located in the cellar of a huge building facing onto the Aurelian Wall, this is a first class restaurant that accepts orders until 1am. An ideal place to come back to after a night of revelry if you have a lingering hunger. The food is mainly veal and beef grilled on a spit over an open wood fired oven. Prior to the meats you can indulge in melon, Parma ham and *ovoline* (small mozzarella cheeses). The servings are large and so are the prices, and befitting its location near the Via Veneto the service is excellent.

Beside the food you'll enjoy the rustic atmosphere, with hams hanging in the entrance way along with a table filled with fresh produce. In the dining area bottles of wine line the walls above the tables, and the wood paneling adds to the peasant appeal at princely prices.

67. AL MORO, *Vicolo delle Bollette 13 (off Via del Lavatore), Tel. 06/678-3495. Closed Sundays and the entire month of August. No credit cards accepted. Dinner for two L110,000. (Metro-Barberini)*

The food is excellent in the Roman style, the ingredients are all fresh and of the highest quality, but the prices are a little high, and since this a popular eating establishment you'll need to make reservations. I swear the *Spaghetti al Moro* (a light carbonara sauce with cheese, egg, bacon, and red pepper flakes) is the best I've tasted. They make an excellent *all'arrabbiata* (hot and spicy sauce) too. I also enjoyed the *Scampi alla Moro* (broiled shrimp). Other excellent dishes are the *abbacchio romanesco al forno con patate* (roasted lamb with superb roasted potatoes with a sprinkle of rosemary).

The inside front room is dominated by a large picture of Moro himself, long since passed away. The other two rooms have wine bottles surrounding the walls above the tables and are relatively roomy. If you want to sit outside you'll be crowded against a wall on a lightly traveled little *via*. I recommend the inside seating.

68. RE DEGLI AMICI, *Via della Croce 33b, Tel. 06/679-5380 or 678-2555. Credit cards accepted. Closed Mondays and the last three weeks in June. (Metro-Spagna)*

This *trattoria* close to the Spanish Steps has been serving traditional Roman food for years. If you don't want a full meal their antipasto bar will more than suffice. After 7:30pm, you can get one of their excellent pizzas. My favorite is the one named after the restaurant, made with sausage, mozzarella, oregano and tomatoes. The pasta dishes here are also something that shouldn't be missed. Try any of the Roman specialties: *carbonara, amatriciana,* or *arrabiata*.

69. TAVERNA RIPETTA, *Via di Ripetta 158, Tel. 06/6880-2979. Credit cards accepted. Dinner for two L75,000. (Metro-Flaminio)*

This is small restaurant with a Middle Eastern flair. They have couscous, falafel, shish kebab, and tabule as well as a Roman staple such as *sogliola alla griglia* (grilled sole). This is a good place for a light but filling meal with a twist. Vegetarians should love this place since many of the dishes are meatless.

PIAZZA DI SPAGNA AREA

The **Piazza di Spagna** is where it all happens in Rome. You have the best shops, great restaurants, beautiful sights. Stately *palazzos* lining the streets look like an ideal place to live, but today much of the housing has been replaced by offices, shops, boutiques, or restaurants. Only the lucky few can afford an apartment in this location.

This area is home to the **Spanish Steps**, which gets its name from the Piazza, which gets its name from the Spanish Embassy in the square that has been its residence since 1622. The area was adopted by British travelers in the 18th and 19th century, because it was not yet a popular location. Their presence is still here in the form of **Babbington Tea Rooms**, an expensive but satisfying establishment in the piazza; as well as a plaque commemorating the house where Keats died in 1821. The area used to called *il ghetto degli Inglesi* – the English ghetto.

At the beginning of Spring, the steps are laden with banks of flowers that make the whole area look like a garden. Even though you're not supposed to sit and relax on the steps (a rule since 1996), you'll find others doing it. So sit a spell and watch the world walk by.

70. BABINGTON'S TEA ROOMS, *23 Piazza di Spagna, Tel. 06/678-6027. Credit cards accepted. Closed Thursdays. (Metro-Spagna)*

Really a place to grab a spot of tea, except in the mornings when they serve massive breakfasts of scones, shepherd's pie, and other British delights (if there is such a thing). This ancient café, with its heavy furniture, musty decor, and creaky floors has been serving customers for several centuries. The service is out of the 18th century, but the prices are from the 21st. Expect a cup of tea to cost over $5.

71. HASLER, *Piazza Trinita dei Monti 6, Tel. 06/678-2651. Credit cards accepted. Open 7 days a week. Dinner for two L120,000. (Metro-Spagna)*

If you have the money to spend, the view down the Spanish Steps from the glassed-in and air-conditioned terrace is worth every penny. You can pick out the Castel Sant'Angelo, the Jewish Ghetto's synagogue, the Pantheon, and the Quirinale Palace from the terrace. The food used to be passable, but now its Italian and Continental menu has begun to sparkle. The multilingual waiters will tell you that the *abbacchio al forno* is excellent, and I'd agree. There are many fine dishes on the menu, so you can order anything, but remember it's expensive.

72. OTELLO ALLA CONCORDIA, *Via Della Croce 81. Tel. 06/679-1178. No credit cards accepted. Closed Sundays. Dinner for two L80,000. (Metro-Spagna)*

This is a family-run small trattoria set off of the main road Via della Croce. This location used to render it unnoticed, but now it seems to be crowded all the time. And with good reason – the food is excellent. You go through a tiny entrance off the main road then through a small shady garden to get to the restaurant. They have now made the garden eating area enclosed in removable glass, so people can eat out here all year round. In the summer it's especially nice. On the inside the walls are filled with countless oil paintings, many received as trade for a good meal by a struggling artist. The prices are perfect and the food is simple, basic, and good. I loved the *abbacchio arrosto can patate* (roast lamb with grilled potatoes). The pasta dishes are not that good, which is strange for Rome, but if you stick with the meat dishes and vegetables you'll have a great meal. They open at 7:30pm. Make sure you get there early or else you'll have a wait. The help is surly, but in a typical Roman way.

73. PIZZERIA LE GROTTE, *Via delle Vite 37. No telephone. Credit cards accepted. Dinner for two L70,000. (Metro-Spagna)*

This place has a dark rustic appearance complete with partially wood walls. They are known for their excellent antipasto bar that could fill you up for the rest of the meal. I've had the *spaghetti alla vongole verace* (spicy clam sauce) and the *pollo arrosto* (spit roasted chicken) and loved them both. The food is down-to-earth peasant in the Roman fashion, and mixes well with the decor.

PIAZZA NAVONA & CAMPO DEI FIORI AREA

Piazza Navona is the perfect place to explore Rome's historical tapestry. Just outside Navona in the **Piazza Tor di Sarguinana**, you'll find ancient Roman ruins completely surrounded by the "modern" baroque buildings of Piazza Navona. The square itself has a charm that makes you want to come back over and over again. It is like a living architectural gallery, with its baroque churches and buildings lining the square and the immense statues standing majestic in the square itself.

On a hot day, the fountains here are a visitor's oasis, allowing for needed foot soaking refreshment. But before you take your shoes off and relax your sore feet by soaking them in one of the fountains, stroll to the center of the piazza and take note of the magnificence of Bernini's **Fontana Dei Quattro Fiumi** (Fountain of Four Rivers). Navona is filled with wonders. You'll find some of the ice cream Navona has become famous for, as well as the carnival of life swirling around you. You might see fire-eaters, painters, jugglers, caricaturists, tourists, rampaging Italian children, and much more here.

And from mid-December to mid-January, the square becomes a giant Christmas market with booths and stalls selling stuffed animals, toys, handicrafts, and candy that looks like coal.

This Navona area is basically an extension of the Campo dei Fiori area in character. They are both genuinely picturesque and intriguing neighborhoods, with a maze of interconnecting narrow streets and *piazzetta* (small squares), and each has a reputation of becoming a haven for hashish sellers late at night. This commercial aspect goes hand in hand with the Campo dei Fiori (literally translated means "field of flowers") flower and produce market every morning. Both areas evoke a feeling of what Rome used to be like many centuries ago, with the centuries-old buildings and the peddlers, carts, and small stores lining the narrow streets.

74. LA CARBONARA, *Campo dei Fiori 23, Tel. 06/654-783. Credit cards accepted. Closed Tuesdays. Dinner for two L90,000.*

Located in the best piazza for dining, and the food's not bad either. As could be expected, *pasta alla carbonara* is the house specialty so give that a try here. Here it is prepared to perfection with *rigatoni* in a rich peppery sauce of egg, cheese, and bacon. They also make the best *spaghetti alla vongole verace* (spicy clam sauce) I've ever had. The *fritto misto* (lightly fried mixed vegetables and cheese) is excellent since most of the produce comes in directly from the *mercato* in the square. The market can be a problem at early lunch since there are still discarded veggies on the ground where the tables should be. There's no smell, but the sight isn't too appetizing. I love the *abbacchio alla griglia* (roast baby lamb) and the roasted potatoes.

75. GINO AI FUNARI, *Via dei Funari. Closed Wednesdays. American Express accepted. Dinner for two L65,000.*

Another inexpensive place, this one located in the Jewish ghetto. The decor is simple and basic but the food is good and cheap. They have the basic Roman pastas (*carbonara, amatriciana, vongole verace, and arrabiata*) but I jumped over them to try the *coniglio alla cacciatore* (rabbit hunter style made with brandy tomatoes and spices). It is superb.

76. HOSTARIA GUILIA, *Via della Barchetta 19, Tel. 06/6880-6466. Dinner for two L65,000.*

They have a beautiful arched interior with brown tiled floors that emits all the character of Rome. The dishes are basic but great Roman fare too, like the *Penne all'arrabbiata* or the *Spaghetti alla Vongole*. Besides the pasta they have fresh fish and grilled meats. These guys are off the beaten track and their prices are great. Give them a try if you're in the neighborhood.

77. ORSO "80", *Via dell'Orso 33, Tel. 06/656-4904. Credit cards accepted. Closed Mondays. Dinner for two L85,000.*

This is a fine Roman restaurant, a place to come for some classic pasta dishes, good fresh fish, and juicy meats. They bake their breads on-site in their red-brick pizza oven. Basically this is a restaurant with a little bit of everything for everybody. Pasta, pizza, fish, grilled meats, home-made breads, extensive antipasto, etc. I really like the Roman favorite *spaghetti alla carbonara* as well as the *abbacchio alla griglia* (grilled baby lamb). The place always seems to be crowded even though it's large, so try to get there early. Located near Piazza Navona, Pantheon, and Campo dei Fiori.

78. VECCHIA ROMA, *Piazza di Campitelli 18, Tel. 06/656-4604. No credit cards accepted. Closed Wednesdays. Dinner for two L85,000.*

The setting of the piazza with its Baroque church and three beautiful palazzos makes your meal worthwhile, even if the buildings are covered in grime. This menu changes constantly, but the basics are the wide variety of antipasto (which could be a meal in itself), as well as *agnello* (lamb) and *capretto* (goat) or their grilled artichokes. You have to try the artichoke, since this is the Jewish ghetto and the dish is a local favorite.

PIAZZA DEL POPOLO TO THE PANTHEON

This historic area shares many of the flavors of the bordering Piazza Navona area. It is filled with a delightful mixture of artisan's shops and modern commercial stores. When you stray off the Via del Corso, this section's eastern boundary, you'll enjoy meandering through narrow streets lined with small shops and boutiques.

The focal point of the area is the **Pantheon**, built almost two thousand years ago by Consul Marcus Agrippa as a pantheistic temple, hence its name. The city's population was centered in this area during the Middle Ages, and except for the disappearance of a large fish market, the area has remained virtually unchanged.

79. DA ALFREDO ALL'ANGOLETO, *Piazza Rondanini 51 Tel. 06/ 686-8019, 06/686-1203. Credit cards accepted. Closed Mondays and August 11- 15. Dinner for two L100,000.*

A vibrant and noisy trattoria specializing in fish. Try to resist the lure of the innumerable, mouth-watering *antipasti* or you won't have room for the superbly fresh fish, the enormous Mediterranean prawns, or the still live lobsters in the display case awaiting your cooking instructions. This tentatively can be called the best seafood restaurant in Rome. Mushrooms are another Alfredo specialty from late summer to late autumn. I recommend you try any of their seafood dishes, roast meats, or pastas.

There is outside seating on a small piazza as well as air-conditioned inside seating. The decor is simple, with wine bottles lining the shelves set above the tables. Come here for great food and go away satisfied.

80. ALFREDO ALLA SCROFA, *Via della Scrofa 104, Tel. 06/654-0163. Closed Tuesdays. Credit cards accepted. Dinner for two L110,000.*

There are photographs of the very rich and famous literally papering the walls. The restaurant has been in business for over half a century and was even frequented by Douglas Fairbanks and Mary Pickford. All the pasta dishes are superb, especially *Fettucine al triplo burro* (with triple butter sauce). The wine list is excellent and so are their house variations. If you like music with your meal, there is a strolling guitarist inside.

81. DAL BOLOGNESE, *Piazza del Popolo 1-2, Tel. 361-1426., 06/322- 2799. Closed Mondays and Sunday evenings, and August 9-25. Credit cards accepted. Dinner for two L85,000. (Metro-Flaminio)*

The cooking is Bolognese in style, which some claim is the best in Italy. Why? Because of the *Parmigiano Reggiano* cheese and the *Prosciutto di Parma*, as well as their affinity for pastas that use one or both of these ingredients. They have a menu in English to help you search through their great dishes. The *fritto misto alla Bolognese*, which includes fried cheeses, meats and vegetables, is great. The *Misto di Paste* (mixed pasta and sauces) was filling enough for two. By ordering this dish you get to sample a variety of dishes while only ordering one. They have outside seating, perfect for people watching, but the intimacy of their inside rooms decorated with a fine collection of modern paintings appeals to me more. Also inside, you don't have to breathe exhaust fumes while you eat.

82. LA BUCA DI RIPETTA, *Via di Ripetta 36, Tel. 06/678-9528. Closed Mondays and the whole month of August. No credit cards accepted. Dinner for two L70,000. (Metro-Flaminio)*

This is a very small, friendly trattoria, where you must arrive early if you have not made a reservation. This place is immensely popular for its food, reasonable prices, and festive atmosphere. Also, the jovial *padrone* is in constant attendance. The food is basic, straightforward Roman fare. Try the *Lasagna al Forno, Saltimbocca alla Romana,* or the *ossobuco di vitello.* They take their food seriously, so if you want to eat the Roman way with course after course, this is the place to do it. The restaurant is only one tiny room, its high walls covered with cooking and farming paraphernalia like enormous bellows, great copper pans, etc. When in Rome, you simply must dine here.

83. HOSTARIA LA NUOVA COMPANNINA DA ENRICO E VITTORIO, *Piazza delle Coppelle 8, Tel. 06/6880-3921. Dinner for two L60,000.*

This is a country restaurant transplanted into the city, with country prices and country accents. I couldn't understand the waiters half the time and I speak Italian. They have outside seating in a little *piazza* that helps you escape the hordes of tourists. If for nothing other than the quaint small *piazza*, come here for a meal. A perfect respite from a day's touring. Try the *vitello arrosto con funghi* (roasted veal with mushrooms) or the *Ossobuco alla Romana*. Did I forget the primo? Yes. This place makes great meats, but they don't know diddly about pasta – so stick to an antipasto and a secondo.

84. LA FONTANELLA, *Largo Fontanella Tevere 86, Tel. 06/678-3849. Closed Mondays. Credit cards accepted. Dinner for two L85,000.*

A simple enjoyable restaurant with a distinctive Tuscan flair. Their specialties are game when it's in season. The charm of the restaurant is distinctively old world, with a gleaming wood floor and flowers on every table. Their pastas are also good and they have all the basic Roman staples: *Tortellini alla panna, penne all'arrabbiata,* etc.

85. LA SACRESTIA, *Via del Seminario 89, Tel. 679-7581. Closed Wednesdays. No credit cards accepted. Dinner for two L85,000.*

Close to the Pantheon, this restaurant has over 200 places for seating, and offers good food at reasonable prices. The decorations leave much to be desired, especially the garish ceiling and fruit clustered grotto. Come for their pizzas, served both during the day and at night, an unusual offering for an Italian restaurant. They also serve good cuts of grilled meat, and the pasta is typically Roman also, which naturally makes it good.

86. OSTERIA DEL TEMPO PERSO, *Via dell'Oca 43, Tel. 06/322-4841, 6/322-0947. All credit cards accepted. Dinner for two L65,000.*

Great rustic, succulent Roman fare, a stone's throw away from the Piazza del Popolo – and at great prices too. The restaurant has a small outside seating area enclosed by planters in which you can eat your meals on wooden tables. There is also some seating inside, but in the summer, the terrace is the best place to be. This *osteria* is not haute cuisine, but every dish is excellent. They have the largest selection of pastas, pizzas and meat dishes I have seen anywhere in Italy, so if you can't find something you like here, you don't like to eat.

Come here for the Roman specialties such as *spaghetti alla carbonara, penne all'arrabiata*, or *bucatini all'amatriciana*; or really treat yourself and sample the super-fantastic *tagliatelle ai funghi porcini* (with porcini mushrooms) with the most succulent sauce you can find anywhere. For seconds, the *abbacchio arrosto con patate* (lamb with rosemary potatoes) is exquisite as is the *vitello arrosto con patate* (veal with rosemary potatoes). Mimmo, the head waiter, is perfectly attentive, and since he was married to an American he speaks good English. While in Rome, definitely try this place.

OUTSIDE OF TOWN

Motivating yourself at the end of a tiring day to sample these restaurants may be difficult, but I believe they will be worth your while. The food at each is stupendous, and the settings uniquely Roman, making for a fabulous dining experience!

87. IL CASALE, *located 10 kilometers outside of Rome on the Via Flaminia. Tel. 06/3361-9806. Closed Tuesdays and August. Best way to get there is by cab. Cost for the cab should be around L20,000 each way. Dinner for two L90,000. Credit cards accepted.*

Excellent outdoor dining, especially during the summer months. The restaurant's location offers a respite from the hectic Roman crowds. Housed in a renovated farm house with roaring fires, looking out over expansive grounds, creates a terrific ambiance for a wonderful evening. The grounds are perfect for children to explore while their parents wile away the hours with a good Italian wine after dinner. An enormous table of antipasto is the perfect first course, since you can help yourself as often as you want. For the main course, grilled meats are the specialty, especially veal, lamb, and beef. All are prepared with exquisite care over their roaring grills, and could be the finest servings of succulent meat south of Florence.

My recommendations for a pasta dish are either the *penne all'arrabbiata* or *tortellini alla panna* (meat or cheese tortellini in a thick cream sauce), *spaghetti alla vongole verace* (with spicy clam sauce), *tagliolini ai funghi porcini* (pasta with porcini mushrooms). Recommendations for meat dishes: *Lambata di Vitello* (Veal Chop), *Lambatta alla Griglia* (Grilled Veal), *maiale alla griglia* (Grilled Pork), *maialino alla griglia* (grilled baby pork, more juicy and flavorful than *maiale*).

88. ER CUCURUCU, *Via Capoprati 10, Tel. 06/325-2571. Closed Mondays and Sundays too in the summer. Dinner for two L100,000.*

The subtitle of this place is "An oasis of calm in the middle of Rome" and they are right. Located directly on the river Tiber, there are plenty of tables out in the open to enjoy the weather and the view. The service is efficient and courteous even when this place is packed, which it usually is. The antipasto buffet is huge and could be your whole meal, but as in most places in Italy they frown on that. So for *primo piatto* try their exquisite *fettucine con porcini* (pasta with porcini mushrooms) or their delectable *fettucine can vongole verace* (with spicy clam sauce).

For seconds, try their *petto di vitello alla fornara* (succulent grilled veal cutlet) or their grilled *bistecca di manzo* (steak). To get here hop in a cab or catch bus 90 from Piazza Flaminio all the way to its terminus.

14. SEEING THE SIGHTS

There are several approaches to sightseeing in Rome. The chief difficulty, most visitors find, is that there is so much to see that even a month's concentrated touring would only scratch the surface. If your time is limited, a sightseeing tour, or series of tours by bus, is perhaps the one way you can be sure to see at least the greatest sights in Rome and its environs. There are a variety of tours available through **CIT** (the official Italian tour company), *Piazza della Repubblica 64*; **American Express**, *Piazza di Spagna 38*; **Thomas Cook**, *Via Vittorio Veneto 9/11*; or **Wagon-Lits**, the French travel company, *Via Boncompagni 25*.

If you have more time, or prefer to set your own pace, the best approach —indeed the only workable approach in Rome — is to choose only what you're really most interested in and not force yourself to visit something that doesn't appeal to you merely because "everybody" goes to see it. A map of Rome, some walking shoes, and a spirit of adventure are all you need to explore the innumerable *piazzas*, churches, galleries, parks, and fountains of this unique city. If you saunter through the narrow streets of old Rome, behind the **Piazza Navona**, for example, or along the **Via Giulia** or near the **Pantheon**, you'll get many unexpected and revealing glimpses of flower hung balconies, inner courtyards, and fountains. Here, perhaps more than in the impressive ruins of antiquity, you will get a little of the feeling of this city where civilizations have been built on the ruins of the previous ones for centuries, an ancient city whose vitality seems to be renewed perpetually.

Most, if not all, of these sights follow the Italian siesta system, which means that they will open at 9:00am until 1:00pm, then close from 1:00pm to 3:00 or 4:00pm. This goes for the museums, sights, monuments, etc. Thereafter they will stay open until 6:00pm or 7:00pm. So plan your tours accordingly. All museums, buildings, and monuments will charge a small fee to enter, mostly around L5,000 (or $3), so be prepared for that also.

To help you find your way around Rome, we include a metro map on page 147; maps featuring sights (and hotels and restaurants) are in Chapter 12; the list of sights by map is on page 149.

TEN MUST-SEE SIGHTS IN ROME

The Vatican Museums alone can take you an entire day to work through, so don't believe that you can do all of these places justice in a few short days. Also, when you visit Piazza Navona, Piazza di Spagna, and Trevi Fountain, you will get a different experience depending on the time of day you go. At night each of these places livens up with Italians of all ages strolling, chatting, sipping wine, strumming guitars, while during the day they may only be swarmed by tourists.

Take your time – don't do too much. These ten could easily last you a week.

Sistine Chapel – Site of Michelangelo's magnificent frescoed ceiling and walls.

Vatican Museums – Everything you could imagine including Egyptian, Greek & Roman artifacts, as well as the best collection of paintings and sculptures anywhere in the world.

St. Peter's – The world's largest cathedral, exquisitely decorated.

Castel Sant'Angelo – The fortress that used to protect the Vatican, now houses a wonderful armaments museum.

Imperial and Roman Forums – The center of ancient Roman life. A great place for people of all ages to explore.

Capitoline Museum on the Campidoglio – The second best museum in Rome, with many fine sculptures and paintings.

Piazza Navona – In what used to be the place for naval gladiatorial battles is now a lively piazza filled with wonderful fountains, churches, and palazzi as well as good cafés and restaurants.

Piazza di Spagna – Walk to the top and get a great view of the city. Sit by the fountain during siesta and enjoy Rome as it passes you by.

Trevi Fountain – One of the most beautiful fountains in Italy. At night, when lit up it is a magnificent sight.

Saint Paul's Outside the Walls – Location of many buried Saints, some fine sculptures and mosaics. Walls ringed with portraits of all the popes.

ANCIENT ROME
THE IMPERIAL FORUMS

Via dei Fori Imperiali. Admission L5,000. Tel. 06/699-0110. Open 9:00am to an hour before sunset. Metro-Colosseo.

The **Imperial Forums** were built in the last days of the Republic, when the Roman Forum became inadequate to accommodate the ever-increasing population, and the emperors began to celebrate their own magnifi-

SEEING THE SIGHTS 147

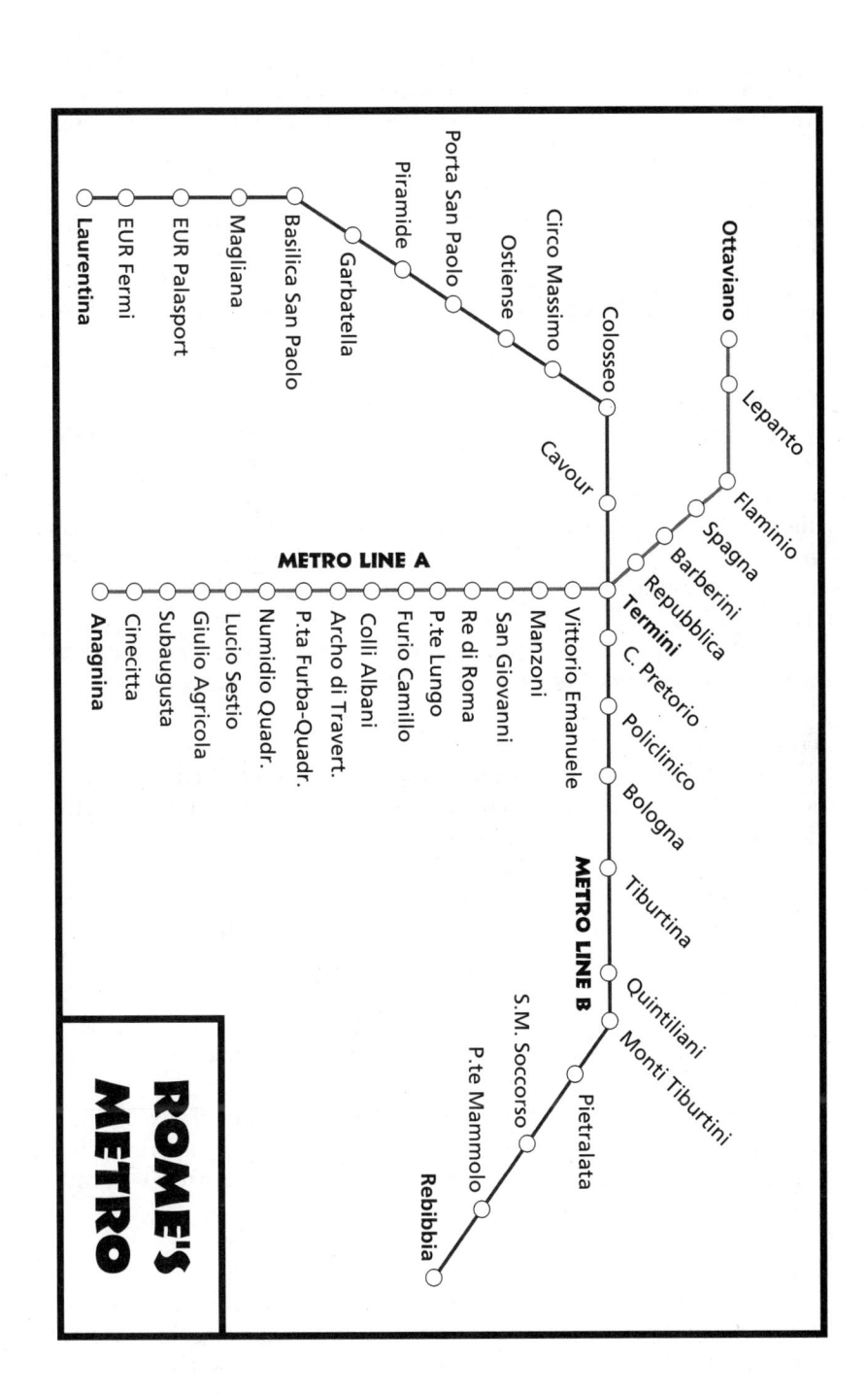

ROME'S METRO

METRO LINE A: Ottaviano — Lepanto — Flaminio — Spagna — Barberini — Repubblica — Termini — Vittorio Emanuele — Manzoni — San Giovanni — Re di Roma — P.te Lungo — Furio Camillo — Colli Albani — Arco di Travert. — P.ta Furba-Quadr. — Numidio Quadr. — Lucio Sestio — Giulio Agricola — Subaugusta — Cinecitta — Anagnina

METRO LINE B: Laurentina — EUR Fermi — EUR Palasport — Magliana — Basilica San Paolo — Garbatella — Piramide — Porta San Paolo — Ostiense — Circo Massimo — Colosseo — Cavour — Termini — C. Pretorio — Policlinico — Bologna — Tiburtina — Quintiliani — Monti Tiburtini — Pietralata — S.M. Soccorso — P.te Mammolo — Rebibbia

cence. These forums were used as meeting places for Romans to exchange views, as lively street markets, or as places where official announcements could be proclaimed to the populace. The first was built by Julius Caesar, and those that followed were created by Augustus, Vespasian, Domitian, Trajan, Nerva, and Hadrian.

After the fall of the Roman Empire, these places of great import fell into disrepair and during the Middle Ages and the Renaissance all that was left are the ruins we see today. Gradually, over the centuries, these monumental ruins became covered with soil until they began to be excavated in 1924.

Trajan's Forum
Located below current street level, this is the most grandiose of the Forums of the imperial age and reflects the emperor's eclectic taste in art and architecture. Here you can see one of the finest monuments in these Imperial Forums, **Trajan's Column**, built to honor the Victories of Trajan in 113. It is over 30 meters high and is covered with a series of spiral reliefs depicting the military exploits of the Emperor against the Dacins in the 1st century CE.

At the summit of this large column is a statue of St. Peter that was placed there by Pope Sixtus V in the 17th century.

Trajan's Market
This is a large and imposing set of buildings attached to Trajan's Forum, where people gathered and goods were sold. In the vast semi-circle is where the merchants displayed their wares.

Forum of Caesar
Located to the right of the Via dei Fori Imperiali (the road itself was built in 1932 on the site of a far more ancient road to more adequately display the monuments of ancient Rome), this was the earliest of the Imperial Forums. It was begun in 54 BCE to commemorate the Battle of Pharsalus, and finished in 44 BCE. Trajan redesigned many parts of this Forum to meet his needs in 113 CE.

For example, Trajan added the **Basilica Argentaria** (Silver Basilica) that was a meeting place for bankers and money changers. Originally a bronze statue of Julius Caesar stood in the center of this Forum; currently it is located in the Campidoglio.

Forum of Augustus
Built around the time of Christ's birth, this Forum commemorates the deaths of Brutus and Cassius (the traitors who allied against Caesar) at the Battle of Philippi in 42 BCE. Here you'll find some remains of the

LIST OF SIGHTS BY MAP

Sight	Map	Sight	Map
Imperial Forums	D	Borghese Gardens	A & C
Trajan's Forum and Market	D	Galleria Borghese	A
		Vitt. Eman. Memorial	D
Forum of Caesar	D	Piazza del Popolo	C
Forum of Augustus	D	Via Veneto	A
Basilica of Maxentius & Constantine	D	Via Appia Antica	D
		Trastevere	B
Colosseum	D	Isola Tiberina	B
Arch of Constantine	D	Ponte Frabricio	B
Roman Forum & Palatine Hill	D	Jewish Ghetto	B
		Palazzo Barberini	A
Baths of Caracalla	D	Palazzo Farnese	B
Baths of Diocletian	D	Gianicolo	B
Campidoglio	D	St. Paul's Outside The Walls	D
Circus Maximus	D		
Catacombs	D	S Maria Sopra Minerva	C & B
Altar/Mausoleum of Augustus	C	S Pietro in Vincoli	A
		SM Maggiore	A & D
Pyramid	D	S Giovanni in Laterano	D
Ponte Milvio	A	S Clemente	D
Aurelian Wall	A,B,C,D	S Cecilia in Trastevere	B
Column of M. Aurelius	C	SM in Trastevere	B
Temple of Hadrian	C	Capitoline Museum	D
Castel St. Angelo	C	National Museum	A
St. Peter's	C	Galleria Borghese	A
Vatican City	C	Villa Giulia	C
Piazza Navona	C	Vatican Museums	C
Piazza di Spagna	A	Museo della Civilta Romana	D
Campo dei Fiori	B		
Trevi Fountain	A		
Pantheon	C & B		

Maps can be found on the following pages:
Map A: pages 104-105
Map B: pages 118-119
Map C: pages 122-123
Map D: pages 152-153

Temple of Mars Ultor, the god of war, including a high podium and some trabeated (horizontal) columns. To the side of the temple you'll find the remains of two arches of triumph and two porticos.

Basilica of Maxentius & Constantine

This large building was begun by Maxentius between 306-312 CE and eventually completed by Constantine. It was used as a court of law and a money exchange, as were all Roman basilicas. It faces the Colosseum and is one of the best preserved of the buildings in the Imperial Forums. In its prime, the building was 100 meters long and 76 meters wide and divided into three naves, most of which remains to this day.

THE COLOSSEUM

Piazza del Colosseo. Admission L8,000. Hours in the summer 9:00am-7:00pm. In the winter 9:00am-4:30pm. Sundays and Wednesdays 9:00am-2:00pm. Catch buses 11, 27, 81, 85, 87. Metro-Colosseo.

The **Colosseum** (*Flavian Amphitheater*) remains the most memorable monument surviving from ancient Rome. Its construction began in 72 CE by Vespasian on the site of the *Stagnum Neronis*, an artificial lake built to be viewed by one wing of Emperor Nero's house on the adjacent Oppian Hill. The Colosseum was eventually dedicated by Titus in 80 CE. It is recorded that at the building's opening ceremony, which lasted three months, over 500 exotic beasts and many hundreds of gladiators were slain in the arena. These types of spectacles lasted until 405 CE, when they were abolished. The building was severely damaged by an earthquake in the fifth century CE and since then it has been used as a fortress and as a supply source for construction material for papal buildings.

What we see today is nothing compared to what the building used to look like. In its prime it was covered with marble, and each portico was filled with a marble statue of some important Roman. The Colosseum used to be fully elliptical and could hold over 50,000 people. Each of the three tiers is supported by a different set of columns: Doric for the base, Ionic for the middle and Corinthian for the top. Inside, the first tier of seats was reserved for the knights and tribunes, the second tier for citizens, and the third tier for the lower classes. The Emperor, Senators, Government Officials and Vestal Virgins sat on marble thrones on a raised platform that went around the entire arena.

Inside the arena we can see vestiges of the subterranean passages that were used to transport the wild beasts. Human-powered elevators were employed to get the animals up to the Colosseum floor. At times the arena was flooded to allow for the performance of mock naval battles.

Unremarkable architecturally, the Colosseum is still an engineering marvel to admire.

ARCH OF CONSTANTINE

Piazza Colosseo. Catch buses 11, 27, 81, 85, 87. Metro-Colosseo.

Located near the Colosseum, this monument was built in 312 to commemorate the Emperor's victory over Maxentius at the Ponte Milvio (a bridge that still stands today and as such is the oldest bridge in Rome) and is comprised of three archways. This is the largest and best preserved triumphal arch in Rome. The attic is not continuous but is broken into three parts corresponding to the placement of the arches. Even though this is the Arch of Constantine, the attic panels are from a monument to Marcus Aurelius. On one side of the attic the bas-reliefs represent Marcus Aurelius in his battle with the Dacians, and on the opposite side there are episodes of deeds by Marcus Aurelius and Constantine. On the lower areas there are bas-reliefs from earlier arches of Trajan and Hadrian.

THE ROMAN FORUM, PALATINE HILL & NEARBY SIGHTS

Via dei Fori Imperiali. Tel. 699-0110. Admission L12,000. Open in the winter 9am to an hour before sunset, and in summer 9:00am-6:00pm. Closed Sunday afternoons. Catch buses 11, 27, 85, 97, 181, 186, 718, and 719. Metro-Colosseo.

The best way to get an overall view of the **Roman Forum** is to descend from the Piazza del Campidoglio by way of the Via del Campidoglio, which is to the right of the Senatorial Palace. You get a clear view of the Forums in the front, with the Colosseum in the background, and the Palatine hill on the right. The entrance is some distance down the Via dei Fori Imperiali. You can also enter from the Via di San Gregario near the Colosseum.

The Roman Forum lies between the Palatine and Quirinale hills and was first a burial ground for the early settlers of both locations. Later the area became the center for the religious, commercial and political activities of the early settlers. The surrounding area was greatly expanded in the Imperial era when Roman emperors began building self-contained

---

REALLY SEEING THE SIGHTS

*If you are interested in seeing the Eternal City from a bird's eye view, **Umbria Fly** offers airborne tours of Rome. You will snap some memorable photos from this tour! Each 20 minute flight offers the best views of Rome for only L100,000 per adult and L50,000 per child accompanied by an adult. For more information on how to get the Urbe Airport (Via Salaria 825) and times of departures each day, call 06/8864-1441.*

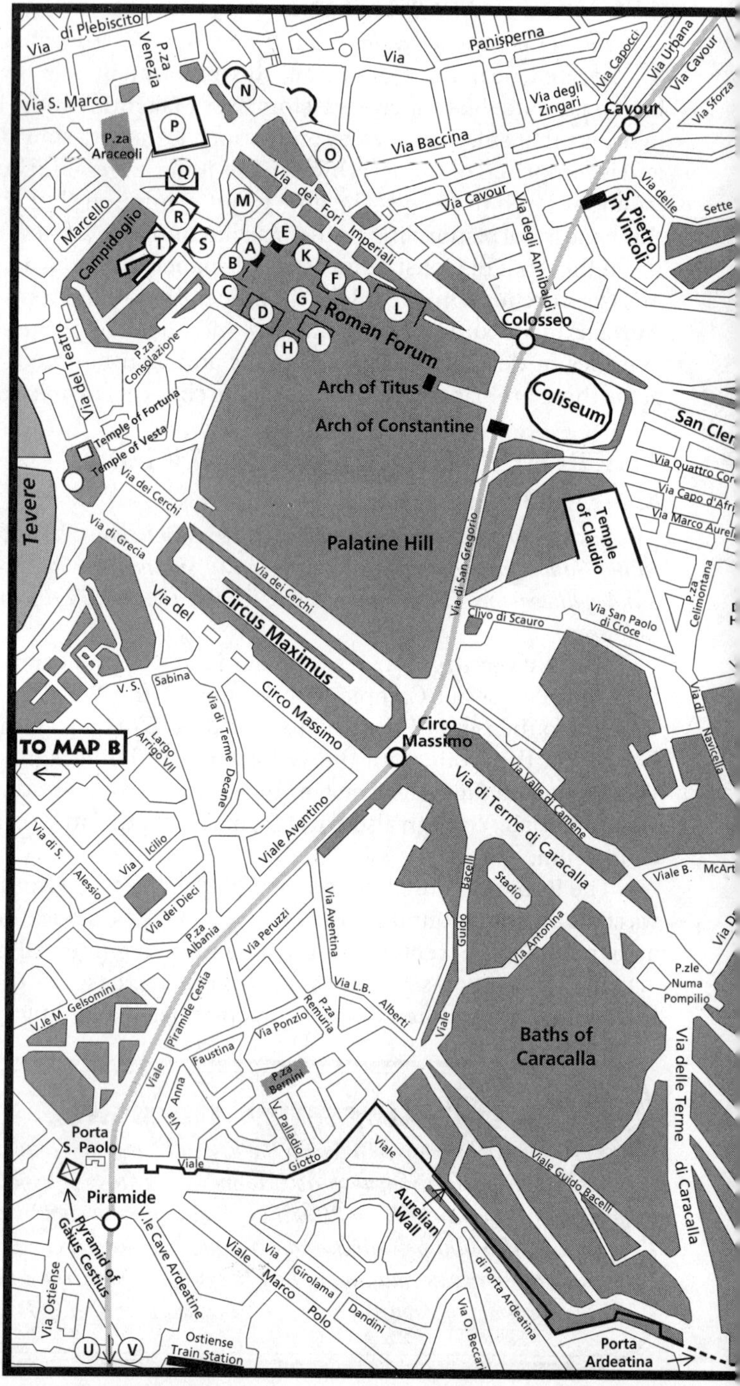

Via di Plebiscito
P.za Venezia
Via S. Marco
P.za Araceoli
Via Panisperna
Via Urbana
Via Cavour
Via Capocci
Via degli Zingari
Via Sforza
Cavour
Via Baccina
Via dei Fori Imperiali
Via Cavour
Via degli Annibaldi
S. Pietro In Vincoli
Via delle Sette
Marcello
Campidoglio
Roman Forum
Colosseo
Coliseum
Arch of Titus
Arch of Constantine
San Cle
Via del Teatro
P.za Consolazione
Temple of Fortuna
Temple of Vesta
Tevere
Via dei Cerchi
Via di Grecia
Via Quattro Cor
Via Capo d'Afri
Via Marco Aurel
Temple of Claudio
Palatine Hill
Via di San Gregorio
Via dei Cerchi
Circus Maximus
Via del
Clivo di Scauro
Via San Paolo di Croce
P.za Celimontana
V. S. Sabina
Via di Terme Decane
Circo Massimo
Circo Massimo
TO MAP B
Largo Arrigo VII
Via di Navicella
Via Valle di Camene
Via di Terme di Caracalla
Viale Aventino
Via di S. Alessio
Via Icilio
Via dei Dieci
P.za Albania
Via Peruzzi
Via Aventina
Guido Baccelli
Stadio
Via Antonina
Viale B. McArt
P.zle Numa Pompilio
V.le M. Gelsomini
Piramide Cestia
Via L.B. Alberti
P.za Remuria
Via Ponzio
Faustina
Viale
Via Anna
P.za Bernini
V. Palladio
Viale
Baths of Caracalla
Via delle Terme di Caracalla
Porta S. Paolo
Viale Giotto
Viale
Aurelian Wall
Viale Guido Bacelli
Piramide
Pyramid of Gaius Cestius
V.le Cave Ardeatine
Viale Marco Polo
Via Girolama Dandini
di Porta Ardeatina
Via O. Beccari
Via Ostiense
Ostiense Train Station
Porta Ardeatina

SEEING THE SIGHTS 153

SIGHTS

A. Arch of Septimus Severus
B. Rostra
C. Temple of Saturn
D. Basilica Giulia
E. Curia (Sentate House)
F. Temple of Anthony & Foustina
G. Temple of Caesar
H. Temple of Castor & Pollux
I. House of the Vestal Virgins
J. Temple of Romulus
K. Basilica Emilia
L. Basilica of Maxentius
   & Constantine
M. Caesar's Forum
N. Trajan's Fourm/Column/Market
O. Augustus' Forum
P. Vitt. Emanuele II Monument
Q. S.M. d'Araceoli
R. Capitoline Museum
S. Senatorial Palace
T. Conservatorio
U. St Paul's Outside the Walls
   Metro - San Paolo
V. Museo della Civilta Romana
   Metro - EUR Palasport or Fermi

ROMA
MAP D

Fora in their own honor. The entire area has been decimated by war, used as a quarry for other buildings in Rome, and has been haphazardly excavated, but is still a wonder to behold.

In the Roman Forum, you'll find the following sights and more:

Arch of Septimus Severus

Built in 203 CE to celebrate the tenth anniversary of the Emperor Septimus Severus' reign. This triumphal arch is constructed with two lower archways flanking a larger central one and is the one of the finest and most imposing structures remaining from ancient Rome. Over the side arches are bas-reliefs depicting scenes from victorious battles fought by the Emperor over the Parthians and the Mesopotamians.

In 1988, in pure Italian fashion, half the arch was cleaned to allow citizens to decide whether the complete structure should be cleaned. By 1998, they finally were getting around to cleaning the other half.

Rostra

Located directly to the left of the Arch of Septimus Severus, this building was decorated with the beaks of ships captured by the Romans at Antium in 338 BCE. It was the meeting place for Roman orators. In front of it is the **Column of Phocas**, erected in honor of the Eastern Emperor of the Roman Empire in 608 CE. The column was the last monument to be erected in the Forum.

Temple of Saturn

Built in 497 BCE, it was restored with eight ionic columns in the 3rd century CE. In the temple's basement was the Treasury of State.

Basilica Giulia

Started in 54 BCE by Julius Caesar and completed by Augustus, it was destroyed by fire and restored by Diocletian in 284 CE. The building served as a large law court.

Basilica Emilia

Located to the right of the entrance to the Forum, it was erected in 179 BCE, and because of the ravages of fire, destruction by "barbarian hordes" and neglect, little remains today. Together with the Basilica Giulia, it was one of the largest buildings in Rome and was used by money-changers and other business people.

The Curia

Founded by Tullus Hostilius and built between 80 BCE and 44BCE, this was the house of the Senate, the government of Rome in the

Republican period, and the puppet government during the empire. It was once covered with exquisite marble but is today a combination of stucco and brick. The structure was rebuilt after a fire in 283 CE, and converted into a church in the seventh century CE. The interior is still a large plain hall, with marble steps that were used as the senator's seats.

Temple of Anthony & Faustina
Built by Antonius Pius in honor of his wife Faustina, the temple was later converted to a church in the 11th century, **San Lorenzo in Miranda**. All that remains of the original Roman temple are the ten monolithic columns that are 17 meters high, and an elegant frieze. The baroque facade is from the 1600s.

Temple of Caesar
Near the Arch of Augustus and past the Temple of Castor and Pollux you'll find the Temple of Caesar, built in 42 BCE by Octavius. It was on this site that Caesar's body was cremated.

Temple of Castor & Pollux
Built in 484 BCE and restored by Hadrian and Tiberius. The three Corinthian columns in the podium are from that period of restoration. It was originally built to pay homage to the Gods Castor and Pollux who, according to legend, aided the Romans against their enemies.

House of the Vestal Virgins
This is where the vestal virgins lived who dedicated themselves to maintaining the sacred fires in the nearby **Temple of Vesta**. A portico of two stories adorned with statues of the Vestals surrounded an open court that was decorated with flower beds and three cisterns. In the court you can still see the remains of some of the statues and the pedestals on which they sat.

Arch of Titus
Erected to commemorate the victories of Vespasian and Titus, who conquered Jerusalem. The arch contains bas-reliefs of the Emperor and of soldiers carrying away the spoils of Jerusalem. One of the most imposing structures remaining from ancient Rome.

Temple of Romulus
Built by the Emperor Maxentius who dedicated it to his deified son Romulus. A circular building that was converted to a church in the sixth century.

The Palatine Hill

This is one of the seven hills of Rome and was the residence of the Roman Emperors during the Golden Age and Imperial Period. It was here, in 754 BCE, that Romulus is said to have founded the city of Rome. But actual records and not just myth have indicated that settlement was actually established in the 9th century BCE. Aristocratic families also resided here, leaving behind wonderful architectural relics that have mostly all been excavated today, making the Palatine Hill one of the must-see places when you tour the Forum. It is also a wonderful respite from the hectic pace of Rome, filled with lush greenery and plenty of shade; it's a great place to have a picnic or go on a relaxing walk through history.

Here you'll find the baths of Septimus Severus, the Stadium of Domitian, the Farnese Gardens, the House of Livia, the Flavia Palace, the House of Augustana, and more. Many of the ruins are under excavation and as such are only occasionally accessible for foot traffic, but all can be viewed.

BATHS OF CARACALLA

Via Terme di Caracalla, Tel. 574-0796. Admission L8,000. Hours Monday–Saturday 9:00am–3:30pm. Sundays 9:00am–1:00pm. Catch buses 90, 90b, 118. Metro-Circo Massimo.

Built in 217 CE by the Emperor Caracalla, these baths were second in size only to the Baths of Diocletian. They were used until the sixth century when they were destroyed by Gothic invaders, and today it takes quite an imagination to reconstruct the building mentally. The baths were once rich with marble and statues and decorated with stucco and mosaic work. All that remains are the weathered remains of the massive brick structure which offers an insight into the scale of the baths, but doesn't offer a glimpse of their beauty. Today, on cool summer evenings, opera performances are held among the ruins of the **Calidarium**, the circular vapor bath area.

BATHS OF DIOCLETIAN

Catch buses 57, 64, 65, 75, 170, 492, and 910. Metro-Repubblica.

These were the most extensive baths of their times in which more than 3,000 bathers could be accommodated at one time. They were built by Maximilian and Diocletian from 196–306 CE. Today the **National Museum** is located within their walls, as is the **Church of Santa Maria Degli Angeli**.

CAMPIDOGLIO
Piazza del Campidoglio. Catch buses 94, 95, 713, 716. Metro-Colosseo.
The Capitoline Hill is one of the seven hills of Rome. It forms the northwest boundary of the Forum and today is home to the **Capitoline Museum, Senatorial Palace**, the **Palace of the Conservatori**, the **Church of Santa Maria D'Aracoeli** (formerly the Temple of Juno Moneta), and the bronze **statue of Marcus Aurelius** which recently underwent a cleansing. The Palazzo di Senatori (Senatorial Palace) was finished in the beginning of the 14th century; the statue was placed there in 1528, and the piazza along with the other two buildings were completed in 1570. These last three structures were based on a design developed by Michelangelo, who died in 1564 not seeing his plan completed.

The **Capitoline Museums** were founded by the Popes Clement XII and Benedict XIV and house some exquisite works (see Capitoline Museum in the *Museums* section below).

To ascend the hill, take either the steep stairway that leads to the church, the winding ramp of the Via delle Tre Pile, or from between the two of these by way of the monumental stairs, Cordonate, which were designed by Michelangelo. At the entrance to these stairs you'll find two imposing Egyptian lions and at the top the statues of Castor and Pollux.

The church of Santa Maria D'Aracoeli was originally a pagan temple, then converted for use as a Christian church. In the 12th century it was given its present form with a colonnade of mismatched ancient columns and wide nave. The enormous set of stairs in front are one of the church's main features.

You must try and visit the museums on this hill, since they are second in magnificence only to the Vatican Museums, and certain exhibits are even better. Also, the photo op with the large pieces of Constantine's statue is a must.

CIRCUS MAXIMUS
Catch buses 15, 90, 90b, 94. Metro-Circo Massimo.
This circus (race-track) was established on the flat lands to the south of the fortified Palatine Hill. It was erected in 309 CE by the Emperor Maxentius in honor of his deified son Romulus, whose temple is nearby. Then in Imperial times it was expanded, destroyed, enlarged and used as a quarry until little is left of the original marble. But today its shape is clearly visible underneath the contoured grass and earth, and some of the original seats remain at the turning circle of the southwestern end. The slight hump running through the center marks the location of the *spina*, around which the chariots, and at times runners, would race. In its prime the Circo Massimo could hold between 150,000-200,000 spectators, more than most modern stadiums.

CATACOMBS

Saint Callistus (Via Appia Antica 110, Tel. 06/513-6725. Closed Wednesdays.)
San Sebastian (Via Appia Antica 132, Tel. 06/788-7035. Closed Thursdays.)
Santa Domitilla (Via di Sette Chiese 282, Tel. 06/511-0342. Closed Tuesdays.)
Entrance for each L8,000. Hours for each 8:30am-12:00pm and 2:30pm-5:00pm.
Catch buses 118 and 218.

Located next door to one another on and around the Via Appia Antica south of the city, these tombs were originally an ancient Roman necropolis, then they were used by the early Christians as a meeting place as well as a place of worship, and a haven from prosecution. Here you can visit the **crypts of the Popes**, the crypt of Saint Cecilia, the crypt of Pope Eusebius, as well as frescoes dating back to the 3rd century CE. All three are an eerie reminder of the time before Christianity dominated the Western world.

ALTAR OF AUGUSTUS & MAUSOLEUM OF AUGUSTUS

Lungotevere in Augusta/Via di Ripetta. Altar open 9:00am-2:00pm. Closed Sundays. Buses 81, 90, 119, 926. Metro-Spagna.

Located near the exquisite restaurant Pizzeria La Capricciosa, this is an excellently preserved altar built from 13-9 BCE. Reconstructed and housed in this glass building in 1938 by Mussolini to glorify Italy's past, this marble structure is essentially a wall with a doorway that encloses the raised altar itself. The carved friezes on the walls were created by Greek masons imported to Rome.

The mausoleum of Augustus is the circular structure nearby overrun with grass and shrubs. It used to be a series of intricate passageways where niches of urns filled with funeral ashes were located, and it used to be topped with a large statue of Augustus. It has been used as a fort, a bull ring, a theater and a concert hall. In 1938 when the museum of Augustus was dedicated inside, the medieval buildings were cleared away and the present piazza was created.

PYRAMID OF GAIUS CESTIUS

Near Porta San Paolo. Buses 13, 23, 57, 95, 716. Metro-Piramide.

Built in 12 BCE as a tomb for the Praetor Gaius Cestius, this structure is a prime example of the influence that Egypt and its religion had on ancient Rome. During early Rome a cult of Egyptology was one of the largest of the pagan religions. Built of brick and rock and covered with limestone, this is one of the more striking structures left from ancient Rome and as such is a great photo op.

PONTE MILVIO

Via Flaminia/Piazza Cardinale Consalvi. Take the 225 bus to piazza Mancini and walk to Piazza Cardinale Consalvi, or take the 201 bus from piazza Mancini.

Ponte Milvio was the first Roman bridge over the Tiber built in 109 CE, located north of the Aurelian and Servian walls. This bridge was the location of much military activity throughout Italian history, including one battle that helped establish Christianity as the world's dominant religion. Here in 312 CE the Christian Emperor Constantine defeated forces led by Maxentius who was then thrown into the river.

The current bridge has been destroyed and rebuilt countless times but retains its original form. It was last destroyed in 1849 when Garibaldi's troops blew it up to prevent the advance of the French army. In 1985 it was closed to vehicular traffic for restoration.

AURELIAN WALL

Built from 272-279 CE, this wall is a testament to the fading glory of the Roman Empire. Built to protect Rome from an incursion of Germanic tribes, one of the best places to witness its protective shield is at the top of the Via Veneto at the **Porta Pinciana**. The walls enclosed not only the old city of Rome but also included land outside of the developed areas.

Today the walls extend to the Baths of Caracalla in the south, Piazza del Popolo in the north, Trastevere and Saint Peter's in the west, and the University and Stazione Termini in the East. They have a total length of about 12 miles; the walls of concrete rubble encased in brick are almost 12 feet thick and 25 feet high. Today their height is 50 feet after extensions in 309-12 and 402-3 CE. There is a parapet running across the top and there are 380 square towers interspersed along its length. These towers are a distance of two arrow shots apart, which was one hundred ancient Roman feet or just under 30 meters, which strangely enough is about 100 modern American feet.

There were 18 main roads where gates were built, many of which have been rebuilt to accommodate different defense strategies throughout the ages; most recently they were adapted for the onslaught of automobile traffic. The ones that are the best preserved with most of their Roman features are the **Porta San Sebastiano** (take bus 188 from San Giovanni in Laterano), **Porta Asinara** (next to Porta San Giovanni) and the **Porta Toscolana** (behind the train station).

COLUMN OF MARCUS AURELIUS
Piazza Colonna. Buses 56, 60, 62, 85. Metro-Barberini.
Carved between 180 and 196 CE, this column is a continuous spiral of sculptures celebrating Marcus Aurelius' military victories. It used to be surrounded by buildings from its own era but only the ruins of the Temple of Hadrian in the wall of the *Borsa* remain (see description below). Statues of Marcus Aurelius and his wife used to adorn the top of the column, but they were replaced by St. Paul in the 16th century.

TEMPLE OF HADRIAN
Piazza di Pietra. Buses 56, 60, 62, 85. Metro-Barberini.
Located near Piazza Colonna and the Via del Corso, this is a fantastic example of architectural *pastiche*, where structures from different eras are molded and blended together into one building. In this case, one wall of the Roman Stock Exchange (*Borsa*) has eleven Corinthian columns that remain from the temple dedicated by Antonius Pius to his father Hadrian in 145 CE. This is a great place for photos of how Rome's history is woven together with the present.

CHRISTIAN ROME
CASTEL SANT'ANGELO
Lungotevere Castello. Admission L8,000. Tel. 06/687-5036. Open 9:00am–2:00pm. Last entrance time is 1 hour before closing. Catch buses 23, 34, 64, 280, 982. Metro-Lepanto.
Also known as the **Mausoleum of Hadrian** since it was built for Hadrian and his successors. For eighty years it was used as a funeral monument where the ashes of the Roman emperors were stored. As the papacy began to establish itself near the tomb of St. Peter's, during the Middle Ages the structure was converted into a fortress for the Popes. During that period the bulky battlements and other military fortifications were added. A covered walkway leads from Saint Peter's to the Castel Sant'Angelo and, because of the volatile political situation in Italy for many centuries, this walkway was used more than once to protect the Pope. Since then it has been used as a residence for popes and princes, as a prison, and as a military barracks.

On the summit of the building is the statue of an angel (hence the name of the castle), and rumor has it that in 590 CE, Gregory the Great saw a vision with an avenging angel sheathing its sword at the summit of the castle. He took this to mean the plague that had ravaged Rome was over. To commemorate this event he placed an angel on top of the building. Today the castle houses a museum with one of the best collections ever assembled of armaments from the Stone Age to the

> **PROPER ATTIRE, PLEASE!**
>
> When you're visiting most museums and monuments in Italy, follow these necessary rules: **Women:** don't forget to wear either long pants or a long skirt or dress, and a top with sleeves. **Men:** wear long pants and no tank tops.
>
> You will be denied entry to St. Peter's for sure, and to many other sights as well, if you're wearing shorts!

present day. There are also some nondescript art exhibits and luxuriously preserved Papal apartments. A must-see when in Rome.

SAINT PETER'S

Piazza San Pietro. Hours 9:00am–6:00pm. Catch the Metro to Ottaviano or buses 19, 62, 64, or 492. Metro-Ottaviano.

Located in the monumental square **Piazza San Pietro**, Saint Peter's is a masterpiece created by **Bernini** between 1655 and 1667, and is the largest church in the world. The square itself is oval and 240 meters at its largest diameter. It is composed of 284 massive marble columns, and 88 pilasters forming three galleries 15 meters wide. Surrounding the square, above the oval structure are 140 statues of saints.

In the center is an obelisk 25.5 meters high with four bronze lions at its base, all of which were brought from Heliopolis during the reign of Caligula (circa 40 CE) and which originally stood in the circus of Nero. It was placed here in 1586. Below the monument you can see the points of the compass and the names of the winds. To reach Saint Peter's you must pass the obelisk and walk up a gradual incline.

The church rises on the site where Saint Peter is buried. The early Christians erected a small oratory on the site of the tomb, but that was destroyed in 326 when Constantine the Great erected the first Basilica on this site. Over the centuries the church began to expand and became incongruously and lavishly decorated, so that by 1452 Nicholas V decided to make it more uniform. He commissioned Bernardo Rossellino to design a new structure. When the Pope died three years late this work was interrupted, but in 1506 Pope Julius II, with the assistance of Bramante, continued the work on a grander scale.

Bramante died in 1514 before his work could be finished. His successor was Raphael, and when he died four years later, Baldassare Peruzzi and Antonio de Sangallo the Younger took over the responsibility jointly. Work was interrupted by the sack of Rome in 1527, then again in

1536 when Peruzzi died. When Sangallo died in 1546, the project was taken over and modified by the 72 year old **Michelangelo**. Before he died eight years later, he had modified Bramante's plan for the dome and we are blessed with his pointed Florentine version today. After he died, the plans he made for St. Peter's were more or less adhered to by his successors Vignola, Pizzo Ligorio, Giacomo dell Porta, Domenico Fontana, and finally Carlo Maderno, who designed the facade according to his plan. On November 1, 1626, **Urbano VIII** dedicated the Basilica as we know it today.

The Facade

Rounding off, the **facade** is 115 meters long and 45 meters high, and is approached by a gradually sloping grand staircase. At the sides of this staircase are the statues of **Saint Peter** (by De Fabis) and **Saint Paul** (by Adamo Tadolini). On the balustrade, held up by eight Corinthian columns and four pilasters, are the colossal statues of the Savior and St. John the Baptist surrounded by the Apostles, excluding Saint Peter.

There are nine balconies, and from the central one the Pope gives his Christmas and Easter benedictions. There are five doors from which to enter the church, but today only the large central one is used.

The Interior

The church is more than 15,000 square meters in area, 211 meters long and 46 meters high. There are 229 marble columns: 533 of travertine, 16 of bronze, 90 of stucco, and 44 altars. On the floor of the central nave you'll find lines drawn identifying where other churches in the world would fit if placed in Saint Peter's. Kids love to explore this aspect of the basilica.

Also on the floor, near the front entrance, is a disk of red porphyry indicating the spot where **Charlemagne** was crowned Holy Roman Emperor by Leo III on Christmas Day in 800 CE. To the right of this, in

---

FREE TOURS OF ST. PETER'S

One of the best ways to see St. Peter's and one of the least known is on an English-language tour of the basilica by trained volunteer guides. Available seven days a week, Monday-Saturday at 3pm and Sundays at 2:30pm, the tour lasts an hour and a half and offers an in-depth historical and religious perspective of this magnificent church. The tours start at the information desk to the right as you enter the portico of St. Peter's. For more information, call 06/6972.

the first chapel, is the world famous *Pieta* created by Michelangelo when he was only 24, in 1500 AD. In the niches of the pilasters that support the arches are statues of the founders of many religious orders. In the last one on the right you'll find the seated bronze statue of Saint Peter. The statue's foot has been rubbed by so many people for good luck that it has almost disappeared.

Just past the statue is the grand **cupola** created by Michelangelo. One of the most amazing architectural wonders of all times, it is held up by four colossal spires which lead to a number of open chapels. Under the cupola, above the high altar rises the famous **Baldacchino** (or Grand Canopy) made by Bernini. It's made from bronze taken mainly from the roof of the Pantheon. In front of the altar is the **Chapel of Confessions** made by Maderno, around which are 95 perpetually lit lamps illuminating the **Tomb of Saint Peters**. In front of the shrine is the kneeling statue of Pius VI made by Canova in 1822.

Throughout the rest of the Basilica you'll find a variety of superb statues and monuments, many tombs of Popes, and a wealth of chapels, not the least of which is the **Gregorian Chapel** designed by Michelangelo and executed by Giacomo della Porta. It is rich in marbles, stuccos, and mosaics, all put together in the creative Venetian style by Madonna del Soccorso in the 12th century.

If you grow tired of the many beautiful works of art and wish to get a bird's eye view of everything, you can ascend into Michelangelo's Cupola either by stairs (537 of them) or by elevator. If you come to Saint Peter's, you should do this.

VATICAN CITY

Piazza San Pietro. Buses 19, 62, 64, or 492. Metro-Ottaviano. The city is generally inaccessible except for official business, but you can look into gardens from the cupola of St Peter's.

Vatican City sits on the right bank of the Tiber river, in the foothills of the Monte Mario and Gianicolo section of Rome. In ancient Rome this was the site of the Gardens of Nero and the main circus where thousands of Christians were martyred. Saint Peter met his fate here around 67 CE. Today it is the world center for the Catholic Church, rich in priceless art, antiques, and spiritual guidance.

The Vatican (officially referred to as **The Holy See**) is a completely autonomous state within the Italian Republic and has its own radio station, railway, newspaper, stamps, money, and diplomatic representatives in major capitals. Though it doesn't have an army, the **Swiss Guards**, who are volunteers from the Swiss armed forces, guard the Vatican day and night.

PIAZZAS, FOUNTAINS, MONUMENTS, PALAZZI & GARDENS
PIAZZA NAVONA
Catch buses 70, 81, 87, 90.

The piazza is on the site of a stadium built by Domitian in 86 CE that he used for naval battles and other gladiatorial contests, as well as horse races. The stadiums north entrance has been excavated and you can see the stone arch of the entrance outside of the Piazza Navona toward the Tiber on the south side of the Piazza di Tor Sanguigna.

At first the piazza was lined with small squatters' homes which followed the tiers of the stadium, but with the wide open space it soon became a prime spot for large palazzi. Today the style of the piazza is richly Baroque, featuring works by two great masters, **Bernini** and **Borromini**. Located in the middle of the square is Bernini's fantastic **Fontana Dei Quattro Fiumi** (Fountain of Four Rivers), sculpted from 1647-51. The four figures supporting the large obelisk (a Bernini trademark) represent four rivers: the Danube, the Ganges, the Nile, and the Plata Rivers. The concept of the statue is to show that the Catholic church reigns triumphant over the world.

Besides the statue's obvious beauty and meaning, Bernini has hidden a subtle treasure in this piece. When visiting Rome, notice the figure representing the Nile. Some historians interpret the position of the figures hand shielding its eyes from the facade of the church it is facing, **Santa Agnese in Agone**, as a statement of revulsion. This church was designed by Bernini's rival at the time, Borromini, and Bernini, as the story is told, playfully showed his disdain with his rival's design through the sculpted disgust in his statue. Others claim the revulsion comes from the fact that the church, built as a family chapel for Pope Innocent X's Palazzo Doria Pamphili, is located on the site of an old neighborhood brothel.

To the south of the piazza is the statue of Il Moro (actually a knockoff of the original) created by Bernini from 1652-54. To the north is a basin with a 19th century sculpture of Neptune struggling with a sea monster.

To savor the artistic and architectural beauty, as well as the vibrant nightlife of the Piazza, choose a table at one of the local bars or cafés and try some ice cream, grab a coffee, or have a meal, and watch the people go by. Navona has been one of Rome's many gathering spots for people of all ages since the early 18th century. You'll find local art vendors, caricaturists, hippies selling string bracelets, and much more. This is a place you cannot miss if you come to Rome.

PIAZZA DI SPAGNA
Catch buses 52, 53, 56, 58, 60, 61, 62, 71, 81. Metro-Spagna.

This is one of the most beautiful and visited spots in Rome. It is named after the old Spanish Embassy to the Holy See that used to stand on the site. The 137 steps are officially called the *Scalinata della Trinita dei Monti*, and are named for the church which they lead to at the top. But most people just call them the **Spanish Steps**. The fountain in the middle of the piazza is known as the **Barcaccia** and was designed in 1628 by Pietro Bernini in commemoration of the big flood of 1598. To the right is the column of the **Immaculate Conception** erected in 1865 by Pius IX.

The Spanish Steps were built in the 17th century. Besides being the location of fine works of art and architecture, it is also a favorite meeting spot for Italians of all ages. You used to find musicians, artists, caricaturists, palmists, tourists, and many others assembled together which made this place perfect for people watching. Now since you cannot sit and congregate anymore, the Steps have lost a little of their feel. But just for a little while, sit down as others do, ignore the no-congregating edict and watch the world go by.

CAMPO DEI FIORI
Catch buses 46, 62, 64.

This is a typically Roman piazza that hosts a lively flower and food market every morning until 1:00pm. Here you'll find the cries of the vendors blending with the bargaining of the customers. A perfect place to see and smell the beauty of Rome. This used to be a square where heretics were burned at the stake and criminals were hanged. The monument in the middle is in memory of Giordano Bruno, a famous philosopher who was burned here in 1600.

This is another place to come at night, since there are plenty of impromptu concerts and a great restaurant, **La Carbonara**, that serves the best *Spaghetti alla Vongole Verace* I've ever had, and a great Irish Pub, **The Drunken Ship**.

TREVI FOUNTAIN
Catch buses 52, 53, 56, 58, 60, 61, 62, 71, 81. Metro-Barberini.

Another meeting place for Italians in the evenings. You'll always find an impromptu guitar solo being performed as well as wine being savored by many. A great place to hang out in the evenings and make new friends. This is the largest and most impressive of the famous fountains in Rome and is truly spectacular when it is lit up at night. Commissioned by Clement XII, it was built by Nicola Salvi in 1762 from a design he borrowed from Bernini and takes up an entire wall of the Palazzo Poli built in 1730. In the central niche you see Neptune on his chariot drawn by marine horses preceded by two tritons. In the left niche you see the statue representing Abundance, and to the right Health. The four statues up top depict the seasons and the crest is of the family of Clement XII, Corsini.

There is an ancient custom, legend, or rumor, that says that all those who throw a coin into the fountain are destined to return to Rome. So turn your back to the fountain and throw a coin over your left shoulder with your right hand into the fountain and fate will carry you back. That is if you can get close enough. In the summer, and especially at night, this place is packed wall to wall with people. Also, please don't try and recreate Anita Ekberg's scene in the film *La Dolce Vita* when she waded through the fountain to taunt Marcello Mastroiani. It is completely illegal to walk in the fountain, and the authorities enforce this regulation severely. If they didn't, the local kids would all swim in and collect the coins thrown by tourists.

PANTHEON

Piazza Rotonda. Open Monday-Saturday 9:00am-6:30pm, Sundays 9:00am-1:00pm. At 10:00am on Sundays is a mass. Tel. 06/6830-0230. Catch buses 70, 81, 87, 90.

Located in a vibrant piazza frequented by the locals and tourists alike, the **Pantheon** is one of the most famous and definitely the best preserved monuments of ancient Rome. Besides the architectural beauty, the entrance area to the Pantheon is by far the coolest place in Rome during the heat wave of August. So if you want to relax in cool comfort in the middle of a hot day, park yourself just in front of the entrance under the portico .

First constructed by Agrippa in 27 BCE, it was restored after a fire in 80 CE and returned to its original rotunda shape by the Emperor Hadrian. In 609 CE, it was dedicated as a Christian Church called Santa Maria Rotunda, and in the Middle Ages it served as a fortress. In 1620 the building's bronze ceiling was removed and melted into the cannons for Castel Sant'Angelo and used for Bernini's Baldacchino (Grand Canopy) in Saint Peter's that marks the site of the saint's tomb.

But during all this pillage the Pantheon was never left to ruin. It always remained in use and thoroughly maintained. The building is made up of red and gray Egyptian granite. Each of the sixteen columns is 12.5 meters high and is composed of a single block.

You enter the building by way of the cool and comfortable portal area and the original bronze door, and you can feel the perfect symmetry of space and harmony of its architectural lines. This feeling is somewhat lessened by the fact that the Roman authorities (in their infinite wisdom) have started charging for entrance to the building, and have placed a ticket booth inside along with a small souvenir stand all of which detracts from the perfection of the structure. Sad. Nonetheless you will still be awed by the marvelous dome (diameter 43 meters) with the hole in the middle.

There are three niches in the building, two of which contain **tombs**: the tomb of **Victor Emmanuel II** (died 1878), one of Italy's few war heroes, and the tombs of **Umberto I** (died 1900) and **Queen Margherita** (died 1926), and in another niche the tomb of renowned artist **Raphael Sanzio** (died 1520).

THE BORGHESE GARDENS
Catch buses 95, 490, 495, 910. Metro-Spagna.

The most picturesque park in Rome, complete with bike and jogging paths (you can rent bikes in the park), a lake where you can rent boats, a wonderful museum – **Galleria Borghese** – lush vegetation, large grass fields, the Roman **zoological park**, a large riding ring, and more.

This is the perfect place to come and relax in the middle of a hard day of touring. Kids of all ages will love to wander all over the park or simply cuddle up together and take a quick siesta.

The gardens are a great sanctuary just outside the ancient walls of Rome. If you only want an afternoon's respite from the sights of the city, or you're tired of spending your time in your hotel room during the siesta hours, escape to these luscious and spacious gardens.

To get to the gardens is simple enough: either exit the old walls of Rome through the gates at the Piazza del Popolo or at the top of the Via Veneto. From the Piazza del Popolo exit, the gardens will be on your right through the iron gates just across the busy Piazzale Flaminio. Once you enter you will be on the Viale Washington. Anywhere to the left of you, after a few hundred meters, will be prime park land. From the Via Veneto exit, cross the major thoroughfare in front of you and you're in Borghese. From here stroll to your right and you will instantly find a pleasant area to picnic or take a small nap for the afternoon.

The Borghese Gardens house Rome's **zoo**, several museums (including Galleria Borghese and the Galleria Arte Moderna), playing fields for *calcio*, a small lake, an amphitheater, and many wooded enclaves to have a wonderfully secluded picnic (look out for those heated Italian couples).

Galleria Borghese
One of Rome's finest museums is in the Borghese Gardens, the **Galleria Borghese**. For those of you that entered the Gardens from Piazza del Popolo, it will be a long hike up the Viale Washington to the lake, and around it to the Viale Dell'Uccelleria (the zoo will be on your left) which leads directly to the Galleria Borghese.

From the Via Veneto it is not quite as long. From where you first entered the gardens, there is a road, Viale Del Museo Borghese, on your right. Take this all the way to the Galleria.

The Galleria Borghese was built by Dutch architect Hans van Santes during the 1820's. It houses a large number of rare masterpieces from many disciplines and countries. There are classical works of Greeks and Romans, along with 16th and 17th century paintings by such notables as Raphael, Titian, Caravaggio, and Antonella da Messina. Sculptures are also featured with works by Lorenzo Bernini, Pietro Bernini, and Houndon.

For more details, see the Galleria Borghese description below under *Museums*.

VITTORIO EMANUELE II MONUMENT

Piazza Vittorio Emanuele. Catch buses 70, 81, 87, 90.

A monument to the first king of Italy who died in 1878. Work started in 1885 but was not finished until 1910. It is an inflated version of the Temple of Fortune on the hillside at Praenestina. To all in Rome it is affectionately called "The Wedding Cake," since its shape and white marble make it look eerily like a larger version of one. The monument is also home to the tomb of the unknown soldier.

ISOLA TIBERINA

Catch buses 44, 75, 170, 710, 718, 719.

Halfway across the river going towards Trastevere, this island used to be a dumping ground for dead and sick slaves. At that time there was a cult of healing *(aesculapius)* located here in the 3rd century BCE, and currently half the island is taken up by a hospital. The church in the island, San Bartolomeo was built in the 12th century, and was substantially altered in the seventeenth. One of the bridges to the mainland, **Ponte Fabricio**, is the oldest in Rome.

PONTE FABRICIO (DEI QUATTRO CAPI)

Now the oldest span in Rome, the bridge is still in use. Its predecessor, the Pons Aemilius, an arch of which is still visible south of the Isola Tiberina, was washed away in 1598 and never rebuilt. This is a good place to cross the Tiber going towards Trastevere after you've been exploring the Jewish Ghetto.

PALAZZO BARBERINI

Via Quattro Fontane, 13. Tel. 854-8577. Admission L4,000. Hours 9:00am–7:00pm, Holidays 9:00am–1:00pm. Closed Mondays. Catch buses 95, 490, 495, 910. Metro-Barberini.

Located just off the Piazza Barberini on the Via Quattro Fontane, this baroque palace was started by Carlo Maderno in 1623 with the help of Borromini and was finished in 1633 by Bernini. When the entrance was rearranged to the south from the north-east in 1864, the baroque iron gates were designed, built and installed by Francesco Azzuri.

One wing of the palace is the site of the **Galleria Nazionale d'Arte Antica**. Besides the wonderful architecture which is impossible to miss, the gallery has many wonderful paintings such as *Marriage of St. Catherine* by Sodoma, *Portrait of a Lady* by Piero di Cossimo, and *Rape of the Sabines* by Sodoma.

PALAZZO FARNESE

Piazza Farnese. Hours 9:00am–Noon. Monday–Thursday. Catch buses 23 or 280.

This palace represents one of the high points of Renaissance architecture. It was started in 1514 by Antonio da Sangallo the Younger for Cardinal Alessandro Farnese (later Pope Pius III), and was continued by Michelangelo who added the large window, the molding on the facade, the third floor of the court, and the sides. It was finally finished by Giacomo della Porta. As well as being an architectural wonder, there is a first floor gallery of frescoes depicting mythological subjects by the painters Carracci, Domenichino, and Reni.

The palace became the French Embassy in 1625 and remains so today. As such it is not open to the public unless you get written permission from the French government.

ROMAN NEIGHBORHOODS
PIAZZA DEL POPOLO

Catch buses 90, 119. Metro-Flaminio.

This impressive piazza, and the ascent to the **Pincio**, a relaxing area of Rome where you can get some great views of the city, was consolidated as a piazza in 1538 during the Renaissance. In 1589, the **Egyptian Obelisk** which is 24 meters high and came from Egypt during the time of Ramses II in the 8th century BCE, was moved from the Circus Maximus and erected in the middle of the square. The present layout was designed by G. Valadier at the beginning of the 19th century and is decorated on its sides with two semi-cycles of flowers and statues. During this re-design the obelisk was placed in a new fountain with the present sculpted lions.

There are two symmetrical baroque churches at the south end of the piazza flanking the intersection of the Via del Corso. These two churches, **Santa Maria dei Miracoli** (1678) and **Santa Maria in Monesanto** (1675) both have picturesque cupolas that were begun by C. Rainaldi and finished by Bernini and Carlo Fontana.

Eerie Roman Trivia: There is a movie theater directly next to Santa Maria dei Miracoli that played the first run release of the *Exorcist* when it came out in the 1970's. During the first showing of the film, the cross on the top of the church dislodged itself from its perch and shattered itself directly in front of the movie theater. No one was hurt but all of Italy was shocked. This is a true story.

VIA VENETO
Catch buses 52, 53, 56, 58. Metro-Barberini.

Definitely the most famous and most fashionable street in Rome. It used to be the center of all artistic activities as well as the meeting place for the jet set, but it doesn't quite have the same allure it used to. Nonetheless, it's still a great place to wander up the road, which is flanked by hotels, stores, and cafés.

At the bottom of the street is the **Piazza Barberini**, where you'll find the graceful **Fontana delle Api** (Fountain of the Bees) as well as the more famous **Fontana del Tritone**, both designed and sculpted by Bernini. Both sculptures were created celebrate the Barberini family and their new palace just up the Via delle Quattro Fontane.

Right at the bottom of the Via Veneto you will find the famous 'Church of Bones,' **Santa Maria della Concezione**, which has a macabre arrangement of over 4,000 skeletons of friars who have died over the centuries in the adjoining convent. The bones are located below the church in the **Cappucin crypt**. Up a little way is the grandiose **Palazzo Margherita**, built by G. Koch in 1890 and now the home of the American Embassy. You'll recognize it by the armed guards out front.

VIA APPIA ANTICA
Catch buses 118 and 218.

This celebrated of all Roman roads was begun by Appius Claudius Caecus in 312 BCE. The road has been preserved in its original character as have the original monuments. Originally it was the chief line of communication between Rome and Southern Italy, Greece, and the eastern possessions of the Roman Empire.

Now it is a well traveled picturesque road to the country and the famous Roman/Christian catacombs.

TRASTEVERE
Catch buses 44, 75, 170, 710, 718, 719.

This is the perfect place for exploring the way Romans actually live. **Trastevere** literally means "across the river" and this separation has allowed the area to remain virtually untouched by the advances of time. Until recently it was one of the poorest sections of Rome, but now it is starting to become gentrified. Yet these changes have not altered Trastevere's charm. You'll find interesting shops and boutiques, and plenty of excellent restaurants among the small narrow streets and *piazzette* (small squares). The maze of streets is a fun place to wander and wonder where you're going to end up.

During the month of July the *Trasteverini* express their feeling of separation from the rest of Rome with their summertime festival called **Noiantri**, meaning "we the others," in which they mix drunken revelry with religious celebration in a party of true bacchanalian proportions. *Trasteverini* cling to their roots of selling clothing and furnishings to make ends meet by continuing to hold the **Porta Portese** flea market on Sundays. The market and event are true Trastevere.

This area offers some of the best dining and casual night life in town. Here you can sit in a piazza bar sipping Sambuca or wine and watch the life of Rome pass before your eyes. To accommodate this type of activity many stores have begun to stay open later. Trastevere is a great place to enjoy for a day or even more, because it is the way Rome used to be.

JEWISH GHETTO
Catch buses 780, 774, 717.

Located west of city center, next to the Tiber just across from Trastevere, you'll find the old **Jewish Ghetto** where Rome's Jewish population was forced to live for centuries. To find out more about this period check out the **Jewish Museum** in the **Sinagoga** *(Tel. 06/684-0061. Fax 06/6840-0684)* that has a plan for the original ghetto, as well as artifacts from the 17th century Jewish community and more.

Besides learning about the history of the ghetto, you can find some of Rome's truly great restaurants here as well as see many ancient Roman buildings, arches, and columns completely incorporated into modern day buildings. It seems as if many structures were better preserved here, since the locals did not have the resources to tear them down and replace them.

GIANICOLO
Catch bus 41.

Offering one of the best panoramas of Rome, **Gianicolo hill** is located between Trastevere and the Vatican, across the river from the old city of Rome. At the terrace of the Piazzale del Gianicolo, you'll find the equestrian statue of Giuseppe Garibaldi and a perfect photo opportunity. The walk may be a little tiring but the view is calming and serene, as is the lush vegetation.

CHURCHES
SAINT PAUL'S OUTSIDE THE WALLS

Via Ostiense. Church open 7:00am–6:00pm. Cloisters Open 9:00am–1:00pm and 3:00pm–6:00pm. Metro-San Paolo.

Located a short distance beyond the Porta Paolo, **St. Paul's Outside the Walls** (San Paolo Fuori le Mura) is the fourth of the patriarchal basilicas in Rome. It is second only in size to St. Peter's and sits above the tomb of St Pauls. It was built by Constantine in 314 CE and then enlarged by Valentinian in 386 CE and later by Theodsius. It was finally completed by Honorius, his son.

In 1823, the church was almost completely destroyed by a terrible fire and many of its great works of art were lost. Immediately afterward, its renovation began and today it seems as magnificent as ever. (So much so that every time my family returns to Rome, whoever is left lines up just inside to the left of the entrance to the *quadroportici* with its 150 granite columns and get our picture taken with the palm trees in the background. We've been doing this since the 1950's and in that time the palms have grown from stubby bushes into gigantic trees.) With the beautiful garden surrounded by the great rows of columns, the palms growing in the center, the gigantic statue of St. Paul, and the facade with mosaics of four prophets (Isaiah, Jeremaih, Ezekial, and Daniel), just getting inside this church is a visual treat.

The interior is 120 meters long and has four rows of columns and five naves. The columns in the central nave are Corinthian that can be identified by their splendidly ornate capitals. The walls contain Medallion Portraits of the Popes from Saint Peter to Pius XI. On the High Altar still sits the ancient Gothic tabernacle of Arnolfo di Cambio (13th century) that was saved from the fire in 1823. Saint Paul rests beneath the altar in the confessional. The mosaic in the apse, with its dominating figure of Christ, was created by artists from the Republic of San Marino in 1220.

To the left of the apse is the **Chapel of St. Stephen**, with the large statue of the saint created by R. Rainaldi, and the **Chapel of the Crucifix** created by Carlo Maderno. This chapel contains the crucifix which is said to have spoken to Saint Bridget in 1370. Also here is St. Ignatius de Loyola, who took the formal vows that established the Jesuits as a religious order. To the right of the apse is the **Chapel of San Lorenzo**, the **Chapel of Saint Benedict** with its 12 columns. One other place of note in the church are the cloisters that contain fragments of ancient inscriptions and sarcophagi from the early Christian era.

SANTA MARIA SOPRA MINERVA

Piazza della Minerva (behind the Pantheon). Hours 7:00am–Noon and 3:30pm–7:00pm. Catch buses 70, 81, 87, 90.

Built on the pagan ruins of a temple to Minerva (hence the name Saint Mary above Minerva) this church was begun in 1280 by the Dominican Order which also commissioned the beautiful Santa Maria Novella in Florence. With their wide Gothic vaulted nave and aisles, the two church are much alike in design. The facade was created during the Renaissance by Meo del Caprino in 1453.

You can find many tombs of famous personages of the 15th through the 16th centuries as well as valuable works of art. Saint Catherine of Siena, who died in Rome in 1380, lies beneath the high altar. To the left of the altar is the statue of *Christ Carrying the Cross* created by the great Michelangelo in 1521. The bronze drapes were added later for modesty.

Behind the altar are the tombs of Pope Clement VII and Leo X which were created by the Florentine sculptor Baccio Bandanelli. In the Sacristy is a chapel covered with frescoes by Antoniazzo Romano, brought here in 1637 from the house where Catherine of Siena died.

In front of the church is a wonderful sculpture designed by Bernini and carved by Ercole Ferrata called *Il Pulcino* of an elephant with an obelisk on his back. In the same piazza is a restaurant that serves magnificent food, is wonderfully relaxing at night, but with horrendous service. The wait staff seem to do everything to discourage foreign patrons, so avoid this place at all costs.

SAN PIETRO IN VINCOLI

Piazza di San Pietro in Vincoli. Hours 7:00am–12:30pm and 3:30pm–6:00pm. Metro-Cavour.

Located only a few blocks from the Colosseum, this church was founded in 442 by the Empress Eudoxia as a shrine dedicated to preserving the chains with which Herod bound St. Peter in Jerusalem. These chains are in a crypt under the main altar.

But the reason to come to this church is the tomb of Julius II. Not really the tomb itself, because the great patron of the arts Julius is actually interred in St. Peter's, but come for the unforgettable seated figure of *Moses*. Created by the master himself, Michelangelo, this statue captures the powerful personification of justice and law of the Old Testament.

In fact, Moses appears as if he is ready to leap to his feet and pass judgment on you as you stand there admiring him. You can almost see the cloth covering his legs, or the long beard covering his face move in the breeze. Flanking Moses are equally exquisite statues of Leah and Rachel also done by Michelangelo. Everything else was carved by his pupils. Because of this one work, this church is definitely worth your time.

SANTA MARIA MAGGIORE

Piazza di Santa Maria Maggiore. Hours 8:00am-7:00pm. Catch buses 4, 9, 16, 27, 714, 715. Metro-Termini.

Like St. Paul's Outside the Walls, St. Peter's, and St. John Lateran, this is one of the four patriarchal basilicas of Rome. It is called *Maggiore* since it is the largest church in Rome dedicated to the Madonna. The facade, originally built in the 12th century, was redone in the 18th century to include the two canon's houses flanking the church. It is a simple two story facade and such is nothing magnificent to look at, and as result, if you are not going out of your way to come here, many people simply amble on by.

But the interior, in all its 86 meters of simplistic splendor, is interesting and inspiring mainly because of the 5th-century mosaics, definitely the best in Rome, and its frescoes. On the right wall of the **Papal Altar** is the funeral monument to Sixtus V and on the left wall the monument to Pius V, both created by Fontana with excellent bas-reliefs. Opposite this chapel is the **Borghese Chapel**, so called since the sepulchral vaults of the wealthy Borghese family lie beneath it. Here you'll view the beautiful bas-relief monumental tombs to Paul V and Clement VIII on its left and right walls. Towards the west end of the church is the **Sforza Chapel** with its intricately designed vault.

SAN GIOVANNI IN LATERANO

Via dei Querceti. Hours 6:00am-12:30pm and 3:30pm-7:00pm. Catch buses 16, 85, 87, and 650. Metro-San Giovanni.

Another of the great basilicas of Rome, this is the actual cathedral church of Rome and of the whole Catholic world, and not St. Peter's. Bet you didn't know that! Established on land donated by Constantine in 312 CE. That building is long gone after many reconstructions, fires, sackings and earthquakes over the centuries. Today, the simple and monumental facade of the church, created by Allessandro Galiliei in 1735, is topped by fourteen colossal statues of Christ, the Apostles, and saints. It rises on the site of the ancient palace of Plautinus Lateranus (hence the name), one of the noble families of Rome many eons ago.

To get inside, you must pass through the bronze door that used be attached to the old Roman Senate house. The interior of the church, laid out in the form of a Latin cross, has five naves filled with historical and artistic objects. In total it is 150 meters long, while the **central nave** is 87 meters long. This central nave is flanked by 12 spires from which appear 12 statues of the Apostles from the 18th century. The wooden ceiling and the marble flooring are from the 15th century.

The most beautiful artistic aspect of the church is the vast transept, which is richly decorated with marbles and frescoes portraying the

Leggenda Aurea of Constantine. One piece of historical interest is the wooden table, on which it is said that Saint Peter served mass, which you'll find in the **Papal Altar**.

SAN CLEMENTE

Via di San Giovanni Laterano. Admission L3,000. Hours to visit the basement 9:00am–1:00pm. Not on Sundays. Catch bus 65. Metro-San Giovanni.

Located between the Colosseum and St. John Lateran is the beautiful **San Clemente**. One of the better preserved medieval churches in Rome, it was originally built in the fifth century. The Normans destroyed it in 1084 but it was reconstructed in 1108 by Pachal II. Today when you enter you are in what is called the **Upper Church**, a simple and basic basilica divided by two rows of columns. The altar is intricately inlaid with a variety of 12th century mosaics.

The thrill of this church is that all you have to do is descend a set of stairs to the **Lower Church**, which was discovered in 1857, and immediately you have left the Middle Ages and are now surrounded by early Christian frescoes and a small ancient altar. Then you can descend a shorter set of stairs and go to the third level where a small temple and a meeting room still exist from the days when Christians had to practice their religion below ground for fear of prosecution.

The temple is Mithraic, a lost religion known for their evil blood rites. Below this level are still more ruins that are in the process of being excavated. This church is perfect for a descent into four different levels of Roman/Christian history.

SANTA CECILIA IN TRASTEVERE

Via Anicia. Hours 10:00am–Noon and 4:00pm–6:00pm. Catch buses 181, 280, 44, 75, 717, 170, 23, 65.

Normally visitors don't go to Trastevere to visit churches. Instead they are attracted by the more secular delights of this part of Rome. But if you're interested in beautiful churches, **Santa Cecilia** is one to visit in Trastevere; the other is Santa Maria.

Santa Cecilia was founded in the fifth century and had a make-over in the ninth century as well as the 16th. A baroque door leads to a picturesque court, beyond which is a baroque facade, with a mosaic frieze above the portico, and a beautiful bell tower erected in the 12th century. There are several important works of art to be found in the church, not the least of which is the expressive statue of Santa Cecilia by Stefano Maderno. It represents the body of the saint in the exact position it was found when the tomb was opened in 1559.

Another place of interest to visit on the church grounds is the Roman house where Santa Cecilia suffered her martyrdom by being exposed to hot vapors. There are two rooms preserved, one of them the bath where she died. It still has the pipes and large bronze cauldron for heating water. A great church to visit, not just for the art, but also for the history.

SANTA MARIA IN TRASTEVERE

Piazza Santa Maria in Trastevere 1. Hours 7:00am–7:00pm. Mass at 9:00am, 10:30am, noon, and 6:00pm. Catch buses 181, 280, 44, 75, 717, 170, 23, 65.

A small church in Trastevere, in a piazza of the same name that is the most frequented by locals and tourists alike, making the church one of the most visited. Around this church are some of the best restaurants and cafés in all of Rome, a popular English language theater, a handsome 17th century fountain where hippies hang out at all night long, and the Palace of San Calisto.

This was one of Rome's earliest churches and the first to be dedicated to the Virgin Mary. It was built in the 4th century and remodeled between 1130-1143. It is best known for its prized mosaics, especially the 12th and 13th century representation of the Madonna which adorns the facade of the church. The Romanesque bell-tower was built in the 12th century. The interior is of three naves separated by columns purloined from ancient Roman temples.

On the vault you'll find exquisite mosaics depicting the Cross, emblems of the Evangelists, and Christ and the Madonna enthroned among the Saints (created by Domenichino in 1140). Lower down, the mosaics of Pietro Cavallini done in 1291 portray, in six panels, the life of the Virgin.

MUSEUMS
CAPITOLINE MUSEUM

Piazza del Campidoglio. Tel. 6710-2071. Admission L10,000. Hours 9:00am–1:30pm. Sundays 9:00am–1:00pm. Tuesdays and Saturdays also open from 5:00pm to 8:00pm. Closed Mondays. Catch buses 44, 46, 56, 57, 90, 90, 94, 186, 710, 713, 718, 719. Entrance L10,000.

The **Capitoline Museum** is actually two museums, the **Capitoline** and the **Palazzo dei Conservatori**.

The **Capitoline** is the perfect place to come to see what ancient Romans looked like. Unlike Greek sculpture, which glorified the subject, Roman sculpture captured every realistic characteristic and flaw. There are rooms full of portrait busts dating back to the republic and imperial Rome, where you have many individuals of significance immortalized here, whether they were short, fat, thin, ugly. Here they remain, warts and all. Because of these very real depiction's of actual Romans, and many other more famous sculptures, this museum ranks only second in importance to the Vatican collections.

Besides the busts, you'll find a variety of celebrated pieces from antiquity including *Dying Gaul*, *Cupid and Psyche*, the *Faun*, and the nude and voluptuous *Capitoline Venice*. Then in the **Room of the Doves** you'll find two wonderful mosaics that were taken from Hadrian's Villa many centuries ago. One mosaic is of the doves drinking from a basin, and the other is of the masks of comedy and tragedy. Besides these items in the interior, the exterior itself was designed by none other than the master himself, Michelangelo.

The **Palace of the Conservatori** is actually three museums in one, the **Museum of the Conservatori**, the **New Museum**, and the **Pinocoteca Capitolina**. It too was also constructed by a design from Michelangelo. Their draw to me, and most people young at heart, are the largest stone head and stone foot you're ever likely to see. A great place to take a few pictures. These pieces are fragments from a huge seated statue of Constantine. Wouldn't that have been a sight to see whole?

You could wander here among the many ancient Roman and Greek sculptures and paintings but remember to see the famous *Boy with a Thorn*, a graceful Greek sculpture of a boy pulling a thorn out of his foot, the *She-Wolf of the Capitol*, an Etruscan work of Romulus and Remus being suckled by the mythical world of Rome, the death mask bust of Michelangelo, the marble *Medusa* head by Bernini, the celebrated painting *St. Sebastian* by Guido Reni that shows the saint with arrows shot into his body, and the famous Caravaggio work, *St. John the Baptist*.

NATIONAL MUSEUM - MUSEO DELLE TERME

Baths of Diocletian, Viale di Terme. Admission L2,000. Hours 9:00am–2:00pm. Sundays until 1:00pm. Closed Mondays. Catch buses 57, 64, 65, 75, 170, 492, 910. Metro-Repubblica.

If you like sculpture you'll love this collection of classical Greek and Roman works, as well as some early Christian sarcophagi and other bas-relief work. Located in the **Baths of Diocletian**, which are something to see in and of themselves, this museum is easily accessible since it is located near the train station and right across from the Repubblica Metro stop. Since there are so many fine works here, you should spend a good half day perusing the items, but remember to start with the best, which are located in the *Hall of Masterpieces*. Here you'll find the *Pugilist*, a bronze work of a seated boxer, and the *Discobolus*, a partial sculpture of a discus thrower with amazing muscle development.

At the turn of the century this collection was graced with the Ludovisi collection, collected by Cardinal Ludovico Ludovisi, and by a number of Roman princes. There are many fine works of art, the most inspiring of which is the celebrated *Dying Gaul and His Wife*, a colossal sculpture from Pergamon created in the third century BCE. The collection also contains the famous Ludovisi throne, created in the 5th century BCE and is adorned with fine Greek bas-reliefs.

Another must-see in the museum is the *Great Cloister*, a perfectly square space surrounded by an arcade of one hundred Doric columns. It is one of the most beautiful architectural spaces in Rome, which is something to say. Rumor has it that it was designed and built by Michelangelo in 1565, which may be the case, but since he was so busy many experts believe that it is actually the work of one of his more famous, and possibly intimate pupils, Jacopo del Duca.

Another great museum to see in Rome.

GALLERIA BORGHESE

Villa Borghese, Piazza dell'Uccelliera 5. Tel. 845-8577. Admission L4,000. Hours 9:00am-7:00pm. Holidays 9:00am-1:00pm. Closed Mondays. Catch buses 95, 490, 495, 910. Metro-Spagna.

Located in the most picturesque public park in Rome, this is a gallery to visit before or after a nice picnic lunch in the shade of the many trees or by the large man-made lake in the center of the park. Housed in a beautiful villa constructed in the 17th century, on the ground floor of the museum is their sculpture collection, which would be considered superb if not for the fact that it is located in Rome. The sculptures are just the appetizer because the main draw of this museum is the beauty of the gallery of paintings on the first floor.

But before you abandon the sculptures, take note of the reclining *Pauline Borghese*, created by Antonio Canova in 1805. She was the sister of Napoleon, married off to one of the wealthiest families in the world at the time to ensure peace and prosperity. She looks quite enticing posing half naked on a lounge chair. Another work not to miss is *David and the Slingshot* by Bernini in 1619. It is a self-portrait of the sculptor.

On the first floor there are many great paintings especially the *Madonna and Child* by Bellini, *Young Lady with a Unicorn* by Raphael, *Madonna with Saints* by Lotto, and countless works by Caravaggio.

MUSEUM OF VILLA GIULIA

Piazza di Villa Giulia. Admission L8,000. Hours 9:00am-7:00pm. Holidays 9:00am-1:00pm. Closed Mondays. Catch buses 19b or 30b. Metro-Flaminio.

Located in the Palazzo di Villa Giulia, which was built in 1533 by Julius III. This archaeological museum contains ancient sculptures, sarcophagi, bas-reliefs, and more, and is separated into five sections consisting of 34 rooms. Items of interest include the archaic statues created in the 5th century BCE of a *Centaur*, and *Man on a Marine Monster*; Etruscan clay sculptures of *Apollo, Hercules with a Deer*, and *Goddess with Child*; objects from the Necropoli at Cervetri including a terra-cotta work of *Amazons with Horses* created in the 6th century BCE and a sarcophagus of a "married couple," a masterpiece of Etruscan sculptor created in the 6th century BCE.

VATICAN MUSEUMS
Viale Vaticano. Tel. 6988-3333. Admission L13,000. From November to the first half of March and the second half of June through August open 8:45am-1:00pm. From the second half of March to the first half of June and September and October open 8:45am to 4:00pm. Closed most Sundays and all major religious holidays like Christmas and Easter. The last Sunday of every month in January, February, April, May, July, Aug, September, October, November and December are open and the entrance is free. Catch buses 19, 23, 32, 45, 51, 81, 492, 907, and 991. Metro-Ottaviano.

There are a number of self-guided tours available that take you through different sections of the Vatican Museums. Touring the Vatican Museum is almost like an amusement park ride, except the sights you see are amazing works of art. There are also tapes and cassette players you can rent to guide yourself through the museums. These are the best way to get an insight into the many splendid works you are witnessing.

Pinacoteca Vaticana
A wonderful collection of masterpieces from many periods, covering many styles all the way from primitives to modern paintings. Here you can find paintings by Giotto (who was the great innovator of Italian painting since prior to his work Italian paintings had been Byzantine in style), many works by Raphael, the famous *Brussels Tapestries* with episodes from the Acts of the Apostles created by Pieter van Aelsten in 1516 from sketches by Raphael, and countless paintings of the Madonna, Virgin, Mother and Child, etc.

Pius Clementine Museum
Known mainly as a sculpture museum, it was founded by Pius VI and Clement XIV. You can also find mosaic work and sarcophagi from the 2nd, 3rd and 4th centuries. One mosaic in particular is worth noting, the *Battle between the Greeks and the Centaurs*, created in the first century CE. The bronze statue of Hercules and the **Hall of the Muses** that contain statues of the Muses and the patrons of the arts are also worth noting. You

can also find many busts of illustrious Romans including Caracalla, Trajan, Octavian and more.

In the **Octagonal Court** are some of the most important and the beautiful statues in the history of Western art, especially the *Cabinet of the Laocoon*. This statue portrays the revenge of the gods on a Trojan priest, Laocoon, who had invoked the wrath of the gods by warning his countrymen not to admit the Trojan horse. In revenge the gods sent two enormous serpents out of the sea to destroy Laocoon and his two sons.

Chiaramonti Museum

Founded by Pope Pius VII, whose family name was Chiaramonti, this museum includes a collection of over 5,000 Pagan and Christian works. Here you can find Roman Sarcophagi, *Silenus Nursing the Infant Bacchus*, busts of Caesar, the Statue of Demosthenes, the famous *Statue of the Nile* with the 16 boys representing the 16 cubits of the annual rise of the Nile, as well as a magnificent Roman chariot recreated in marble by the sculpture Franzone in 1788.

Etruscan Museum

If you can't make it to any of the Necropoli around Rome, at least come here and see the relics of a civilization that preceded Ancient Rome. Founded in 1837 by Gregory XVI, it contains objects excavated in the Southern part of Etruria from 1828-1836, as well as pieces from later excavations around Rome. Here you'll find an Etruscan tomb from Cervetri, as well as bronzes, gold objects, glass work, candelabra, necklaces, rings, funeral urns, amphora and much more.

Egyptian Museum

If you can't make it to Cairo to see their splendid exhibit of material excavated from a variety of Egyptian tombs, stop in here. Created by Gregory XVI in 1839, this museum contains a valuable documentary of the art and civilization of ancient Egypt.

There are sarcophagi, reproductions of portraits of famous Egyptian personalities, works by Roman artists who were inspired by Egyptian art, a collection of wooden mummy cases and funeral steles, mummies of animals, a collection of papyri with hieroglyphics, and much more.

Library of the Vatican

Founded through the efforts and collections of many Popes, this museum contains many documents and incunabula. Today the library contains over 500,000 volumes, 60,000 ancient manuscripts, and 7,000 incunabuli. My favorite are the precious manuscripts, especially the *Codex Vaticanus B* or the 4th century Bible in Greek.

Appartamento Borgia

Named after Pope Alexander VI, whose family name was Borgia, since he designed and lived in these lavish surroundings. (What about that vow of poverty?) From the furnishings to the paintings to the frescoes of Isis and Osiris on the ceiling, this little "museum" is worth a look.

Sistine Chapel

This is the private chapel of the Popes but it is famous for some of the most wonderful masterpieces ever created, many by **Michelangelo** himself. Michelangelo started the ceiling in 1508 and it took him four years to finish it. On the ceiling you'll find scenes from the Bible, among them the *Creation*, where God comes near Adam, who is lying down, and with a simple touch of his hand imparts the magic spark of life. You can also see the *Separation of Light and Darkness*, the *Creation of the Sun and Moon*, *Creation of Trees and Plants*, *Creation of Adam*, *Creation of Eve*, *The Fall and the Expulsion from Paradise*, the *Sacrifice of Noah and his Family* and the *Deluge*.

But on the wall behind the altar is the great fresco of the *Last Judgment* by Michelangelo. It occupies the entire wall (20 meters by 10 meters) and was commissioned by Clement VII. Michelangelo was past 60 when he started the project in 1535. He completed it seven years later in 1542. Michelangelo painted people he didn't like into situations with evil connotation in this fresco. The figure of Midas, with asses' ears, is the likeness of the Master of Ceremonies of Paul III, who first suggested that other painters cover Michelangelo's nude figures.

This eventually was done by order of Pius IV, who had Daniele da Volterra cover the most prominent figures with cloth. These changes were left in when the entire chapel underwent its marvelous transformation a few years back, bringing out the vibrant colors of the original frescoes that had been covered by centuries of dirt and soot.

Rooms of Raphael

Initially these rooms were decorated with the works of many artists of the 15th century, but because Pope Julius II loved the work of Raphael so much, he had the other paintings destroyed and commissioned Raphael to paint the entire room himself. He did so, but spent the rest of his life in the task. Not nearly as stupendous as the Sistine Chapel work by Michelangelo, but it still is one of the world's masterpieces.

Chapel of Nicholas V

Decorated with frescoes from 1448-1451 by Giovanni da Fiesole. The works represent scenes from the life of Saint Stephan in the upper portion and Saint Lawrence in the lower.

The Loggia of Raphael
Divided into 13 arcades with 48 scenes from the Old and New Testaments, these were executed from the designs of Raphael by his students, Giulo Romano, Perin del Vaga, and F. Penni. The most outstanding to see are the *Creation of the World, Creation of Eve, The Deluge, Jacob's Dream, Moses Receiving the Tablets of Law, King David*, and the *Birth of Jesus*.

Grotte Vaticano
The Vatican caves seem to be a well-kept secret even though they've been around for some time. I think that's because you need special permission to enter them, and if you haven't made plans prior to your arrival it is quite difficult to gain access at short notice. To gain permission you need to contact the **North American College** in Rome *(Via dell'Umita 30, Tel. 672-256 or 678-9184)*. The entrance to the Grotte is to the left of the basilica of St Peter's where the Swiss Guards are posted. The Grotte were dug out of the stratum between the floor of the actual cathedral and the previous Basilica of Constantine. This layer was first excavated during the Renaissance. After passing fragments of inscriptions and mosaic compositions, tombstones, and sarcophagi, you descend a steep staircase to get to the Lower Grottos, also called the **Grotte Vecchie** (the Old Grottos).

Here you'll find pagan and Christian Necropoli dating from the 2nd and 3rd century. The Grotte are divided into three naves separated by massive pilasters that support the floor of St. Peter's above. Along the walls are numerous tombs of popes and altars adorned with mosaics and sculptures. At the altar is the entrance to the **Grotte Nuove** (New Grottos), with its frescoed walls, marble statues, and bas-reliefs.

MUSEO DELLA CIVILTA ROMANA
Viale della Civilta Romana. Metro-EUR Palasport (Marconi) or Fermi.

If you've always wanted to see a scale model of ancient Rome, you have to visit this museum. In it you'll find a perfect scale model replica of Rome during the height of empire in the 4th century BC. This piece, called *Modello Plastico* (plastic model), is an exquisitely detailed plaster model that brings ancient Rome to life. It really helps to bring some sense to the ruins that now litter the center of Rome. Even if you are not a museum person, this exhibit is well worth seeing. Ideal for kids of all ages.

The rest of the museum contains little original material, and is made up of plaster casts of Roman artifacts. The museum is located in the section of Rome called **EUR** (Esposizione Universale di Roma), which was built as an exposition site for an event that was to take place in 1941. It is a perfect example of grandiose fascist architecture and its attempt to intimidate. Built with Mussolini's guidance halfway between Rome and its old port of Ostia and was an attempt to reclaim some of Rome's glory and add to its grandeur. EUR has none of the human feel of the rest of Rome, since it is in essence an urban office park with a connected suburban residential ghetto eerily similar to American suburbs, but with more style.

WALKING TOUR OF MICHELANGELO'S ROME

Even though he was Tuscan born and bred, and is still considered Florence's native son, Rome helped develop Michelangelo Buonarotti into the world's greatest artist, and in Rome he spent most of his adult life. Michelangelo specialized in four distinct art forms – sculpture, painting, architecture, and poetry. Rome at that time was a run-down faded city, but it was where Michelangelo became the wonder of his time, and the master of all ages.

The Fabric of Rome in the Mid-Fifteenth Century

At the age of 21, in June 1436, Michelangelo Buonarotti arrived in the city of Rome. The contrasts between Rome, a dirty, noisy, chaotic place, practically in a state of complete disrepair, and Florence, where order, reason, and beauty were cherished and cultivated, were immense. Many tourists today still consider this to be true.

This once vast city had turned to pasture lands outside the Roman walls. Sheep grazed among the ruins of ancient Rome, and the population, which had shrunk to a mere 50,000 from its height of over 1 million inhabitants, was beset with disease and a lack of potable water. But even in this setting Michelangelo blossomed, and Rome is where he created many of his most memorable masterpieces. Uncovering these works from the many corners of Rome can be the highlight of any trip to Italy, and I've laid it out for you in a special walking tour of Michelangelo's Rome.

The Search

For most people, the **Vatican** and **St. Peter's** offer the extent of Michelangelo's influence on Rome. But Vatican City holds just the beginning of the fabric Michelangelo wove into the tapestry of Roman life. It is true that nothing yet conceived can rival the magnificence of the **Sistine Chapel**, which is dominated by Michelangelo's powerful ceiling, made even more so by the recent cleaning that again allow the colors to jump out at you. And you also shouldn't miss the apocalyptic *Last Judgment*, located on the immense wall above the main altar. Every time I return to Rome I visit these two masterpieces to reassure myself that their beauty is not just a figment of my imagination.

These two works seem to epitomize the contrasts of Michelangelo's long career, which seem to coincide with the rise and fall of the Renaissance itself. *The Last Judgment*, begun when Michelangelo was in his 60's, marks the end of his life's work, and the Renaissance's magnificence, while the glorious Sistine Ceiling commemorates the peak of excellence.

These two works, coupled with *La Pieta* located just to the right of the entrance inside St. Peter's, completes for most visitors to Rome the extent of Michelangelo's influence on the Eternal City. Remember to wear long pants, men, otherwise the Vatican guards will not allow you entrance into St. Peter's. By the way, this holds true for most, if not all, monuments and museums in Rome.

Other Works

Michelangelo's Roman tapestry spreads over the entire city. To attempt to see every piece of Michelangelo's work would be virtually impossible, therefore we cover only the most important pieces in this little tour. Get your walking shoes on.

To begin, return to the Vatican, to the art works overlooked by most. The **Vatican Museum** houses two definite musts for any Italian expert and lover. The beautiful sculpture *Apollo Belvedere* should be viewed even if you will be visiting, or have seen, the godlike *David* in Florence. The Apollo's importance stems from the fact that it was Michelangelo's inspiration for his ageless *David*.

Palazzo Farnese

To get to our next destination, cross the **Ponte Vittorio Emanuelle** and walk down the Corso Vittorio Emanuelle on the right hand side. Follow this street, then turn into **Campo dei Fiori** after you pass the Palazzo Della Cancelleria. The Campo dei Fiori was once the site of brutal executions, but now is the home to a beautiful open air market every morning.

Walk through the Campo dei Fiori and you'll find the **Palazzo Farnese** at the other end. Situated in one of Rome's most picturesque quarters, the Palazzo Farnese is one of the most unexplored examples of Michelangelo's work, since it now houses the French Embassy.

The Palazzo was begun in 1514 by Antonio Sangano, The Younger, and was then passed onto Michelangelo's creative genius and imagination to develop the finishing touches. Just prior to overall completion, Michelangelo handed over the reins of design to Giacamo Della Porta, but many of the master's inclusions were left untouched. The most apparent Michelangelo marks are the pieces above the main doorway, but if you have any diplomatic pull (possibly a brother or cousin who happens to be a US Senator) or more realistically try to get a note from your Congressman, you should be able to get yourself inside to see the elegant third floor. A bribe to the French won't help, incidentally, since the French government rents this exquisite building for the incredible fee of only one lira a year.

Since it is hard to get inside, go around the left of the building to the **Arch of the Palazzo Farnese** over Via Guilia. This bridge was designed by Michelangelo and connects the Piazza Farnese with its satellite houses that were originally on the river's edge, but now are restricted by the high walls and roadway of the Lungotevere. Michelangelo's plan had been to connect the Palazzo Farnese with its cousin in Trastevere, the Villa Farnesina, by a private bridge. Unfortunately for the French, and the rest of us, the bridge was never built.

On to the Piazza Navona

From here, stroll through the aforementioned Campo dei Fiori, across the Via Vittorio Emanuelle II, onto the small Via Cuccogno and into the elegant **Piazza Navona**. On a hot day, the fountains here are a visitor's oasis, allowing for needed foot-soaking refreshment. But before you take your shoes off and relax your sore feet by soaking them in one of the fountains, stroll to the center of the piazza and take note of the magnificence of Bernini's **Fontana Dei Quattro Fiumi** (Fountain of Four Rivers). The fours figures supporting the large obelisk (a Bernini trademark) represent four rivers, the Danube, the Ganges, the Nile and the Plata Rivers; see the story behind this statue in the *Piazza Navona* section above.

Even though this has close to nothing to do with Michelangelo, it is one of the many pieces of Roman history intertwined almost inconspicuously with its present. And it's a good place for a refreshing break. Try the *gelato* (ice cream) at the small *gelateria* a few paces down the small unnamed road to the left of **Le Tre Scalini**, one of Rome's best attractions. True, the *gelato* at Le Tre Scalini is also good, if you are willing to pay an exorbitant price for a small scoop. That's why it's wise to simply walk down the road to a smaller, better, less expensive gelato place. With ice cream in hand you can sit in the piazza, soak your feet if you wish, and partake in the Roman tradition of people watching.

Santa Maria Sopra Minerva

The last stop on today's *passegiatta* involves a short walk to the **Piazza Della Minerva** and the church of **Santa Maria Sopra Minerva**. To get there, leave the Piazza Navona via the exit directly across from Le Tre Scalini. As you exit, bear to your left and go down the Via di Crescene to the piazza directly in front of the imposing **Pantheon**. If you haven't seen the Pantheon yet, stay awhile and go inside. It's a beautiful sight and pleasantly cool in the interior. The Piazza Della Minerva is around the left of the Pantheon.

Santa Maria Sopra Minerva is a combination of an early Renaissance exterior and an austere Gothic interior. Besides displaying splendid frescoes by Fillipino Lippi and elaborate marble tombstones made by Michelangelo of two Medici popes (Leo X and Clement VII, who played large roles in the sculptor's life), the masterpiece of the church to the left of the main altar is Michelangelo's *Christ Bearing the Cross*. This obviously spiritual sculpture epitomizes how much the church meant to Michelangelo.

More Buried Treasure

The next day's itinerary is much shorter and begins at the church of **San Pietro in Vincoli** near the Cavour Metro stop. Here you can admire Michelangelo's glowering, biblical figure *Moses*, which emphatically demonstrates the qualities of excellence, perfection, and intensity that make Michelangelo's works so memorable.

From here, grab the Metro at Cavour and take it to Termini. From Termini transfer to Linea A and go one stop to Repubblica. In the **Piazza della Repubblica** is the church of **Santa Maria Degli Angeli**, whose interior was created by Michelangelo out of the ruins of the enormous **Diocletian Baths**. Even though the interior was modified in the 18th century, Michelangelo's creative transformation is still very apparent.

The monumental task of reconstructing a church's interior contrasts well with our next stop, a virtually unknown and infinitely smaller creation. Go up the Via VE Orlando to the **Piazza San Bernardo**, where you'll find the national Catholic church of Americans in Italy, **Santa Susanna**. Its baroque exterior and interior, rich paintings, stucco work, and ornaments has played host to many a visiting American dignitary, with OJ Simpson and George Wallace visiting when I was there. (I got both their autographs; I think OJ's might be worth something now.) Also, in case you were paying attention, as we go through the Piazza San Bernardo, there is a copy of the figure Moses we just saw.

The paintings inside Santa Susannas, though created many years after the life of Michelangelo, and have nothing to do with this tour except to show you some more of Rome's glory, are exquisitely beautiful and can be fully enjoyed with the realization that many casual visitors to Rome never witness their grandeur. What we came to see is not these paintings, but the small **well** in the adjacent courtyard. Surrounded by what was once the convent of the sisters of San Bernardo, this well is one of the smaller threads of Michelangelo's tapestry in Rome. The architrave (main form and structure) and pilaster (rectangular column work on the well) were created by the master himself. And to think that after Mass every other

Sunday, we the parishioners of Santa Susanna would congregate here for coffee and donuts. Isn't Rome magnificent?

Well, that's the last stop. As you can see, Michelangelo's works spread like a tapestry over all of Rome. I hope you enjoyed finding them. If you find others along the way, please send me your information.

LITERARY ROME

For centuries Rome has lured artists from all over the world to bathe in its charms, especially writers seeking inspiration. Here you can explore the city and imagine that Virgil, Robert and Elizabeth Browning, Hans Christian Anderson, Henry James, Lord Byron, Mark Twain, Goethe and more all traced the same steps you are taking.

If you are interested in following almost exactly in these famous writers' footsteps, read on, for we are going to trace for you the paths taken, the places stayed and the restaurants/cafés frequented by literati of times gone by.

Start at the **Piazza di Spagna**. In the 18th and 19th century this piazza was literally (no pun intended) the end of the line for many traveling coaches entering the city. Near the western end of the piazza, the **Via delle Carrozze** (Carriage Road) reminds us that this is where these great coaches tied up at the end of their long journeys. More often then not, travelers would make their homes in and around this area.

ROME'S BEAUTIFICATION PROGRAM

To celebrate two thousand years of Christianity, the Roman authorities have restored the Spanish Steps and outlawed eating, drinking, or loitering on them. In theory this is wonderful, but in true Italian fashion, just after the newly renovated steps had been opened in December 1995, natives and tourists alike could be seen eating sandwiches and drinking soda while the police looked on passively. But don't try and bend the rules too far, like bringing a bottle of wine, a guitar, and some long haired friends with you. Then the police will intervene.

To open up the city even more to the many admirers from all over the world who will descend to celebrate the beginning of the third millennium, another metro line is being built from the Colosseum to Saint Peter's, traveling under the Old Town of Rome. This will afford quicker access, for those intimidated by taking the bus, to the Pantheon, Piazza Navonna, and Campo dei Fiore, as well as the nightlife of Trastevere across the river.

With the fear of further traffic congestion playing on their minds, authorities have also approved a tunnel along the Tiber to bypass Castel Sant'Angelo and Saint Peter's. The entire area is being envisioned as a vast pedestrian paradise, which would completely enhance the beauty that is Rome. So if you're coming to Rome at the turn of the century, be prepared to see a few changes in the eternal city.

At *Piazza di Spagna #23*, you'll find **Babbington's Tea Room** (see Chapter 12, *Where to Eat*) where Byron, Keats, Shelley, and Tobias Smollett all shared at one time or another some afternoon tea. Across the piazza, *at #26*, is the **Keats/Shelley Memorial** where Keats spent the three months before his death in 1821 at the age of 25. The memorial contains some of Keats' manuscripts, letters and memorabilia, as well as relics from Shelley and other British writers. Keats and Shelley still reside in Rome, in the **Protestant Cemetery** near the metro stop Piramide. Located on the *Via Ciao Cestio 6*, it is open all day, but visitors must ring the bell for admittance. Next, *at #66 in the piazza*, the grand poet George Gordon (Lord) Byron took lodging in 1817 and performed work on *Child Harolde's Pilgrimage*.

From here, you can explore the **Via Condotti**, Rome's center for consumerism. **Caffe Greco**, *at #86*, is where, in its double row of interconnecting rooms you could have found Goethe, Hans Christian Anderson or Mark Twain sipping an aperitif and other drinks that were a little stronger than can be found at Babbington's. In 1861, one of the upper rooms was also the lodgings for Hans Christian Anderson of *Ugly Duckling* fame. A little further along, *#11 Via Condotti*, poet Alfred Lord Tennyson and writer William Thackeray made their home when they visited Rome.

Just off the Via Condotti, *at Via Bocca di Leone #14*, is the **Hotel D'Inghlitera** where Mark Twain scratched many pages for *Innocents Abroad* in 1867 and where Henry James initially stayed during his forays into the Eternal City. Later on, James would reside at the **Hotel Plaza** *at Via del Corso 126* where he began his work *From a Roman Notebook*, which described his exploration of the city, its culture, history, and expatriate social activities.

Further down the Corso, *at #20*, is where the German poet Goethe made his home from 1786 to 1788. Here is penned his immortal travel diary *Italian Journey*. Goethe's old house now contains a small museum of photographs, prints, journals, books, and other material relating to the poet's travels in Italy.

At *Bocca di Leone, #43*, you'll see where Robert and Elizabeth Browning lived in 1853. This is where Robert got the inspiration for his epic poem *The Ring and the Book*, a tragic tale of the murder of the Comparini family and their daughter Pompilia (who had lived on the Via Bocca di Leone in 1698), by Pompilia's husband, Count Franchescini.

Another famous writer who resided in Rome was the magnificent Charles Dickens, who wrote part of his *Pictures From Italy* at Via del Babuino 9. If you get a chance, try and read this book, since it brings the Rome of that time to life as vividly as he brought London to life in his many other books.

15. NIGHTLIFE & ENTERTAINMENT

Rome is filled with many discos, pubs, and *birrerias* (bars) where you can spend your evening hours having wild and raucous times. If that's what you want to do, I've compiled a list of the best places to go. But if you want to do like (most of) the Romans do, seat yourself at a bar/café or restaurant, and savor the beauty that is Rome. Linger in the evening air while recalling the day's events or planning tomorrow's. Slow down your pace. Adapt to the culture. Be one with the Force, and so on. You get the picture.

Anyway, there are a few places in Rome in which you can do just that, become part of the culture. The best is in **Trastevere** at one of the little open air cafés where you can either stay all night sipping a few glasses of wine, or visit after you've had your dinner in one of the restaurants around the piazza (see Trastevere in Chapter 13, *Where to Eat*). This is definitely THE best place to go for a night out in Rome.

Another is **Campo dei Fiori**, which also has many cafés and restaurants where you can sit while you watch the life of Rome amble past. The other nightspot is around **Piazza Navona**, of course, where you can admire the fine sculpture, the beautiful people, and the many different life forms comprising the streetlife of Rome.

But if this sedate, appreciative, slow-paced lifestyle is not for you, by all means try one of the following. I found them all perfect for letting off some steam.

IRISH-STYLE PUBS

TRINITY COLLEGE IRISH PUB, *Via del Collegio Romano 6, Tel. 678-64-72. Open 7:30am to 3:00pm and 8:00pm to 2:00am. Harp, Kilkenny, Guinness on tap. Before 8:00pm Harp and Kilkenny Pints are 5,000 and half pints L2,500, after 8pm Pints are L8,000 and half pints L5,000. Before 8:00pm Guinness Pints are L6,000 and half pints are L3,000; after 8:00pm Pints are L8,000 and half pints L5,000. Credit cards accepted.*

This is more of a place to come for a good meal and a few pints rather than a watering hole in which to drink the night away. The menu comes complete with pub fare such as sandwiches, Shepherd's Pie, salads, hamburgers, hot dogs, french fries and more, as well as an extensive and excellent Roman menu. The atmosphere and ambiance are impeccably upper crust Irish. A great place to come for an intimate meal or some early evening drinks and relax over one of the many complimentary newspapers in a variety of languages. Another plus: in summer, the air conditioning is cranked, so it's the perfect spot to escape the heat of Rome.

NED KELLY'S AUSTRALIAN PUB AND RUGBY CLUB, *Via delle Coppelle 15, Tel. 685-2220. Open 6:30pm to 2:00am week days and 3:00pm on weekends. Lunch open M-F 12:30-3:30. L6,000 for bottled beer. L7,000 Pint of Castleman XXXX, L8,000 Pint of Carlsberg Elephant, Devil's Kiss and Tetleys.*

A small hole in the wall place that is the unofficial rugby and darts bar in Rome. Two boards are to the right as you walk in; there is league play in the winter. Their are four owners, two of which do most of the bar work. David, the lone American, helps draw some local foreign students and Tony, the manager of the local rugby club, draws the Italian rugby community. This mix of fifty-fifty Italian/foreigners makes for a fun place in the evenings. Then at lunch from 12:30pm to 3pm, they have one of Rome's best salad bars. Located a stone's throw from Oliphant.

THE DRUNKEN SHIP, *Campo dei Fiori 20/21, Tel. 683-00-535. Open 1pm-2am. Somedays (the schedule changes) they open at 6:00pm for the night crowd. Happy Hour 6:00-9:00pm L5,000 pints, L3,000 half pints; L5,000 Nachos and Salsa.*

The best bar in the best location in Rome. Owner Regan Smith has created a wild and raucous American style bar in one of Rome's oldest piazzas. Loud music, rowdy crowd, great drinks, draft beer and bilingual and beautiful waitresses. The crowd is mainly Italian with a sprinkling of foreign students and travelers. All adventurous and fun. You'll love the Jello shots and adorable English speaking waitresses and bartenders. The decor is dark wood and the whole place has a slight tilt to it befitting, I suppose, a drunken ship. This is the place to come for a pint or two in the early evenings as well as the best place to party the night away. They have specials every night to keep you coming back for more.

OLIPHANT TEX MEX RESTAURANT, *Via delle Coppelle 31/32, Tel. 686-14-16. Open 11:00am to 2:00pm. Happy hour 6:00-8:00pm Pitcher L20,000, Cocktails L6,000. Regular pitcher Harp, Kilkenny or Guinness L30,000. Small beer L5,000, Pint L7,000, Cocktails L10,000.*

Besides the Tex Mex menu, this place is also a really great sports bar. TVs are everywhere in the bar area and there's an American flag fluttering in the middle of the restaurant, a crew boat hanging from the wall, a cut-out of Michael Jordan by the bar, surfboards precariously placed all over and other athletic memorabilia thrown in for that authentic sports bar feel. The menu is super-extensive, complete with nachos (L5,000), quesadilla (L14,000), BBQ back ribs (L25,000), burgers (L13,500) and hot dogs (L15,000). The beautiful bartender Valentina will cater to your every need.

THE BLACK DUKE, *Via della Maddelena 29, Tel. 6830-0381. Open for lunch in the summers, and until 2:00am all year long, every day. Harp and Harp Strong, Guinness, Kilkenny and Kilkenny Strong, Strongbox Cider L5,000 half pint; L8,000 pint.*

Located near the Pantheon there is outside seating bordered by large shrubs that separate you from the street. You can also sit inside in the large downstairs dining and bar area that seat 120 people. The air circulation is not that great so non-smokers beware ... even in the small area designated for your use, breathing can be quite difficult. Here you can savor a full menu of authentic pub grub in the traditional dark and dinghy (yet clean and comfortable) English/Irish pub setting of dark wood decor and furnishings.

THE FIDDLERS ELBOW, *Via dell'Olmata 43, Tel. 487-2110. Open 7 days a week 5:00pm -1:15am. Harp, Kilkenny and Guinness served. Pints L8,000, half-pints L5,000*

Rome's oldest authentic pub, with knock-offs in Florence and Venice, this place has a slightly run-down feel but that gives it a truly Irish flavor. Located near the Piazza Santa Maria Maggiore, you'll get a taste of home here but no real food. Only snacks like potato chips, peanuts and salami sticks are served. A little off the beaten path, unless you are staying near the Train Station, this is not really a place to go out of your way to visit.

FLAN O'BRIENS PUB, *Via Napoli 29/34. Tel. 488-0418. Open all day everyday from 9:00am to 1:00am. Harp, Kilkenny and Guinness on tap. Pints L8,000. Half-pints L5,000.*

The backroom bar of the cafe of the same name on Via Nazionale, this place has the look and feel of a real Irish upscale pub. There is an all wood decor, rather brightly lit, with polished brass fitting, framed pictures of Irish origin, stained glass windows, and a quaint floral patterned wallpaper. Frequented by tourists from the four star Hotel Britannia just up the road and an upwardly mobile, young Italian crowd in the evenings, especially Friday and Saturday. Lunch time is basically dead since they only serve meager pub fare.

MISCELLANEA PUB, *Via delle Paste 110A. No telephone. Open 12:30pm - 2:00pm and 6:00pm to 3:00am. Bottled beer: Bud, Sol, Kronenbourg, Labatts L6,000. Beer on Tap: original Budweiser from Germany (much better than the American brand). Sandwiches L5,000, Salads L7,000.*

The unofficial international student's pub. It is the preferred meeting place for all the expatriate college and high school students in Rome. Only around 15-25% Italians. An intimate dive bar atmosphere with the friendliest owner around, Michy. Many special theme nights like beach nights with bikini-clad women or Mardi Gras celebrations. The beer flows like water here and the crowd gets boisterous. More for the younger set but really fun.

FOUR GREEN FIELDS, *Via Morina. Tel. 372-5091. Open 10:00pm to 2:00am every day. Kilkenny and Guinness on tap. Pints L8,000. Half-pints L5,000.*

This is two pubs in one. There are two floors each with their own balcony. The top floor is for quiet relaxation and drinking one of their exotic cocktails from a lengthy list of options, and/or eating some quality food from their extensive menu. The bottom floor is for drinking and dancing to loud live music. Since this place is only open four hours a day, it gets wild for that time. Crowded, chaotic, but fun.

MAD JACK'S, *Via Arenula 20, Tel. 06/6880-8223. Open Mon. - Fri. 11:00am-2:00am, Sat. and Sun. 4:00pm-:002am. Harp, Kilkenny and Guinness served. Pints L8,000, half-pints L5,000. Credit cards accepted.*

In one of Rome's best nighttime neighborhoods is this pub decorated in classic Irish style. They serve up all manner of Irish imbibement as well as many traditional offereings from the kitchen. Thursdays I avoid the place because of their disco night, but some of you may enjoy that.

THE DOG AND DUCK, *Via delle Luce 70. Tel. 06/589-5173. Kilkenny and Guinness on tap. Pints L8,000. Half-pints L5,000. Open 7:00pm to 2:00am.*

Located in Trastevere, this tiny little place is a local pub that is great on the weekends. Upstairs is microscopic, but the downstairs opens up a little. It's kind of like drinking in a bomb shelter. Not much other than drinks and intimate atmosphere offered, so if you want some food, try elsewhere.

THE JOHN BULL PUB, *Corso Vittorio Emanuele II 107a, Tel. 06/687-1537. Open 12:00pm to 2:00am. John Bull draughts (Ale, Stout, Lager) served for L8,000 a pint and L5,000 a half pint.*

The English John Bull company's version of what the Irish Guinness is promoting all over the world: authentic pub experience to sell their beer. There is wood, brass, glass, and mirrors, and English knickknacks everywhere. Totally British, including the friendly service. Ideally located near Piazza Navona, The Pantheon and Campo dei Fiori on the main street Vittorio Emanuele, this is a fun place to come for a few drinks or their extensive antipasto spread at happy hour. Besides that you can muster up some sandwishes, salads, or other basic pub food for around L5,000.

NIGHTLIFE & ENTERTAINMENT

> ### WHEN IN ROME ... DO AS THE IRISH DO!
>
> When you think of Rome, you picture magnificent monuments, savory food, wonderful wine, flavorful gelato, and most importantly romantic moons hovering over picturesque piazzas stirring long forgotten passions. To that list you can add Irish pubs and cold Guiness on draught, because everywhere you look in the Old City of Rome you'll find quaint, authentic Irish-style pubs, jam packed with customers, the majority of whom are Italian. From Campo dei Fiori, to the Pantheon, to Via del Corso, to Trastevere and beyond, stopping in a local pub for lunch or a pint in the evening has become a facet of daily life in Rome.
>
> Only a few years ago there were but a few seedy, vaguely pub-style bars, mainly catering to the foreign population. Today you can find authentic Irish-style pubs everywhere, filled to capacity with Italians enjoying the time honored Anglo-Saxon tradition of bellying up to the bar and throwing down a few pints.
>
> Just as we in the States have adopted coffee bars into our culture, so have the Italians incorporated Irish-style pubs into the fabric of their everyday lives.

NIGHTCLUBS & BARS

JACKIE O, *11 Via Bon Compagni, Tel. 06/488-5457. Open 8:00pm-3:00am. All credit cards accepted.*

This place has been famous for years and the fact that it is located just off the Via Veneto makes their prices sky high. The place is a combination, in three different areas, of a piano bar, a disco, and restaurant, so conceivably you can go to dinner, grab an after dinner drink, then dance the night away at the same place. It claims to be Rome's most prestigious and best loved nightclub, with members of the jet set visiting whenever they're in Rome, and from the atmosphere I can see why. Besides the high class but bawdy decor, you can expect discreet and professional service while at Jackie O's.

BIRRERIA LOWENBRAU MUNCHEN, *Via delle Croce 21, Tel. 06/679-5569. Open 11:00am-11:00pm. All credit cards accepted.*

You can eat here if the need for Viennese cuisine creeps up on your stomach (you'll find plenty of German tourists here enjoying the staples from their homeland), but I find it's a perfect place to have the best German beer on tap. It's a festive place to throw down a few pints with your travel partners. They serve their large beers in glass boots which adds to the charm of this *birreria*. In conjunction you're in one of the best nighttime areas in Rome, around the Piazza di Spagna, where you can go for a casual stroll before or after your drinking adventure.

NIGHT AND DAY, *Via dell'Oca 50. Pints L8,000. Half Pints L5,000. Open until 5:00am. All credit cards accepted.*

Yes, it's open until 5am, so put your drinking hat on. They also serve a lovely lunch from 12:30pm until 3:30pm with great salads and shepherd pies. You'll find their Guiness on tap 'for strength', as well as a nice assortment of local Frascati wines graciously served to you by the owners Stefano and Simone.

BIRRERIA TRILUSSA, *Via Aruleno Dello Sabino 29P, Tel. 06/7154-2180. Pints L8,000. Half Pints L5,000. All credit cards accepted.*

Located a stone's throw away from the Campo dei Fiori, you can see a few shady characters in here, but all are having fun. So if you want a little adventure, and desire to be a part of the in-crowd in Rome, give this place a try. (But do not buy anything illegal from anyone in there, no matter how nicely they offer. The laws are very strict in Italy, i.e. incarceration for many months before you even go to trial. Here you're guilty until proven innocent). That being said, have a pint for me.

RADIO LONDRA CAFFE, *Via di Monte Testaccio, 65B. Tel. 06/575-0044. Open 9am to 3am, and Sat. until 4am. All credit cards accepted.*

Recommended to me by a wine importer friend, who said it was wild. Well, he was way off base. It's totally insane, and crowded, and loud, and completely out of this world. You have segments of all parts of society here, making for a complete viewing pleasure. If the goings-on inside the inferno gets too hot, you can always sojourn to one of the tables on the terrace. A great place to meet other single people, not necessarily tourists. The interior is complete with an 18th century vaulted ceiling and 1940s style decor. They offer live music Tuesday through Friday. Food spcialties are house pizza and grilled steaks.

LOWENHAUS, *Via della Fontanella 16b, Tel. 06/323-0410. Open Tues.-Sun. 12:00pm-3:30pm, and 6:00pm to 3:00am. Closed Mondays. All credit cards accepted.*

For a traditional German stube atmosphere, this place near the Piazza del Popolo really rolls out the barrel. You'll find the best beer Lowenbrau has to offer and you can dine or snack on typical German specialties such as roast pig, wurstel, or goulash.

THE NEW FOX PUB, *Via di Monterone 19, Tel. 06/6889-2646. Open 9:00pm to 3:00am.*

A small Italian attempt to create a pub, but instead this is a good place to watch live music or listen to the juke box. With a disco ball in the main upstairs room and bright colors with the neon lights, the ambiance is upbeat and caters to a late night crowd. It doesn't start hopping until midnight or so. The crowd is about half Italian. Downstairs they have space for live music.

MOVIES IN ENGLISH

Look for listings for both of these in local papers or contact each cinema for a list of movies.

PASQUINO, *Vicolo del Piedo 19A, Tel. 06/580-3622.*

Located just off the Piazza Santa Maria in Trastevere, this is the only true English language cinema in Rome since this is all they show. So if you are in need of a little touch of back home, come here and enjoy. Beware of the changing of the reels in inclement weather. Since there is only one projector, they have to change reels when one ends, and when they do they usually open the skylight roof and sometimes forget it is pouring outside.

Despite the possibility of a drenching by coming to the Pasquino, you will probably witness the last remaining true cinema intermission, complete with intermission girls walking around selling popcorn, candy, and ice cream.

MAJESTIC, *Via S Apostoli 20, Tel 06/679-4908.*

They show first run English-language films only on Mondays.

ALCATRAZ, *Piazza M del Val 14, Tel 06/588-0099.*

They show films in their original language that have been dubbed into Italian. Only on Mondays.

16. SHOPPING

Store hours are usually Monday through Friday 9:00am to 1:00pm, 3:30/4:00pm to 7:30/8:00pm, and Saturday 9:00am to 1:00pm. This may vary in Milan and/or Turin, where sometimes the lunch break is shorter so shops can close earlier.

The big Italian chain stores are **La Rinascente**, **Coin**, **UPIM**, and **STANDA** (see sidebar on page 202). In Coin, UPIM, and STANDA, you will also find supermarkets filled with all manner of Italian delectables. In a few pages I'll make some suggestions about what you can buy at a local Italian *Supermercato* or *Alimentari* (smaller food store) to bring home with you so you can make a fine Italian meal with authentic ingredients!

Besides food and clothing, Italy has a wide variety of handicrafts. Any one of Italy's crafts would be a perfect memento of your stay. Stores in Rome sell works in alabaster and marble from Florence, Milan, and Venice; wood carvings from Southern Italy; beautiful glasswork from Venice and Pisa; embroidery and lace from all over Italy; and rugs, straw bags, hats, and mats from Sardinia and Florence.

Gold and silver jewelry is also available, as is hand-wrought iron work as well as beautiful tiles. And finally, the main fashion centers in Italy are, of course, Milan, Florence and Rome, with Florence specializing in shoes and gloves, and Milan and Rome everything else.

TAX-FREE SHOPPING

Italian law entitles all non-European Union residents to a **VAT (IVA) tax refund** with a minimum purchase exceeding L300,000. Ask for an invoice (*fattura* in Italian) or a Tax-Free Check when completing a purchase. Upon departure from Italy, purchased goods must be shown to a customs agent at the airport or border station and a customs stamp must be obtained no later than three months after the date of purchase. The stamped invoice must be returned to the store or the VAT Refund Companies Office in Italy no later than four months after the date of purchase.

GET YOUR TAX REBATE ON PURCHASES

*If you acquire products at the same merchant in excess of L300,000 (about $180), you can claim an **IVA** (purchase tax) **rebate**. You must ask the vendor for the proper receipt (**il ricetto per il IVA per favore**), have the receipt stamped at Italian customs, then mail no later than 90 days after the date of the receipt back to the vendor. The vendor will then send you the IVA rebate. I know it's complicated, but if you spend a fair chunk of money in Italy on clothing or other items, this is a good way to get some money back.*

Direct refunds at the airport or the border are only offered by Tax-Free for Tourists. You will usually see their signs in most upscale stores. Shop at them if you want instant refunds when you leave Italy.

LITTLE ITALIAN STORES

Since there are no 24-hour pharmacies or convenience stores that carry everything under the sun, like we have in North America, shopping for the basic necessities can be a little confusing. Listed below are specifc types of shops and what you can find in them:

Cartoleria

Shopping at a *cartoleria* brings you face to face with Italian make-work programs, since most are not self-service. Some products you can pick out what you want, others you will have to enlist a stockboy/girl to help you get it. But you don't bring the products up to the register. In most cases you will have it tabulated for you by the stockperson. Then you bring your purchases up to the register and another person rings them up for you.

pen	*penna*
pencil	*mattita*
notebook	*quaderno*
paper	*carta*
envelope	*borsa per un lettera*
binder	*classificatore*
calendar	*calandra*
wrapping paper	*carta da regalo*

Alimentari

When shopping at an *alimentari* some products are self-service and some have to be prepared for you. Most meats, cheeses and breads are not pre-packaged and therefore you will have to talk to someone behind a glass counter to get you what you want. Other goods, like mustard and water, are self-service. When ordering meats, cheeses or breads, you will get the products and the receipt for the products from the person behind the counter. Bring the receipt and all your other products to the cashier, and then you pay.

mustard	*senape*
mayonnaise	*maionese*
tomatoes	*tomaté*
olive oil	*olio d'oliva*
salami	*salame* (the best types are *Milanese* or *Ungherese*)
cheese	*formaggio*
mineral water	*aqua minerale*
wine (red/white)	*vino (rosso/bianco)*
beer	*birra*
potato chips	*patate fritte*
cookies	*biscotti*
roll	*panino*
bread	*pane*
butter	*burro*

Sometimes *alimentari* do not have bread. If that is the case you'll need to find a *panificio* (bakery). Same type of service here as in an *alimentari*.

Farmacia

Shopping in a pharmacy is full service; you have no access to anything. If you want anything you have to ask the pharmacist or his/her assistant.

toothpaste	*dentifricio*
razor	*rasoio*
deodorant	*deodorante*
comb	*pettine*
rubbers	*profilattici*
toothbrush	*spazzolino*
aspirin	*aspirina*
tampon	*tampone*

Tabacchaio

Most everything but the tobacco products and stamps are self-service in a *tabacchaio*.

stamps	*francobolli*
newspaper	*giornale*
pen	*penna*
envelopes	*buste per lettere*
postcards	*cartoline*
cigars	*sigaro*

cigarettes	*sigarette*
cigarette paper	*cartina*
pipe tobacco	*tabacco da pipa*
matches	*fiammiferi*
lottery ticket	*biglietto di lotteria*
lighter	*accendino*

SIZES

Below is a comparison guide between US and Italian sizes. Many sizes are not standardized, so you will need to try everything on in any event. The following conversions should help you out in your shopping quest:

WOMEN'S CLOTHING SIZES

US	2	4	6	8	10	12	14	16
Italy	36	38	40	42	44	46	48	50

Continued

US	18	20	24
Italy	52	54	56

WOMEN'S SHOE SIZES

US	5 1/2	6 1/2	7	7 1/2	8	8 1/2	9	10
Italy	35	36	37	38	38 1/2	39	40	41

WOMEN'S HOSIERY SIZES

US	Petite	Small	Medium	Large
Italy	I	II	III	IV

MEN'S SUITES, OVERCOATS, SWEATERS, & PAJAMAS

US	34	36	38	40	42	44	46	48
Italy	44	46	48	50	52	54	56	58

MEN'S SHIRTS

US	14	14 1/2	15	15 1/2	16	16 1/2	17	17 1/2
Italy	36	37	38	39	40	41	42	43

MEN'S SHOES

US	6	6 1/2	7	7 1/2	8	8 1/2	9	9 1/2
Italy	30	40	40 1/2	41	41 1/2	42	42 1/2	43

Continued

US	10	10 1/2	11-11 1/2
Italy	43 1/2	44-44 1/2	45

MEN'S HATS

US	6 7/8	7	7 1/8	7 1/4	7 3/8	7 1/2	7 5/8	7 3/4
Italy	55	56	57	58	59	60	61	62

CHILDREN'S SIZES

US	1	2	3	4	5	6	7	8
Italy	35	40	45	50	55	60	65	70

Continued

9	10	11	12	13	14
75	80	85	90	95	100

CHILDREN'S SHOES

US	4	5	6	7	8	9	10	10 1/2
Italy	21	21	22	23	24	25	26	27

Continued

11	12	13
28	29	30

KEY SHOPPING & BARGAINING PHRASES

Italian	English
Quanto costa?	How Much is This?
E Troppo	That's too much
No Grazie	No thank you
Voglio paggare meno	I want to pay less
Che lai questo pui grande?	Do have this in a bigger size?
..... *pui piccolo*	..... in a smaller size
..... *in nero*	..... in black
..... *in bianco*	..... in white
..... *in roso*	..... in red
..... *in verde*	..... in green

WHEN TO BARGAIN

In all stores, even the smallest shops, bargaining is not accepted, just like here in North America. But you can bargain at any street vending location, even if they have placed a sign indicating the price. Don't be afraid to bargain, otherwise you'll end up spending more than you (ahem) 'bargained' for.

Most Italian vendors see foreigners as easy marks to make a few more *lire* because they know it is not in our culture to bargain, while in theirs it is a way of life.

ITALIAN SOCCER ATTIRE

If you or someone you know is a soccer nut, you may want to get them a jersey, hat, or scarf from one of the local teams. Most cities and towns in Italy have a soccer team, whether in the **Serie A** *(First Division) or in the three lower divisions. The games are played from September to June and are the best places to get low cost, high quality merchandise.*

Outside of most games vendors are selling everything from key rings to official soccer jerseys, all at a low price. The Italian soccer teams are starting to open their own stores featuring their specially-licensed products, like **Milan Point**, *for one of the teams in Milan, but those prices will be about four times as much as at the stadium.*

The best way to bargain, if the street vendor doesn't speak English, is by writing your request on a piece of paper. This keeps it personal too in case you're embarrassed about haggling over money. You and the vendor will probably pass the paper back and forth a few times changing the numbers before a price is finally agreed upon. And of course, the Italian vendor will be waving his arms about, jabbering away, most probably describing how you're trying to rip him off, all in an effort to get you to pay a higher price. Remember, this is all done in fun – so enjoy it.

BRINGING BACK PURCHASES THROUGH CUSTOMS

You can bring back to the US $400 worth of goods duty free. On the next $1,000 worth of purchases you will be assessed a flat 10% fee. These product must be with you when you go through customs.

You can mail products duty free, providing the total value of each package sent is not more than $50 *and* no one person is receiving more than one package a day. Also, each package sent must be stamped "Unsolicited Gift" and the amount paid and the contents of the package must be displayed. They'll be able to tell you all this again at the post office.

What you can't bring back to North America are any fruits, vegetables, and in most cases meats and cheeses, even if they're for your consumption alone, and even if they are vacuum sealed. Customs has to do this to prevent any potential parasites from entering our country and destroying our crops. Unfortunately, this means all those great salamis and cheeses you bought at those quaint outdoor food markets and had on one of your picnics will not be let back into the North America.

But there are some things you can buy. In most supermarkets you can find salamis and cheeses that have been shrink-wrapped, which customs should let through. Good luck!

ITALIAN DEPARTMENT STORES

It's always fun to go to supermarkets and department stores in other countries to see what the natives like. Even if you don't buy anything, it's still fun to browse and not be followed around the store, as you would in one of the smaller boutiques by one of the vulture-like owners or staff. Both STANDA and UPIM are designed for the Italian on a budget, while Rinascente is a little more chic.

STANDA, Viale di Trastevere 60 and Via Cola di Rienzo 173.

Italy's largest food market, the perfect place to find that food product to bring back to the States with you. Since most of their stuff is vacuum sealed and pre-packaged you should not have any problems with customs. STANDA also has a large selection of housewares and clothing. This is the combined K Mart and Safeway of Italy, with slightly better quality products.

UPIM, Via Nazionale 111, Piazza Santa Maria Maggiore and Via del Tritone 172.

This department store is just like STANDA, except without the food.

LA RINASCENTE, Piazza Colonna on the Via del Corso and Piazza Fiume.

This is much more upscale than the other two and has about the same prices as boutiques, and even has some of the vultures hanging around too.

Because the very best of Italian design and craftsmanship are conveniently located in one small area, Rome is one of the finest shopping cities in the world. You can find beautifully made items made from the very best material, and as such this is not the place to look around for cut-price bargains. Leather and silk goods predominate, but Rome is also an important location for jewelry, antiques and general top of the line *pret-a-porter* (ready to wear) fashion.

The main shopping area is a network of small and large streets containing the famous **Via Condotti**. The shopping area boundaries extend over to **Via della Croce** in the north to **Via Frattina** in the south, and **Via del Corso** in the west to **Piazza di Spagna** in the east.

Romans, like other Italians, prefer to shop in boutiques, and the Via Condotti area has these quaint little shops selling everything from shirts to gloves. This specialization originates in the craft shops from which the smart shopping village has grown, and generally ensures top quality and personal service. In Italy, **department stores** are the exception rather than the rule, but in this shopping area there are some that warrant a look, like **La Rinascente**, **STANDA**, **UPIM**, and **Coin**.

To get the instant smile and respect you expect when you shop in most stores in America, you may have to dress the part here in Italy. It's not like in the malls back home where it doesn't matter how you dress; here in Rome the wealthier you look the better assistance you'll get. Unfortunately as tourists we usually leave our best attire back home, but try the best you can. Shorts and tank tops usually will get you no respect at all, particularly if you're shopping on the Via Condotti and Via Borgognona. This holds true, and I can vouch for this personally, if you're shopping on some of the parallel streets like Via Frattina, some of the little cross-streets, and even in Piazza di Spagna or Via del Babuino.

SHOPPING STREETS

Top of the Line Shopping – Via Condotti, Via Borgognona, Via Bocca di Leone

Middle Range Fashion – Via Nazionale, Via del Corso, Via Cola di Rienzo, Via del Tritone, and Via Giubbonari

Antiques – Via del Babuino, Via Guilia, Via dei Coronari.

Food Stores – Via del Croce

Inexpensive Shoes – Fontana di Trevi area

Leather goods and apparel – Via due Macelli, Via Francesco Crispi

Straw and Wicker Products – Via dei Deiari, Via del Teatro Valle

---

Other shopping districts are less formal, and many of these are worth investigating if you have time, for here is where you'll find the real bargains. **Via del Tritone** and the streets around the **Trevi Fountain**, **Via Cola di Rienzo** across the Tiber and north of the Vatican, **Piazza San Lorenzo** in Lucina and the streets around **Piazza Campo dei Fiori** are all areas where you will find cheaper leather bags and shoes. **Via Veneto** also has more of an international flavor, but boy, is it expensive.

Besides these areas, Rome also has many colorful street markets offering a vast selection of top quality fruit, flowers, vegetables, prosciutto, salami, cheeses, meat and fish, as well as cheap (that's inexpensive and sometimes just plain cheap) clothes. Because of this proliferation of shops and markets, and the Italian penchant for shopping in them, there are few department stores or supermarkets in the city center.

Straight bargaining is an accepted practice in clothes markets, but elsewhere transactions are conducted in a more roundabout way. At food stalls, cheeses and other weighed items have *prezzi fissi* (fixed prices), and in nearly all clothes shops, you can try asking for a *sconto* (discount). Reasons for meriting a *sconto* may be numerous – buying two articles at once is a good example – but if you are bold you will ask for a *sconto* for no good reason at all, and will usually get one. This practice applies to all but the very grandest of shops.

Surprisingly few shopkeepers speak English, but in the larger shops there is usually one person on hand who understands enough to be able to help you. Try to get your shopping done in the morning hours, when the stores are not so busy. At night, traditionally when Italians shop, it is so crowded it is difficult to get assistance.

ANTIQUES

Today, the typical Roman antique can be either a precious Roman artifact or pieces in the baroque and neoclassical style. There are also many French and English antiques masquerading as Italian. One thing that they all have in common is that they are extremely expensive.

The best antique shops in Rome can be found in the **Via del Babuino** and the **Via Margutta**. Other shops can be found on the **Via dei Coronari**, and the **Via Guilia**. And don't forget to check out the **Porta Portese** Sunday market *(open 6:30am–2:30pm)*. You'll find some interesting antiques there, but not too many.

OUTDOOR MARKETS

Many natives buy their vegetables, fruits, flowers, meats and cheeses from one of the many street markets held daily all over the city. Stalls of

> ### CLASSY CONSIGNMENT SHOP
> *Chimera (Via del Seminario 121, Tel. 06/679-2126; open Mon. 3:15pm-7:30pm, Tuesday-Saturday 10:00am-7:30pm; closed Sundays) is a consignment shop that specializes in collector's items and objects like paintings, drawings, porcelain, silver, jewelry, art, coins, and much more. A short walk from the Pantheon, located in the basement of a 16th century palazzo, this is where Rome's well-heeled pawn their family heirlooms so they can continue living the life of luxury. Remember to bargain.*

inexpensive clothing are also available, but there are whole markets devoted specifically to clothing. The food and flower markets are the best, and I advise you not to miss the opportunity to wander through one in the mornings, since they are usually closed in the afternoons.

Here are some of the better markets:

Campo dei Fiori, *Piazza Campo dei Fiori. Open 6:00am–2:00pm. Closed Sunday.*

Rome's oldest market held in the cobblestoned square in the center of Rome's old medieval city. You can buy flowers (the name Campo dei

SHOPPING

Fiori means fields of flowers), fruits and vegetables, all delicately presented under makeshift awnings or giant umbrellas. Surrounding the square are some *Alimentaris* where you can pick up cold cuts, cheeses, and bread for picnics.

Piazza Vittorio Emanuele, *Open 7:00am–2:00pm. Closed Sundays.*

Stretching all the way around this large piazza is the city's largest market. Clothes and leather goods are displayed along the south side, with some fine bargains to be found. The food stalls on the north side are known by their specialization: one stall will sell only fresh tuna, another calves livers, another tangerines. The crowing of the cocks and scuttling of crabs really adds to the atmosphere of this market. You can find some very unusual food in these stalls as well as some exquisite cheeses and salamis.

Porta Portese, *Ponte Sublico. Open 6:30am–2:30pm, Sundays only.*

This flea market stretches along the Tiber from Ponte Sublico (where the Porta Portese is) in the north to the Ponte Testaccio in the south. That's roughly south of the center of Trastevere along the river. It is not even on most maps, but tell a cab driver where you're going and he'll know.

It is truly a Roman institution where anything and everything under the sun is sold: from live rabbits to stolen atniques to trendy clothes to kitchen items and all sorts of odds and ends. The clothes and accessories are inexpensive but are not of the highest quality, as befits most flea markets. Not many tourists venture here, but it's safe (beware of pickpockets), and if you like flea markets, it is a whole lot of fun. And it goes without saying that you have to bargain.

Via Andrea Doria, *Open 8:00am–1:00pm. Closed Sundays and Mondays.*

Filling almost the entire length of the Via Andrea Doria, as well as spilling into many side streets, this is a large and lively food market. The stalls are laid out in artistic arrangements to attract buyers. You can find strings of onions, cheeses, bottled oils, salamis, sausages, cheeses, etc. all laid out perfectly for the customer.

Via Sannio, *Open Monday through Friday 8:00am–1:00pm, Saturdays 8:00am–7:00pm. Closed Sundays.*

Most of these clothes sellers move their wares to the Porta Portese on Sundays, so if you can't make it there try to make it here. To get here by Metro, go two stops past the Piazza Vittorio Emanuele.

Mercato de Stampe, *Piazza Fontanella Borghese, Monday–Saturday 9:00am–6:00pm.*

A small outdoor market based at the end of the square that specializes in old prints, stamps, postcards, assorted books, and knickknacks that could be considered antiques. The prices tend to be high, especially if you're pegged as a tourist, so bargaining is essential.

BOOKSTORES WITH ENGLISH LANGUAGE TITLES

American Book Shop, *Via della Vite 27 & 57, Tel. 06/583-6942. American Express, Diners Club, Mastercard and Visa accepted. Open Mondays 4:00pm–8:00pm, Tuesday–Saturday 10:00am–1:00pm and 3:30pm–7:30pm.*

A small English-language only new bookstore that has almost everything you could want. It's a little pricey but that's to be expected.

Ancora Book Shop, *Via della Conciliazione 63, Tel. 06/656-8820. American Express, Diners Club, Mastercard and Visa accepted. Monday-Friday 9:00am–1:00pm, and 3:30pm–7:30pm. Saturdays 9:00am–1:00pm.*

Mainly a Catholic religious bookstore, but they have English language titles upstairs as well as a good selection of travel guides.

Anglo-American Bookstore, *Via delle Vite 102. Tel. 06/679-5222. Credit cards accepted. Monday–Friday 9:00am–1:00pm, and 3:30pm–7:30pm. Saturdays 9:00am–1:00pm.*

Located between the Spanish Steps and the Trevi Fountain, this bookstore caters to all manner of bibliophiles and computer nerds too. As well as a full selection of travel books, paperbacks, history books, etc. They have a multimedia computer center too.

The Corner Bookshop, *Via del Moro 48, Tel. 06/583-6942. Mastercard and Visa accepted. Open Mondays 3:30pm–7:30pm, Tuesday–Saturday 10:00am–1:00pm and 3:30pm–7:30pm.*

Located in Trastevere, near the renowned night spot Piazza Santa Maria in Trastevere, this is a relatively new bookstore featuring English-language titles exclusively. Owned by the very knowledgeable, helpful, and friendly Claire Hammond, you can almost always find what you want. They're stocked with hardbacks, paperbacks in non-fiction, fiction, general interest and more. A great place to meet other ex-pats or fellow travelers. Say hello to Claire for me when you see her.

Economy Bookstore and Video Center, *Via Torino 136, Tel. 06/474-6877. Credit cards accepted. Mondays 3:00pm–7:30pm, Tuesday–Saturday 10:00am–1:00pm and 3:30pm–7:30pm.*

The best place to find a novel in English, and now they rent movies too. This mainstay of the English-speaking community for the past three decades has recently moved from Piazza di Spagna to this new location (I almost didn't find it again). They buy and sell second-hand English language paperbacks and have an excellent selection of both new and used books, including everything from fiction to non-fiction, children's, science fiction, best sellers and mysteries. They also carry a complete range of guide books on Rome and Italy.

Libreria Internazionale Rizzolo, *Largo Chigi 15, Tel. 06/679-6641. Credit cards accepted.*

The largest store of Italy's largest bookstore chain. It has a great selection of artistic and cultural books. On the ground floor and in the basement there is also an adequate selection of guidebooks and paperbacks in English.

NEWSPAPERS

The *International Herald Tribune* is published jointly by the Washington Post and The New York Times and printed in Bologna for distribution throughout Italy. You can also find a condensed version of *USA Today*. There used to be the local English language paper for Rome, *The Daily American*, but that perished from competition years ago. Besides these two, you can also find newspapers from all over the world at almost any newsstand.

FOOD STORES & MARKETS

As mentioned above in the section on outdoor markets, the best places to get your fresh fruit, cheese, salami, ham, turkey, and bread for a picnic would be at any of the markets mentioned above in this section under *Outdoor Markets*. If you can't make it to one of these, here's a list of some small *Alimentaris* and wine stores from which you can get all you need.

Campo dei Fiori, *Open Air Market, Piazza Campo dei Fiori. Open 6:00am–2:00pm.*

You can get salamis, cheeses, breads, and fruit here. A few stores on and around the Via Sistine.

Piazza Vittorio Emanuele, *Open 7:00am–2:00pm. Closed Sundays.*

You can find many specialty food items here, especially cheeses, breads, and salamis.

Other small stores include one on Via Laurina, and another small store, near both entrances to the Borghese Gardens, is in the middle of the Via Della Croce.

Wine

Antica Bottigleria Placidi, *Via del Croce 76, Tel. 679-0896. Expensive. All credit cards accepted. Closed Sundays.*

Opened in 1860, until a few years ago this was an old fashioned, ancient really, wine store selling local vintages directly from large vats. You would walk past the huge wooden doors and into the cool, dark, and damp store lined with shelf upon shelf of wine and oil, and it would seem as if centuries had been erased. Now it's a yuppified fern-filled wine bar. They actually have plants in the vats where once I was served some of the choicest vintages. Not that it's all that bad, for a faux wine bar, they do serve palatable side dishes. I just wish they had kept the vats in use.

Interesting Little Shops

Check out any **Cartolerie** (Bookstores), the perfect places to buy unique school supplies for the kids, or yourself, such as pens, notebooks, stationary, pencils, etc. I've been using foreign made notebooks bought in these shops for my journal entries for many years. Cartolerie are all over town.

For specific stores you simply must visit the following:

Ai Monestari, *Via dei Coronari*, located just outside the Piazza Navonna. A tiny shop of monk-made products including my favorite, **L'Amaro Francescano di Assisi** liqueur. Another fun place is **Terecotte Persiane**, *Via Napoli 92, Tel. 06/488-3886, Open 10:00am–1:30pm and 3:30pm–8:00pm*. Eclectic mix of terra cotta figures, tiles, masks, planters and post boxes. Located in a small courtyard just down from the American church in Rome, Santa Susanna's, the place is packed with everything terra cotta you can imagine. Even if you don't want to buy, come and browse.

And finally, for the most amazing, colorful and oh so collectible, painted prints of the piazzas, monuments, and buildings of Rome, in all shapes and sizes, framed or unframed, visit L'Impront**a** at *Via del Teatro Valle 53, Tel. 06/686-7821*. It's an adventure to find since it is tucked away on a cute side street between the Pantheon and Piazza Navona.

ALIMENTARI

These are small shops that serve up Italy's famous salamis, meats, cheeses, and breads for you to snack on or take on a picnic. I've listed some of my favorites that are dispersed all over the city, but you only need to find one closest to your hotel for a culinary treat.

Via Principe Amadeo 61 (Termini). *Next to Fiorino Hotel.*
Valeria Basconi, Via Firenze 53 (Via Nazionale). *Near Hotel Alda.*
**Salumeria, Via Sardegna 20 (Via Veneto/Trevi Fountain).*
Via degli Avignonesi 25 (Via Veneto/Trevi Fountain)
Via Laurina 36 (Piazza di Spagna) – *Meats, cheeses, breads*
Via Laurina 39 (Piazza di Spagna) – *fruits and vegetables and wine*
Via di Ripetta 233A (Pantheon/Navona) – *large meat, cheese, bread, and wine store.*
Via della Scrofa 100 (Piazza Navona/Pantheon) – *meats and cheeses. If you want some prosciutto this small shop will have it cut by hand for you in the window for all to see.*
Via della Scrofa 32 (Piazza Navona/Pantheon)– *hot and cold take out of pastas and soufflés as well as salami, cheese and wine.*

17. CULTURE & ARTS

FROM ETRUSCANS TO THE RENAISSANCE

Italy is perhaps best known for its great contributions to painting and sculpture; and many art lovers have described the country as one vast museum. Italy gave birth to such world renowned artists as Giotto, Donatello, Raphael, Michelangelo, Leonardo da Vinci, and Botticelli, known all over the world.

The oldest works of art in Italy are those of the **Etruscans**, and they date back to the 9th century BCE. This mysterious society's main cities and art centers were in the middle of the peninsula, between Rome and Florence, mainly in the province now know as Tuscany (the region was named after them ... Etruscans ... Tuscany). In Tarquinia, Volterra, Cerveteri, and Veio, the Etruscans have left behind magnificent temples, sculptures, and bronzes as well as other fascinating testimonies to their presence. In the Vatican in Rome, the best museum collections of Etruscan art can be found in the **Etruscan Museum**.

Italy is also know as being a repository of ancient Greek art. During the time of the Etruscans, the Greeks established colonies in the south of modern-day Italy. Magnificent ruins of temples exist today in some of these Greek colonies: **Syracuse**, **Agrigento**, and **Taormina** in Sicily; and **Paestu** and **Coma** in Campania. There are good collections of Hellenic art in the **National Museum of Naples**, and in the museums in Palermo, Syracuse, Reggio Calabria, Paestum, and Taranto.

After the Greeks and Etruscans, the Roman Empire left its lasting impression all over Italy. There are still roads, bridges, aqueducts, arches, and theaters built by the Romans. The most extensive excavations have been made at the **Forum** in Rome, at **Ostia** near Rome by the beach, and at **Pompeii** and **Herculaneum**, the cities that the volcanic Mount Vesuvius buried. For a first-hand, up-front feel of what life was like in the Roman Empire, don't miss these sites.

After the fall of the Roman Empire, the Byzantine Empire ruled many parts of the southern and eastern regions of Italy. This period left behind many churches, with their glorious mosaics, like those of the 6th century in Ravenna near the east coast; as well as the morbid-but-can't-miss site of the **catacombs** outside of Rome.

Then the Renaissance came. This artistic period, meaning "rebirth," began in Italy in the 14th century and lasted for two hundred years. The Renaissance left us an extensive array of churches, palaces, paintings, statues, and city squares in almost every city of Italy. The main cities of Florence, Rome, Venice, Milan, and Naples have most of the treasures and beauty of this period, but smaller towns like Ferrara and Rimini also have their share. In Rome, the best museums for viewing Renaissance art are in the **Vatican** and the **Borghese Galleries** (in the Borghese Gardens just outside Rome's walls).

After the Renaissance, **baroque art** became fashionable. And Rome, more than any other Italian city, contains a dazzling array of churches, paintings, and statues recalling the splendor of such famous artists as Bernini, Borromini, and Caravaggio of the late 16th and 17th centuries.

RENAISSANCE PAINTING

In Italy (with France and Germany soon following suit) during 14th and 15th centuries, the Renaissance was a period of exploration, invention, and discovery. Mariners from all over Europe set sail in search of new lands. Scientists like **Leonardo da Vinci** studied the mysteries of the world and the heavens. Artists found the human body to be a marvel of mechanics and beauty (but had to secretly study it, as Michelangelo did, lest the Church condemn them for heresy). This was undoubtedly one of Italy's most exciting periods in the history of artistic and scientific advancement. Florence is the best place to view Renaissance art, but Rome has its share of great Renaissance artworks as well.

Three of the most famous Renaissance artists were **Raphael**, **Leonardo da Vinci**, and **Michelangelo**. Raphael was mainly known for his paintings of the Madonna and Child, from which our concept of the Mother of Jesus is largely based. But all of his paintings reflect a harmony that leaves the viewer with a warm feeling.

Leonardo da Vinci is most well known for his *Mona Lisa*, painted in Tuscany in 1505-06 and now hanging in the Louvre, but he was also a versatile architect and scientist as well. Leonardo studied botany, geology, zoology, hydraulics, military engineering, anatomy, perspective, optics, and physiology. You name it, he did it – the original Renaissance Man!

Another versatile artist of the Italian Renaissance, and definitely its most popular (he was always being commissioned to paint or sculpt all the wealthy people's portraits) was Michelangelo Buonarroti. Although he considered himself chiefly a sculptor – he trained as a young boy to become a stone carver – he left us equally great works as a painter and architect. As a painter he created the huge **Sistine Chapel** fresco, encompassing more than 10,000 square feet in area. As an architect he helped complete the designs for **St. Peter's**, where his world renowned statue, *La Pieta*, currently resides.

RENAISSANCE SCULPTURE

Besides painting and architecture, **Michelangelo Buonarroti** was also the pre-eminent sculptor of the Renaissance. By the age of 26 he had carved *La Pieta*, his amazing version of Virgin Mary supporting the dead Christ on her knees; and was in the process of carving the huge and heroic marble *David*. His greatest but lesser known work is his majestic *Moses* designed for the tomb of Pope Julius II. Today this great statue can be viewed at the basilica of **San Pietro in Vincoli** in Rome.

Even though Michelangelo was commissioned to create many works by Popes themselves, he had learned his amazing knowledge of the human anatomy by dissecting cadavers in his home town of Florence as a young man, a crime punishable by death and/or excommunication at the time.

During the Renaissance there were many other sculptors of note, but Michelangelo was truly the best. One of the others was **Lorenzo Ghiberti**, who died a few years before Michelangelo was born. For 29 years he labored to produce ten bronze panels, depicting Biblical episodes, for the doors of the Baptistery of Florence. Michelangelo was said to have been inspired to become a great artist because of these beautiful bronze doors.

MUSIC

Italy also has a great tradition in music. Even today, Italian folk music has made a resurgence, mainly because of the theme song for the *Godfather* movie series. Can't you just hear it playing in your head right now?

Italian Opera & Musical Concerts

Besides the folk music and Gregorian chants, Italy is known for its opera. If your appetite cannot be satiated without the shrill explosion of an *aria* try these famous opera houses covered by this book: **The Opera** in Rome, **The San Carlos** in Naples, and **The Petruzzelli** in Bari. There are also many opera festivals all over Italy virtually year-round.

As the birthplace of opera, Italy offers visitors a variety of choices during the operatic seasons, which are almost year-round. In the summer months there are wonderful open-air operas presented at the **Terme di Caracalla** (Baths of Caracalla) in the center of Rome near the main train station from July to August, and from June through August there are concerts in the Basilica Maxentius. In general, the opera season lasts from December to June.

Italian opera began in the 16th century. Over time such composers as Gioacchino Rossini, Gaetano Donizetti, and Vincenzo Bellini created **bel canto** opera – opera that prizes beautiful singing above all else. Singers were indulged with *arias* that gave them ample opportunity for a prominent display of their vocal resources of range and agility.

Rossini, who reigned as Italy's foremost composer of the early 19th century, was a master of both melody and stage effects. Success came easily, and while still in his teens he composed the first of a string of 32 operas that he completed by the age of 30. Many of these are comic operas, a genre in which Rossini excelled, and his masterpieces in this form are still performed and admired today. Among them is one you probably recognize (even I know this one): *The Barber of Seville* (1816).

Rossini's immediate successor as Italy's leading operatic composer was **Donizetti**, who composed more than 70 works in the genre. A less refined composer than Rossini, Donizetti left his finest work in comic operas, including *Don Pasquale* (1843) and *Lucia di Lammermoor* (1835).

Although he lived for a shorter time than either Rossini or Donizetti and enjoyed a far briefer career, **Bellini** wrote music that many believe surpassed theirs in refinement. Among the finest of his ten operas are *La sonnambula* (The Sleepwalker, 1831), *Norma* (1831), and *I Puritani* (The Puritans, 1835), all of which blend acute dramatic perceptions with florid virtuosity.

From these roots came Italy's greatest opera composers of all times, **Puccini** and **Verdi**. Giacomo Puccini lived from 1858-1924 and composed twelve operas in all. Considered by many to be a close second to Verdi in skill of composition, Puccini's work will remain alive because of his enduringly popular works such as *Madame Butterfly* and *La Boheme*. Even though Puccini was the fifth generation of musicians in his family, he was mainly influenced to pursue his career after hearing Verdi's still popular *Aida*.

Giuseppe Verdi lived from 1813-1901, and is best know for his operas *Rigoletto* (1851), *Il Trovatore* and *La Traviata* (both 1853), and what could be the grandest opera of them all, *Aida* (1871). Verdi composed his thirtieth and last opera *Falstaff* at the age of 79. Since he mainly composed out of Milan and many of his operas opened at La Scala opera house in that city, today a Verdi museum has been established there to honor his work.

CULTURE & ARTS 213

> **OPERA ADDRESSES & PHONE NUMBERS**
> *Teatro dell'Opera*, Piazza D. Gigli 1, 00184 Roma. Tel. 06/481-601, Fax 06/488-1253
> *Teatro San Carlo*, Via San Carlo 98f, 80132 Napoli. Tel. 081/797-2331 Or 797-2412, Fax 081/797-2306
> *Teatro Massimo*, Piazza Verdi, 90139 Palermo. Tel 091/605-3111, Fax 091/605-3325 or 605-3324

If you wish to obtain tickets to opera performances, concerts, ballet, and other performances you can either write directly to the theater in question or ask your travel agent to obtain the ticket for you. Currently there is no agency in the US authorized to sell concert and/or opera tickets, so this is the only way. When you are in Italy, your hotel should be able to assist you in obtaining tickets for performances in their city.

REGIONAL & NATIONAL FOLK FESTIVALS

Despite the encroachment of the modern world, the traditional festivals and their accompanying costumes and folk music have survived surprisingly well all over Italy. In many cases they have been successfully woven into the pattern of modern life so as to seem quite normal. Despite all possible modern influences these festivals (both secular and religious) have preserved their distinctive character. Two of the most famous, the secular festivals of the Palio in Siena and of Calcio in Costume in Florence, both outside the scope of this book.

With Italy the home of the Catholic church, religious festivals also play a large part in Italian life. Particularly interesting are the processions on the occasion of **Corpus Christi**, **Assumption**, and **Holy Week**. In Italy, holiday times such as Easter and Christmas have not lost their religious intent as they have in most other places. In Italy, commercialism takes a back seat to the Almighty.

The items below marked by an asterisk are the ones you simply cannot miss. Plan your trip around them.

JANUARY
- **New Year's Day**, *Rome*: Candle-lit processional in the Catacombs of Priscilla to mark the martyrdom of the early Christians
- **January 5**, **Rome*: Last day of the Epiphany Fair in the Piazza Navona. All throughout the piazza a fair filled with food stands, candy stands, toy shops opens to the public. Lasts a week. A must see.

FEBRUARY/MARCH

During February or March in *San Remo*, the Italian Festival of Popular Songs is celebrated.
- **February 24-26**, *Oristano*: "Sa Sartiglia" medieval procession and jousting of masked knights dressed in Sardinian and Spanish costumes.
- **19 March**, *Many places*: San Giuseppe (St. Joseph's day)

MARCH/APRIL

During March or April, *Rome* celebrates the Festa della Primavera (Spring Festival).
- **Palm Sunday**, *Many places, particularly Rome and Florence*: Blessings of palms, with procession
- **Wednesday before Easter**, *Many places, particularly Rome*: Mercoledi Santo (lamentations, Miserere)
- **Thursday Before Good Friday**, *Many places, particularly Rome and Florence*: Washing of the Feet, burial of the sacraments
- **Good Friday**, *Many places, particularly Rome and Florence*: Adoration of the Cross. *Taranto*: Procession of the Mysteries (Solemn procession with many beautiful period costumes).
- **Easter Saturday**, *Many places, particularly Rome and Florence*: Lighting of the Sacred Fire
- **Easter Day**, *Rome*: Papal blessing; *Florence:* Scopplo dei Carro ("Explosion of the Cart" – A pyramid of fireworks is set off in the Cathedral square to commemorate the victorious return of the first Crusade.

MAY

- **First Saturday in May**, *Naples*: San Gennaro (feast of St. Januarius)
- **May 7**, *Bari*: Festival of St. Nicholas (procession of fishing boats with people in costumes)
- **May 26**, *Rome*: San Filippo Neri

JUNE

- **Mid-June**, *Many places*: Corpus Domini (Ascension processions)
- **June 23-24**, *Rome*: Vigilia di San Giovanni Battista (St. John's Eve, fireworks, eating of snails, song competition)
- **June 29**, *Rome*: Santi Pietro e Paulo (feast of Saints Peter and Paul); *Genoa*: "Palio Marinaro dei Rioni." Rowing race in ancient costumes.

JULY

- **July 10-15**, *Palermo*: Feat of Saint Rosalia with processions, bands, fireworks etc., all decorated in honor of the patron saint of the city.
- **July 16**, *Naples*: Feast of Santa Maria del Carmine

CULTURE & ARTS

- **July 19-26,** *Rome*: Festa de' Noantri folklore festival of old Rome in Trastevere, Rome's oldest habitable section, which includes a colorful procession, folk dances, songs, carnival floats, and fireworks. Everybody gets real worked up for this. A must see.

AUGUST
- **15 August,** *Many places*: Assumption (processions and fireworks)

SEPTEMBER/OCTOBER
- **September 5-7,** *Naples*: Madonna della Piedigrotta Folk Song Festival
- **September 19,** *Naples*: Festival of San Gennaro. Religious ceremony honoring the patron saint of the city.
- **October 1,** *San Marino*: Installation of Regents

NOVEMBER/DECEMBER
- **November 22,** *Many places*: Santa Cecilia (St. Cecilia's day)
- **December 25,** *Rome*: Papal blessing
- **Mid-December to mid-January,** Many places: Christmas crib (Nativity Scenes)

CRAFTS

Hundreds of thousands of skillful Italian artisans are the heirs of a 2,000-year tradition of craftsmanship. Their products – fashioned of leather, gold, silver, glass, and silk – are widely sought by travelers to Italy. Cameos made from seashells, an ancient Italian art form, are as popular today as they were in the days of the Roman Empire. The work of Italian artists and artisans is also exported for sale in the great department stores of France, Germany, the United Kingdom, and the United States.

Italian clothing designers are world famous, especially for precise tailoring, unusual knits, and the imaginative use of fur and leather.

The best place to see Italian artisans at work is in the glass blowing factories of Venice. There you'll be amazed at how easily they can manipulate molten balls into some of the most delicate, colorful, and beautiful pieces you've ever seen. Each chapter in this book highlights specific traditional crafts by region.

LITERATURE

Perhaps Italy's most famous author/poet is **Dante Aligheri**, who wrote the *Divine Comedy*, in which he describes his own dream-journey through Hell *(l'Inferno)* Purgatory *(Purgatorio)*, and Paradise *(Paradiso)*. At the time it was extremely controversial, since it is a poem about free will and how man can damn or save his soul as he chooses, which was contrary to church teachings. Even today it sparks controversy since it seems apparent that Dante's description of Purgatory is actually describing the life we all lead on earth, and shows his belief in reincarnation.

Two other notable Italian writers (you should remember these for quality cocktail party conversation) are **Petrarch**, famous for his sonnets to Laura, a beautiful girl from Avignon who died quite young, and is known as the "First of the Romantics;" and **Boccaccio**, the Robin Williams of his time (except he wrote, not performed) his famous *Decameron*, a charming and sometimes ribald series of short stories told by ten young people in a span of ten days – sort of the Chaucer of Italy.

Among contemporary Italian writers, **Umberto Eco** stands out on his own. You may know two of his books that have been translated into English: *The Name of the Rose* and the more recent *Foucault's Pendulum*. If you are looking for complex, insightful, intriguing, and intellectual reading, Eco's your man. Last but not least, one Italian writer whom children all over the world should know is **Calo Collodi**, the author of *Pinnochio*.

SHAKESPEARE'S ITALY

The Immortal Bard chose Italy as the setting for a number of his best-known masterpieces: **Othello** *takes place in part in Venice, and features both honorable and conniving Venetians;* **Two Gentlemen from Verona** *and* **Romeo & Juliet** *take place in Verona (the latter was pretty much lifted from Luigi da Porto's identical story, and today you can visit Juliet's House in Verona);* **The Merchant of Venice** *of course takes place in Venice;* **The Taming of the Shrew** *concerns the doings of rich Paduans, Pisans, and Veronans; about half of* **A Winter's Tale** *takes part in Sicily; all of* **Much Ado About Nothing** *takes place in Sicily; and finally,* **All's Well That Ends Well** *has one part set in Florence.*

Ancient Rome and the ageless themes of power, love, and intrigue also held great allure for Shakespeare: pick up **Julius Caesar, Titus Andronicus, Troilius & Cressida,** *or* **Coriolanus** *for some light reading about the tragic nature of the men and women who made the Roman Empire the world's first superpower!*

18. SPORTS & RECREATION

There are many different sporting activities to participate in and around Rome, since the city is only 15 miles from the beach and 65 miles from great skiing country. Below is a list of possible activities:

AMUSEMENT PARK

For people with a lot of money in their pockets, there is a permanent amusement park, **Luna Park**, in EUR. To get there take the Metropolitana on Linea B to the EUR stop. EUR stands for *Esposizione Universale Romana*, a grandiose project sponsored by Mussolini as a permanent exhibition to the glory of Rome. The park is to your left as you enter EUR along the Via Cristoforo Colombo.

BICYCLING

Reckless Roman drivers can make biking on the city streets dangerous if you're not careful, and especially if you're a young North American used to the defensive drivers in the States and Canada.

But you can rent bicycles at many different locations (see *Getting Around Town*) and take them for a trip through the **Borghese Gardens** (see *Seeing the Sights*).

BOATING

Rowboats can be rented at the **Giardino del Lago** in the Villa Borghese. You can also rent dinghies at **Lago di Bracciano** and **Lido di Ostia** (see *Day Trips & Excursions* below).

BOWLING

There are two particularly good bowling alleys *(bocciodromi)* in Rome. Unless you have your own car, both of these places are far outside of the old walls of the city and thus rather difficult to get to except by taxi.
- **Bowling Brunswick**, *Lungotevere Aqua Acetosa, Tel. 396-6696*
- **Bowling Roma**, *Viale Regina Margherita 181, Tel. 861-184*

GOLF

There are a variety of 18 hole and 9 hole courses all around Rome:
- **L'Eucalyptus Circolo del Golf**, *Via della Cogna 3/5, 04011 Aprilla. Tel. 06/926-252. Fax 06/926-8502*. Located 30 km from Rome, this is an 18 hole par 72 course that is 6,372 meters long. It is open all year except on Tuesdays. They also have a small executive course, driving range, pro shop, tennis courts, swimming pool, guest quarters, and a restaurant/bar.
- **Golf Club Torvalaianica**, *Via Enna 30, 00040 Marina di Ardea. Tel. 06/913-3250. Fax 06/913-3592*. Located 25 km from Rome this is a 9 hole par 31 course that is 2,208 meters long. It is open all year except Mondays. They have a driving range as well as a restaurant/bar.
- **Golf Club Castel Gandolpho**, *Via Santo Spirito 13, 00040 Castel Gandolpho. Tel. 06/931-2301. Fax 06/931-2244*. This is an 18 hole par 72 course near the Pope's summer residence that is 5,855 meters long. It's open all year except on Mondays. They have a driving range, carts, pro shop, swimming pool, and a restaurant/bar.
- **Circolo del Golf di Fioranello**, *Via della Falcognana 61, 00134 Roma. Tel. 06/713-8080 or 731-2213. Fax 06/713-8212*. Located 17 km from the center of Rome, this is an 18 hole par 70 course that is 5,417 meters long. It is open all year except for Wednesdays. They also have a driving range, pro shop, swimming pool, and a bar/restaurant.
- **Macro Simone Golf Club**, *Via di Marco Simone, 00012 Guidonia. Tel. 0774/370-469. Fax 0774/370-476*. Located 17 km from Rome, this is an 18 hole par 72 course that is 6,360 meters long. It is open all year except for Tuesdays. They also have an 18 hole executive course, driving range, pro shop, swimming pool, tennis courts, massage room, sauna, gymnasium, and an excellent restaurant and bar.
- **Golf Club Parco de' Medici**, *Viale Parco de' Medici 20, 00148 Roma. Tel. 06/655-33477. Fax 06/655-3344*. Located 10 km outside of the city center, this is an 18 hole par 72 course that is 5,827 meters long. It is open all year except on Tuesdays. They also have a driving range, swimming pool, tennis courts, and a restaurant/bar. This is the course most accessible and nearest the city center.
- **Circolo del Golf di Roma – Aqua Santa**, *Via Appia Nuova 716 or Via Dell'Aquasanta 3, Roma 00178, Tel. 06/780-3407. Fax 06/7834-6219*. Located 11 km from Rome, this is an 18 hole par 71 course that is 5,825 meters long. It is open all year except on Mondays. They have a driving range, putting green, swimming pool, and a restaurant/bar.
- **Olgiata**, *Largo Olgiata 15, Roma 00123, Tel. 06/378-9141. Fax 06/378-9968*. Located 19 km from the center of Rome, in a housing development similar to many golf courses in the U.S. At Olgiata there is an 18 hole par 72 course that is 6,396 meters long and a 9 hole par

34 course that is 2,968 meters long. The course is open all year except on Mondays. They have a driving range, pro shop, swimming pool and a bar/restaurant.

RIVER TRIPS

In July and August you can take a river trip through central Rome. The trips are organized by the **Amici del Tevere**. Check the journal *This Week in Rome* for details, available in most hotels.

SPECTATOR SPORTS

If watching from the sidelines is more up your alley, Italy goes **soccer** crazy every Sunday from September to May. Virtually every city and every town has a team that plays professionally. The Italian league is separated into four divisions, or *Serie*. The first division is *Serie A*, which plays the best soccer in the world, and the bottom division is *Serie D*.

Some cities have several teams, like Rome which has two *Serie A* teams (**Lazio** and **Roma**), three from *Serie C*, and one from *Serie D*. The Serie A and B games are the most fun to go to since the fans are so passionate. Tickets can be hard to come by since the games are so popular, but contact your hotel's concierge and s/he may be able to scrape (scalp?) some up for you from a relative.

If you don't want to go into the stadium you might want to go to the game to get some great gifts from the vendors that sell team paraphernalia outside. Certain types of product piracy is legal in Italy, and putting the names and logos of sports teams on unofficial products is one of them. The quality of the shirts, hats, and scarves is just as good and about one fourth the price of the official products.

Surprisingly enough, **basketball** and **baseball** both have professional leagues. Most major cities now have teams. Professional baseball has been around for only about twenty years, and is still at the level of minor league play in the US, but is starting to catch on in popularity. Ask your concierge about upcoming games.

SWIMMING

The major outdoor pool in Rome is at the **Foro Italico** (*Tel. 396-3958*), open June to September. An indoor pool at the Foro Italico is open November to May.

The best beach is at **Lido di Ostia**, less than an hour west-northwest of Rome. The beaches are clean and large. They have plenty of *cabanas* to rent where you can change your clothes, and there are some excellent seafood restaurants where you can leisurely eat, sip wine, and enjoy the beautiful Italian summers.

TENNIS

The following public courts require reservations:
- **Circolo Montecitorio,** *Via Campi Sportivi 5, Tel. 875-275*
- **EUR,** *Viale dell'Artigianato 2, Tel. 592-4693*
- **Foro Italico,** *Tel. 361-9021*
- **Tennis Belle Arti,** *Via Flaminia 158, Tel. 360-0602*

19. PRACTICAL INFORMATION

ATM MACHINES

ATM (**Bancomat machines**)has arrived in Italy. If you have an ATM card it is now possible to withdraw money directly from your checking account at home. One drawback is that you can only withdraw up to L500,000 each day. But the advantages of using an ATM over traditional travelers checks is easy to discern.

The ATM gives you excellent, up to date exchange rates better than most exchange offices. For example, when I used one, the official exchange rate was L1,640 per dollar, I got L1,615 from the ATM and the going rate at exchange places was L1,570. There is a bank fee, a fixed rate of $1 to $3 which is usually lower than the fees charged by exchange places. Another advantage is that you are not constrained by bank hours.

But do bring some travelers checks with you, since if there is a bank strike (and that could happen at any time in Italy), the ATMs won't be filled up with cash.

BABYSITTERS

A list of reliable, English-speaking babysitters can be obtained through the **American Women's Association of Rome** (AWAR), *Tel. 06/482-5268*. In addition the American Embassy also has babysitter listings.

BANK HOURS & CHANGING MONEY

Banks are open Monday through Friday from 8:30am to 1:30pm and some do reopen from 2:45pm or so to 3:45pm or so. Some exceptions to that rule are:
- **American Express**, *Piazza di Spagna 38, Tel. 06/67-64-1. Open weekdays 9:00am to 5:30pm, and Saturdays from 9:00am to 12:30pm.*
  American Express is always a great option, especially if you have their travelers checks. But remember, the lines here are long, since every other guide book in the world suggests going to AMEX. But if you're

adventurous and looking to interact with other travelers, these lines are great meeting spots.
- **Banco Nazionale del Lavoro**, *Via Veneto 11, Tel. 06/475-0421. Open 8:30am to 6:00pm Monday through Saturday.*
- **American Service Bank**, *Piazza Mignanelli 15. Open 8:30am to 6:30pm Monday through Saturday.*

Besides banks, there are plenty of exchange bureaus (*casa di cambio*) around some of which actually offer great rates and low service charges. When using these tiny, hole in the wall yet completely reputable places, if you are changing small amounts (i.e. $20) look for ones that offer a low percentage transaction fee (i.e. 1% to 2% of the amount you're exchanging), and if you are changing large amounts, find one that has a reasonable set fee (i.e. L3-5,000). One such exchange place that is open until 9:00pm on weekdays, and until 2:00pm on Saturdays, is in the **Stazione Termini**. But use this as a last resort since the lines are always ridiculously long, just like American Express.

Another option, if all else is closed, is to simply change your money at your hotel or any of the four star hotels that line the Via Veneto. You won't get the best rate but at least you'll have money.

Credit Card Lost?
If you lose your credit card, these numbers will come in handy:
- **American Express**, *Tel. 06/72282*
- **Bank Americard**, *Tel. Toll Free 167/821-001*
- **Mastercard** or **VISA**, *Tel. Toll Free 167/868-086*
- **Diner's Club**, *Tel. Toll Free 167-864064*
- **Citibank**, *Tel. 06/854-561*

BUSINESS HOURS

From October to June, most shops are open from 9:00am to 1:00pm and from 3:30pm to 7:30pm, and are closed all day Sundays and on Monday mornings. Then from June to September, when it really starts to get hot in Rome, the morning hours remain the same, but the mid-day siesta time is slightly extended to 4:00pm and sometimes 4:30pm, which then pushes closing time back to 7:30pm or 8:00pm. In conjunction with the Sunday/Monday mornings closed, shops also close for half days on Saturday. Is that clear?

Food stores, like an *alimentari*, generally are open from 8:30am to 1:30pm (so stock up on your picnic supplies before you need them) and from 5:00pm to 7:30pm, and during the winter months they are closed on Thursdays.

PRACTICAL INFORMATION 223

CHURCH CEREMONIES IN ENGLISH

- **All Saints'** (Church of England), *Via del Babuino 153b, Tel. 06/3600-2171. Sunday Mass 8:30am and 10:30am (sung)*
- **Methodist Church**, *Via del Banco di Santo Spirito 3, Tel. 06/686-8314. 10:30 Sunday Service*
- **Rome Baptist Church**, *Piazza San Lorenzo in Lucina 35, Tel. 06/687-6652. 10:00am Sunday worship*
- **St. Andrews** (Scottish Presbyterian), *Via XX Settembre 7, Tel. 06/482-7627. Sunday Service at 11:00am*
- **St. Patrick's** (English-speaking Catholic), *Via Boncompagni 31, Tel. 06/488-5716. Sunday mass at 10:00am*
- **St. Paul's** (American Episcopal), *Via Napoli 58, Tel. 06/488-3339. Sunday Mass 8:30am and 10:30pm (sung)*
- **San Silvestro** (English-speaking Catholic), *Piazza San Silvestro 1, Tel. 06/679-7775. Sunday Mass at 10:00am and 6:00pm*
- **Santa Susanna** (American Catholic), *Piazza San Bernardo, Tel. 06/488-2748. Sunday Mass at 9:00am, 10:30am, and noon. Saturdays at 6:00pm*
- **Synagogue**, *(No services in English) Via Lungotevere dei Cenci, Tel. 06/687-5051*

COMPUTER STORES & INTERNET ACCESS

If you decide to bring your laptop, remember to carry along a three pronged adapter so you can plug it into the wall for re-charges. You can get them at most hardware, Circuit City or Radio Shack stores in North America.

If you can't find these devices, you can order them from the **Franzus Company**, (pronounced Francis), *Murtha Industrial Park, PO Box, 142, Beacon Falls, CT 06403, Tel. 203/723-6664, Fax 203/723-6666*. They also have a free brochure, *Foreign Electricity Is No Deep Dark Secret,* that can be mailed or faxed to you.

If you forget, most computer stores in Italy carry them too but at a much higher price. You will also need an adapter to plug in your modem cable to access your e-mails. Some of the plugs look like they'll fit but they don't.

Also, when dialing out you may have to add a prefix "8" to your modem string in the software setup. Most hotels in Italy require an "8" to be dialed for you to access an outside line.

The only access number I am aware of is for **America Online**. That number is in Milan, *Tel. 02/9530-1301*.

DOCTORS & DENTISTS (ENGLISH-SPEAKING)

In case of need, the **American Embassy** *(Via Vittorio Veneto 119, Tel. 06/46741)* will gladly supply you with a recommended list of English-speaking doctors and dentists. A hospital where English is spoken, **Salvator Mundi**, is at *Viale della Mura Gianicolensi 67, Tel. 588-961.* I had my tonsils out there and am doing fine today. Another place is the **Rome American Hospital** at *Via VE Longoni 69, Tel. 06/22551.* They have a physician on call 24 hours a day.

An organization that can hook you up with physicians all over the world is **Personal Physician Worldwide**, run by Myra Altschuler. Her opinion is "This is a 'just in case' type of planning that makes a lot of sense. You never know where you'll be when you need the care of a competent doctor." You can reach them toll-free at *Tel. 888-657-8114* or: *Fax 301-718-7725; e-mail myra@personalphysicians.com; www.personalphysicians.com.*

A recommended heart specialist is **Aleardo William Madden, MD**, a Fellow in the American Heart Association. For an appointment, call *06/7049-1747 (Via Baldo degli Ubaldi 272.)*

An American trained, English speaking dentist recommended by the American community in Rome is **Dr. Daniel Giacomuzzi**, *Via Benedetto Croce 22 (near Luna Park in EUR), Tel. 06/540-7883.* There is free valet parking. Another recommended dentist is **Dr. John Costanzo**, *Via Friggeri 55, Tel. 06/3545-4172.*

EMBASSIES & CONSULATES

- **United States**, *Via Veneto 199, Tel. 06/46741*
- **Canadian Embassy**, *Via Conciliazione 4D, Tel. 06/68-30-73-16*
- **United Kingdom**, *Via XX Settembre 90, Tel. 06/482-5441*
- **Australia**, *Via Alessandro 215, Tel. 06/852-721*
- **New Zealand**, *Via Zara 28, Tel. 06/440-2928 or 440-40-35*
- **Ireland**, *Largo del Nazereno, Tel. 06/678-25-41*
- **South Africa**, *Via Tanaro 14, Tel. 06/841-97-94*

EMERGENCIES

To call the local police in case of an emergency, the **Polizia Municipiale** are at *Tel. 06/676-91* and are located at *Via delle Consolazione 4.*

FESTIVALS IN ROME

- **January 1**, Candle-lit processional in the Catacombs of Priscilla to mark the martyrdom of the early Christians.
- **January 5**, Last day of the Epiphany Fair in the Piazza Navona. A carnival celebrates the ending.

- **January 21**, *Festa di Sant'Agnese*. Two lambs are blessed then shorn. Held at Sant'Agnese Fuori le Mura.
- **March 9**, *Festa di Santa Francesca Romana*. Cars are blessed at the Piazzale del Coloseo near the church of Santa Francesca Romana.
- **March 19**, *Festa di San Giuseppe*. The statue of the saint is decorated with lamps and placed in the Trionfale Quarter, north of the Vatican. There are food stalls, sporting events and concerts.
- **April**, *Festa della Primavera* (festival of Spring). The Spanish Steps are festooned with rows upon rows of azaleas.
- **Good Friday**, The Pope leads a candlelit procession at 9pm in the Colosseum.
- **Easter Sunday**, Pope gives his annual blessing from his balcony at noon.
- **April 21**, Anniversary of the founding of Rome held in Piazza del Campidoglio with flag waving ceremonies and other pageantry.
- **May 1**, *Festa del Lavoro*. Public Holiday
- **First 10 days of May**, international horse show held in the Villa Borghese at Piazza di Siena.
- **May 6**, Swearing in of the new guards at the Vatican in St Peter's square. Anniversary of the sacking of Rome in 1527.
- **Mid-May**, Antiques fair along Via dei Coronari
- **First Sunday in June**, *Festa della Repubblica* involving a military parade centered on the Via dei Fori Imperiali. It's like something you'd see in Moscow during the Cold War.
- **June 23-24**, *Festa di San Giovanni*. Held in the Pizza di Porta San Giovanni. Traditional food sold: roast baby pig and snails.
- **June 29**, *Festa di San Pietro*. Festival to Saint Peter. Very important religious ceremony for Romans.
- **July**, *Tevere Expo* involving booths and stalls displaying arts and crafts, with food and wine lined up along the Tiber. At night there are fireworks displays and folk music festivals.
- **July 4**, A picnic organized by the American community outside Rome. Need to contact the American Embassy *(06/46741)* to make reservations to get on the buses leaving from the Embassy.
- **Last 2 weeks in July**, *Festa de Noiantri* involving procession, other festivities, feasting and abundance of wine all in Trastevere.
- **July & August**, Open air opera performances in the Baths of Caracalla.
- **August 15**, *Ferragosto*. Midsummer holiday. Everything closes down.
- **Early September**, *Sagra dell'Uva*. A harvest festival with reduced price grapes and music provided by performers in period costumes held in the Roman Forum.
- **Last week of September**, Crafts show held in Via dell'Orso near Piazza Navona.

- **Early November**, Santa Susanna Church Bazaar. Organized by the church for the Catholic American community to raise money for the church. Great home-made pies and cookies as well as used books and clothes. Auction of more expensive items held also.
- **December 8**, Festa della Madonna Immacolata in Piazza di Spagna. Floral wreaths inlaid around the column of the Madonna and one is laid at the top by firefighters.
- **Mid-December**, Start of the Epiphany Fair in the Piazza Navona. All throughout the piazza a fair filled with food stands, candy stands, toy shops opens to the public. Lasts a week. A must see.
- **December 20-January 10**, Many churches display elaborate nativity scenes.
- **December 24**, Midnight Mass at many churches. I recommend the one at Santa Maria Maggiore.
- **December 25**, Pope gives his blessing at noon from his Balcony at St. Peter's. The entire square is packed with people.
- **December 31**, New Year's Eve. Much revelry. At the strike of midnight people start throwing old furniture out their windows into the streets, so be off the streets by that time, or else your headache from the evening's festivities will be much worse.

LAUNDRY SERVICE
- **Uondo Blu**, *Principe Amadeo 70, near Termini Station*. Coin operated laundry open until 1am. If you need clean clothes, this is the only place to come that is inexpensive. Otherwise it's the wash-in-the-sink-action-and-let-them-dry-for-days scenario.

PAPAL AUDIENCES

General audiences with the Pope are usually held once a week (Wednesday at 11:00am) in Vatican City. To participate in a general audience, get information through the **North American College** *(Via dell'Umita 30, Tel. 06/679-0658, Fax 06/679-1448)*, the American seminary in Rome. Catholics are requested to have a letter of introduction from their parish priest. Ticket pickup is the Tuesday before the Wednesday audience.

During the audience women should dress modestly, with arms and head covered, and dark or subdued colors are requested. Men are asked to wear a tie and a jacket.

Also at noon, every Sunday the Pope addresses the crowds gathered beneath his window in St. Peter's square.

During the latter part of the summer, because of the heat in Rome, and now more so for tradition, the Pope moves to his summer residence

PRACTICAL INFORMATION 227

at **Castel Gandolpho** in the Alban Hills about sixteen miles southeast of Rome. Audiences are also regularly held there.

POSTAL SERVICES

You can buy stamps at local tobacconists (they are marked with a "T" outside) as well as post offices. Mail boxes are colored red, except for the international ones which are blue. Post offices are open from 8:25am to 1:50pm on weekdays, and 8:25am to 11:50am Saturday. Some, like the one on Via Firenze, near the Economy bookstore are open until 5pm Monday through Saturday. The two exceptions to this rule are: the **main post office** (Piazza San Silvestro), which is open Monday through Friday from 9:00am to 6:00pm, Saturday from 9:00am to 2:00pm, and Sundays from 9:00am to 6:00pm; and the branch at **Stazione Termini** that keeps the same hours.

If you want to have your postcards mailed by the Vatican, with their official stamp, go to the offices off the right hand collonnade of St. Peter's square near the newsstand, and to the left of St. Peter's square near the Information Office. They keep the 9:00am to 2:00pm hours.

PHARMACIES

Farmacia are open from 9am to 1pm and reopen from 3:30pm to 7:30pm. At nights and on Sundays and holidays, one pharmacy in each district remains open on a rotating schedule. For information, dial 192 then 1 through 5 depending on the zone (see phone book for zones) for location of the pharmacy nearest you. Also a list of open pharmacies for holidays and Sundays is published in the Rome daily, *Il Messagero*.

POLICE

- **Pubblica Sicurezza**, *Tel. 06/4686* (for theft, lost and found, petty crimes)
- **City Police** (Vigili Urbani), *Tel. 06/67691* (for car towings)
- **Carabinieri**, *Tel. 112* (for emergencies, violent crimes, etc.)
- **Highway Police** (Polizia Stradale), *Tel. 06/557-7905* (for parking tickets, etc.)

PUBLIC RESTROOMS

These are scarcer than flying pigs, but for the year 2000 more are being established all over Italy. When in need, there are always McDonalds, which have sprouted up all over Rome and Italy after they bought out the Italian burger chain *Burghy*.

If no McDonalds is evident, try a well-heeled restaurant or hotel. Ask for the *servizio*, or *toilette*.

SUPERMARKETS

You can usually find all the food you need at an *alimentari*, but if you want a wider selection, here are some supermarkets close to the center of Rome (hours 7:30am to 1:30pm and reopen from 4:00pm to 7:30pm. Closed Thursday afternoons in winter and Saturday afternoons in summer):
- **Maxi Sidis**, *Via Isonzo 21D*
- **Supermex**, *Viale Liegi 29*
- **Standa**, *Viale Regina Margherita 117*

TOURIST INFORMATION & MAPS

You can buy maps and guide books at most newsstands and bookstores. This may be necessary even though the tourist offices give away free maps for the subway, buses, as well as an extensive map of the streets of Rome. Most of the time, especially in high season, they are out of all of the above. And in Grand Italian Fashion, nothing gets done about it. So newsstands are your only recourse.

Below are some sources for tourist information:
- **American Express**, *Piazza di Spagna 38, Tel. 06/676-41*
- **Rome Provincial Tourist Board** (**EPT**), *Via Parigi 5, Tel. 06/488-3748*
- **EPT Termini**, *between tracks #2 and 3, Tel. 06/487-1270*
- **EPT Fiumicino**, *just outside customs, Tel. 06/601-1255*
- **Italian Government Travel Office** (ENIT), *Via Marghera 2, Tel. 06/49711*
- **Enjoy Rome**, *Via Marghera 2, Tel. 06/446-3379 or 444-1663*
- **Centro Turistico Studentesco e Giovanile**, *66 Via Nazionale, Tel. 06/467-91*

TOUR COMPANIES

Some of the companies that offer you comfortable, air-conditioned modern buses and complete guided tours of Rome, the countryside and beyond, are listed below. Most are open Monday through Friday 9:00am-5:30pm, Saturday 9:00am-12:30pm and closed on Sundays.
- **American Express**, *Piazza di Spagna 38, Tel. 06/676-41. For Lost Travellers checks (toll free) 167-872000. For lost/stolen cards, Tel. 06/7228-0371*
- **Carrani Tours**, *Vie V.E. Orlando 95, Tel. 06/488-0510. Fax 06/4890-3564*
- **Thomas Cooke Travel**, *Piazza Barberini 21A, Tel. 06/482-81-82*
- **Wagon-Lit**, *Via Gradisca 29, Tel. 06/8-54-38-86*

20. EXCURSIONS FROM ROME

I've planned some fun nearby excursions for you: Tivoli Gardens, Castel Gandolfo, Frascati, Ostia Antica, Lago di Bracciano and Cervetri.

TIVOLI GARDENS

Tivoli has about 45,000 inhabitants. It stands on the **Aniene**, a tributary of the Tiber, and overlooks Rome from its place on the **Sabine hills**. This town is where the wealthy Romans built their magnificent summer villas. The three main attractions are **Villa Adriana** (Hadrian's Villa), **Villa d'Este**, and **Villa Gregoriana**.

The **Villa Adriana's** main attraction is its huge grounds, where you and lizards can bask in the sun. There are plenty of secluded spots to relax or enjoy a picnic on the grass. The building itself was begun in 125 CE and completed 10 years later, and was at the time the largest and most impressive villa in the Roman Empire. From his travels **Hadrian**, an accomplished architect, found ideas that he recreated in his palace. The idea for the **Poikile**, the massive colonnade through which you enter the villa, came from Athens. And the **Serapeum** and **Canal of Canopus** were based on the Temple of Serapis near Alexandria, Egypt.

The **Villa D'Este's** main draw are its many wonderful fountains. The villa itself was built on the site of a Benedictine convent in the mid-16th century. The **Owl Fountain** and **Organ Fountain** are especially beautiful, as is the secluded pathway of the **Terrace of the Hundred Fountains**. If you make it out to Tivoli, these gardens and their fountains cannot be missed, especially at night during the months of May through September when they are floodlit.

The **Villa Gregoriana** is known for the **Grande Cascata** (the Great Fall), which is a result of Gregory XVI diverting the river in the last century to avoid flooding. The park around the cascade has smaller ones as well as grottoes. This is the least interesting of the three villas.

230 ROME & SOUTHERN ITALY GUIDE

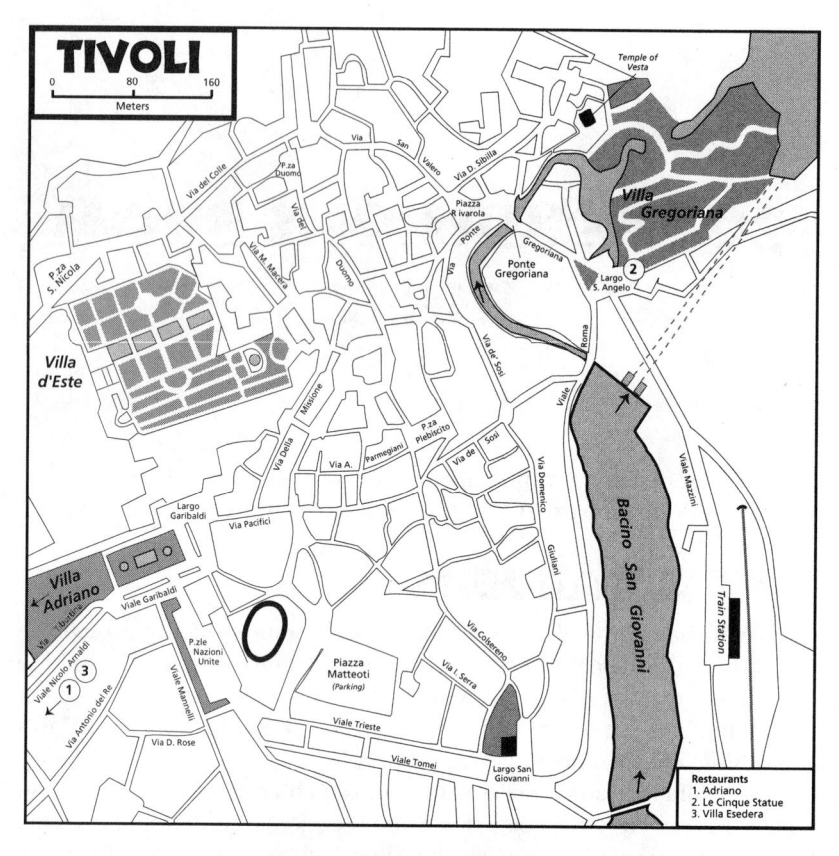

The addresses and hours of the three villas are:
- **Villa Adriana**, *Bivio Villa Adriana, 3.5 miles southwest of Tivoli. Open Tuesday-Sunday, 9:30am-1 hour before sunset. Closed Mondays. Small fee required.*
- **Villa D'Este**, *Viale delle Centro Fontane. Open Tuesday-Sunday, 9:30am to 1.5 hours before sunset. May-September also open 9:00pm-11:30pm with the garden floodlit. Closed Mondays. Small fee required. Sundays free.*
- **Villa Gregoriana**, *Largo Sant'Angelo. Open Tuesday-Sunday 9:30am to 1 hour before sunset. Closed Mondays. Small fee required. Sundays free.*

ARRIVALS & DEPARTURES

Tivoli is about 23 miles east of Rome.

By Car

Take the Via Tiburtina (SS5). The Villa Adriana lies to the right about 3.5 miles before the town.

By Train
From Stazione Termini the trip takes about 40 minutes.

WHERE TO EAT

Tivoli simply abounds with restaurants, many offering a magnificent panoramic view of Rome. Here are some of my suggestions.

1. ADRIANO, *(near Hadrian's Villa), Via di Villa Adriana 194, Tel. 0774/529-174. Closed Sunday nights. All credit cards accepted. Dinner for two L130,000.*

Basically at the front of the entrance to Hadrian's Villa, this restaurant attached to a hotel has a beautiful garden terrace. They make excellent *crostini di verdure* (fried dough with vegetables inside), *raviolini primavera con ricotta e spinaci* (ravioli with spring vegetables, spinach and fresh ricotta), *tagliata di coniglio alle erbette* (rabbit with herbs) and more. The prices are a little rich for my blood, especially with the L6,000 for *coperto* (just sitting down and ordering).

2. LE CINQUE STATUE, *Largo S Angelo 1, Tel. 0774/20366. Closed Fridays. Dinner for two L110,000. All credit cards accepted.*

In front of the entrance to Villa Gregoriana this place has outside seating where you can enjoy the local cuisine. They make many of their pastas in house so they're sure to be fresh. They also specialize in meats, especially the *maialino* (baby pork) and *abbacchio* (lamb) *arrosto* as well as their *verdure fritte* (fried vegetables).

3. VILLA ESEDRA, *(near Hadrian's Villa), Via di Villa Adriana 51, Tel. 0774/534-716. Closed Wednesdays. Dinner for two L70,000. All credit cards accepted.*

You can get some interesting antipasti like the *insalatine di pesce* (small fish salad), then you can move on to their pastas, which are all made in house, and are all superb, especially the *spaghetti all'amatriciana* (with tomatoes, cream and spices) and the *penne all'arrabbiata* (with tomatoes, garlic oil and hot pepper). The meats are a little suspect, so you may get away with a less expensive bill if you only try the pastas.

CASTEL GANDOLPHO

Beautifully located above **Lake Albano**, is **Castel Gandolpho**, the location of the summer residence of the Pope. From up at the Castel Gandolpho, you can enjoy a wonderful view of the wooded slopes that fall swiftly down into the murky waters of a volcanic crater.

The one real sight to see is the **Palazzo Pontificio** (Papal Palace), built in 1624. During the summer months when the Pope is in residence, every Sunday at noon His Eminence gives an address in the courtyard of the palace. No permit is required to enter. First come, first served is the rule.

ARRIVALS & DEPARTURES

Castel Gandolpho is about 15 miles east of Rome.

By Car
Take the Via Appia Nuova (SS7) for about 30 minutes.

By Train
From Stazione Termini, it's about 35 minutes. From the station you will have to take a local taxi up to the Castel, unless you feel adventurous and want to walk the three kilometers uphill. Just follow the signs on the side of the road.

WHERE TO EAT

ANTICO RISTORANTE PAGNANELLI, *Piazza A Gramsci 4, Tel. 06/936-0004. Closed Tuesdays. Dinner for two L90,000. All credit cards accepted.*

This restaurant with a nice view of the lake has been in existence since 1882, and they still serve all the traditional dishes made with produce from the local countryside. They make a wonderful *strozzapreti all'amatriciana* (pasta with tomatoes, cream and spices), *risotto al'erbe* (rice dish with herbs), *maialino arrosto* (roast baby pork), *bracciole di cinghiale* (roast boar "arms"), and other savory dishes. Rumor has it that the Pope even has stopped in once or twice.

FRASCATI

If wine is what you're looking for, **Frascati** is where you want to be. This town's wine is world famous, and something you simply cannot miss. The ambiance of this hill town is magnificent.

Frascati is a great place to stay while visiting Rome if you can't stand the urban hustle and bustle. Since it's only 30 minutes and $5 away, Frascati's relaxing pace, scenic views, quaint little wine shops, excellent local restaurants, and winding old cobblestone streets should be seriously considered as an alternative to downtown Rome.

Since this is still primarily an excursion, I've listed the restaurants first and hotels second for this beautiful town – even though I hope some of you will opt to stay here and enjoy Frascati's many charms.

ARRIVALS & DEPARTURES

Frascati is roughly 14 miles southeast of Rome.

By Car
Take the Via Tuscolana (SS215) up to the hill town (25 minute drive).

EXCURSIONS FROM ROME 233

FRASCATI

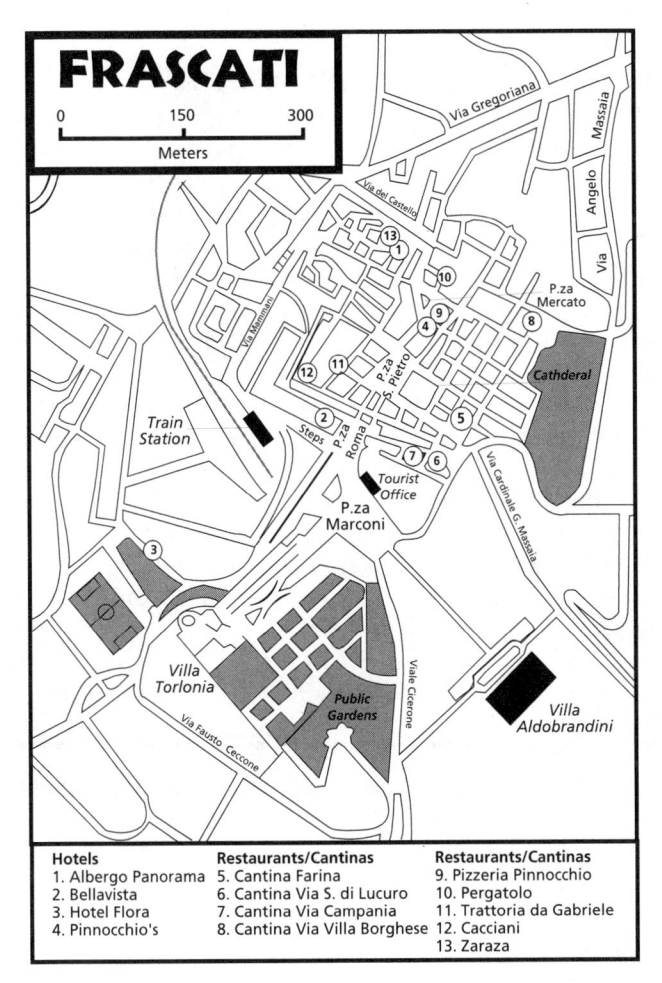

0 — 150 — 300 Meters

Hotels
1. Albergo Panorama
2. Bellavista
3. Hotel Flora
4. Pinnocchio's

Restaurants/Cantinas
5. Cantina Farina
6. Cantina Via S. di Lucuro
7. Cantina Via Campania
8. Cantina Via Villa Borghese

Restaurants/Cantinas
9. Pizzeria Pinnocchio
10. Pergatolo
11. Trattoria da Gabriele
12. Cacciani
13. Zaraza

By Train

From Stazione Termini, board a local train that leaves every forty minutes or so from Track 27. The ride lasts a little over 35 minutes. Cost L4,500.

WHERE TO STAY

1. ALBERGHO PANORAMA, *Piazza Carlo Casini 3, Frascati 00044. Tel. 06/942-1800 or 941-7955. 9 rooms, two with bath. Single with bath L68,000-90,000; Single without bath L50,000-70,000; Double without bath L60,000-90,000. L15,000 for an extra bed. L30,000 for all meals. No credit cards accepted.* **

Situated in the centro storico with a beautiful panoramic view of Rome. This is a small but comfortable hotel for those on a budget.

> **CONSIDER FRASCATI!**
>
> If you are someone who would rather not experience the hectic pace of a big city, but you still want to see all that Rome has to offer, stay in Frascati. This quaint, charming, quiet, little hill town is the perfect place to get away from it all while still having access to everything. The town is only 35 minutes away by train (the fare is L4,500) and the trains run every 45 minutes or so until 10:00pm. Granted there might be a concern if you want to take a nap in the middle of the afternoon, but that is what the Borghese gardens are for. Bring a picnic lunch and take a little siesta in the shade in one of the prettiest and peaceful gardens in any city in the world.
>
> In Frascati, you'll be able enjoy many good restaurants, sample the fine local wines from quaint little wine stores that are located all over the city. They serve you glasses or carafes from huge vats. You'll also be able to savor the ambiance of an ancient medieval town, with its cobblestone streets and twisting alleys. Here you'll be able to gaze out your windows and see lush valleys below, instead of looking out onto another building as you would probably do in Rome. And if you come in October, you'll be able to experience a wine festival of bacchanalian proportions.
>
> So if you are used to the calm serenity of country life, but still want to experience the beauty that Rome has to offer, Frascati may be your answer.

2. BELLAVISTA, *Piazza Roma 2, 00044 Frascati. Tel. 06/942-1068 or 942-6320. Fax 06/942-1068. 13 rooms all with bath. Double L140,000-160,000. Breakfast L10,000. All credit cards accepted.* ***

You have room service, TV in your room, and a hotel bar, as well as a nice view of the valley. The rooms are clean and comfortable as befits a good country three star. The building is quite quaint, and old but restored perfectly for your comfort. I love the high ceilings in the rooms, making them feel much larger.

3. HOTEL FLORA, *Via Vittorio Veneto 8 00044 Frascati. Tel. 06/941-6110. Fax 06/942-0198. 33 rooms only 30 with bath. Single L120,000; Double L150,000. Breakfast L12,000. All credit cards accepted.* ***

An old hotel decorated with style, located in a central position in Frascati. Much better amenities than the Bellavista, but not as good a view. Located a little ways outside of town, this hotel is set in a wonderfully tranquil environment. A good place to stay.

4. PINNOCCHIO'S, *Piazza del Mercata 20, Tel. 06/941-7883. Fax 06/941-7884. Single L60,000-80,000 (Double used as a single); Double L100,000-130,000. Seven rooms all with bath, mini-bar, and TV. No credit cards accepted.* **

Large comfortable rooms with gigantic bathrooms. Upstairs from the restaurant, so you can grab yourself a snack until late in the evening. The office is in the restaurant so you'll need to enter there to get your key. Perfectly located on the central market square. A sight you have to see while in Frascati and a great place to get some fruits, vegetables (you can even get fresh bags of mixed salad), meats, and cheeses. The place is alive with bargaining and local greetings.

WHERE TO EAT/WINE BARS

Some of the wine bars are so small and so nonchalant about the tourist trade that they don't even have names. Also many of the places do not have telephones. One of the owners explained to me, *"Why should we have telephones when we can walk over and talk in person?"* That makes sense, since Frascati is such a small intimate little town.

Don't be put off by this casual hill town attitude, since the ones without names or phones are some of the best places to visit. Enjoy.

5. CANTINA FARINA, *Vini Propri, Via Cavour 20. No Telephone.*

A real wine bar, not a fern infested one. With a tile floor, collapsible wooden tables and chairs and great wine served from vats, here you can get a real taste for how the Italians enjoy life. Located near a school, so it can get periodically noisy during the day.

6. CANTINA VIA SEPULCRO DI LUCURO, *Via Sepulcro di Lucuro 6. No Telephone.*

Located just off the main road (Via Catone), this place has a small area for seating outside separated from the rest of the world by large planters. The inside is quite cool, like a wine cellar. Just inside the door is an antique wine press that they still use during the pressing season. Inside or out you'll get some of the best wines Frascati has to offer here.

7. CANTINA VIA CAMPANIA, *Via Campania 17. No Telephone.*

Just down the road from the wine bar listed above, this place has one and a half of its four inside walls covered with wine vats, and the rest of the space taken up with strange looking tools used in the wine trade, as well as large empty bottles that you only wish you could take home with you ... full. The owner is quite friendly and if it's not too crowded will sit down and chat. Great wine. Wonderful atmosphere.

8. CANTINA VIA VILLA BORGHESE, *Via Villa Borghese 20. No Telephone.*

Small wine store filled with large 1,000,000 liter barrels called *botte*, and 500,000 liter barrels called *mezza botte*. Each cask is numbered and initialed with the vineyard it came from. Not very scenic atmosphere and no tables to sit at, but they will sell you a bottle of their finest for only L2,000. That's $1.50 for an excellent bottle of Frascati wine.

9. PIZZERIA/BIRRERIA PINNOCCHIO, *Piazza del Mercato 20, Tel. 06/941-6694 or 942-0330. Dinner for two L55,000.*

A large statue of Pinnocchio advertises this superb restaurant in Frascati's quaintest and most vibrant square (it's actually a triangle). There is outside seating with large planters separating you from the pace of this market-dominated piazza. Inside you'll find tiled floors and wood paneling giving the place a nice rustic flair. They serve great *canneloni ai quattro formaggi* (with four cheeses), as well as great Roman staples such as *amatriciana, carbonara, and vongole.*

For seconds try their *scampi alla griglia* (grilled shrimp) which is reasonably priced at only L16,000. If you find you've lingered too long over your Sambuca, Pinnocchio's has some wonderful rooms upstairs.

10. PERGATOLO, *Via del Castello 20, Tel. 06/942-04-64. L13,000-Cold plate with wine and bread; L20,000-First course of pasta, pizza, or meat, second course of the cold plate with wine and bread.*

Wild and fun atmosphere, a little on the touristy side with singers serenading the diners. You can either enjoy or ignore it in this large and spacious restaurant that has a deli counter displaying all the available meats, cheeses, breads, salamis, etc., that you'll be served. There are roaring fires behind the counter where your meats are all prepared.

If you've come to Frascati for the day or the week, this is one place you have to try, just for the fun of it. Say hi to the beautiful manager Tiziana for me.

11. TRATTORIA/PIZZERIA DA GABRIELE, *Via Solferino 5. No telephone. No credit cards. Dinner for two L35,000.*

You ladies will love the charming part owner Raphaele. He looks like something out of a movie with his piercing dark eyes and sultry glances. You can get pizza until 1:30am at wonderfully inexpensive prices. Just off the main piazza, this is a fun place to come in the late evening. Try their *pizza can salsiccia* (with sausage) or *con porcini* (mushrooms). I asked them to put both together, with extra cheese, and the pizza came out wonderfully.

12. CACCIANI, *Via Alberto Diaz 13, Tel. 06/942-0378. Closed Mondays. Holidays January 7-15 and 10 days after Ferragosto. Dinner for two L110,000. All credit cards accepted.*

One of the most famous restaurants in this region. It has a beautiful terrace that offers a tranquil and serene atmosphere. For starters, try the *crostini con verdure* (baked pastry appetizer filled with vegetables). Then try the home-made *fettuccine alla Romana* (made with tomatoes, chicken and spices) or *spaghetti con le vongole verace* (with clams in a hot oil and garlic sauce). For the entrée try the *fritto misto di carne* (mixed fried meats) the *saltimbocca*, or any of their grilled fish.

13. ZARAZA, *Viale Regina Margherita 21, Tel. 06/942-2053. Closed Mondays and the month of August. Dinner for two L70,000. Visa accepted.*

Traditional *cucina Romana* where you can get *bucatini all'amatriciana* (pasta with tomatoes, cream and spices), *gnocchi al ragu* (potato dumplings with tomato-based meat sauce), *capaletti in brodo* (pasta shaped like little hats in soup), *trippa alla Romana* (tripe with a tomato-based sauce) *abbacchio al forno* (grilled lamb), as well as some other Roman specialties such as *spaghetti all'amatriciana* and *penne all'arrabbiata* (with a hot spicy tomato based sauce), as well as *lombata di vitello* (grilled veal chop) and *misto arrosto* (mixed roast meats).

A simple rustic atmosphere with a few tables outside offering a limited view of the valley below. Inside tables are located in the basement of (but separate from) the Albergho Panorama hotel. It's warm and inviting in the winter, with the heat from the kitchen, the brick pillars, the whitewashed arched walls, and the friendly family service.

SEEING THE SIGHTS

If you've driven, you've seen the lovely scenic route to Frascati along the old **Appia Antica**, past the Catacombs and ruined tombs. The town is perched halfway up a hill, and on a clear day you will have splendid views of all of Rome and its scenic countryside.

Besides the great views, the wine, and the chance for some relaxation, Frascati has a wealth of villas and spacious parks that were formerly residences of princes and popes. One of these residences, **Villa Aldobrandini**, sits just above the town, and has a magnificent garden in which you can find solitude. To enter the villa's grounds you need to first get a free pass from the **Aziendo di Soggiorno e Turismo**, in Frascati's Piazza Marconi. *The hours are Monday-Friday 9:00am-1:00pm.*

Besides the beauty of its old villas, many of which were damaged in Allied bombings because the Germans had taken over the town for their headquarters, Frascati's draw is the fine **white wine** that bares its name. All wines seem to lose a special *qualcosa* when they travel, so if you are a wine lover, do not miss out on this chance to drink Frascati's wine directly at the source.

To enjoy this succulent nectar, there are old, dark wine stores, with heavy wooden tables and chairs located all over town. At one of these you can sip and enjoy this unspoiled and inexpensive wine, the way the natives have been doing it for centuries. The **Cantina Vanelli**, just off Piazza Fabro Filzi, is a prime example of one such wine store, and a fine traditional location to sample Frascati's produce. Just ask for a *bicchiere di vino* (glass of wine). An alternative to the cramped quarters of these wine stores but with quite a bit less atmosphere would be to sit at one of the sidewalk cafés offering superb views along with great wine.

Frascati is the perfect place to wander through, getting lost in the alleys, side streets, steps leading nowhere, and winding roads (all cobblestoned). If you follow the sporadically placed yellow signs that say *Ferario Pedonale*, you'll be guided through all the major sights and sounds of this hill town. One distinguishing feature is that there seem to be more *alimentari* (little food stores) per person than in any other city I've ever seen.

If you are fortunate enough to be in Frascati in the fall, specifically during the month of October, the town celebrates a **wine festival** of pagan proportions that lasts several days and nights. Come out to witness and partake in the debauchery, but please do not drive back to Rome afterwards – take the train.

LAGO DI BRACCIANO

Bracciano is a place to visit if you desperately need to go swimming, or entertain the kids for a little while. There are sights to see in the main town, with its imposing castle, but the distance and time to get here, and lack of adequate restaurants makes it a destination only if you feel the need to swim in fresh water. Even so, **Ostia Lido** is closer and much more easily accessible if you want to go swimming.

One of the best sights on the way to Bracciano, whether by car or train (since the train follows the roadway) is a still functional ancient **Roman aqueduct** that slices through lush green fields. When you get to the town Bracciano, you need to drive or walk down the hill to get to the **lake**. It's about a 15 minute walk and a three minute drive.

The lake is about 22 miles in circumference, and its shoreline boasts the town of **Bracciano**, standing high above the lake; the picturesque village of **Trevignano**; and the popular resort of **Anguillara**. The shores of the lake, planted with pine and olive groves, make pleasant picnic spots and swimming areas. Bracciano seems dominated by the **Castello Orsini**, the castle of the former landlords of the town. The structure, completed around 1485, is a magnificent example of a private Renaissance castle. It has a polygonal shape accompanied by five slender circular towers rising from it. Many rooms open to public still display the original frescoes and contain some quite good Etruscan relics and a fascinating collection of arms and armor. *Tel. 902-4003. Open Tuesday to Sunday 10:00am–Noon and 3:00pm–6:00pm in the summer, and Tuesday – Sunday 9:00am–Noon and 3:00pm–5:00pm in the winter. Admission L7,000.*

While at Bracciano you can also rent dinghies and paddle out on the water. There's not much to do or see, and the beach space is relatively limited, so try to come during the week and not on the weekends.

EXCURSIONS FROM ROME 239

ARRIVALS & DEPARTURES
Bracciano is 26 miles north northwest of Rome.

By Car
Drive about 45 minutes up the Via Cassia (SS2) to Madonna di Bracciano, then take route 493 to the lake.

By Train
From Stazione Ostiense it takes about 1 and a quarter hours and costs L8,400. In Rome, take the metro to the Piramide stop, and walk through the underpass at the "Ple Partigiani" exit to the Ostiense station. Buy your ticket at this station.

WHERE TO EAT
In all honesty I cannot recommend any of the restaurants in Bracciano, but if you haven't prepared a picnic lunch or didn't buy supplies in the town to bring down to the beach area, there are plenty of little bars and cafés lining the main road around the beach, and a few floating restaurants you might brave.

CERVETRI

Cervetri used to be the Etruscan capital of **Caere**, which the Romans at one point overran on their rise to power long before the Roman Empire. But Cervetri is not known today for the town of the living, but the towns of the dead the Etruscans built. These **Necropoli** are large circular mounds of tombs laid out in a pattern of a street, like houses in a city.

Today their round roofs are densely covered with grasses and wild flowers. Inside they have been furnished with replicas of household furnishings carved from stone. Most of the original artifacts are in the **Villa Giulia Museum** or the **Vatican Museums** in Rome. *The site is open Tuesday to Sunday 9:00am–4:00pm. Admission L6,000.*

After viewing the necropolis you can settle down among the mounds and have a picnic lunch, and imagine what life would be like during that time. After sightseeing you can return to the town by taxi, or by car if you have one, and take in the limited sights the little town has to offer. From the crowded main piazza you can climb steps to a **museum** with a lovely medieval courtyard.

ARRIVALS & DEPARTURES
Cervetri is about 28 miles west northwest of Rome.

By Car
A 45 minute drive up the Via Aurelia (SS1), which will give you a more scenic view, or the Autostrada A12, which connects to the 'beltway' around Rome by route 201.

By Train
From Stazione Termini it takes 1 hour and 10 minutes; from Roma Tiburtina it takes 50 minute to get to Cervetri-Ladispoli. Once in the town, to reach the **Necropolis** you can grab a local taxi, or take the two kilometer walk along a quiet little road. There are signs on the road to guide you where you're going. If in doubt stay to the right at the fork in the road.

WHERE TO EAT
DA FIORE, *near Procoio di Ceri, Tel. 06/9920-4250. Closed Wednesdays. Dinner for two L60,000. No credit cards accepted.*

A simple little local *trattoria* in the open country not far from the ruins and only four kilometers from the Via Aurelia. They make great pastas like *penne al funghi* (with mushrooms) *al ragu* (with tomato and meat sauce) or *con salsiccia* (with sausage), as well as grilled meats and their famous *bruschetta* (garlic bread as an appetizer) and pizza – all cooked in a wood burning oven.

OSTIA ANTICA & LIDO DI OSTIA
Ostia Antica
Founded in the fourth century BCE, **Ostia Antica** feels about as far away from Rome as you can get. As with excursions to Pompeii or Herculaneum, you get the sensation that the clock has been turned back nearly 2,000 years. But actually it is only 15 miles southwest of the city, a mere 45 minutes by subway (don't take your car or you'll defeat the purpose of relaxation).

This city was once the bustling port of Ancient Rome, but today it is calm and serene, and it is only busy with quiet. It is well preserved despite having been subject to repeated attacks by pirates and hostile navies. The only invasions it undergoes now are from packs of marauding Italian school children, on their cultural outings, rampaging through its archaeological excavations – the main reason to come here (see below).

ARRIVALS & DEPARTURES
Ostia Antica is about 15 miles southwest of Rome.

By Car
Take the Via del Mare (SS8) for about 25 minutes.

By Metro & Train

Buy a metro ticket and take Linea B to the Magliana station, and catch the train to Ostia Antica or continue to Lido di Ostia (the beach). It takes about 45 minutes from Stazione Termini. You'll have to pay a new fare (L3,000) to take the beach train since the Metro and the train systems are different animals.

WHERE TO EAT

There's really only one to recommend if you haven't packed yourself a picnic lunch. All the other restaurants are by the beach, so if you're heading that way see the listings under Lido di Ostia.

IL MONUMENTO, *18 Piazza Umberto I, Tel. 06/565-0021. Closed Mondays. Holidays Aug. 15 - Sept. 15. Dinner for two L90,000. Credit cards accepted.*

A simple seafood restaurant with quaint outside seating on the main piazza. Try the *spaghetti "Monumento"* with seafood and shrimp, as well as the *spaghetti con cozze* (with muscles) either in their light white sauce or their spicy red sauce. For seconds try any of the fish, which they either bake in the oven or grill on an open fire.

SEEING THE SIGHTS

You enter the excavations in Ostia at the **Porta Romana** from which you follow the **Decumanus Maximus**, the old city's main street. You will encounter the well-preserved old **Theater**. From here you overlook the **Piazzale dei Corporazione** (Corporation Square), a tree-lined boulevard once filled with over seventy commercial offices of wine importers, ship owners, oil merchants, or rope makers. The well-preserved laundry and wine shop should be visited. These offices are tastefully decorated with mosaic tiled floors representing the trades of each location (If you will not have a chance to visit Pompeii, this will give you the taste and feel, on a smaller scale, of that famous city). The chief commodity was corn, but there were also such imported luxuries as ivory (depicted by an elephant).

Farther down the Decumanus Maximus you arrive at the **Capitolium**, a temple dedicated to Jupiter and Minerva, located at the end of the **Forum**. The **insulae** (apartment blocks) are of particular interest since they are often four or five stories high. This is where the regular people and smaller merchants lived. Only the most wealthy of the merchants were able to build themselves villas. The *insulae* were well lighted, had running water, and had a means for sanitation (i.e., garbage removal) on each floor.

Two private home of interest that should be visited are the **House of the Cupid and Psyche**, which is west of the Capitolium, and the **House of the Dioscuri**, which is at the southwest end of town.

The excavation site is open daily 9:00am–6:00pm in summer, 9:00am–4:00pm in winter. Admission L10,000.

Lido di Ostia

Lido di Ostia is the beach about four kilometers from the ruins of Ostia Antica. Take the same route that you took to the ruins but continue on a little farther either by car or by train (see *Arrivals & Departures* above for more details). This is a perfect place to visit after a tough day of walking through the buildings and Necropoli of the Old City.

Treat yourself to a seaside celebration. There are rafts to rent, umbrellas to use, *cabanas* to change in, restaurants to go to, and hotels to stay at if you get to tired and don't want to get back to Rome. Lido di Ostia is a typical Italian beach and it's close to Rome. But don't go on the weekend unless you like mobs of people.

WHERE TO STAY

If you find you've lingered over the wine and the seafood a little too long, here are some hotel suggestions:

ROME AIRPORT PALACE HOTEL, *Viale Romagnoli 165, Lido Di Ostia. Tel. 06/569-2341. Fax 06/569-8908. 260 rooms, 230 with bath. All credit cards accepted. Single L200,000; Double L320,000.* *****

Don't let the name fool you, this place is quiet and it is also close to the beach. Also it's the only five star deluxe hotel in the area. They have everything you could need or want like a bar, restaurant, reading room, air conditioning, and more.

SATELLITE PALACE HOTEL, *Via delle Antille 49, Lido Di Ostia. Tel. 06/569-3841. Fax 06/569-8908. 283 rooms all with bath. All credit cards accepted. Single L200,000; Double L320,000. Air conditioning.* ****

Even though the star rating is one below it's cousin just around the corner, the Rome Airport Palace Hotel, the service and prices are exactly the same. They even have more, like a disco, swimming pool, audio video equipment, a sauna, a solarium, and so on, so I don't know why they don't have that last and final deluxe star.

HOTEL KURSAAL 2000, *Via F d'Aragona 10, Lido Di Ostia. Tel. 06/567-0616. Fax 06/567-0547. 38 rooms, 8 suites, all with bath. All credit cards accepted. Double L125,000.* ***

A good deal in a very tranquil location right near the beach. They have their own piano bar and restaurant so you don't have to stray too far at night. The rooms are all air conditioned, clean and tidy, and each has the necessary amenities to make this a three star hotel.

HOTEL LA RIVA, *Piazzale Mageliano 22, Lido Di Ostia. Tel. 06/562-2231. Fax 06/562-1667. 15 rooms all with bath. Single L99,000-120,000; Double L128,000-148,000. All credit cards accepted.* ***

Located near the beach, this is a good but not great three star hotel that overlooks the sea in the front and has a tranquil garden in the back. You also have prompt room service, air conditioning, a good restaurant and a small but comfortable bar.

LIDO, *Lungomare Toscanelli 78, Lido di Ostia. Tel. 06/562-5679/560-1892. Fax 06/560-1823. 28 rooms all with bath. Single L70,000; Double L110,000.* **

Situated right next door to the Tirrenia and located directly by the beach, this is a two star with A/C, and phone, TV and refrigerator in the room. Remodeled in 1989, they have taken pains to make the place as clean and comfortable as possibly. The only common area is a small bar. A good place for a short stay or for budget travelers.

TIRRENIA, *Lungomare Toscanelli 74, Lido di Ostia. Tel. 06/5630-4192. Fax 06/5632-4850. 9 rooms all with bath. Single L70,000-80,000; Double L95,000-110,000.* **

Established in 1924 and remodeled in 1993, this place is located by the beach right next door to the Lido Hotel. Quaint and comfortable, the only real drawback is that there is no AC, which is a necessity in the summer. They do have phone, refrigerator and TV in the rooms, all of which have been modernized. A great feature is a beautifully cool garden setting where you can relax in the evenings. They also have private parking which the Lido does not.

WHERE TO EAT

LA CAPANNINA DA PASQUALE, *Lungomare Vespucci 156, Tel. 06/567-0143. Closed Mondays. Holidays in November. All credit cards accepted. Dinner for two L110,000.*

A little expensive but the location is supreme, especially the outside seating right on the sea. They have a superb antipasto table which could serve as your whole meal if you're not too hungry. Their pastas and rice dishes are also good since many of them have been home-made at the restaurant. Try the *risotto ai frutti di mare* (rise with seafood ladled over the top). They are known for their seafood dishes so try anything *al forno* (cooked over the grill), with their wonderfully grilled potatoes. The service is stupendous, as it should be based on the price.

CHIARALUCE, *Via Ponte di Tor Boacciana 13, Tel. 06/569-1302. Closed Wednesdays. No credit cards accepted. Dinner for two L60,000.*

A little off the beaten track with tranquil outside seating. This is a small local place that prides itself on making superb food. They make a great *sauté di vongole* (sautéed clams) as well as *spaghetti con vongole* (with clams), and a huge mixed fried seafood platter (*frittura mista*). They also make perfectly grilled fish that goes well with their excellent house wine. The food is very good here.

PECCATI DI GOLA, *Corso Regina Maria Pia 19, Tel. 06/560-1233. Closed Mondays. No credit cards accepted. Dinner for two L70,000.*

On a street parallel to the beach, this is (surprise) another great fish restaurant that also serves well prepared meat dishes. You can watch through the glass partition as the cooks make each dish. If you're looking for light fare try their *insalata di mare* (mixed seafood salad).

TRE PULCINI, *Viale della Pineta di Ostia 30, Tel. 06/562-1293. Closed Mondays. All credit cards accepted. Dinner for two L110,000*

A simple family run place with mama Antoinetta in the kitchen and Renato in the restaurant. Here you'll experience some true down home Italian cooking. Try their *sauté di cozze e vongole* (sautéed muscles and clams), *zuppa di pesce* (fish soup), or their *fritto misto* (mixed fried seafood). You can also get some home-made *gelato* (ice cream) as dessert which is made daily by the daughter Cristina. You can enjoy all of this either outside on the balcony or in the air conditioned comfort of the interior.

VILLA IRMA, *Corso Regina Maria Pia 67, Tel. 06/560-3877. Closed Tuesdays. Holidays December 20-30. All credit cards accepted. Dinner for two L150,000.*

Super expensive but superb restaurant, some say the best in Ostia. You can enjoy the ambiance of the patio or the comfort of air conditioning inside while you dine on the wonderfully prepared seafood dishes. Anything here on the grill (*alla griglia*) or fried (*fritta*) is great. The service is four-star perfect. The place to come if you want to be treated like royalty.

RURAL RETREATS AROUND ROME

I've provided a three day escape if you ever get tired of the Eternal City, or are simply starting to feel overwhelmed by all the hustle and bustle of Rome. Peace and tranquillity are but a drive away in the hills around Rome. Some of these excursions are mentioned in greater detail above.

Day One

The perfect place to start is **Tivoli**, an ancient vacation spot famous for its large villas, lush gardens and picturesque waterfalls. The best way to get out to Tivoli from Rome is to make your way to the Raccordo Annulare, the beltway around the city. Follow this east until you get to the Via Tiburtina exit. This will take you all the way out. If it is easy for you to get directly on the Via Tiburtina downtown do so instead.

Drive first to **Villa d'Este**. Originally built as a Benedictine convent, it was transformed into a sumptuous villa by Cardinal Ippolito II of Este. Here you will be transfixed with the stunning beauty of the lush gardens and beautiful fountains.

After wandering the paths that cut through the vegetation, get back in the car for the short jaunt up to the **Villa Gregoriana**, in the town of Tivoli itself. Walking along the dirt path in the Villa's grounds you pass the Grotta delle Sibille and then are able to witness the panorama of the Grande Cascata with it's wonderful waterfall.

After bathing in the beauty of these two villas it's time for some repast before you venture into the third, Hadrian's Villa.

For lunch stop in **Adriano** (*Via di Villa Adriano 194, Tel. 0774/529-174*) located just outside of Hadrian's Villa. Sample some of their *crostini di verdure* (fried dough with vegetables inside), or *raviolini primavera con ricotta e spinaci* (ravioli with spring vegetables, spinach and fresh ricotta).

After lunch venture onto the grounds of Hadrian's Villa. The building itself was begun in 125 CE and completed 10 years later, and was at the time the largest and most impressive villa in the Roman Empire. From his travels Hadrian, an accomplished architect, found ideas that he recreated in his palace.

Once you have satisfied all your architectural voyeurism, it's onto **Frascati** where we will spend the night.

To get to Frascati, take route 636 under the A24 highway, past the Via Prenestina and the Via Casalina. Once there we will check into out quaint old hotel, the **Bellavista** (*Piazza Roma 2, Tel. 06/942-1068*). Evening is the perfect time to spend at an outside cafe or wine bar in Frascati, savoring the quiet ambiance of this Roman hill town as well as the full bodied white of the region. If you want to be in the center of everything for dinner try **Pizzeria Pinnocchio** (*Piazza del Mercato 20, Tel. 06/941-6694*). If you want a quiet meal overlooking the fields of Frascati, try **Zaraza** (*Viale Regina Margherita 21, Tel. 06/942-2053*).

Day Two

The next day take a leisurely stroll through the thriving gardens of the **Villa Aldobrandini**. Afterwards simply wander the streets of this lovely medieval town, watching the tapestry of daily life unfold around you.

For lunch, let's go to **Pagnanelli** (*Piazza A Gramsci 4, Tel. 06/936-0004*) in **Castel Gandolpho**, only a few minutes drive away. Take route 216 through the town of Marino. There's not much to see here except for the wonderful **Palazzo Pontificio**, the summer resident of the Pope, located in the **Piazza del Plebiscito**. From the piazza and the restaurant you have wonderful views of the lake below. The scene is truly enchanting. After lunch take the car for a spin down to the lake and around the beautiful blue waters.

The afternoon and early evening will be spent getting to **Velletri** and **Anagni** then finally onto **Fiuggi** for the night and their curative baths the next morning. Don't hesitate to stop along the way and take some amazing photos of the picturesque Italian countryside.

To get to **Velletri** from Castel Gandolpho you can either take the less scenic Route 7, or the pleasant route 217. You can get on Route 7 straight from Castel Gandolfo, but to catch the 217 you need to drive down to the lake and go south around it until the junction for 217. In Velletri we can admire the fourth century **Cattedrale di San Clemente** and walk slowly through the historical center of the town, taking in the small details of everyday life.

Next on our tour is **Anagni**, which we arrive at by taking Route 600 north out of town, which hooks up with Route 6 at Collefore and will take us to Anagni. This is a wonderful medieval town with steep, narrow streets winding around beautiful palazzi. The town's cathedral rises solitary on the highest point in town. Beside this eleventh century monument with its simple facade is the powerful twelfth century bell tower. If you're hungry stop for a small snack at one of the cafes in town, but don't eat too much, in Fiuggi we're going to have a great meal.

To get to **Fiuggi**, only a short drive away, we catch the Route 155r. Fiuggi is famous for its curative waters at the **Fonte di Bonifacio** or the **Fonte Anticolana**. The waters and the tranquillity are always an excuse to linger here for a day. We will spend the night at the **Grand Hotel Palazzo Delle Fonte** (*Via dei Villini 7, Tel. 0775/5081*) a spectacular four star hotel, founded in 1913 with tennis courts, indoor and outdoor swimming pools, luscious gardens and more. If you don't want something so upscale, try **Hotel Fiuggi Terme** (*Via Prenestina 9, Tel. 0775/551-212*), another four star that runs about half the price since it has about half the amenities.

Fiuggi is a city split in two: Fiuggi Fonte where the curative waters are, and Fiuggi Citta with its quaint winding streets. We will be eating dinner in the old city at La Torre dal 1961 (P*iazza Trento e Trieste 18, Tel. 0775/ 55382*) so you may want to drive to the restaurant. Eating here at Antonio and Maria Ciminelli's wonderful restaurant is a culinary delight. Everything they serve is exquisite. I especially liked the filet of trout (*filetto di trota*) lightly cooked in extra virgin olive oil.

Day Three

Today will be leisurely spent being 'cured' by the waters, savoring the peace and quiet of the hills, and sampling the fine food and atmosphere of Fiuggi. For lunch try **Villa Hernicus** (*Corso Nuova Italia 30, Tel. 0775/ 55254*) near the waters. Their *spaghetti con vongole e peperoncini verdi* (with clams and green peppers) is wonderful.

After you've had enough peace and quiet to last a life time ... it's back to Rome. We can get back by taking the Via Prenestina all the way.

21. NAPLES & THE AMALFI COAST

This area has got to be one of the most stunning and beautiful in the world. **Naples** is a city teeming with passion and adventure, and in the surrounding area you can find exotic, out-of-the-way islands, and pleasant, peaceful little coastal towns. People from all over the world come to this area of Italy to bathe in the pristine paradise of the islands of **Ischia**, **Procida** and **Capri** and to visit the picturesque towns along the **Amalfi Coast**.

Positano is one of these towns, and once you witness the majesty of the buildings of the village perched precariously on the slope overlooking the water, you will never want to come back. And if you enjoy history, you'll want to see the ancient towns of **Pompeii** and **Herculaneum**, destroyed by the fiery explosion of Mt. Vesuvious nearly 2,000 years ago.

NAPLES

Naples is a welcoming city. In many neighborhoods, life is still lived in the streets, where old and young interact and the day or evening entertainment is right in front of you, whether it's a family quarrel or two lovers at the corner cuddling away from onlookers. As Dickens wrote, Neapolitans don't just live their lives, they enact them. To people here, life is a performance and as such it must be lived with gusto. You'll see this quality all over Naples, especially in its **Centro Storico** (old town), and that's what makes Naples so irresistibly Italian.

Naples is a city that has been conquered, destroyed by wars, and leveled by earthquakes, but it still keeps on ticking. As a port city, Naples is filled with all sorts of characters from all over the world, as well as some great seafood. Though Naples is not really known for its cuisine, you can find some good restaurants and pizzerias. Naples claims that it is the birthplace of the pizza so you'll have to try at least one while here.

There is much to see in Naples if you can get used to the clutter of cars, buses, motorcycles and people all interweaving themselves through the tapestry of life. You can see everything from Roman ruins to medieval castles, and all can be seen by using quick and convenient underground metro or above ground funicular.

> **BE ALERT - BE AWARE**
>
> *During your travels in Naples, the best advice is this: be prepared. For all its charm and vibrancy, Naples at night is not very safe if you do not know where you are going. As a port city, like Genoa, it attracts people from all over the world, some of whom are undesirables. So be aware, be alert, and make sure you perform all necessary safety precautions.*

Brief History

Naples was originally a Greek settlement. In the 8th century BCE, it was called Parthenope and settled by people from Rhodes. Near this site, Ionian settlers founded the 'old town' in 7th century BCE, which they called Palaipolis. In the 5th century BCE, the 'new town' of **Neapolis** was founded by newcomers from Chalcis, and the name, only with slight changes, remains today.

These three settlements interacted freely but never merged. In 326 BCE, they became allies of Rome and united. Though faithful to the alliance, Naples still retained its strong Greek traditions and characteristics until late into the Roman Imperial period. The town itself became a favorite of many wealthy Roman merchants and magistrates because of its beautiful scenery.

But the peace that Rome brought was not to last. In 543 CE, the town fell into the hands of the Goths. Ten years later it was returned to the rule of the Byzantine Empire. After that it began to assert its independence and was free until 1139, when conquered by the Normans and incorporated into the Kingdom of Sicily by Roger II. Frederick the I, Roger II's grandson, founded the **University in Naples** that still exists today. Only forty years later, the capital of the Kingdom of Sicily was moved to Naples.

Still, peace was not to last. Spain gained control of the kingdom from 1503 to 1707, and in 1713 the territory passed to the Hapsburgs. Then in 1748 the Bourbons gained control, and kept control until 1860, when the territory was incorporated into the united Italy we see today.

NAPLES & THE AMALFI COAST

ARRIVALS & DEPARTURES

The best ways to get to Naples from Rome is by car or train. Bus service is slow, out of the way, and inconvenient from Rome. Bus service to and from Naples is mainly used for getting into remote villages inaccessible by train. The only time you would take a bus to Naples from a major city would be if it you're on a tour.

By Car

Located 217 kilometers from Rome, the easiest way to get to Naples by car is via the **A2** (Autostrada #2). If you are looking for a more scenic route, the coast road from Ostia Antica will move you past many scenic seaside resorts, including Anzio and Gaeta. But this will take you 12 hours or more because the roads are small, sometimes only two lanes, and wind endlessly along the coast through little seaside towns. If you have the time, take this route because the sights are wonderful. From Rome directly down the A2 should take four hours at most.

By Train

The train station, **Stazione Centrale FS**, is located at the eastern end of the city. The tourist information office in the station, *Tel. 081/268-779*, can help you locate a hotel if all those in this guide are booked up. Getting from Rome to Naples by train takes 4 hours. If you catch a *rapido* you can shave an hour off that time.

GETTING AROUND TOWN

By Bus

Buses can take forever to get you where you want to go, especially at rush hour, but there are times you'll need to take them. For example, when you want to get up to Campodimonte and the National Gallery. The buses congregate at the Piazza Garibaldi outside the train station and each route is posted on the signs at all bus stops for ease of use. You can also get a convenient map from the tourist office that details the main map routes, or you can buy an even better one from a newsstand that lists all the bus routes.

To use the map simply find where you are and where you want to go. Then match up the black numbers (which are the numbers of the bus routes) where you are with those located at where you want to go. For example, if you're at Piazza Garibaldi which is marked number 8 on the map, and you want to go to Piazza Municipio which is also marked number 8 on the map, that means the bus number 8 goes from Piazza Garibaldi to Piazza Municipio.

Riding the bus during rush hour is very tight, so try to avoid the hours of 8:00am to 9:00am, 12:30pm to 1:30pm, 3:30 to 4:30pm, and 7:30pm to

8:30pm. They have an added rush hour in the middle of the day because of their siesta time in the afternoon.

By Foot

You'll obviously need to combine the use of one of the above modes of transport with bi-ped movement. You'll love the strolls through the Centro Storico and university area, but always be alert. Don't walk at night, especially alone. Remember, this is a port city. During the day, don't go down alleys that are empty of people. Just play it smart.

By Funicular

These hill-side trams connect the lower city of Naples to the hills of Vomero, where you can see the Castel San Elmo and the Certosa di San Martino. There are three funiculars that can assist in your ascent, the **Centrale** that leaves from Via Toledo, the **Montesanto** that leaves from Piazza Montesanto, and the **Chiai** that leaves from Piazza Amadeo. A one way ticket costs L1,500.

By Metro

You can take the metro almost anywhere you want to go in Naples for only L1,500 a trip each way. It's fast, inexpensive, and safe, but always keep a lookout for pickpockets. They flourish here in Naples.

By Taxi

Naples is a very congested city, and as such it will cost you an arm and a leg whenever you choose to transport yourself by taxi, especially during rush hour. But if you want to spend the equivalent of a meal at a good restaurant just to get from point A to point B, by all means.

The going rate as of publication was L4,500 for the first 2/3 of a kilometer or the first minute (which usually comes first during the rush hours), then its L500 every 1/3 of a kilometer or minute. At night you'll also pay a surcharge of L3,000, and Sundays you'll pay L1,000 extra. If you bring bags aboard you'll be charged L500 extra for each bag.

Besides having to rely on flagging down a cab, there are strategically placed cab stands all over the city.

WHERE TO STAY

1. VESUVIO, *Via Partenope 45, 80121 Napoli. Tel. 081/764-044. Fax the same. 183 rooms all with bath. Single L260,000; Double L390,000. Suites L500,000-1,300,000. All credit cards accepted. Breakfast included.* ****

Located on elite hotel row, this beautifully restored old building houses a truly superb hotel. Decorated elegantly with antiques, the charm and character of this place shine through. You will be offered the most

NAPLES & THE AMALFI COAST 251

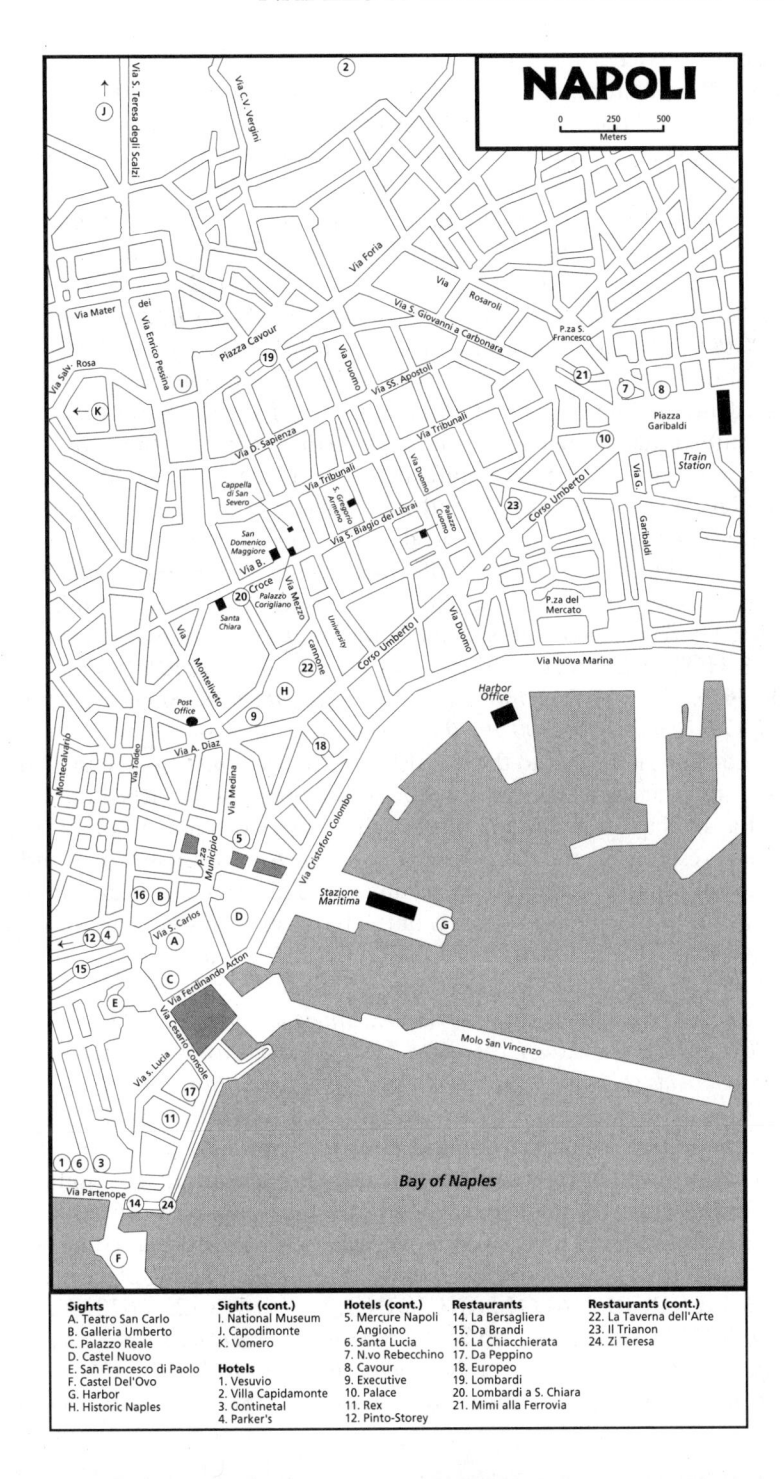

NAPOLI

Sights
A. Teatro San Carlo
B. Galleria Umberto
C. Palazzo Reale
D. Castel Nuovo
E. San Francesco di Paolo
F. Castel Del'Ovo
G. Harbor
H. Historic Naples

Sights (cont.)
I. National Museum
J. Capodimonte
K. Vomero

Hotels
1. Vesuvio
2. Villa Capidamonte
3. Continetal
4. Parker's

Hotels (cont.)
5. Mercure Napoli Angioino
6. Santa Lucia
7. N.vo Rebecchino
8. Cavour
9. Executive
10. Palace
11. Rex
12. Pinto-Storey

Restaurants
14. La Bersagliera
15. Da Brandi
16. La Chiacchierata
17. Da Peppino
18. Europeo
19. Lombardi
20. Lombardi a S. Chiara
21. Mimi alla Ferrovia

Restaurants (cont.)
22. La Taverna dell'Arte
23. Il Trianon
24. Zi Teresa

attentive service while staying here. The restaurant, Caruso, on the top floor offers a stunning panoramic view. For over 100 years this hotel situated along the sea has been the address for many illustrious guests. The rooms are extremely comfortable, decorated with wonderful antiques and colorful wall coverings. The bathrooms have showers and also come with every imaginable amenity. If you're driving, they have an underground garage since parking on the street is impossible.

2. VILLA CAPIDAMONTE, *Via Moiariello, 80121 Napoli. Tel. 081/459-000. Fax 081/229-344. 60 rooms all with bath. Single L120,000; Double L190,000-240,000. Breakfast included. All credit cards accepted.* ****

Situated above the city near the magnificent tranquillity of the park Capidamonte (hence the name), a few minutes from the airport and near the Autostrada, this place is a gem. If you want peace and quiet away from the hectic pace of Neapolitan life, this is the place. Virtually brand new, this place was opened in 1995 and as such it comes with every imaginable creature comfort. You can wind down in the garden, the terrace, the salons, the library or in your comfortable room. Decorated in soft colors to enhance the peaceful tones, most rooms also offer lovely panoramic views. There are also tennis facilities for you to work on your game.

3. HOTEL CONTINENTAL, *Via Partenope 44, 80121 Napoli Tel. 081/764-4636. Fax 081/764-4661. 166 rooms all with bath. Single L200,000-245,000; Double L290,000-395,000. Credit cards accepted.* ****

Located right next to the Excelsior within walking distance to all the sights, but outside of the Centro Storico and business districts directly on the Bay of Naples. A tranquil place with its own swimming pool. Besides a good restaurant, they also have a separate American style bar and a piano bar for your evening's entertainment. This street is a beautiful one to stay on, with a panoramic view of the bay – all hotels on it are superb.

4. PARKER'S GRAND HOTEL, *Corso Vittorio Emanuele, 80121 Napoli. Tel. 081/761-2474. Fax 081/663-527. Toll free in Italy 167013519. 83 rooms, 47 with bath, 36 with shower. Single L180,000-230,000; Double L290,000-330,000; Suite L750,000-1,500,000. Breakfast included. L70,000 extra bed. Kids stay for 10% of cost in you room. Credit cards accepted.* ****

In a renovated historic building, this is a romantic spot with great panoramic views of the harbor and Vesuvius, especially on the top floor. You can get local or international cuisine in the restaurant, and you have entertainment in the piano bar. The rooms are large and comfortable and are decorated with lovely wall coverings. The bathrooms come with whirlpool tubs and every other amenity. A tranquil, relaxing place to stay.

5. MERCURE NAPOLI ANGIOINO, *Via Depretis 123, 80121 Naples. Tel. 081/552-9500. Fax 081/552-5909. 85 rooms all with bath. Single L190,000; Double L230,000. All credit cards accepted. Breakfast included.* ****

Optimum location in the centro storico, near the business district and the Beverello pier where the ferries leave for the islands in the Bay of Naples. Owned by the French chain Mercure, you will receive lavish Gaulish attention. The breakfast room on the first floor is filled to overflowing with the buffet each morning. All the rooms have sound-proofed windows so as to block out the noise that makes its way in from the streets below – a necessity in this ideal location. The rooms are all decorated in delicate colors and some are expressly reserved for non-smokers, a rarity in French hotels. The bathrooms are accommodating and have all amenities necessary. The downstairs bar is a great place to relax in the afternoons, or you can order room service from there without a surcharge. A good place to stay.

6. SANTA LUCIA, *Via Partenope 46, 80121 Naples. Tel. 081/764-0666. Fax 081/764-8580. 102 rooms, 90 with bath, 12 with shower. Single L125,000-250,000; Double L180,000-350,000; Suite L600,000. Breakfast L20,000 extra. Credit cards accepted.* ****

Located within walking distance of the Centro Storico as well as the other major sites, this tranquil romantic hotel is located with a perfect panoramic view of the bay, Mount Vesuvius and Castel dell'Ovo. Like its brethren on the Via Partenope, this is an excellent choice with all the necessary amenities. The only thing it doesn't have is a swimming pool. Opened in 1922, it has been recently renovated and offers as always complete attention to all details. The restaurant is only open in the evenings, but if you make a reservation they accommodate you for lunch too. The breakfast buffet is overflowing. The rooms are very spacious, come with every imaginable comfort, and are decorated in light blue to continue the seascape you have out the window. The bathrooms come complete with courtesy sets of toiletries. And the service is impeccable.

7. NUOVO REBECCHINO, *Corso Garibaldi 356, 80121 Naples. Tel. 081/553-5327. Fax 081/268-026. 58 rooms all with bath. Single L110,000; Double L160,000. All credit cards accepted. Breakfast included.* ***

Convenient location for travelers, right by the station and near the entrance to the Autostrada and with affordable prices. Established in 1890, renovated in 1990. The common rooms are diverse. One is a nice old-fashioned billiard room. Ask for a room on the fourth floor for the best rooms. All are furnished in style and elegance, but some don't have sound-proofed windows so request that too. The bathrooms are clean and comfortable and decorated in soft ceramic colors.

8. HOTEL CAVOUR, *Piazza Garibaldi 32, 80142 Naples. Tel. 081/283-122. Fax 081/287-488. 98 rooms, 40 with bath, 58 with shower. Single L98,000-150,000; Double L150,000-190,000. Suite L200,000-230,000. Breakfast included.* ***

In a renovated historic building in the busy Piazza Garibaldi. They have double paned glass, which keeps out most of the traffic noise from this busy piazza, but some rooms do not. The staff is professional and courteous and do everything to make up for the location. You have air conditioning and satellite TV. The restaurant is run by Signora Tea and she prepares some excellent local dishes.

9. HOTEL EXECUTIVE, *Via del Cerriglio 10, 80134 Naples. Tel. 081/ 552-0611. Fax the same. 19 rooms all with bath. Single L180,000. Double L240,000. Credit cards accepted.* ***

In the Centro Storico in a renovated old building, this place has a gym, sauna, and sun room. It's a good alternative to the larger hotels in Naples. Here you are made to feel special. The rooms are clean and comfortable and have air conditioning, TV, mini bar and more. A romantic place to stay.

10. PALACE HOTEL, *Piazza Garibaldi 9, 80142 Napoli. Tel. 081/267-044. Fax 081/264-306. 102 rooms, 52 with bath, 50 with shower. Single L95,000-150,000; Double L150,000-190,000. Breakfast included. Extra bed L60,000. Credit Cards accepted.* ***

In the busy Piazza Garibaldi, this place has many amenities but they can't make up for the intruding chaos of Naples. The rooms are clean, small, but comfortable. The restaurant serves international and local cuisine and you have air conditioning and TV in your rooms.

11. HOTEL REX, *Via Palepoli 12, 80139 Napoli. Tel. 081/764-9389. Fax 081/764-9227. 40 rooms all with bath. Single L109,000; Double L160,000. All credit cards accepted. Breakfast included.* ***

In a sweet position, near the *lungomare*, this hotel occupies part of the Palazzo Coppedé. The Liberty style furnishings in the common rooms hark back to another era, lending a quaint charming air to this place. The rooms are clean and comfortable with colorful bed coverings. All rooms have sound-proof windows but only a few have views of the Bay of Naples. A great location and a good price.

12. HOTEL PINTO-STOREY, *Via G Martucci 72, 80121 Napoli. Tel. 081/681-260. Fax 081/667-536. 25 rooms all with bath. Single L170,000. Double L220,000. Credit cards accepted.* ***

This is a newly upgraded three star after they equipped their last six rooms with bath facilities. Located in a quiet area of Naples just below the Villa Floridiana, it is only a short walk to the bay. They have air conditioning and TV in the rooms and a small bar downstairs. Clean but only adequate accommodations with different furnishings in each room, sometimes a combination of antique and modern pieces.

WHERE TO EAT

14. LA BERSAGLIERA, *Borgo Marinaro Sant Lucia, Tel. 081/764-6016. Closed Tuesdays and August. Credit cards accepted. Dinner for two L140,000.*

The best thing about this place is its location with a view of the Castel dell'Ovo, especially on their terrace overlooking the water. The food is good, but not for these exorbitant prices. If you want romantic atmosphere, come here. Try their *spaghetti con vongole* (with clams) or their *linguine agli scampi* (with shrimp). For seconds try their fried or grilled fish.

15. PIZZERIA DA BRANDI, *Salita San Anna di Palazzo 1, Tel. 081/ 416-928. Closed Mondays and one week in August. Dinner for two L60,000. Credit cards accepted.*

As you know Neapolitans claim to have made the first pizza, and this place claims to have made the first *Pizza Margherita* (simple pizza with fresh tomato sauce, oil, and mozzarella cheese). This place is famous throughout Naples not only for their *Margherita* but also for their *Pizza Biancha* (dough and olive oil only) which is superb. Located in the Spanish Quarter, it's a little walk from the Centro Storico. If in Naples, you have to try this place.

16. LA CHIACCHIERATA, *Piazzetta M Serano 37, Tel. 081/411-465. Closed Sundays and August. American Express Cards accepted. Dinner for two L60,000.*

A small *trattoria* with only a few tables at the end of the Via Toledo near the Palazzo Reale. They use a lot of vegetables, especially on pizza, where they pile mozzarella and provolone. You can also get some *pasta e fagioli* (pasta and beans), some good *pesce arrosto* (grilled fish), and a some superb *capretto al forno* (baked kid goa). The food here is great.

17. PIZZERIA DA PEPPINO, *Via Palepoli 6a/b, Tel. 081/764-9582. Closed Sundays. American Express card accepted. Dinner for two L80,000.*

In the Santa Lucia area near the Castel dell'Ovo this place is open late for you revelers. Here you not only can get great pizza, but a tasty seafood appetizer, superb *bruschetta* (garlic bread with oil and tomatoes), some *linguine alla putanesca* (whore's pasta made with tomatoes, oil, garlic and tuna), and great grilled or fried fish. A fun place to come any time of day or night.

18. EUROPEO, *Via Marchese Campodisola 4/8, Tel. 081/552-1323. Closed Sundays and two weeks in August. Only open for lunch on Friday and Saturday. American Express and Visa accepted. Dinner for two L80,000.*

This is a small local *trattoria* that is frequented by academics, since it's near the University, as well as manual laborers. Eating here gives you an insight into the people of Naples. They serve a tasty *ostriche e frutti di mare* (oysters and other sea food) appetizer. Then try their *Pizza Margherita* (simple pizza with fresh tomato sauce, oil and mozzarella cheese) or have them put some great sausage on the pizza as well. Or try their superb *spaghetti alla vongole verace* (with spicy clam sauce). For seconds they make a great *frittura di pesce* (fried fish dish).

19. PIZZERIA LOMBARDI, *Via Foria 12, Tel. 081/456-220. Closed Mondays. All credit cards accepted. Dinner for two L55,000.*

Located near the Museo Archeologico Nazionale, this place definitely has the best *Pizza Napoletana* anywhere. Covered in ricotta, mozzarella, vegetables, and almost everything imaginable, this is the tastiest pizza around. If this is a little complicated for you, look over their extensive list of other excellent pizza. You can order anything from the basic *Margherita* to a pizza with wurstel sausage, with local sausage and more. Also, the no smoking signs on the walls .... nobody adheres to them, so take note.

20. PIZZERIA LOMBARDI A SANTA CHIARA, *Via B Croce 59, Tel. 081/522-0780. Closed Sundays and three weeks in August. Credit cards accepted. Dinner for two L65,000.*

Located in the heart of the Centro Storico right next to the Santa Chiara church and their beautiful cloisters, this place makes great pizza of all kinds. For an appetizer try their *mozzarella di bufalo* (buffalo mozzarella) *peperoni, melanzane* (eggplant), and *zucchine* plate. A perfectly situated place to stop for a bite to eat in the middle of a day of touring. The food is excellent and inexpensive.

21. MIMI ALLA FERROVIA, *Via A d'Aragona 21, Tel. 081/553-8525. Closed Sundays and a week in August. Credit cards accepted. Dinner for two L120,000.*

Choose either the terrace or inside in which to dine. At both you will be more than happy. Start with their appetizer of *mozzarella di bufalo*, *peperoni* or *assagi di paste povere* (a tasty sampling of their pasta dishes). For pasta try their *linguine alla Mimi* (which comes with a great shrimp sauce), then move onto their *frutti di mare e pomodorini* (mixed seafood and small tomatoes). The *calamaretti fritti* (fried calamari) is also good.

22. LA TAVERNA DELL'ARTE, *Rampa S. Giovanni Maggiore 1a, Tel. 081/552-7558. Closed Sundays and August. No credit cards accepted. Dinner for two L80,000.*

A small local place situated in the center of the Centro Storico near the University. The service is excellent, either on the terrace or inside. Try the traditional appetizer of *pizze rustiche* (literally country pizza, with a variety of toppings), *salumi artigianali* (literally craftsmen salami – great local salami), *mozzarelle fresche* (fresh mozzarella) and *sformato di cipolle* (baked onions). This will definitely fill you up so move directly to a great main course of *maiale in agrodolce* (a sweet and sour pork dish).

23. IL TRIANON, *Via P Colletta 46, Tel. 081/553-9426. Closed Sundays and for lunch, New Years Eve and Christmas. No credit cards accepted. Dinner for two L50,000.*

Located in the Centro Storico, this is the best pizza in Naples, and that's saying a lot. Besides the many varieties of pizza that come out of their wood burning brick oven, you'll love the high ceilings, slate-yellow walls, tacky print motifs that they call decoration, and the long communal tables. Mainly frequented by University students this place has a fun filled crowd. Try their filling pizza/lasagna that is loaded with sauce, cheese and meat if a pizza sounds too boring to you, but do not miss this place when in Naples. Great food, local atmosphere.

24. RISTORANTE ZI TERESA, *Via Partenope 1, Tel. 081/764-2565. Closed Sunday nights and Saturdays as well as two weeks in August. Credit cards accepted. Dinner for two L130,000.*

Located across from the Castel dell'Ovo on the water, this is a famous and popular eating spot, and because of that it's rather expensive. It's also surrounded by some of the best hotels in the city, like the Excelsior and the Continental which doesn't help keep prices down. Their terrace is a perfectly romantic spot to have lunch or dinner, but remember to reserve well in advance. Start off with their *antipasto di mare* (seafood antipasto), then move on to their *spaghetti alla vongole* (with clam sauce), then if you're still hungry settle on any of their grilled fish.

SEEING THE SIGHTS

Naples has plenty to offer, from high culture like opera, museums, and centuries-old castles and palaces, to the simple pleasures of just strolling along the harbor. Use common sense, don't wander down lonely alleys, and Naples can be a fun town.

A. TEATRO SAN CARLO

Via San Carlo 98f, 80132 Napoli. Tel. 081/797-2331 Or 797-2412, Fax 081/797-2306. Ticket office open Tuesday – Sunday 10:00am–1:00pm and 4:30pm–6pm.

This is the most distinguished opera in house in Italy after La Scala in Milan. Its neoclassic facade dates from its rebuilding in 1816. The season runs from October to June. Most tickets are always sold out, but you can check at the ticket office between 10:00am and 1:00pm and 4:30pm to 6:00pm Sunday through Tuesday during the season.

B. GALLERIA UMBERTO

Between Via San Carlo and Via Toledo. Open 24 hours.

Modeled after the Galleria Emanuelle in Milan, this arcaded shopping area with its glass ceilings is also laid out in a cross pattern. The blending of iron and glass gives it an almost futuristic appeal. A place to visit even if you're going to Milan, just to compare the two structures. And if you like to shop, this should be one of your stops.

C. PALAZZO REALE

Via Ferdinando Acton. Open 9:00am-noon and 3:00pm-5:30pm.

The former **Royal Palace** was begun in 1600 by Domenico Fontana and was restored between 1837 and 1841. You'll see statues of eight former kings who ruled Naples on the facade. This extensive palace contains a magnificent marble staircase built in 1651, 17 heavily decorated apartments, and the **Biblioteca Nazionale** that contains over 1,500,000 volumes as well as many ancient manuscripts and relics. You should come to the Royal Palace just to see the National Library, because it is like nothing you can find in North America.

D. CASTEL NUOVO

Via Ferdinando Acton. Open 9:00am-Noon and 3:00pm-5:30pm.

Behind the palace is the magnificent, five towered **Castel Nuovo**, also referred to as **Maschio Angionino**. This was once the residence of kings and viceroys who ruled the Kingdom of Naples. Built between 1279 and 1283, it pre-dated the Palazzo Reale and was constantly being upgraded. Surrounded by park land, it seems as if it is an oasis in the sea of Neapolitan chaos. An imposing structure that adults and children alike love to explore.

Other gardens you can explore are those located next to the Palazzo Reale near the water. A great place to get away for a few hours.

E. CHURCH OF SAN FRANCESCO DI PAOLO

Piazza del Plebiscito. Open 7:00am-noon and 4:00pm-5:30pm.

The **Church of San Francesco di Paolo** was built between 1818 and 1831, and is a fine imitation of the Pantheon in Rome.

F. CASTEL DELL'OVO

Borgo Marinaro, Open 9:00am-noon and 3:00pm-5:30pm.

If your kids like exploring castles, there is another one near the Castel Nuovo and the Palazzo Reale. The **Castel dell'Ovo** is located off a causeway from the Via Partenope and sits on a small rocky islet. It was begun in the 12th century and completed in the 16th century. It was used as lighthouse and as the first line of defense for the harbor.

G. THE HARBOR

Always a bustle of activity, since Naples is one of Italy's biggest ports. You can get more information about the history of the location at the **Marine Station** on Molo Angionino just past the heliport. From this heliport you can take regular helicopter service to Capri and Ischia as well as the Airport. This is the same location from which you would catch a ferry or hydrofoil over to these two islands.

H. HISTORIC NAPLES – CENTRO STORICO

Located just north of the harbor, this part of Naples is the most fun to walk, since it has winding streets that seem to lead nowhere but to another small local church. A fun place to explore in the day (be careful at night), especially along the old main street through the center.

The old main street is a combination of all the streets, from the Via Toledo, the Via Maddaloni, moving to the Via D. Capatelli, and ending at the **Piazza Nolana** with the Via Nolana. This old main street, as well as the small streets and alleys that are offshoots, is lined with shops of traditional artisans like the **Palace of Strumenti Musical** at Vico San Domenico Maggiore #9 in front of the church of the same name. Up the stairs to the first floor you'll find guitars and other instruments being crafted by hand.

Another unique shop is the **L'Ospedale delle Bambole (The Doll Hospital)**, located on *Via S Biagio dei Librai* in the Centro Storico. This is the world famous shop where you'll find ancient dolls and puppets hanging everywhere or just lying around. Walk in and have a look around, the proprietor is very friendly.

Another can't-miss street in the Centro Storico is the **Via San Gregorio Aremeno**, which is commonly known as the Nativity scene street since they sell figurines for crèches year round.

Via Toledo

Formerly **Via Roma**, this street runs through the heart of the Centro Storico. Sometimes referred to in other guidebooks or on other maps as Via Roma, the natives refer to the street by both names. Officially it is Via Toledo, since it was built by and named after Don Pedro de Toledo.

Montecalvario

On the left of this street is the **Montecalvario** section that rises steeply to the **Via Vittorio Emanuelle**. Many of these 'streets' are actually steps. An interesting place to walk.

NAPOLI PORTE APERTE – OPEN DOOR NAPLES

Be aware that at infrequent times and in true Italian fashion, unannounced, the city opens all of its churches, monuments, and gardens for free. Ask at the tourist office or your concierge whether this rare event will occur during your stay.

Church of Santa Anna del Lombardi
Piazza Monteoliveto, Open daily 7:15am–1line of pm.

This church, in the **Piazza Monteoliveto** just off the Piazza della Carita, is a great collection of Renaissance sculpture. The church was built in 1411 and later continued in the Renaissance style. Here you'll find the *Pieta*, created in 1492 by Guido Mazzoni. You'll also find some wonderful terra cotta statues as well as a beautiful 16th century choir stall.

Church of Santa Chiara & Gesu Nuovo
Piazza del Gesu Nuovo. Santa Chiara open daily 8line of am–12:30pm and 4:30pm–7:30pm. Gesu Nuovo open daily 7:15am–1line of pm and 4line of pm–7:15pm.

Try to see these two churches. The Jesuit **Gesu Nuovo** was erected between 1585 and 1600 and still maintains its triangular grid-like facade. There are also some beautiful cloisters here. The place is full of roses and cats. It's a great place to relax among the Mediterranean-style tiles covered with bucolic scenes of Naples. There are benches on which to sit where you can enjoy the aroma of the roses and escape from the hectic pace of Naples, at least for a few minutes.

The **Santa Chiara** is one of medieval Naples' main monuments. It was built in 1310 and was recreated in the Gothic style after being bombed during World War II. Inside you'll find many medieval tombs and sarcophagi that belong to the house of Anjou. Don't miss the Nun's choir behind the High Altar, where secluded nuns could watch mass without being seen. This church has a wonderful, often empty courtyard. There are beautiful frescoes and a lazy palm leaning in the center. The church also has some great art work on its ceiling. They have thoughtfully placed slanted mirrors for you to see the ceiling without having to crane your neck.

Church of San Domenico Maggiore
Piazza San Domenico Maggiore. Open daily 8:00am–12:30pm and 4:30pm–7:00pm.

From the two churches above, go east down the Benedetto Croce to the next piazza on the left to the church of **San Domenico Maggiore**. Built around 1300, with a Gothic facade added in the 19th century, this is one of the most interesting churches in Naples. It has early Renaissance art as well as over 40 sarcophagi of the Anjou family. Here you'll find a combination of Gothic and Baroque architecture.

Capella di San Severo
Via F de Sanctis. Open Mondays and Wednesday–Saturday 10:00am–5:00pm, Tuesday and Sunday 10:00am–1:30pm. Admission L6,000.

The **Chapel of San Severo** is a short distance east of the church of San Domenico Maggiore, hidden down the small side street of Via F de

Sanctis. Built in 1590 as a burial chamber for the Sangro family, it was embellished with the Baroque style in the 18th century. Now a private museum, the chapel is filled with many fine statues including an eerie *Christ in a Winding Sheet* by Sammartino. You can also find two grisly corpses located downstairs. They are leftovers from the experiments of the Prince Raimondo.

Palazzo Corigliano
Piazza San Domenico Maggiore. Open daily 9:00am-7:00pm.

In the 4th floor library of the **Palazzo Corigliano** (currently a university building dating from the 18th century), located in the Piazza San Domenico Maggiore, you'll find a place to leisurely read a periodical or book and escape the pace of Naples. You can also see the remains of Greek walls in the basement.

Cloisters of San Gregorio Armeno
Between Via Tribunali and Via S. Baglio S. Librai. Hardly ever open. You need to go there and request entrance.

Often closed, you have to ask the nuns if you can enter. But if you gain access you'll adore the beauty of the flowering plants, the splashing fountain, and the comfortable benches. There's a place where you can enter the choir chamber which is all made of wood and peer through the wrought iron grating down onto the church itself. This was where the cloistered nuns celebrated mass, but themselves could not be seen.

Most often they'll only allow women in and usually only on special Sundays, but it doesn't hurt to try. Here you'll be able to see what the life of a cloistered nun is like.

Palazzo Cuomo
Via Duomo. Open 9:00am-2:00pm.

The beautiful Renaissance **Palazzo Cuomo**, built from 1464 to 1490, is located on the corner of the Via Duomo and the Via San Biago ai Librai. The building now houses the **Museo Filangieri** that contains arms and armor, as well as porcelain and pictures.

Duomo
Via Duomo. Open daily 8:00am-12:30pm and 5:00-7:00pm.

Up the Via Duomo from the Palazzo Cuomo is the **Cathedral**. It is dedicated to San Gennaro, the patron saint of Naples. Built over the 4th century ruins of a paleo-Christian basilica, this church was erected between 1295 and 1324 in the French Gothic style. After an earthquake destroyed part of it in 1456 it was rebuilt, restored, and altered. It was further updated in the 19th century when part of the facade was replaced, but the church retains its original doors.

On the main altar you'll find a silver bust of **San Gennaro** that contains his skull. In the tabernacle are two vials of hardened blood from the saint. Believers say that this blood liquefies three times, as well as a few minutes, every morning. To find the saint's tomb, look under the high altar.

Gite Sotteranea – The Underground City

This is one cool sight. You can go on underground tours of two different **catacombs**, as well as **aqueducts**, **cisterns**, and **Roman** and **Greek cities** that lie below Naples. You'll be given candles to help guide you through the slim passages and damp darkness.

One trip starts from the Caffe Gambrinus (there are only a few accessible entrances to the underground city; another entrance is from the Piazza San Gaetano in the Centro Storico). You'll find aqueducts, caves, quarries, Greek markets, medieval houses, Greek tombs, catacombs. There are also special tours that start from the Chiesa di S. Lorenzo. You need to ask a priest to guide you through the courtyard and underground to the location where they are still excavating the jumbled layers of Greek, Roman, and medieval streets, houses, and markets. You have to do a little talking in Italian to get where you want to go but it's worth the trip.

Go to the tourist office in the Piazza del Gesu Nuovo for more complete times, locations, and information about touring the underground city.

I. NATIONAL MUSEUM

Piazza Cavour. Tel. 440-166. Open daily 9:00am-7:00pm. Open September-May, Monday-Saturday 9:00am-2:00pm, Sunday 9:00am-1:00pm. Admission L10,000.

On the northwestern outskirts of the Centro Storico just off of **Piazza Cavour** is the **National Museum**, which boasts one of the world's finest collections of antiquities. The building was originally erected as a barracks in 1586, then was the home of the University from 1616 to 1790. During this time the University began to house the art treasures of the kings of Naples, the Farnese collections from Rome, and material from Pompeii, Herculaneum, and Cumae. A great museum.

J. CAPODIMONTE

Park open daily 7:30am-8:00pm. In off-season open 7:30am-5:00pm. Museum open Tuesday-Saturday 9:00am-2:00pm, Sunday 9:00am-1:00pm. Admission L10,000. Take bus 110 or 127 from the train station or 22 or 23 from Piazza del Plebiscito. If walking, take the Corso Amadeo di Savoia about two

NAPLES & THE AMALFI COAST

kilometers north up the hill from the National Museum to arrive at the park of Capodimonte and the Catacombs of San Gennaro.

The **Catacombs** are only open Saturday and Sunday mornings and like their Roman counterparts, these contain a maze of passageways and tomb chambers. But these are slightly better preserved and have much more artistic representation.

Just across the piazza Tondo di Capodimonte is the entrance to the park. This 297 acre park commands some wonderful panoramic views of Naples. It is a peaceful respite from the hectic pace of Naples. If you don't get to Vomero you must try and get here. Also located at the park is the **Capodimonte Museum** of arms, armor, porcelain, and pictures. In particular, there are some great works by **Titian**.

K. VOMERO & THE SURROUNDING HILLS

Certosa di San Martino, Museum Tel. 578-1769. Open Tuesday-Sunday 9:00am-2:00pm. Admission L8,000; Castel Sant'Elmo, Open Tuesday-Saturday 9:00am-2:00pm, and Sunday 9:00am-1:00pm.

If you want to get away from the smog and congestion of Naples just hop on one of the *funiculars* and enter a calm antidote in a residential district high above the city. The district was built from 1885 onwards. You can also get here by climbing the streets in the Montecalvario section.

The Villa Floridiana public park in the southern part of Vomero has a terrace with a wonderful view overlooking the **Bay of Naples**. You'll also find a small museum, **Duca di Martina Museum**, with paintings, porcelain, ivory, china, and pottery here.

Of great interest is the **Certosa di San Martino**, an old monastery erected in the 14th century and remodeled during the Renaissance and Baroque periods. You should take the time to the see the cloisters because they give you a glimpse into the monastic life of the times. Their museum contains some interesting nativity scenes (crèches).

Just north of the monastery is the **Castel Sant'Elmo** that was built in 1329 and added to between the 15th and 17th centuries. Come here for the view from the ramparts, as well a chance to explore the many passageways that were used for the defense of the harbor.

NIGHTLIFE & ENTERTAINMENT

RIOT, *Located in an old building at Via S Biagio dei Librai 26 in the Centro Storico. Open from 9:00pm until 3:00am. No phone.*

To enter come through a wooden door, cross an open courtyard, climb a staircase, and on the right is the secret garden that is the club. It consists of a few rooms in an old building from the 18th century with tall French windows opening out onto a lush terrace of palm trees, pebble paths, and tables at which to sit and enjoy a drink or a smoke.

During the summer they have art exhibits and late night bands, mostly American blues and jazz. The waitresses here are all hip and have a definite attitude. Even so they will serve you drinks and sandwiches outside. It's a bit expensive but the crowd is fun and the atmosphere is like nothing you'll find in the States. I mean how many nightclubs do you know are in 18th century *palazzi*? It's like something out of an Anne Rice vampire novel. They are so hip they don't have a phone.

Opera
If you are in Naples from December to June, the traditional opera season, have the proper attire (suits for men, dresses for women), and have a taste for something out of the ordinary, try :
• **Teatro San Carlo**, *Via San Carlo 98f, 80132 Napoli. Tel. 081/797-2331 Or 797-2412, Fax 081/797-2306*

SPORTS & RECREATION
Golf
• **Circolo Golf Napoli**, *Via Campiglione 11, 80072 Arco Felice. Tel. 081/526-4296*. Located only 5 km from Naples, this is a 9 hole, par 35, course that is 2,601 meters long. It is open year round except Mondays and Tuesdays. They also have a driving range, pull carts, and a bar/restaurant. A good place to come if you're going through golf withdrawal.

SHOPPING
The main shopping streets with fancy shops are the **Corso Umberto**, **Via Toledo**, and **Via Chiaia**. Along these streets you'll find your international style, upscale, expensive stores. For additional shopping suggestions, see *Seeing the Sights: Historic Naples* above.

English Language Bookstores
• **Feltrinelli**, *Via San T. d'Aquino 70. Open Monday through Friday 9:00am to 8:00pm, Saturdays 9:00am to 1:00pm*. They have an extensive selection of English language travel guides as well as some paperback novels.
• **Universal Books**, *Rione Sirignano*. This store has books in many different languages and only a small selection of paperbacks in English.

PRACTICAL INFORMATION
Bank Hours & Changing Money
Banks are open Monday through Friday from 8:30am to 1:30pm and some do reopen from 2:30pm or so to 4:30pm or so. Most exchange

NAPLES & THE AMALFI COAST

money but strangely enough some do not in Naples. The **Stazione Centrale** has a *cambio* inside that is open from 8:00am to 1:30pm and 2:30pm to 8:00pm.

If you're looking for an **American Express** office you'll have to go all the way to **Sorrento** *(Tel. 081/807-3088).*

Business Hours

From October to June, most shops are open from 9:00am to 1:00pm and from 3:30pm to 7:30pm, and are closed all day Sundays and on Monday morning. Then from June to September, when it really starts to get hot in Naples, the morning hours remain the same, but the mid-day siesta time is slightly extended to 4:00pm and sometimes 4:30pm, which then pushes closing time back to 7:30pm or 8:00pm. And also, in conjunction with being closed on Sunday and Monday mornings, shops are also closed half-days on Saturday.

Food stores, like *alimentari,* generally are open from 8:30am to 1:30pm (so stock up on your picnic supplies before you need them) and from 5:00pm to 7:30pm, and during the winter months they are closed on Thursdays.

Consulates

• **United States**, *Piazza della Repubblica, Naples,* Tel. *081/583-8111*

Postal Services

You can buy stamps at local tobacconists (they are marked with a "T" outside) as well as post offices. Mail boxes are colored red. Post offices are open from 8:00am to 2:00pm on weekdays. The two exceptions to this rule are the **main post office** (**Palazzo delle Poste**) at Piazza Matteoti and the office at the Stazione Centrale, both of which are open Monday through Friday from 8:00am to 7:30pm, and Saturday from 8:00am to noon.

Tourist Information & Maps

The **EPT** has an extensive office at the Stazione Centrale, where you can get some pretty good maps, as well information on ferries, reservations for hotels, and pick up a copy of the necessary *Qui Napoli* publication that tells you what's going on around the city *(Tel. 081/268-779).*

EXCURSIONS & DAY TRIPS: POMPEII & HERCULANEUM

If you have any free time while in Naples, try to visit the two ancient cities of **Pompeii** and **Herculaneum**. They are truly a major wonder of the world: two cities trapped in time by a devastating volcanic eruption. What more could you ask for? The other excursion in this section that you can undertake from Naples as a day trip or a more extensive stay, is the beautiful isle of **Capri**.

Two thousand people died and thousands more lost their homes when **Vesuvius** erupted in 79 CE, submerging **Pompeii**, **Herculaneum**, and **Stabiae** with lava. The lava created an almost perfect time capsule, sealing in an important cross-section of an ancient civilization.

ARRIVALS & DEPARTURES
By Car
From Naples, take the S18 to the S70.

By Train
From Napoli Centrale, go one floor below the Central Station to the Circumvesuviana station for a local high speed train to Ercolano (Herculaneum) or Pompeii Scavi (3 1/2 to 4 hours total journey). Purchase one of the inexpensive maps available so you can find your way through the two ruined cities.

POMPEII
Before the catastrophe, **Pompeii** was an old established city with a diverse population of about 25,000 that reflected successive waves of colonization. By 80 BCE, it was a favorite resort of wealthy Romans.

Although the ruins were discovered in the 16th century and rudimentary excavations began in 1763, systematic excavations did not get under way until 1911. Since then only about three fifths of the site has been freed from the death grip of the lava.

Strolling through this dead city is quite ominous. You can easily imagine yourself living here. Many pieces of regular life remain: the walls are covered in ancient graffiti, ranging from erotic drawings to political slogans, since a local election was taking place when the eruption occurred. There are also abundant frescoes depicting mythological scenes in the wealthier homes, as well as frescoes indicating what form of work the owners of the house partook in.

Some of the best homes to see are the **House of the Faun** and the **House of the Vettii**, both in the residential area north of the Forum. Other homes of interest are the **House of the Melander** (located to the east of the Forum), the **Villa of the Mysteries** (located to the west of the main town), and the **House of Pansa** (located to the north of the Forum) that also included rented apartments.

Also in evidence in the remains are symbols of the cult of Dionysis. But this cult was only one of many that flourished in the city. The **Temple of Isis** (to the East of the Forum) testifies to the strong following that the

Egyptian goddess had here. The public **Amphitheater**, in the east of the city, should not be missed. There are locations on the stage area that if a whisper is spoken, even a person standing at the top-most part of the seating area can hear it clearly. Other attractions are the footprints left in time, the mummified bodies trying to shield themselves from the lava, and more.

Unfortunately, most of the best-preserved artifacts are not in Pompeii anymore, they are in the national Museum in Naples. Also in the past twenty years, due to many different forces – mafia, mismangement, tourists, thieves, pollution, neglect, corruption and uncontrolled weeds – Pompeii is no longer the true wonder it used to be.

World Monuments Watch has declared Pompeii one of the world's most imperiled cultural sites, but the good news is that they are helping to restore Pompeii to the wonder it once was. Even in the state it is in now, Pompeii still is something to behold. It is unique anywhere in the world – where else can you find a city frozen in time as a result of a volcanic erutpion? – and as such it should be visited.

Gates to the site open year round 9:00am to 1 hour before sunset. Admission L15,000.

HERCULANEUM

Seventeen miles northeast of Pompeii is the smaller town of **Herculaneum**. At the time of the eruption it had only 5,000 inhabitants, compared to the 25,000 in Pompeii, had virtually no commerce, and its industry was solely based on fishing. The volcanic mud that flowed through every building and street in Herculaneum was different from that which buried Pompeii. This steaming hot lava-like substance settled eventually to a depth of 40 feet and set rock-hard, sealing and preserving everything it came in contact with. Also the absence of the hail of hot ash that rained down on Pompeii, which smashed its buildings, meant that many of the inhabitants of Herculaneum were able to get away in time, and that complete houses, with their woodwork, household goods, and furniture were preserved.

Although Herculaneum was a relatively unimportant town compared with Pompeii, many of the houses that have been excavated were from the wealthy class. It is speculated that perhaps the town was like a retirement village, populated by prosperous Romans seeking to pass their retirement years in the calm of a small seaside town. This idea is bolstered by the fact that the few craft shops that have been discovered were solely for the manufacture of luxury goods.

Archaeologists speculate that the most desirable residential area was in the southwest part of town which overlooked the ocean in many different housing terraces. Here you will find the **House of the Stags**, famous for its beautiful frescoes, sculpted stags, and a drunken figure of Hercules.

Farther north you can find the marvelously preserved **House of the Wooden Partition**. It is one of the most complete examples of a private residence in either Pompeii or Herculaneum. (Remember that this town was recently discovered which allowed for better preservation efforts, unlike Pompeii which was discovered in the 16th century) Near this house to the north are the **Baths**, an elaborate complex incorporating a gymnasium and assorted men's and women's baths.

Gates to the site open year round 9:00am to 1 hour before sunset. Admission L10,000.

CAPRI

Capri is an island geared completely for the reaping of tourist dollars. That doesn't mean that it is not beautiful, like the **Blue Grotto**, but remember that in the summer the population of Capri fluctuates perhaps more than any other island in the world. This increase is a result of many tourists from the mainland and all over the world, and temporary residents who summer on the island.

In winter, life reverts to the dreamy pace that has been so characteristic of Capri over the centuries. So if you want to see a relatively pristine part of paradise unsoiled by rampant tourism, try to visit in the winter months. Many tourist stores and restaurants will be closed, but you'll have the island almost to yourself.

ARRIVALS & DEPARTURES

By Ferry

Head over to the ferry or hydrofoil docks (they only run in the summer). Go to the Mole Beverello to catch the ferry or hydrofoil (tourist cars are not allowed on the island, so you'll have to leave it in Naples. Not a good idea.)

By Train

From Napoli Centrale the train takes about 2 hours and 30 minutes. Then take a taxi to Molo Beverello in the harbor to catch the ferry or hydrofoil to the island.

WHERE TO STAY

1. QUISISANA E GRAND HOTEL, *Via Camerelle 2, 80073 Capri, Tel. 081/837-0788. Fax 081/837-6080. 150 rooms, 15 suites all with bath. All credit cards accepted. Single L225,000-325,000; Double L330,000-600,000. Closed November 1 to March 31.* *****

You'll stay in the lap of luxury in one of the more famous hotels in the world. An ultra-luxurious hotel with an indoor and outdoor swimming pool, health club, tennis courts, sauna, a great restaurant, as well as excellent views of the whole island. The rooms are large and comfortable and have all the amenities you could expect: mini-bar, TV, air conditioning, room service, hairdryers and even a safe for your valuables. If you have the means, this is *the* place to stay.

2. LA RESIDENZA, *Via F Serena 22, 80073 Capri. Tel. 081/837-0833. Fax 081/837-7564. 114 rooms all with bath. All credit cards accepted. Single L170,000-200,000; Double L260,000-320,000.* ****

The second largest hotel on the island (the Quisisana e Grand Hotel is larger), you'll find everything you could want for your stay on Capri: a good restaurant with a great view, a pool with interesting guests, a hotel bar, location on the sea, clean and comfortable rooms, transport around the island, and more. But if you want the romantic intimacy of a smaller hotel, this is not the place to stay. It's so large that you can get lost in the crowd. But if you want anonymity for you and your special friend, this is a good choice.

3. LA SCALINATELLA, *Via Tragara 10, 80073 Capri. Tel. 081/837-0633. Fax 081/837-8291. 30 rooms all with bath. Single L250,000-400,000; Double L320,000-630,000. All credit cards accepted. Closed November to March.* ****

Located on the sea, this small intimate hotel offers you the charm you're looking for when you think of Capri. Run by the same family that operates the Quisisana, here they can give you much more personal attention since there are only 30 rooms compared to 150. The hotel also has a pool by which you can get your meals served; or you can go to the restaurant that offers perfect views for an intimate dining experience. The rooms are ample, many with great views. They are clean, wonderfully decorated with antiques, and comfortable. This is definitely the most romantic place to stay in Capri.

4. SAN MICHELE DI ANACAPRI, *Via G Orlandi 3, 80071 Capri. Tel. 081/837-1427. Fax 081/837-1420. Single L100,000-140,000; Double L150,000-220,000. Breakfast extra. All credit cards accepted.* ***

Oh my, what a view. Located on the edge of a cliff overlooking the water, almost all the rooms have the most spectacular view you could find anywhere. The excellent restaurant and swimming pool share the same scenery. It doesn't have the intimacy of a smaller hotel, but it has worlds of ambiance, character and charm. The rooms are large and comfortable and bathrooms are immaculate.

5. CERTOSELLA, *Via Tragara 13, 80071 Capri. Tel. 081/837-0713. Fax 081/837-6113. CLosed November and Easter. 12 rooms all with bath. Single L120,000-230,000. Double L 200,000-300,000. All credit cards accepted. Breakfast included.* ***

On the wau to the Belvedere Tragara in a central but tranquil location. Operated by the proprietor of the restaurant Canzone del Mare listed below, the food in their small restaurant, for obvious reasons, is superb. The accommodations are pleasant and comfortable with simple furnishings. Some rooms have terraces which are a great place on which to relax in the evenings. The bathrooms are of medium size and come with hair dryers. They have an ample swimming pool . All the amenities of a three star. A great little hotel.

6. VILLA SARAH, *Via Tiberio 3, 80071 Capri. Tel. 081/837-0689. Fax 081/837-7215. Closed from the end of October until Easter. 20 rooms all with bath. Single L120,000-160,000; Double L200,000-260,000. American Express, Mastercard and Visa accepted. Breakfast included.* ***

A villa with a garden located in a tranquil setting away from the bustling crowds along the road that takes you to the Villa Tiberio. The rooms are ample, bright, come with small terraces, are clean and comfortable and are filled with peace and quiet.The bathrooms are also accommodating and come with all necessary amenities. Agreat place to stay while in Capri.

7. VILLA KRUPP, *Via Matteoti 12, 00871 Capri. Tel. 081/837-0362. Fax 081/837-6489. Closed January. 12 rooms all with bath. Single L100,000; Double L160,000-210,000. Visa accepted. Breakfast included.* **

This place is bucking for three star status but they have a little way to go. But that doesn't mean that a stay here is not pleasant. The hotel is located in a wonderful little villa that was once the home of the writer Massimo Gorky, who was in love with Capri. Situated by the gardens of Augustus and near the center of Capri, but far enough away from all the confusion, the atmosphere is pleasant and welcoming like a good bed and breakfast. There is a large terrace with good panoramic views, a TV room and small bar area downstairs. The rooms are clean, comfortable and accommodating; the bathrooms come with all amenities. TVs are also in the room. A good place to stay at a good price in Capri.

NAPLES & THE AMALFI COAST 271

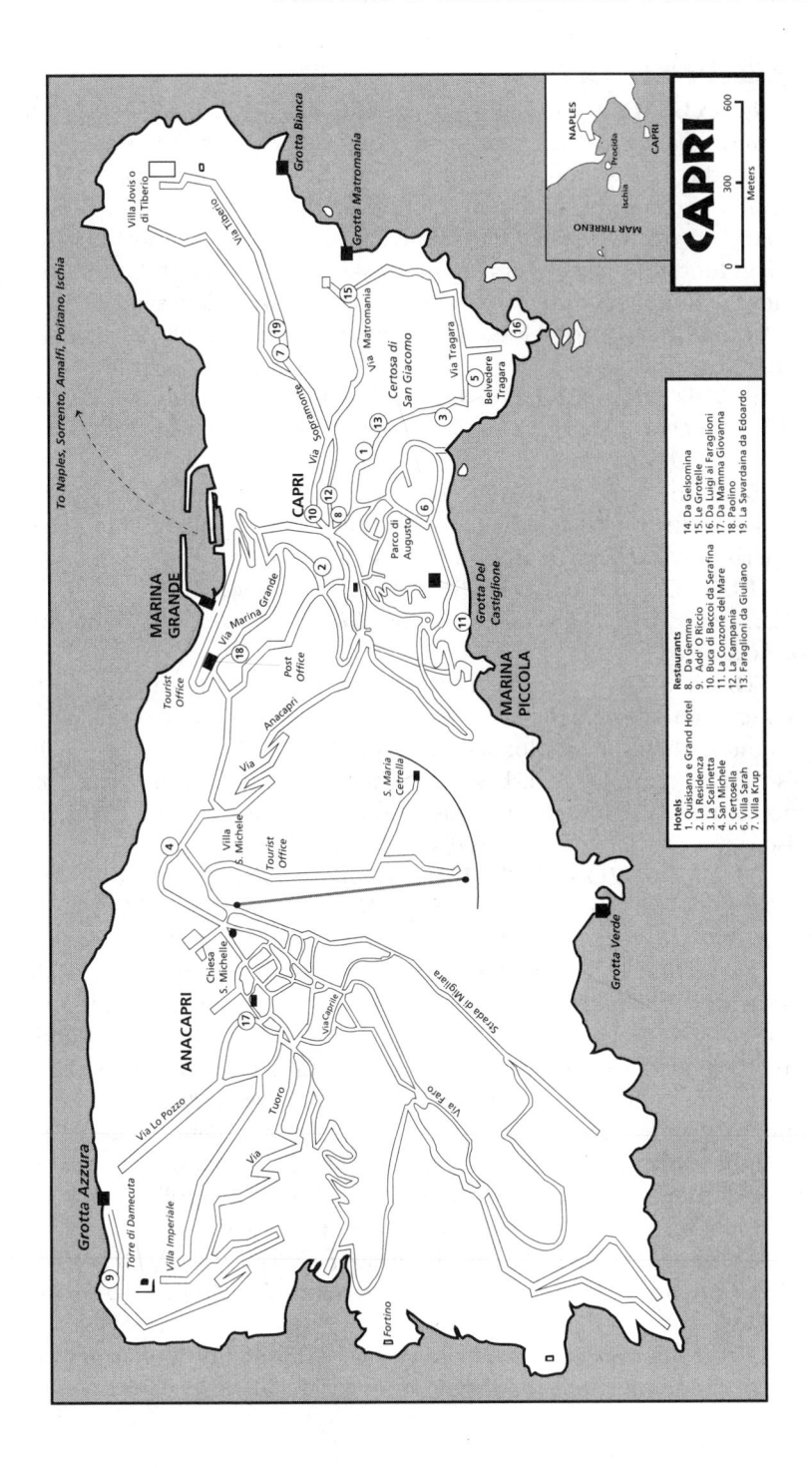

WHERE TO EAT

8. DA GEMMA, *Via Madre Serafina 6, Capri, Tel. 081/837-0461. Closed Mondays and November. Dinner for two L50,000. All credit cards accepted.*

In the hot summer months, come here to enjoy the cool air-conditioned comfort and great food. Even though Gemma is no longer around to run the place, her family continues the tradition of classic Italian food with just enough flair to make them unique and interesting. They are famous for their *spaghetti alla vongole* (with clam sauce) and the *"fritto alla Gemma"* (fried food alla Gemma with mozzarella, zucchini and other vegetables).

9. ADD' O' RICCIO, *Locanda Gradola, Via Grotta Azzurra 4, Tel. 081/837-1380. Open all week. Closed for holidays November 10 - March 15. Dinner for two L110,000. All credit cards accepted.*

Come here for the food as well as the beautiful terrace overlooking the water, the rocks, and the Grotta Azzurra (Blue Grotto). They make a superb *risotto al mare* (seafood rice dish) and grilled or baked fish.

10. BUCA DI BACCO DA SERAFINA, *Via Longano 35, Tel. 081/837-0723. Closed Wednesdays and November. Dinner for two L80,000. All credit cards accepted.*

This is a small pizzeria trattoria with the wood burning oven the center of attention in the place. As you can guess, they make great pizzas. Try one of their specials, loaded with mozzarella and ricotta cheeses. They also make great pasta dishes, including a *pennette alla peperoni* (small tubular pasta in a tomato and sausage sauce). Since they're on Capri, they also serve a variety of seafood dishes for good prices.

11. LA CANZONE DEL MARE, *Via Marina Piccola 93, Tel. 081/837-0104. Only open for dinner. Holidays November to March. Meal for two L110,000. All credit cards accepted.*

Located at the small marina with a beautiful terrace overlooking everything. The perfect place to enjoy a meal and watch the people go by. You can get a variety of food here, including *bruschetta* (toasted Italian bread) loaded with mozzarella, tomatoes and olive oil, as well as a scrumptious club sandwich. Any of their *antipasti di mare* (seafood appetizers) are superb. Try their *spaghetti con pomodoro e basilico* (with tomatoes and basil) or their *spaghetti ai frutti di mare* (with seafood). For seconds they have a great selection of fresh fish, either grilled, cooked in the oven, or *all'aqua pazza* (in crazy water, i.e. boiled).

12. LA CAMPANINA, *Via delle Botteghe 12, Tel. 081/837-0732. Closed Wednesdays and November to Easter. Dinner for two L140,000. All credit cards accepted.*

A fine family-run, upscale, but rustic establishment. You'll enjoy the air conditioning in the heat of the summer. Try their *linguine ai frutti di mare* (with seafood) and their *conniglio "alla tiberiana"* (rabbit stewed with tomatoes and spices). Here you'll get peasant fare for a princely sum.

13. FARAGLIONI DA GIULIANO, *Via Camarelle 75, Tel. 081/837-0320. Closed Mondays and November 15 to March 15. Dinner for two L110,000. All credit cards accepted.*

You can enjoy the traditional cooking either in air conditioned comfort inside or out on their terrace overlooking the street. They make a good *risotto alla pescatore* (rice with seafood), *spaghetti ai frutti di mare* (with seafood) and any of their grilled fish dishes, especially the sole.

14. DA GELSOMINA *(Anacapri) Via Belvedere Migliari, Tel. 081/837-1499. Closed Tuesdays and January 20-31. Dinner for two L70,000. All credit cards accepted.*

Off the beaten path, and quite a hike from Anacapri or Capri, but it's worth the journey. Great peasant food served on a beautiful verandah overlooking the ocean and the lights from Capri below. Try their *spaghetti alla cozze* (with muscles) or their great antipasto table for primo. Then sample their great *conniglio alla cacciatore* (rabbit with a tomato, brandy, and mixed spices - you have to try it).

15. LE GROTELLE, *Via Arco Naturale 5, Tel. 081/837-5719. Closed Thursdays and December 1 - January 3. Dinner for L 100,000. All credit cards accepted.*

Out in the middle of a virtual nature preserve, from the terrace you have a spectacular view of the sea, the stars, and nature. Here you get typical local fare like *pasta e fagioli* (pasta and beans), *ravioli alla caprese* (ravioili with seafood made Capri style), and fish either fried or grilled. If you sit inside, these delicious smells permeate the rooms making your meal all the more enjoyable.

16. DA LUIGI AI FARAGLIONI, *Strade dei Faraglioni, Tel. 081/837-0591. Open only for dinner. Dinner for two L120,000. All credit cards accepted.*

The best terrace in Capri. Out on a small peninsula, you can try some wonderfully prepared seafood dishes like *saute di vongole* (sauteed clams), or *pomodoro "alla Luigi"* (with mozzarella e basil) or *pizza "Monacone"* (filled with vegetables). Come for the romantic view (remember to reserve a spot) and stay for the food.

17. DA MAMMA GIOVANNA *(Anacapri) Via Boffe 3/5, Tel. 081/837-2057. Closed Mondays and the ten days after Christmas. Dinner for two L80,000. All credit cards accepted.*

Located in the heart of Anacapri, this is a small, quaint, local trattoria that makes great pizzas as well as grilled or oven cooked meats and fish. They have a terrace from which you can watch the night pass as you sip your dry house wine and enjoy the food.

18. PAOLINO, *Via Palazzo a Mare 11, Tel. 081/837-6102. Closed Mondays and January 15 to Easter. Dinner for two L120,000. All credit cards accepted.*

They've got old stoves and other cooking devices for the bases of the tables, which lends the place a nice down to earth touch that seems to go well with their sky high prices. Try their *ravioli alla caprese* (ravioili with seafood made Capri style), *spaghetti con pomodoro* (with spicy herbed tomatoes), or *rucola e gamberi* (pasta with shrimp) for primo. For seconds try any of their seafood on the grill.

19. LA SAVARDINA DA EDOARDO, *Via Lo Capo Tiberio 8, Tel. 081/837-6300. Closed November to March. Dinner for two L75,000. All credit cards accepted.*

You can only get here on foot, but it's worth the hike. Some of the best food on the island as well as some of the best prices. The terrace looks out over lemon and other fruit trees making the meal quite tranquil. They make great *fiori di zucchine fritte* (fried zucchini flowers) and *conniglio alla cacciatore* (succulent rabbit cooked in tomatoes, brandy, and spices). A nice place to come for a change of pace.

SEEING THE SIGHTS

To get to the town of Capri after you've made it to the Marina Grande, the main harbor on the island, take the funicular up the mountain. Once you reach the **Piazza Umberto I** you can enjoy the view out onto the Bay of Naples. This is the perfect piazza to have a seat at a cafe and watch the world go by. You'll pay a king's ransom for a coffee but the ambiance and character of the square need to be savored slowly, while seated.

From here it's a long walk northeast to the **Palace of Tiberius**, the biggest and best preserved Imperial villa on the island. You won't find elaborate mosaic floors or statues in place here, and at first the site might seem disappointing. What makes this place special is the sheer extent of the ruins located in such a superb setting. Built in the first century, the villa was initially 12 stories high but only partial remains of three remain. The beehive of passageways leading to many small rooms make it evident that this villa functioned as a mini-city, with baths, store rooms and servants' quarters. The Palace is perched on an imposing hilltop called **Il Salto** (the Leap) from which the Emperor is said to have thrown his enemies (and if you've read any Roman history this is probably true). *Open daily 9:00am until 1 hour before sunset. Admission L5,000.*

On the south edge of town is the **Certosa di San Giacomo**, a 14th century Carthusian monastery that was founded in 1371, destroyed in 1553 and rebuilt soon after. It was used as a prison and a hospice in the 1800s and today houses a secondary school and a library. The cloisters and the dark Gothic church are open to the public. The frescoes in the church are interesting to view but the cloister can be missed, especially the Museo Deifenbach, with its dark and crusty oil paintings.

From the monastery, walk along the Via di Certosa to the **Parco Augusto**. From the terrace there are nice views to the south of the island over the Marina Piccola (small harbor) and the Faraglioni rock formations. Bring your camera. From here you can follow a road that leads to the Marina Piccola and see the private yachts and fishing boats close up.

My favorite part of the island is the town of **Anacapri**. You get here either by bus or taxi from Capri. Anacapri is more relaxed and down-to-earth than Capri. Perched high up on a rocky plateau, its flat-roofed whitewashed buildings are Moorish in style. You can find the 18th century **Church of San Michele**, *open daily 7:00am-7:00pm*, with it sober Baroque design and intricate frescoed floors. The **Villa San Michele** is known for its beautiful gardens (with spectacular views) and vast collection of classical sculpture, *open summer 9:00am-6:00pm, winter 10:00am-3:00pm; admission L12,000*. If you want to go higher, from Anacapri you can walk or take a chair lift up to **Monte Solaro**, which has amazing views over all of Capri. You catch the chairlift from Piazza Vittoria, and the trip up here is equal in spectacle to the trip to the Blue Grotto below. Here you will find one of the world's premier picnic spots, so come prepared. But bring a sweater or jacket even on sunny days, since the wind tends to cool things down slightly.

Finally, visit the famous **Grotta Azzura** or **Blue Grotto**. You can walk or take the bus down the via Grotta Azzura from Anacapri. Once at the bottom you can hire a boat to take you into the grotto, or you can come from Marina Grande by motorboat with a number of other people, then transfer to rowboats to enter the grotto. You will have to sit on the floor of the row-boat as the captain (on his back) leads the boat in by pulling hand over hand on a length of fixed chain. The silver-blue light inside is close to indescribable. Suffice to say it is magnificent. The color of the water is caused by refraction of light entering the grotto beneath the surface. Don't foolishly deny yourself the joy of this excursion for fear of being labeled a tourist. The Blue Grotto really is worth seeing no matter how cheesy it appears. *Open 24 hours. Boat trips from Marina Grande go from 9:00am-6:00pm. Cost L10,000.*

Walking is by far the best way of getting about the island, but horse-drawn carriages, buses and taxis operate, linking Capri and Anacapri. The island seems bigger than its ten square kilometers suggest, due to an undulating landscape resting upon sheer limstone cliffs. If you are walking during the summer months, remember to rest frequently because the hills are very steep, especially in Capri. Anacapri is easier to walk around since it sits on a plateau. Also remember to bring along some water to prevent dehydration even in the cooler, off-season months.

PROCIDA

Located in the Bay of Naples, **Procida's** beauty has achieved worldwide acclaim as a result of the Oscar winning Italian movie, *Il Postino*, partially set on the island. The movie was able to capture the quaint, picturesque quality of this magnificent little island located in the Bay of Naples. The island's tiny towns are strewn with houses of fading pink, blue and yellow all thrown together in a Byzantine labyrinth of cobblestone streets.

Originally a volcano that now has five inactive craters, Procida is awash with vineyards and citrus plantations overlooking a spectacular sea dotted with small fishing boats of green, orange, navy and white collecting the day's catch for the local restaurants and households.

ARRIVALS & DEPARTURES

Take the ferry to the island from Molo Beverello in Naples harbor. The trip takes about an hour and they run almost every hour.

WHERE TO STAY

There are not many upscale places to stay on Procida, but with its newfound popularity this might change. For the most part, people come for a day trip, then go back to Naples, Capri, or Ischia. But if you want a little peace and quiet, here are two comfortable options.

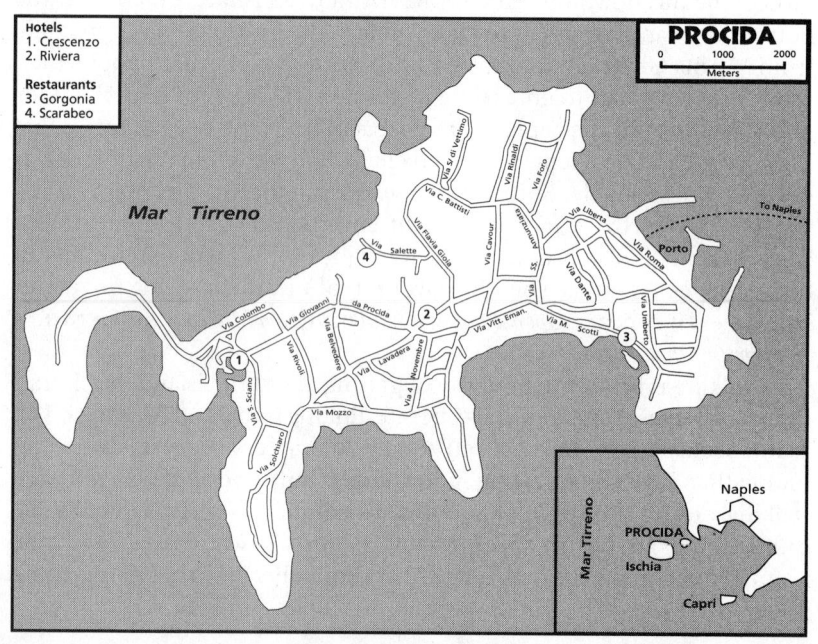

1. **CRESCENZO**, *Via Marina Chiaiolella 33, 80079 Procida. Tel. 081/896-7255. Fax 081/810-1260. 10 rooms all with bath. Double L90,000-116,000. Credit cards accepted. Full board L79,000-109,000.* ***
The best of the few options available on Procida. An adequate three star with air conditioning and TV in the room. This is like an intimate bed and breakfast, but in the middle of the Mediterranean. Relaxing, clean and comfortable.

2. **RIVIERA**, *Via G. da Procida 36, 80079 Procida. Tel. 081/896-7197. 26 rooms all with bath. Single L40,000-45,000; Double L70,000-90,000; No credit cards accepted. Full board L70,000-100,000.* **
A cute little two star with hardly any amenities. There's a TV and phone in the spartan rooms, and a quaint little garden area in which you can relax, but other than that, this place is bare bones. But there are limited options on the island, and you knew it was going to be rustic.

WHERE TO EAT

3. **GORGONIA**, *Marina Corricella 50, Tel. 081/810-1060. Never closed in the summer and only open on the weekends and holidays in the winter. Credit cards accepted. Dinner for two L80,000.*
In the summer you can enjoy a meal outside on the terrace overlooking the sea. A truly relaxing and romantic way to dine. A *gorgonia* is a local sea plant and that maritime theme is played out in the menu. I really like the *linguini al pescatore* ('fishermen's linguine,' meaning it is covered in seafood). And for seconds, any and all grilled fish are superb.

4. **SCARABEO**, *Via Saleto 10, Tel. 081/896-9918. Never closed in the summer and only open on the weekends and holidays in the winter. Closed November. No credit cards accepted. Dinner for two L70,000.*
Located in a splendid little garden, this trattoria is as traditional as you can get. Large and boisterous atmosphere filled with locals and tourists alike – and the food doesn't disappoint either. The antipasto is overflowing, and the pastas superb. I especially like the *linguine con broccoli e cozze* (pasta with broccoli and mussels). For seconds, the fresh fish just out of the bay is fantastic, as is the succulent *conniglio alla cacciatore* (rabbit stewed in a tomato, spices and wine sauce).

SEEING THE SIGHTS

The island is a celebration of natural beauty and uncontaminated locations. Even though it is a popular tourist attraction, Procida has designated a large segment of its mass, the peninsula of Vivara, as a nature preserve. Besides nature walks, Procida offers all sorts of water sports, including wind surfing, water skiing, snorkeling, and more. In conjunction there are sights to see: the castle of **Punta S Angelo**, an ancient prison; the church of **Santa Maria della Pieta**, the **Abbey of Saint Michael the**

Archangel that dates back to the 13th century, and the monastery of **Punta del Monaci**.

Procida is the ideal location to come to witness the way life used to be in Italy (but not in the high season), with fishermen plying their trade, housewives and restaurant owners clamoring over the daily catch, locals congregating in the piazzas, and life slowed down to a human pace. There are scores of amazing vistas on Procida, wide open seascapes and enchanting towns – **Ciraccio, Corricella, Chiaiolella, Pozzo Vecchio** – all bursting with color and alive with activity. Procida has a definite emotional pull with its unhurried pace and friendly attitude. As such, Procida is the perfect antidote for civilization.

PRACTICAL INFORMATION

• **Tourist Information,** *Via Roma (Stazione Maritima), Tel. 081/810-968*

ISCHIA

The island of **Ischia** has been inhabited since prehistoric times, as evidenced by flint and glass instruments dating from 300 BCE being located inland, as well as some Bronze and Iron Age objects. Located in the Bay of Naples, the island was formed by volcanic eruptions, the last of which was in 1301, which caused the inhabitants to flee the island for four years. Today the only remnant of those days are the curative thermal baths that make Ischia so popular. But not with Americans for some reason. Ischia is mainly frequented by Europeans; the Americans go to Capri.

These baths have become the gold mine of the island. In the 1950s and '60s, a hotel boom erupted to capitalize on this natural resource, and today there are many thermal complexes for the public and many private ones attached to hotels. They are open from early April to the end of October and cater to an international clientele.

The tourism 'dollars' generated from the baths is Ischia's main source of revenue. Farming is also an important industry (especially on the southern part of the island which is less developed in terms of tourism than the rest of the island), and strangely fishing comes in a distant third. It could be that most of the fish have been culled from the local waters many centuries ago.

ARRIVALS & DEPARTURES

Take the ferry to the island from Molo Beverello in Naples harbor. The trip takes about an hour and they run almost every hour.

WHERE TO STAY

There are so many hotels to choose from on Ischia, most of them attached to a spa/thermal bath. Many are excellent and high priced in response to that excellence. These are the best three, regardless of star rating or price.

1. GRAND HOTEL EXCELSIOR, *Via Emanuele Gianturco 19, 80077 Ischia. Tel. 081/991-522. Fax 081/984-100. 72 rooms all with bath. Single L210,000-270,000; Double L330,000-540,000. Credit cards accepted. Breakfast included. Full board L240,000-370,000.* *******

A superbly luxurious hotel with every conceivable amenity your little heart could desire. Indoor and outdoor pools, tennis courts, mud baths, saunas, fitness center, massage, and an excellent restaurant with a stunning view that serves fine local cuisine. There's also a private beach, water sport equipment rentals, day care, shuttle bus service and so much more. All of this in a quaint old building filled with the finest furnishings money could buy. The service is impeccable, the ambiance unbeatable ... but all for a very high price.

2. DELLA BAIA SAN MONTANO, *Via San Montano, Commune di Forio, 80075 Ischia. Tel. 081/986-398. Fax 081/986-342. Closed October through April. 20 rooms all with bath. Double L160,000-200,000. Credit cards accepted. Breakfast included. Full board L150,000-180,000.* *****

Located on the splendid bay of San Montano far from all the hubbub of the tourists but right by the sea, this hotel is in a splendid position. You can get a massage, practice windsurfing or simply relax in their garden setting or by the sea. The rooms are spacious: each one has its own little garden, TV, mini-fridge and phone. The bathrooms are a little small. Overall, an excellent place to stay.

3. VILLA ANGELICA, *Via 4 Novembre 28, Lacco Ameno. Tel. 081/994-524. Fax 081/980-184. Closed November 1 to April 15. 21 rooms all with bath. Single L55,000-65,000; Double L110,000-130,000. Discover card accepted. Full board L120,000.* *****

Located in a tranquil side street in Lacco Ameno, you have quiet terraces on which to sunbathe, a swimming pool filled with a spring of naturally heated water, a fine restaurant serving local dishes and some great views over the water. The rooms are somewhat small but all have balconies on which to relax. The bathrooms are no larger but are kept spotless. An inexpensive place to stay, away from all the clamor, with a taste of luxury.

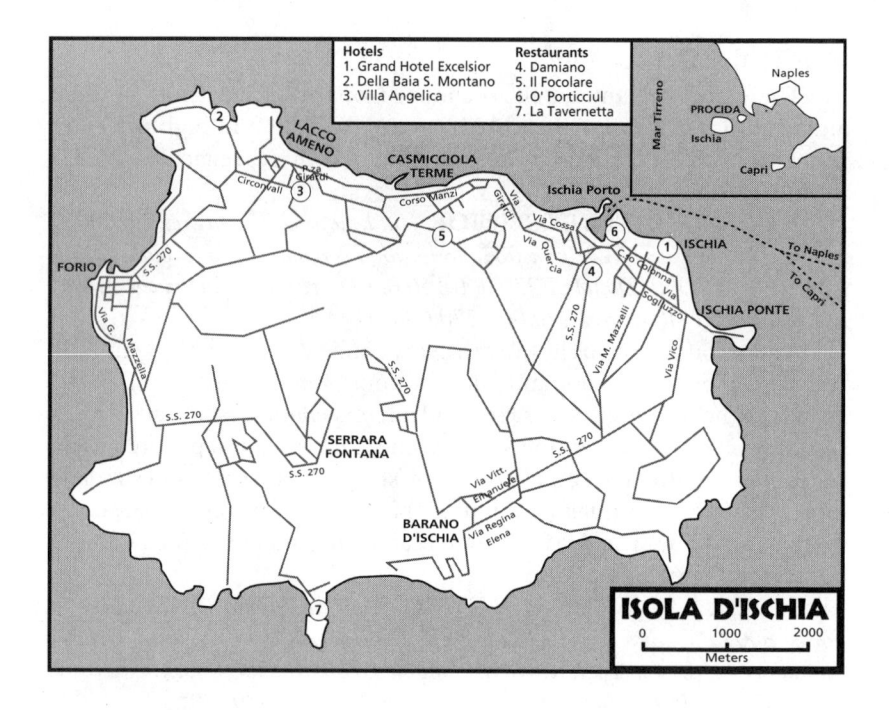

WHERE TO EAT

4. DAMIANO, *Ischia Porto on SS270, Tel. 081/983-032. Only open in the evenings. Closed Nov. 15 to March 30. No credit cards accepted. Dinner for two L120,000.*

Located in a panoramic position above Ischia Porto, this place has wonderful local food and a great atmosphere. They make a great *frutti di mare al gratin* (seafood au gratin), *linguine all'aragosta* (with lobster sauce), *spaghetti alla Maria* (with tomatoes, olive oil and capers), *risotto al pescatore* (seafood rice dish), *calamari ripieni* (stuffed shrimp). The entire menu is superb. They truly take pride in the preparation and presentation of their food.

5. IL FOCOLARE, *Terme via Cretaio 36, Tel. 081/980-604. Open only in the evenings on Saturday and Sunday. Closed Wednesdays (not in summer) and October 31 to December 31. No credit cards accepted. Dinner for two L80,000.*

A fantastic local place situated in the country above Casamicciola whose menu changes based on the seasonal produce and other food items available. In January when the pigs go to slaughter, the restaurant's main dishes are *maiale* (pork). In Spring, vegetables take over. In September, pumpkin plays a large part in the ingredients and October sees the introduction of locally grown mushrooms. Another specialty, whenever they can catch enough, is co*niglio al'Ischiano* (rabbit in a *cacciatore* style sauce with tomatoes, wine and spices). You can also get a fine cut of Angus beef. My favorite desserts are *torte alla frutta* (fruit tarts) or *sorbetto al limone* or *al sambuca* (crushed ice dessert of lemon or the liqueur sambuca). The wines are all locally grown, some produced by the family vines.

6. O PORTICCIUL, *Via Porto 42, Tel. 081/993-222. Closed Mondays (not in summer) and November. From January 31 to August 31 only open Saturday and Sunday evenings. Credit cards accepted. Dinner for two L140,000.*

An expensive option, but with great vistas and equally great food. Feast on classic local cuisine like *antipasto di pesce* (mixed antipasto of fish), *insalata di aragosta* (lobster salad), *frutti di mare a sauté* (sautéed seafood), *zuppa di pesce* (fish soup), *spaghetti alla vongole* (with clam sauce), *bucatini con cozze e pecorini* (pasta with mussels and pecorino cheese), *pesce alla griglia or all'aqua pazza* (grilled or boiled fish). In autumn, the succulent mushrooms are harvested locally. A great place to dine.

7. LA TAVERNETTA, *Via Sant'Angelo 77, Tel. 081/999-251. Closed Wednesdays (not from July 1 to August 31) and October 30 to February 28 (but are open during Christmas season). No credit cards. Dinner for two L60,000.*

For forty years they've been here, on the jetty of Porto Sant'Angelo serving up inexpensive traditional cuisine to locals and tourists alike. Eat on their terrace for a perfect place to have a meal by the sea. Come here if you're on the island, whether it's for a drink, meal, or a light snack. Seafood is the staple and they it's great, whether grilled, boiled, fried, baked, spread over pasta or served as an antipasto. The menu depends on the season and the catch of the day.

SEEING THE SIGHTS

Besides scenic vistas all along the coast, quaint little towns, all manner of water sports, the thermal baths, excellent restaurants and nightlife, Ischia also offers a wide variety of options for sightseeing, since each separate community on Ischia takes pride in its own piece of history.

The **Commune of Ischia** has its 17th century Cathedral with paintings and sculptures from the period, the church of Santo Spirito with some magnificent paintings, the Argonese Castle, and the centuries old wine cellar and modern perfume factory in Ischia Port.

The **Commune of Casamicciola** is famous for its thermal baths and is about to complete a commercial port to rival and compete with Ischia Port. The sights here include the Piazza Marina with its statue of Emanuele II, the church of Santa Maria Maddelena with a high altar constructed in the 1600s, and the Chiesa della Pieta with some wonderful paintings by Andrea Vaccaro.

The **Commune of Lacco Ameno** is famous for its Greek tombs, its beaches, mineral waters, and the Church of Santa Restituta that dates back to the 4th century and the museum attached to it that contains many objects from Ischia's past; the Argonese tower built in the 15th century, the Villa Arbusto built on the site of Neolithic and Bronze Age settlements, and the Negombo Thermal Gardens.

The **Commune of Forio** is the largest borough on the island and contains many churches rich in frescoes and neoclassic domes, 10 ancient watchtowers, and towns with narrow streets and winding alleys. The best churches to see are the Church of Soccorso and the Brotherhood of Saint Mary the Poor. Another interesting sight is La Mortella, a stone quarry that has been transformed into an exotic and luxuriant botanical garden.

The **Commune of Serrara Fontana** is the least populated, mainly with farmers, and is predominantly hilly. The village of Sant' Angelo is a jewel you simply must see if on Ischia. The Piazza Serrara in the town of the same name is worth a see, as is the Hermitage of San Nicolo at the very top of Mount Epomeo and the church of Santa Maria la Sacra, the oldest parish church on the island.

The **Commune of Barano** is predominantly arable farmland but also has many areas dedicated to tourism, including beaches and thermal spas. The Piazza Barano is worth a visit with the churches of San Rocco and San Sebastian on either side.

SPORTS & RECREATION
- **Tennis Club Cartaromana**, *Via Nuova Cartaromana, Tel. 081/993-622*
- **Tennis Club Pineta**, *Corso Vittoria Colonna, Tel. 081/993-300*
- **Tennis Club Residence**, *Via dello Stadio, Tel. 081/981-246*
- **Tennis Communale**, *Via Cristoforo Colombo, Tel. 081/993-416*
- **Boat Rental**, *Porto di Ischia, Tel. 081/992-383*
- **Ischia Diving Center**, *Via Iasolini 106, Tel. 081/985-008*

PRACTICAL INFORMATION
Car Rental
- **Center**, *Via Michele Mazzella 109, Tel. 081/992-451*
- **Ischia**, *Via Alfredo de Luca 61/a, Tel. 081/993-259*

Laundry
- **Lavanderia Aurora**, *Via A. DeLuca 91/a, Tel. 081/991-886.* Laundry and dry cleaning services available.

Tourist Information
- **Tourist Information Office**, *Corso Colonna 16, Tel. 081/991-146*

THE AMALFI COAST

The steep slopes and rugged beauty of the **Amalfi Coast** have enchanted visitors for centuries. Mount Vesuvius reigns majestically in the distance, dominating the scenery as it once controlled the lives of the area's inhabitants with its eruptions. Dotted with little hillside towns, the only way to get to and from them is by car or bus. Neither option is too swift an alternative during the peak summer months, since the serpentine road connecting the towns is bumper to bumper traffic. In the off-season the traffic decreases considerably, but then so does the temperature, and bathing in the sea is one of the attractions of this coastline.

The road, dug almost entirely out of the rock, curves incessantly, but every turn offers coastal panoramic views of unparalleled proportions – which means that sometimes sitting in traffic can be candy for the eyes since you would have flown past the vista if the road was otherwise empty. Each town along the road has its own character but they are all blessed, or some would say cursed, with narrow curving streets and stairs that seem never to end.

The Amalfi Coast is the playground for people of all nationalities because of its unrivaled beauty and holiday options. Filled with high class hotels, excellent restaurants, countless nightlife options, ancient medieval streets and passageways, cultural sights and fun loving effervescent locals, this area is one you will wnat to return to time and time again.

POSITANO

Situated on a hill overlooking ten pristine beaches, **Positano** has been a part of this beautiful landscape for almost a thousand years. When Emperor Tiberius moved to Capri to escape the intrigue and serious threat of poisoning in Rome, he had his flour brought in from a mill in Positano, a mill that is still working today. In the 10th century Positano was one of the most important commercial centers on the Italian peninsula in active trade competition with Venice, Pisa and Genoa. In the 16th and 17th centuries, Positano was incredibly rich from all their trading activities. It was at this time that many of the beautiful Baroque homes scattered on the hills of the town were built.

Because of its timeless beauty, Positano has been the playground of the rich and famous for centuries. Writers, musicians, nobles, aristocrats – all have come here to bathe in the azure waters and relax in the lush green hillsides. Today it is no different. Filled with excellent restaurants, world class hotels, and all manner of water sports, Positano is a perfect holiday destination.

ARRIVALS & DEPARTURES

You can get to Positano by car via the coast road around the tip of the peninsula or the cross peninsula road. If you go by bus from Naples, catch a SITA bus from Piazza Municipio (*Tel. 081/55-22-176*). From Salerno you catch the bus along Via SS Martiri Salernitani (*Tel. 089/22-66-04*).

WHERE TO STAY

1. CASA ALBERTINA, *Via della Tavolozza 3, 84017 Positano. Tel. 089/875-143. Fax 089/811-540. 20 rooms all with bath. Single L120,000-150,000; Double L160,000-180,00. Credit cards accepted. Breakfast included. Full board L120,000-170,000.* ***

The area the hotel is in is quite tranquil, but it is also close to the beach, only some 300 steps down to the water. If you don't want to walk back up they have a small shuttle bus to carry you home after your swim. There are little rooms, a terrace and a solarium for your relaxing pleasure. The rooms are large and well isolated from each other. The bathrooms are a little tight but they do have all the modern amenities. Breakfast is a memorable experience filled with meats, cheeses, breads and more, which you can enjoy either in your room or on their little terrace. The restaurant is superb, with food prepared by Aunt Albertina of the family Cinque that runs the hotel. A true family affair designed to make your stay as relaxing as possible.

2. HOTEL POSEIDON, *Via Pasitea 148, 84071 Positano. Tel. 089/811-111. Fax 089/875-833. 48 rooms all with bath. Double L230,000-290,000. Credit cards accepted. Breakfast included.* ****

Located in the heart of Positano and run by the Aono family, this a fine four star hotel. Each room has a nice view from their little balconies where you can have your breakfast served. The furnishings are all antique but still comfortable. The restaurant in the summer is located in a quiet garden setting, where the solarium and pool are also located. You also have massage, exercise rooms and babysitting service at your disposal.

3. HOTEL LE SIRENUSE, *Via Cristoforo Colombo 30, 84071 Positano. Tel. 089/875-066. Fax 089/811-798. 60 rooms all with bath. Single L350,000-450,000. Double L440,000-600,000. Credit cards accepted. Breakfast included. Full board L360,000-555,000.* *****

Definitely the place to stay in Positano – everything about this place is beautiful. Nothing overly fancy, nothing too ostentatious, just simply radiant. The rooms are furnished with antiques but nothing too frilly. The bathrooms are complete with every conceivable comfort. The breakfast buffet is so ample as to dissuade most from lunch. There is a stunningly

NAPLES & THE AMALFI COAST 285

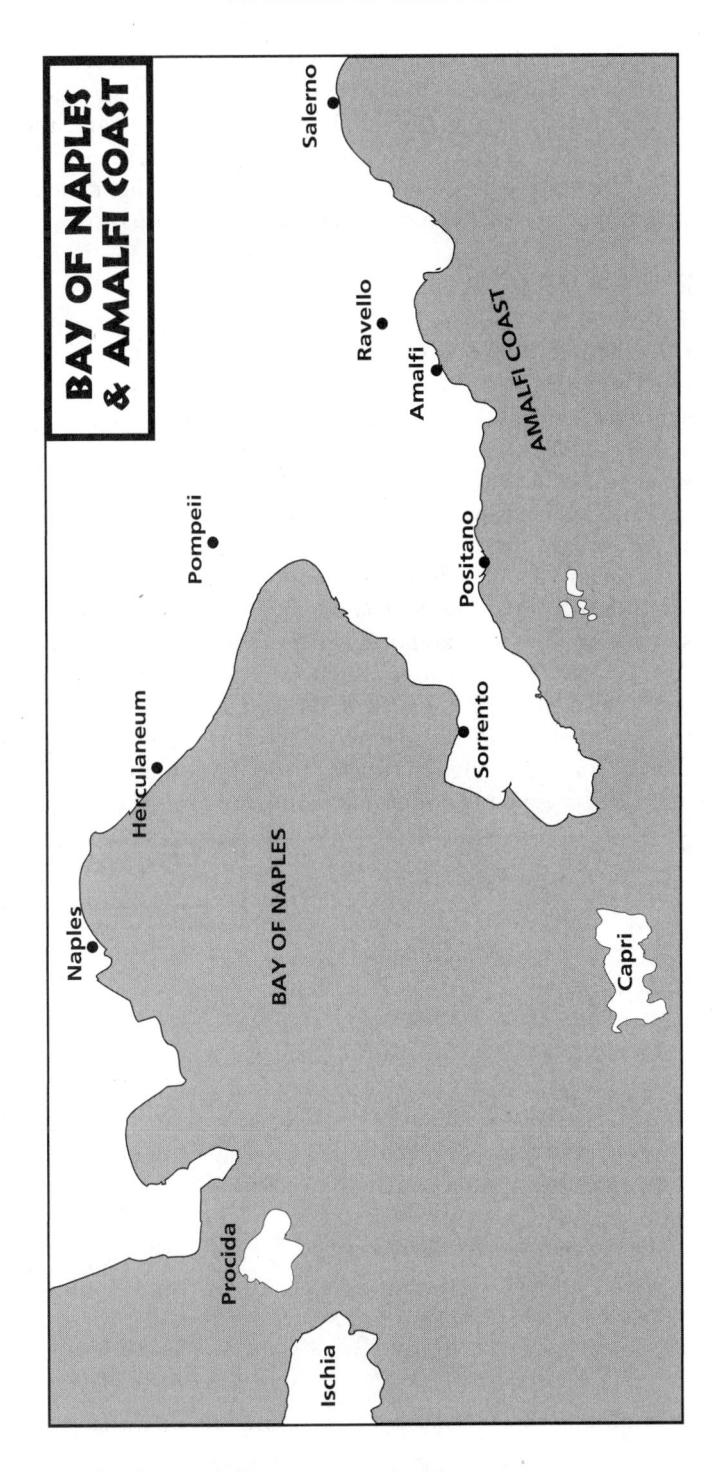

BAY OF NAPLES & AMALFI COAST

- Salerno
- Ravello
- Amalfi
- AMALFI COAST
- Pompeii
- Positano
- Herculaneum
- Sorrento
- Naples
- BAY OF NAPLES
- Capri
- Procida
- Ischia

beautiful pool at your disposal, a sauna, and a small boat to ferry you along the coast. The service here is extremely attentive. Their restaurant is one of the best, if not the best, in the city. Expensive, yes, but when the food is combined with the great views from the terrace, the price is irrelevant. All the food they make here is great, but I believe the chef concocts the best *spaghetti alla vongole* (with spicy clam sauce) in Positano.

WHERE TO EAT

4. DA ADOLFO, *Locanda Laurito, Tel. 089/875-022. Closed November 1 to May 1. Open only for lunch. No credit cards accepted. Meal for two L60,000.*

To get here you need to catch a boat from the beach at Positano. Located in a truly romantic and isolated setting but not too far from town, you have to come here when in Positano. A large place, it seats about 100. The best place to dine is on their extensive balcony overlooking the water. They are usually packed, which is why they only have to be open for lunch and only about half the year. Try some of their flavorful *spaghetti alla vongole* (with clam sauce), *agli zucchine* (with a zucchini sauce), *totani con le patate* (cuttlefish with potatoes), *la parmigiana di melanzane* (eggplant parmesan), or any of their fabulously grilled fish.

5. LA CAMBUSA, *Piazza A. Vespucci 4, Tel. 089/875-432. Closed November 11 to December 20. Credit cards accepted. Dinner for two L140,000.*

Be prepared to be wined and dined in splendor. The perfect place to dine is on the terrace facing the beach. If you don't want to order from the menu they have a daily buffet that features many different plates.

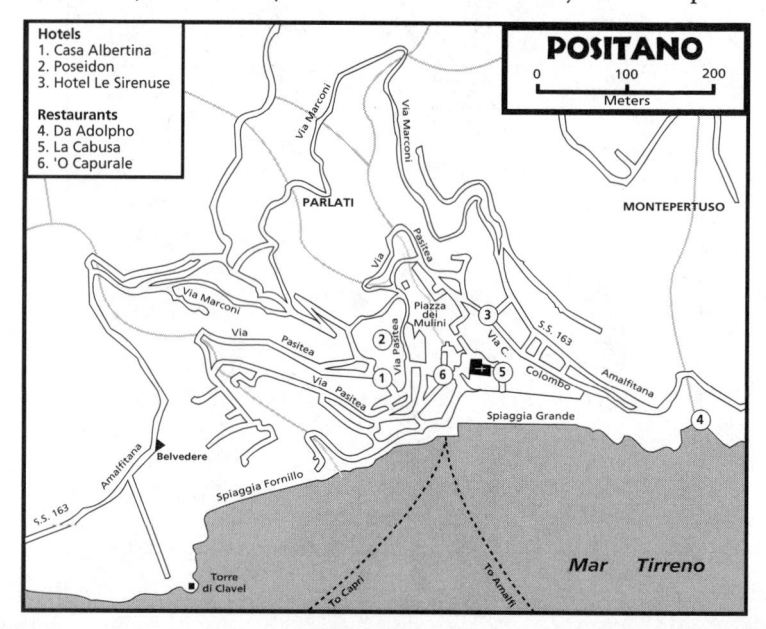

They are known for their great seafood, like *insalata di pesce* (seafood salad) or *di gamberetti* (small prawns). For *primo* try their *linguini con scampi* (with shrimp), *con frutti di mare* (with seafood), or the *zuppa di pesce* (seafood soup). For seconds you must try any of their grilled fish, served with roasted potatoes. A little expensive, but the food and ambiance are worth the price.

6. 'O CAPURALE, *Via Regina Giovanna 12, Tel. 089/811-188. Closed Tuesdays (not in summer) and January. Credit cards accepted. Dinner for two L70,000.*

This place has been in the family for over one hundred years and is part of the life of Positano. You can still find some of the older residents of the town playing cards at some of the tables. People come here for the friendly local atmosphere as well as the fine food. Start off with some *linguine all'astice* (with lobster), *agli scampi* (with shrimp), or *bucatini alla 'caporalessa'* (with mozzarella, tomatoes, eggplant, olives, and capers); then move onto *zuppa di pesce* (seafood soup) and *pesce al aqua pazza* (boiled fish).

SEEING THE SIGHTS

Positano snakes its way up from the **Harbor** (Marina Grande) where ferries dock coming from Sorrento, Capri and Naples. Along the beach by the harbor are many chic boutiques that you can find in any holiday resort. For more historic sights, try the **Santa Maria Assunta**, a 12th century church that dominates the Positano hillside. The ancient floor is a Byzantine mosaic and on the main altar is a relief of the Madonna and Child in black marble. An hour hike up the hill is **Montepertuso** (Hole in the Mountain), where there is a large cliff pierced by a hole. Legend has it that the devil challenged the Madonna to make a hole in the mountain. He failed in ten attempts, while the Virgin Mother's finger easily created the hole and at the same time pushed the devil into the mountain below the hole. Anyway ... from here your vantage point is perfect and the little village quaint. If you don't want to walk you can catch a bus at the harbor piazza (Piazza dei Mulini).

A short hike away from Montepertuso is **Nocelle**, another tiny village with great views and a quiet unassuming life. If you are here on New Year's Day, more specifically at dawn of the New Year, you will stumble onto a huge bonfire and banquet that welcomes in, through copious amounts of revelry, all the possibilities of the future.

AMALFI

Clinging to the rocky coats of the Sorrento peninsula is one of the most beautiful little holiday resorts in Italy, **Amalfi**. Legend has it that the town was established by Constantine the Great as a respite from the intrigue of Rome. By the Middle Ages it had a population of 50,000, but today it is only around 7,000 (when all the tourists leave). During the 16th and 17th centuries it was joined with the other little towns on the Amalfi Coast in competition with the other seafaring states of Venice, Genoa and Pisa.

As a tourist resort, Amalfi offers fine restaurants, wonderful hotels, nightlife, shopping, water sports and sightseeing.

ARRIVALS & DEPARTURES

You can get to Amalfi by car via the coast road or the cross peninsula road. If you go by bus from Naples, catch a SITA bus from Piazza Municipio (*Tel. 081/55-22-176*). From Salerno you catch the bus along Via SS Martiri Salernitani (*Tel. 089/22-66-04*).

WHERE TO STAY

1. LA BUSSOLA, *Lungomare dei Cavalieri 16, 84011 Amalfi. Tel. 089/ 871-533. Fax 089/871-369. 63 rooms all with bath. Single L90,000-120,000; Double L150,000-200,000. Credit cards accepted. Breakfast included. Full Board L110,000-140,000. ****

La Bussola is situated in a fine location directly on the walkway along the sea, where they have a private beach. This hotel is located in an old mill and has been in business since 1962. The rooms are well decorated and all have balconies. The bathrooms are normal with all necessary modern conveniences. The restaurant is large and has a nice view of the water. On the fourth floor is a quiet roof garden where you can relax all day long if desired. A fine three star hotel.

2. CAPPUCCINI CONVENTO, *Via Annunziatella 46, 84011 Amalfi. Tel. 089/871-877. Fax 089/871-886. 42 rooms all with bath. Single L140,000-180,000; Double L180,000-220,000. Credit cards accepted. Breakfast included. Full board L170,000-220,000. *****

From the hotel's terrace you have your own slice of the Amalfi Coast to enjoy all to yourself. This ex-monastery, built in the 1200s, is so beautiful, so quaint, so filled with character that many couples have their weddings set here. The rooms are what once were the cells for the monks that lived here, all updated with modern conveniences of course. They have a babysitting service and a fine restaurant. A peaceful place to stay. A wonderful hotel.

3. LUNA CONVENTO, *Via Comite 33, 84011 Amalfi. Tel. 089/871-002. Fax 089/871-333. 45 rooms all with bath. Double L180,000-220,000. Credit cards accepted. Breakfast included. Full board L180,000-210,000. *****

Located in convent built in 1222, this place is filled with charm. The library is the old cloisters where you can enjoy a quiet read amongst the white columns and archways. There are two restaurants to choose from, each with its own magnificent view of the water and the hotel's private beach area. There is also an outdoor pool in a garden setting to enjoy. The rooms are large and all furnished differently with pieces made by local artisans, and each has its own little terrace with a view of the water. There are fifteen internal cells turned into rooms that do not have a view. The bathrooms were modernized in 1994 so they have all modern amenities. The staff is professional and courteous.

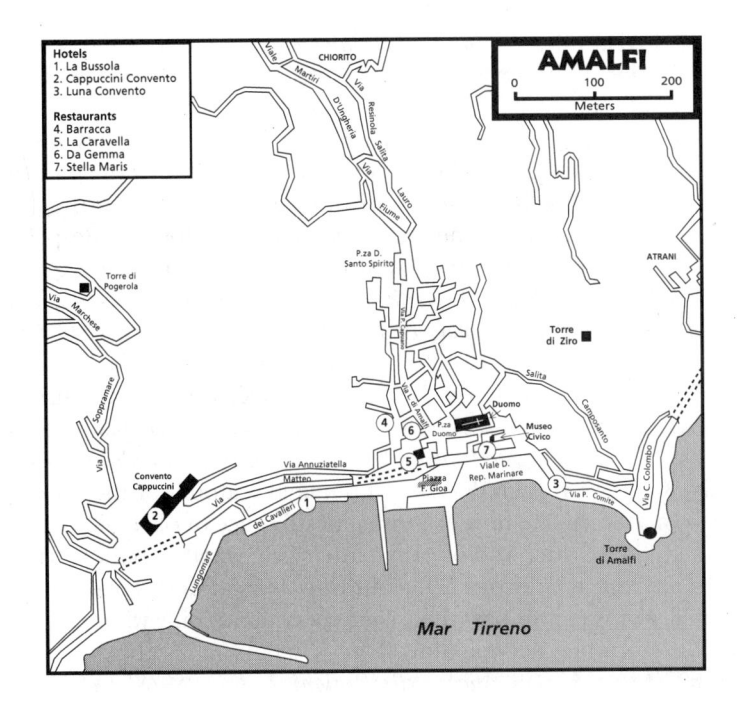

WHERE TO EAT

4. BARRACCA, *Salita Pizzo 13, Tel. 089/871-285. Closed Wednesdays (not from June 15 to September 15) and January 15 to February 15. Credit cards accepted. Dinner for two L90,000.*

Classic seafood cooking prepared with attention and served perfectly. You must try the *spaghetti alla vongole* (with a spicy clam sauce with some tomatoes added for color), *risotto alla pescatore* (fisherman's rice) and for the main course the succulent *gamberini e calamari alla griglia* (grilled shrimp and octopus) or any of the grilled fish they serve. For an after-dinner drink try one of their home made aromatic liqueurs.

5. LA CARAVELLA, *Via Matteo Camera 12, Tel. 089/871-029. Closed Wednesdays (not in the summer) and November. Credit cards accepted. Dinner for two L150,000.*

Franco Di Pino opened this place back in 1959 and now his wife concocts local specialties in the kitchen. She also makes all the pasta and desserts herself. Fish is the staple of this menu, whether in the pasta, grilled, or fried. The atmosphere is relaxing and comfortable despite the presence of a main road nearby. A little pricey but worth the expense.

6. DA GEMMA, *Via Fra' Gerardo Sasso 10, Tel. 089/871-345. Closed Wednesdays (not in the summer) and November and January. Credit cards accepted. Dinner for two L110,000.*

This place represents the best of the local, traditional cuisine in Amalfi. Their *antipasto di mare* (seafood appetizer), *zuppa di pesce* (seafood soup), *linguine all'aragosta* (with lobster sauce), *spaghetti alla cozze* (with mussels), *spaghetti ai frutti di mare* (with mixed seafood) or the *penne alla Genovese* (macaroni-like noodles with a pesto sauce of olive oil, basil and garlic) are all fantastic. And of course their fish, whether boiled, fried or grilled is all fresh and flavorful. Their terrace is a wonderful place to enjoy your meal. For the most part their wine list contains only whites, but that is sensible since they serve mainly fish.

7. STELLA MARIS, *Viale delle Regioni 2, Tel. 089/872-463. Closed Thursdays (not at Easter). American Express and Visa accepted. Dinner for two L90,000.*

Right on the sea, in the center of Amalfi, this is a great trattoria with great food. The first impression you get is that of a tourist restaurant that only has a superb view of the water and a great terrace, but they also serve great food. Their *spaghetti alla vongole* (with clam sauce), and *sogliola alla griglia* (grilled sole) are the perfect meal. Seafood is also the mainstay of this place. Great atmosphere. Great food.

SEEING THE SIGHTS

Some of the sights you can see are the **Duomo** of Sant'Andrea built in the Lombard Romanesque style in 1203. Its fine portico with pointed arches was totally rebuilt in 1865. On the west side is a bronze door that was cast in Constinantinople in 1066. In the crypt you will find the remains of the Apostle, Saint Andrew.

Near the Duomo is the tiny **Museo Civico** that does its best to offer a history of the town. If you have nothing else to do you may want to try here. High above the town, reachable by a steady hike, is the **Capuccinni Monastery** that offers fine views of the city. Now a hotel, some areas will be off limits to visitors who are not guests of the hotel.

A 15 minute boat ride away is the **Grotta di Amalfi**, an ancient stalactite cave on the coast. The boat ride itself offers fine vistas, so don't forget your camera. One kilometer away along the coast road is the tiny little village of Atrani, picturesquely sitting along the mouth of a rocky gorge. In the main piazza is the 10th century **church of San Salvatore**, complete with Byzantine bronze doors cast in Constinantinople in 1087.

RAVELLO

About five kilometers from Amalfi is **Ravello**, a superb little hill town in one of the most enchanting spots in the world. Perched on a 350 foot high cliff overlooking the azure sea of the Amalfi Coast, Ravello has preserved its historical monuments through the ages and incorporated them into everyday life.

ARRIVALS & DEPARTURES

You can get to Ravello by car via the coast road or the cross peninsula road. If you go by bus from Naples, catch a SITA bus from Piazza Municipio *(Tel. 081/55-22-176)*. From Salerno, catch the bus along Via SS Martiri Salernitani *(Tel. 089/22-66-04)*. From Amalfi, buses leave from Piazza Flavio Gioia *(Tel. 089/87-10-09)*.

WHERE TO STAY

CARUSO BELVEDERE, *Via San Giovanni del Toro 52, 84010 Ravello. Tel. 089/857-111. Fax 089/857-372. 24 rooms all with bath. Double L169,000-217,000. Credit cards accepted. Breakfast included. Full board. L150,000-235,000.* ****

In a truly historic building, this hotel has been open for 102 years but has every modern convenience possible. The rooms may be sparsely furnished but they are wonderfully comfortable. From their stunning garden you have amazing vistas of the water and surrounding area. Everything about this place is designed to relax, from the view of the coast in the restaurant (which is quite good), to the study room with daily newspapers from around the world.

VILLA MARIA, *Via Santa Chiara 2, 84010 Ravello. Tel. 089/857-255. Fax 089/857-071. 18 rooms all with bath. single L120,000-130,000; Double L190,000-210,000. Credit cards accepted. Breakfast included. Full board L105,000-195,000* ***

This is a four star masquerading as a three star. They have a heated pool, a garden terrace area for relaxing, rooms filled with antique furnishings, bathrooms with every modern convenience, beautiful balconies (Room Number 3's is huge), professional service, and a relaxing atmosphere like a bed and breakfast. You can eat inside or out on the terrace with its stunning views over the sea. You also have access to tennis courts only 100 meters down the road.

WHERE TO EAT

CUMPA COSIMO, *Via Roma 44, Tel. 089/857-156. Closed Mondays (not in Spring and Summer). Credit cards accepted. Dinner for two L80,000.*

On the walls are photographs of the many personalities who have enjoyed the simple local cooking and the hospitality of the Bottone family. For p*rimo* try the *pasta al pesto* (home made pasta with garlic, oil and basil sauce), or *agli zucchine* (with zucchini sauce), or *ai peperoni* (with peppers). For seconds the *agnello, salsicce* and other grilled meats (lamb, sausage, etc., all supplied by the butcher shop run by the same family) are fantastic. You should also try the fresh fish caught daily right in the Bay. For dessert you might want to try some of their *torte* (cakes) and *sorbetti* (Italian ices) made from locally grown oranges. A great little trattoria.

SEEING THE SIGHTS

One of the most important monuments is the **Cathedral**, founded in 1086. Here you can admire the Byzantine mosaic work on the pulpit, the bronze doors, and the civic museum located in the crypt. **Villa Rudolph** is another sight to behold, especially in July when the views are complimented with music at the Wagner Festival. **Villa Cimbrone** also contains lush gardens and is known for its breathtaking views, which have been described by many as the best in the world.

Other sights to see while in Ravello are the church of **San Giovanni del Toro** with its mosaic pulpit; the **Villa Episcopio** where King Vittorio Emanuele abdicated the throne; the cloister of the 13th century **convent** of St. Francesco with its amazing library; and the scenic **Piazza Fontana Moresca**.

SALERNO

At the north end of the Gulf of Salerno sits the town of the same name. An industrial center, **Salerno** still has an old town that merits a look because of its winding medieval streets and steps, but mainly it is just another southern Italian port city, devoid of charm. Near the old town, off of the Piazza Amendola, are the public gardens, on the west side of which is the **Teatro Verdi** where many operas are performed. In the middle of the maze of the old town is the **Duomo** built in 1086, restored in 1768 and then in 1945 after allied bombing took its toll on the facade. Inside a flight of steps leads up to an atrium that has 28 ancient columns and 14 sarcophagi purloined from Paestum. The magnificent bronze doors were cast in Constinantinople in 1099.

A little ways north in the Largo Plebiscito is the **Museo Duomo** that contains many relics from Salerno's past. West along Via San Michele is

NAPLES & THE AMALFI COAST

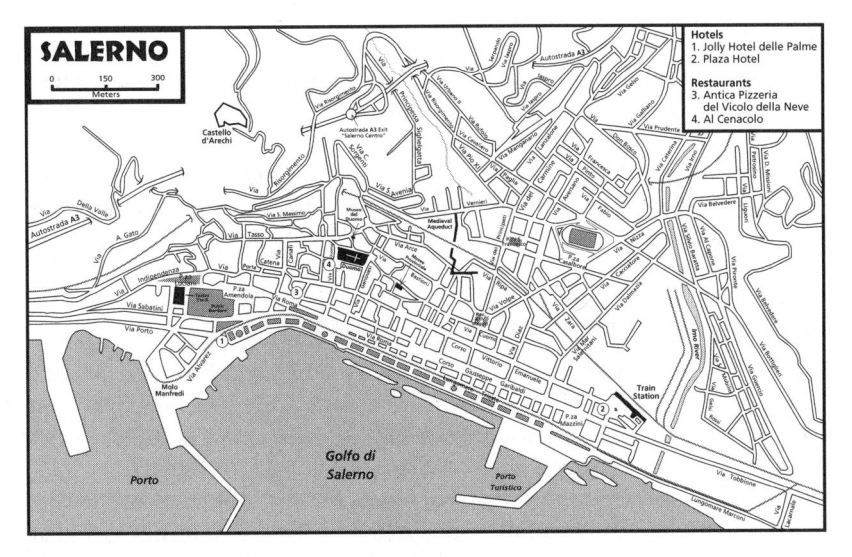

the **Museo Provinciale** with many antiquities, including a huge bronze head of Apollo cast in the 1st century BCE.

ARRIVALS & DEPARTURES

You can get to Salerno by train from Naples in under an hour, or you can take the Autostrada A3 from Naples. There are also ferries from Capri and Naples that will bring you here.

WHERE TO STAY

1. JOLLY HOTEL DELLE PALME, *Lungomare Trieste 1, 84100 Salerno. Tel. 089/225-222. Fax 089/237-571. Toll free in Italy 167-017703. Toll free in US and NYC 1-800/221-2626. Toll free in NY State 1-800/247-1277. 104 rooms all with bath. Single L177,000-197,000; Double L197,000-232. Credit cards accepted. Breakfast included. Full board L190,000-295,000.*
****

The best hotel in Salerno, which says a lot about the types of hotels in the city. Located at the end of the Lungomare along a busy thoroughfare. The rooms have pastel colored curtains to contrast with the white furniture. The double windows are needed to block out the sounds of the street below. The bathrooms are ample with large windows and every modern convenience. All Jolly hotels have professional service, as well as stale North American-style hotel lack of ambiance.

2. PLAZA, *Piazza Via Veneto 42, 84100 Salerno. Tel. 089/224-477. Fax 089/237-311. 42 rooms all with bath. Single L85,000; Double L120,000. Credit cards accepted. Breakfast L12,000.*

A simple basic three star located near the station. The accommodations in Salerno are not that upscale, and this is the best three star in town. Located in a building built in the 1800s, you can also see some ancient architectural features that the structure was built around. In an ideal location at the beginning of the walking street area (*zona pedonale*) where you can head out for your evening stroll. The common areas are pleasant enough with plants and flowers as adornment. The rooms are simple with modern furnishings and are comfortable with satellite TV, air conditioning and minibar.

WHERE TO EAT

3. ANTICA PIZZERIA DEL VICOLO DELLA NEVE, *Vicolo della Neve 24, Tel. 089/225-705. Closed Wednesdays, two weeks in August and Christmas. Open only in the evenings. American Express accepted. Dinner for two L70,000.*

In one of the areas with the most character and ambiance in the city, this rustic little locale is an ideal place to have typical Salernese food at honest prices. Some dishes to try are: *verdure al forno* (grilled vegetables), *funghi al forno* (grilled mushrooms), *melanzane alla parmigiana* (eggplant parmesan), *calzone* (baked dough stuffed with veggies and meat) and all manner of pizzas.

4. AL CENACOLO, *Piazza Alfano I 4/6, Tel. 089/238-818. Closed Sunday evenings and Mondays, as well as August 8-22 and December 25 to February 1. Credit cards accepted. Dinner for two L90,000.*

Basically right in front of the Duomo, this local favorite owned by Pietro Rispoli is a sure thing when it comes to finding fine food and good atmosphere. They have a fixed menu for L45,000 that comes with antipasto, first, second, and dessert. If you want to order on your own try some of these dishes: *alici marinate* (marinated anchovies), *gamberi in salsa di limone e zucchine* (shrimp in a lemon/zucchini sauce), *ravioli di pesce con vongole e zucchine* (fish stuffed ravioli in a clam/zucchini sauce), or *cannelloni con le melanzane* (cannelloni with eggplant). For seconds they grill a variety of meats and fish. For dessert, their *mousse al ciocolato* (chocolate mousse) is simply sinful.

22. SOUTHERN ITALY & SICILY

SOUTHERN ITALY

Southern Italy is still a land of immigrants waiting to move, but today instead of moving to America like their great grandfathers or grandfathers would have, they move to northern industrial cities like Milan or Turin. Without jobs in the south, Southern Italians are forced to move even if they know they will be cursed because of their accents and their place of birth. The discrimination against Southern Italians from too many of their cousins in the north is unfortunately still alive and well.

The main work for people in the south is still in small-scale agriculture, local fishing activities, and small-scale crafts manufacturing, with a smattering of limited industrial activities. Despite its poverty, Southern Italy can be a wonderful place to visit for an experienced Italy traveler. The sights to see, many of which have a definite Middle Eastern or Moorish influence, are few and far between.

But if you've never been to Italy, or still haven't seen all there is to see in Rome, Florence, Venice and other cities, Southern Italy would not be a vacation for you. Southern Italy is only for the hardiest travelers. In 1993, two American tourists, roaming the quaint country roads of Southern Italy, suddenly stumbled into a situation they weren't supposed to see in a small village (it was reported to be Mafia related). They didn't come back alive. So don't wander aimlessly through Southern Italy.

BARI

Bari is known in Italy as the 'gateway to the East' because as a port city it is heavily involved in trade with the Eastern Mediterranean. Bari also is the chief embarkation point for passenger ships to Greece and beyond, as it was an embarkation point centuries before for many of the Crusades.

> **BARI'S SANTA CLAUS**
>
> Have you ever wanted to see Santa? In Italy he is the patron saint of seafarers, prisoners, and children. **Saint Nicholas of Bari** is buried in the **Church of San Nicola**. Better known to us as Saint Nick or Santa Claus, here's your chance to finally see that portly, paramount, patriarchal provider of presents.

Because of its location and port, Bari became the cornerstone of several ancient empires and was a major stronghold of Byzantine power. The old city still has some remnants of the look and feel of many centuries ago and should be explored – during the day, not at night. Like Naples, this is a port city.

As the capital of **Apulia**, Bari also is the seat of an archbishop, a major university, and a naval college. Besides shipping, the city's other industries include shipbuilding, petrochemical refinement, and tourism. Bari also is the site of Italy's first atomic power station.

Not far away from Bari are two other attractions: the **Castellana Grottoes**, limestone caves that are 48 km (30 miles) south, and the Apulian **Trulli** dwellings – rock houses built in a spiral design, thought to have been influenced by ancient Middle Eastern structures (in **Alberobello**, just a few miles farther south of Castellana). On your way to Bari, look out the car or train window for a sight of some of these Trulli dwellings. They look like something from another planet. Other regional sights you'll see on your way to Bari are fields upon fields of olive trees.

In all, Bari is a good place to stay and explore the region and its local flavor. It's also a perfect place to stop over on your way to points east.

Again, a word of warning: This is a port city like Genoa and Naples and as such you need to be aware of your surroundings. The crime that comes with a port city is doubled since this is the country's poorest region. Don't wear flashy jewelry, carry your handbag on the arm that is not towards the street, and always walk down streets that are populated.

The most important rule you can follow is do not go into the Old City after dark, ever. They don't call Bari *scippoladdri* (the land of petty thieves) for nothing.

ARRIVALS & DEPARTURES

Bari is 262 kilometers from Naples and 458 kilometers from Rome. The main form of transport into and out of the city is still the railroad. Since the journey is long and tedious, the train is the fastest most efficent means of getting here. By train from Rome, which usually comes through

Naples, takes seven or eight hours. From Naples it would only be four hours.

If you decide to come by car from the north, the Autostrada A14 lets you off on the outskirts of the city. If you're coming from Barletta or Trani the coast highway 16, which runs parallel to the Autostrada, would be the path to follow. The same time allotment as the train would apply when coming from Rome or Naples.

Ferries to Greece

One of the main reasons people come to Bari is use their **ferry** and **hydrofoil** system to get to Greece. Your Eurorail or Interrail pass does not give you a discount on the fares, but most ferry lines offer discounts for students as well as for round-trip tickets. You have to ask for these discounts since they don't automatically offer them to you.

For all information about prices and schedules, go to the **Stazione Maritima** *on Molo San Vito in the port* (not the Stazione Maritima for trains on the Corso Vittorio Veneto) and check with the different ferry lines. Below is a list of the main offices ferry lines. They also have a ticket window at the **Stazione Maritima**.
- **Marlines**, *Car Ferry Terminal Box 3-4, Tel. 080/521-76-99*
- **Poseidon**, *Corso de Tullio 40, Tel. 080/521-0022*
- **Ventours Ferries**, *Corso de Tullio 16, Tel. 080/521-05-56*
- **Yasco**, *Corso de Tullio 40, Tel. 080/521-0022*

Taking the hydrofoil is much quicker than the ferry. While the ferries take most of a 24 hour day to reach their destinations, the hydrofoils get you there in five hours. They cost twice as much, but if you're in a hurry they're perfect.

STOP OVER IN BARI

The city has a program by just that name (Stop Over In Bari), which is in place from June to September and assists all travelers under 30 who are not residents of the region in finding inexpensive lodging or camp sites. You can also get information about food stores, restaurants, Laundromats, and more when you arrive in Bari. You can get all this information at the **Information Office** *in the train station at the* **Stazione Maritima** *or at their main office on Via Dante Alighieri 111 (Tel. 080/521-45-38). This program is designed to encourage travelers to stay a few extra nights in Bari and it seems to be working. During the summer, Bari has become a backpackers heaven and is a great place to find a party and a companion.*

WHERE TO STAY

1. PALACE HOTEL, *Via Lombardi 13, 70122 Bari. Tel. 080/521-6551. Fax 080/521-1499. 197 rooms all with bath. Single L160,000-225,000; Double L210,000-275,000. All credit cards accepted. Breakfast included.* ****

The Palace is a prestigious hotel in Bari. It is elegant, refined, and filled with antique furnishings and decorations. Each room is designed differently with precious antiques, but despite all this finery are quite comfortable and accommodating. Where the rooms are all different, the bathrooms are all the same with courtesy toiletry sets that come with everything, including face cream for the lady and slippers for the man. Breakfast is a buffet feast and is served in an exquisitely elegant salon. Situated between the centro storico and the business district, you could not find a better location. But despite being in the midst of it all, you'll not be disturbed by the traffic or nightlife, since each room's windows are sound-proof. The Palace and the Villa Romanazzi Carducci are the places to stay in Bari.

2. JOLLY HOTEL BARI, *Via G. Petroni 15, 70122 Bari. Tel. 080/536-4366. Fax 080/536-5219. Toll free in Italy 167-017703. Toll free in US and NYC 1-800/221-2626. Toll free in NY State 1-800/247-1277. 164 rooms all with shower. Single L110,000-210,000; Double L150,000-275,000. Credit cards accepted.* ****

Jolly hotels are everywhere in Italy, and most are close to the train station; this one is no exception. This is a modern hotel, preferred by traveling businessmen because of the convenience and service. The rooms are clean, comfortable, filled with modern furnishings, and come with air conditioning, satellite TV and room service but are not as large as we may be used to in North America. The hotel restaurant is good enough to sample since they make some good local dishes. The Manager Gabriele Delli Passeri really makes an effort to ensure your stay is pleasant.

3. VILLA ROMANAZZI CARDUCCI, *Via G. Capruzzi, 70057 Bari. Tel. 080/522-7400. Fax 080/556-0297. 89 rooms all with bath. Single L135,000-200,000; Double L200,000-300,000. All credit cards accepted. Breakfast included.* ****

An elegant hotel, refined and located on a tranquil site. It's the only one in Bari that is surrounded by a sea of green vegetation. And how beautiful it is! Besides that, the hotel is located in a building filled with character that was built in 1850, and the restaurant is located in the old stables. (It may sound a trifle odd, but the ambiance is wonderful. No horse hockey pucks anywhere.) The rooms are large and comfortably appointed with wonderful marble floors. The entrance hall itself is quite elegant with carpets, divan seats and a sculpture in the center. The bar is

SOUTHERN ITALY & SICILY 299

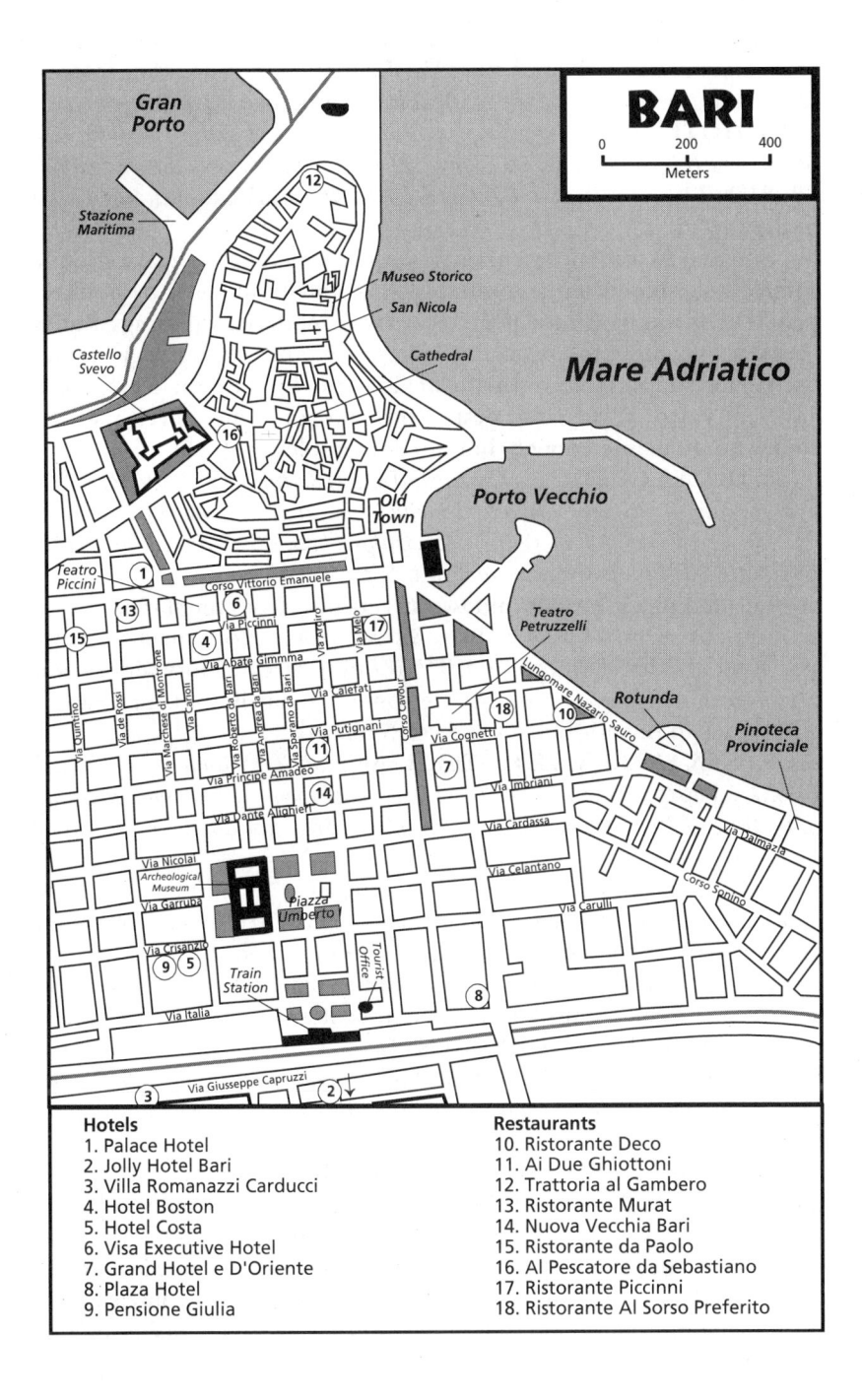

Hotels
1. Palace Hotel
2. Jolly Hotel Bari
3. Villa Romanazzi Carducci
4. Hotel Boston
5. Hotel Costa
6. Visa Executive Hotel
7. Grand Hotel e D'Oriente
8. Plaza Hotel
9. Pensione Giulia

Restaurants
10. Ristorante Deco
11. Ai Due Ghiottoni
12. Trattoria al Gambero
13. Ristorante Murat
14. Nuova Vecchia Bari
15. Ristorante da Paolo
16. Al Pescatore da Sebastiano
17. Ristorante Piccinni
18. Ristorante Al Sorso Preferito

well stocked and is located in the park area around the hotel. Your abundant buffet breakfast is served in the refined elegance of an interior salon, and the private garage is ideal for automotive travelers.

4. HOTEL BOSTON, *Via Piccinni 155, 70122 Bari. Tel. 080/521-6633. Fax 080/524-6802. 70 rooms, 20 with bath, 50 with shower. Single L100,000-140,000; Double L160,000-210,000. Breakfast included. Credit cards accepted.* ***

Situated in a modern building, with all amenities to make it quite comfortable. Based on its location it is mainly frequented by business people. The rooms are adequately sized with modern furnishings. Buffet breakfast is continental and comes with cereal, fruit, cheese, yogurt, rolls, butter, and jam and is served in the small room near the entrance. You can also rent videos at the front desk. Not really for family travel since the rooms are not large enough, but fine for couples or singles.

5. HOTEL COSTA, *Via Crisanzio 12, 70122 Bari. Tel. 080/521-9015. Fax 080/521-0006. 23 room, only 18 with bath. Single without bath L55,000-65,000; Single L65,000-90,000; Double without bath L85,000-97,000; Double L97,000-120,000. Credit cards accepted.* ***

Located two streets up and two streets over from the station, this is an inexpensive hotel option in Bari. All the amenities of a small city three star hotel like direct dial phones, TV, room service, laundry service, but no air conditioning. The rooms are somewhat small but kept clean. A good place to stay for budget and convenience.

6. VISA EXECUTIVE HOTEL, *Corso Vittorio Emanuele 201, 70122 Bari. Tel. 080/521-6810. Fax 080/524-5178. 21 rooms all with shower. Single L80,000-140,000; Double L120,000-180,000. Breakfast L5,000 extra. Credit cards accepted.* ***

Located in a renovated older building near the Municipio (Town Hall), this is a businessman's hotel that also caters to tourists. The rooms are immaculate but small as are the bathrooms, and the amenities are simple but good. There are direct dial phones, air conditioning, TV, room service, and a downstairs bar. For the price it is a good place to stay.

7. GRAND HOTEL E D'ORIENTE, *Via Cavour 32, 70121 Bari. Tel. 080524-4011. Fax 080/524-3914. 120 rooms, 60 with bath, 60 with shower. Single L80,000-160,000; Double L160,000-300,000. Credit cards accepted.* ***

On the upscale Via Cavour near the beach, here you can have all the amenities of a four star hotel, in a three star hotel – with four star prices. Does that makes sense to you? The only reason they're a three star is that their rooms have showers, a minus mark in the ratings game. Located in a renovated historical building, the rooms here are impeccably clean and perfectly comfortable, and staff bends over backwards to make you feel comfortable.

8. PLAZA HOTEL, *Piazza Luigi di Savoia 15, 70057 Bari. Tel. 080/524-6777. Fax 080/524-1761. 40 rooms all with bath. Single L74,000-150,000; Double L100,000-200,000. All credit cards accepted. Breakfast L15,000. Closed August 5-25 as well as December 23rd to February 1.* ***

Near the station in the center of the new town, the Plaza is mainly a businessperson's hotel. The bar area is also utilized for the breakfast buffet. The rooms are not all the same; the best ones are located on the inner courtyard and these are the most quiet. Each room has a balcony and is filled with modern furnishings. An adequate place to stay, better than most in Bari.

9. PENSIONE GIULIA, *Via Crisanzio 12, 70122 Bari. Tel. 080/521-6630. Fax 080/521-8271. 14 rooms only 10 with shower. Single without bath L50,000; Single L65,000; Double without bath L70,000; Double L90,000. Breakfast included. Credit cards accepted.* **

This is definitely the best budget traveler's alternative in Bari, with its location a few blocks up and over from the train station. It's in a safe and quiet neighborhood and the prices are good. You don't have air conditioning and need to make reservations for the rooms with bath, but this is good place to stay. The rooms are clean if a little worn, and they're comfortable. There is a little sitting room and bar area.

WHERE TO EAT

10. RISTORANTE DECO, *Largo Adua 5, Tel. 080/524-6070. Closed Mondays and August. Credit cards accepted. Dinner for two L120,000.*

A good restaurant inside an interesting structure that makes some great *cucina nuova* dishes made mainly with the ingredients that are found locally, such as leafy greens, other vegetables, fresh pasta, local cheeses and meats in large quantities. Creatively rustic servings that change all the time.

11. AI DUE GHIOTTONI, *Via Putignani 11, Tel. 080/523-2240. Closed Sundays and two weeks in August. All credit cards accepted. Dinner for two L120,000.*

What a perfect name, *The Two Gluttons*, for the restaurant that is the symbol of the city for the Barese (i.e., the people of Bari). Here you had better come ready to eat since their portions are large. Heck, you wouldn't even be able to finish your antipasto if it was your main meal. They make excellent pasta dishes, as well as a variety of fish plates. When in Bari, eat at least one meal here.

12. TRATTORIA AL GAMBERO, *Corso de Tullio 8, Tel. 080/521-6018. Closed Sundays, Christmas and August. No credit cards accepted. Meal for two L90,000.*

Located deep in the heart of the old city, I recommend you eat lunch here, not dinner, but eat here you must. Their terrace has a wonderful view of the port area and they make superb *spaghetti alla cozze* (with mussels), *alla vongole verace* (with a spicy clam sauce) and *al frutti di mare* (with a variety of sea food). They always have a fire burning outside where they cook the specialty of the region, grilled fish. In the winter they still cook outside, but mainly meats like *vitello* (veal).

13. RISTORANTE MURAT, *Via Lombardy 13, Tel. 080/521-6551. Closed Sundays and August. All credit cards accepted. Dinner for two L120,000.*

One of the finer restaurants in Bari. This place is refined and elegant both on the terrace and inside. They have a great gourmet menu with wine included for L60,000 per person that includes native dishes and some simple *cucina nuova* creations. Try some of their *minestra di verdure* (vegetable soup), *stracceti di pasta alla cozze* (pasta with mussels), *filetto di spigola gratinato con mozzarella* (sea bass au gratin with mozzarella).

14. NUOVA VECCHIA BARI, *Via Dante Alighieri 47, Tel. 080/521-6496. Closed Tuesdays and three weeks in August. Credit cards accepted. Dinner for two L90,000.*

A rustic location in the new city, this place is famous for its ancient local cuisine creations. All the specials are made in the tradition of regional Apulian cooking. Try some great game dishes and their fresh home-made pasta with a spicy tomato-based sauces, as well as an excellent vegetable soup.

15. RISTORANTE DA PAOLO, *Via Q Selia 13a, Tel. 080/521-1662. Closed Mondays and the last two weeks of August. Credit cards accepted. Dinner for two L80,000.*

Located in the center of new Bari, this restaurant, owned by Paolo Anaclero, makes excellent food despite the thoroughly modern decorations. And at great prices. Try some of his famous *spigola al sale* (sea bass with salt) and the scrumptious *misto di pesce arrosto* (mixed roasted fish).

16. AL PESCATORE DA SEBASTIANO, *Via Frederico II di Svevia 6, Tel. 080/523-7039. Closed Mondays. All credit cards accepted. Meal for two L120,000.*

Located in the old town right by the castle, this is a place to come for lunch, not dinner. A good restaurant that cooks mainly fish and seafood over an open fire, but they also specialize in some great home-made pasta dishes. The best place to sit in the summer is outside on their terrace where you can gaze at the majestic Castle across the piazza.

17. RISTORANTE PICCINNI, *Via Piccinni 28, Tel. 080/521-1227. Closed Sundays and August. All credit cards accepted. Dinner for two L140,000.*

The ambiance here is refined, elegant, and discreet, especially in their inside garden seating area. One of the higher-end restaurants in Bari. Here you'll find many of the magistrates from the town hall just down the road. The menu consists of a variety of local, national, creative and international dishes. Sample dishes include *filetto di Angus al pepe verde* (filet of Scottish Angus beef with pepper), *spaghetti con fiori di zucchine* (with zucchini flowers), and *pappardelle con radicchio e gamberi* (wide strips of pasta with radish and shrimp). There's something for everyone here, but you'll pay the price.

18. RISTORANTE AL SORSO PREFERITO, *Via de Nicolo 46, Tel. 080/523-5747. Closed Sundays and 15 days in August. Credit cards accepted. Dinner for two L100,000.*

Located near the Porto Vecchio, this is a well respected local place that serves both local and national dishes. They feature a wide variety of pasta dishes as well as a great *bistecca alla fiorentina alla brace* (steak cooked over an open flame), and my favorite *agnello al forno* (lamb cooked over a fire pit). The prices are a little high but the food is superb.

SEEING THE SIGHTS

Bari is an easy town to walk around and enjoy the town's castles, churches, and harbor front area. In Bari there is a new town and an old town. Most of the interesting sights are located in the **old town** and around the **Porto Vecchio (Old Port)**.

NEW TOWN

The main feature of the new town is the palm-shaded **Piazza Umberto I**, located two blocks in front of the train station. Another sight to see in the new town is the **Teatro Piccinni**, which is located in the **Town Hall (Municipio)** in the **Piazza della Liberta** and on the Via Vittorio Emanuele I (*Corso Vittorio Emanuele. Tel. 521-3717. Concert season is in the spring; the rest of the year the theater is closed*). This is the city's busiest streets and it conveniently divides the new town from the old town. Another theater to see is the **Teatro Petruzzelli**, which was almost completed destroyed by insurance-related arson, located on the Corso Cavour (*Concert season is in the spring; the rest of the year the theater is closed*).

Behind the theater is the **Lungomare Nazario**, a beautiful sea front promenade that runs past the old harbor. If you go in the other direction you'll find the **Pinoteca Provinciale** in its gray and white towered building, about a kilometer down the promenade. This is the home of the provincial picture gallery with works by Tintoretto, Bellini, Vivarini, and Veronese (*Lungomare Nazario Saura. Tel. 392-421. Open Tuesday-Saturday, 9:00am-1:00pm and 4:00pm-7:00pm. Sunday 9:00am-1:00pm.*)

LEVANT FAIR

Fair takes place in the fairground by the municipal stadium, off of Lungomare Starita.

This is the annual fair that runs for 10 days in mid-September, located about 2.5 kilometers from the center of town. This is the largest fair in southern Italy; goods from all over the world are exhibited and sold here. A festive atmosphere. Don't miss it if you're in Bari while it's being held.

OLD TOWN

Around the old city is a peaceful seaside promenade. Strolling here is the perfect way to get a feel for Bari as it used to be. To the left of the old city is the **Gran Porto (Grand Harbor)**, where the big liners and ferries dock. To the right of the old city is the **Porto Vecchio (Old Port)** that evokes a feel of sailors past.

CATHEDRAL

Piazza Duomo. Open daily 8:00am-noon and 4:00pm-7:00pm.

This 12th century church with a Romanesque facade and Baroque influences resides in the center of the old city. You can find in the crypt an ornate painting of the Virgin from Constinantinople, and the church's archives contain many large scripture rolls from the 11th century. Also notice the Romanesque architecture characteristic of the choir and chapel protruding ever so perfectly from the Nave.

CHURCH OF SAN NICOLA

Via Palazzo Citta. Open daily 8:00am-noon and 4:00pm-7:00pm.

This is a large church built over an ancient Byzantine castle that once occupied the site. The funding came from Crusaders' and pilgrims' money in 1087, but it sat incomplete until the late 13th century. Besides being one of the finest achievements of Romanesque architecture in the region, the church contains the remains of **Saint Nicholas of Bari**. This patron saint of seamen, prisoners, and children, better known to us as **Saint Nick** or **Santa Claus** (ignore those northern European claims to Sinter Klaas, Father Christmas, and all their other Santa Claus allegations – this is the real deal, or so my Bari sources tell me!). So if you or the kids really want to see Santa, bring them to San Nicola here in Bari.

CASTELLO SVEVO

Piazza Federico II di Svevia. Museum open daily 9:00am-1:30pm and 3:30pm-7:00pm. Admission L5,000.

The **Castle** is located on the outskirts of the old town, almost directly in front of the Cathedral. Begun by Frederick II in 1233 and converted into a palace by Bona Sforza, the wife of Sigismund II of Poland and the last duchess of Bari in the 16th century (her remains are located in San Nicola). It was later used as a prison and a light house/signal station. Recently a **Roman city** was discovered on the site. There is also a small **museum** containing copies of Apulo-Norman sculpture.

PRACTICAL INFORMATION
Bank Hours & Changing Money
    Banks are open Monday through Friday from 8:30am to 1:30pm and some do reopen from 2:30pm or so to 4:30pm or so. The **Stazione Centrale** has a *cambio* inside that is open from 8:00am to 1:30pm and 2:30pm to 8:00pm Monday through Saturday.
• **American Express**, *Corso de Tullio in the offices of Morfimare at #40, Tel. 080/521-0022, near the Stazione Maritima.*

Business Hours
    From October to June, most shops are open from 9:00am to 1:00pm and from 3:30pm to 7:30pm, and are closed all day Sundays and on Monday mornings. Then from June to September, when it really starts to get hot in Southern Italy, the morning hours remain the same, but the mid-day siesta time is slightly extended to 4:00pm and sometimes 4:30pm, which then pushes closing time back to 7:30pm or 8:00pm.
    In conjunction with being closed on Sunday and Monday mornings, shops are also close half-days on Saturdays. Food stores, like a*limentari* generally are open from 8:30am to 1:30pm (so stock up on food if you're taking a picnic) and from 5:00pm to 7:30pm, and during the winter months they are closed on Thursdays.

English Language Bookstores
• **Feltrinelli**, *Via Dante Alighieri 91. Open Monday through Friday 9:00am to 8:00pm, Saturdays 9:00am to 1:00pm.* They have an extensive selection of English language travel guides as well as some paperback novels. Located a half block away from Stop Over in Bari's main office.

Postal Services
    You can buy stamps at local tobacconists (they are marked with a "T" outside) as well as post offices. Mail boxes are colored red. Post offices are open from 8:00am to 2:00pm on weekdays. The one exception to this rule is the **main post office** (**Palazzo delle Poste**) located behind the university at **Piazza Batista** *(Tel. 080/521 0381)* which is open Monday through Friday from 8:00am to 7:30pm, and Saturday from 8:00am to noon.

Tourist Information & Maps
• **Stop Over in Bari**, *Via Dante Alighieri 111, Tel. 080521-4538. Open Monday through Saturday 9:00am-8:00pm and Sundays 10:00am to 5:00pm.* They also have offices in the Stazione Centrale and Stazione Maritima. They can supply you with all the information you need to know.
• **EPT**, *Piazza Aldo Moro 33A, Tel. 080/524-2244.* Located just to the right as you leave the station. In perfect Italian disorganization, the

government is sponsoring two different agencies to give out virtually the same information. If you don't get everything you need from **Stop Over in Bari**, try here.

BARLETTA

Barletta is small compact town and is one of the principal ports in the region. It has a few sights of interest and can be easily walked. If you're up for swimming in the Adriatic Sea, here's your opportunity.

ARRIVALS & DEPARTURES

Barletta is 40 minutes from Bari by train (L5,000) or 50 minutes by car, taking the coastal highway 16.

WHERE TO STAY

1. HOTEL ARTU, *Piazza Castello 67, 70051 Barletta. Tel. 0883/332-121. Fax 0883/332-214. 32 rooms, 8 with bath, 24 with shower. Single L120,000; Double L190,000. Breakfast included. Credit cards accepted.* ****

Located right in the center of all the sights that Barletta has to offer, you are also close to the beach at this hotel. This is a renovated old building that is perfect for a romantic weekend. All the amenities are here, including a restaurant that features local and international cuisine as well as great pizzas, and a piano bar for nightly entertainment. The rooms are super clean and very comfortable.

2. HOTEL ROYAL, *Via L. De Nittis 13, 70051 Barletta. Tel. 0883/531-139. Fax 0883/531-466. 34 rooms all with bath. Single L50,000-98,000; Double L100,000-160,000. All credit cards accepted. Breakfast included.* ***

Located in the center of Barletta in an older building, the rooms are all different and all face into an inner atrium which makes them quiet and relaxing. Furnished with modern pieces, the rooms are comfortable but lack character. The bathrooms come with a courtesy set of toiletries and are clean and ample. A good place to stay when in Barletta.

WHERE TO EAT

3. ANTICA CUCINA, *Via Milano 73, Tel. 0883/521-718. Closed Sunday nights and Mondays as well as the last week in January and the month of July. Dinner for two L140,000. Credit cards accepted.*

This place has sort of a rustic sophisticated charm with its antiques hanging on the wall and tables laid out for an elegant dinner. Open for a little over ten years, this is one of Apulia's best restaurants. Their cooking is an expression of the region with the traditional dishes they make and the local ingredients they use. If you like anchovies try their *alici marinate in olio e aceto* (anchovies marinated in oil and vinegar) or the *melanzane arrosto con polpa di granchio e merluzzo* (roasted eggplant covered with crab meat and pulped cod meat). Their *spaghetti con fiori di zucchine al profumo d'aglio* (with zucchini flowers and garlic) is also good, as is the *Frittura alla Barlettana* (local fried seafood: calamari, octopus, mullet, and whatever else is caught that day).

4. RISTORANTE BACCO, *Via Sipontina 10, Tel. 0883/571-000. Closed Sunday nights and Mondays, as well as August. Dinner for two L160,000. Credit cards accepted.*

Another great restaurant in the city, as well as the region. The owner, Franco Ricatti, recently opened a second Bacco in Rome, so business must be good. The atmosphere is always friendly and the menu includes two different gastronomic options, so you can sample a wide variety of food at a lower cost. They make traditional dishes as well as creative ones. Their *zuppetta di fagioli e cozze* (soup of beans and muscles) is particularly good as is the *fusilli al ragu di scorfano* (twisted pasta with a ragu sauce of scorpion fish).

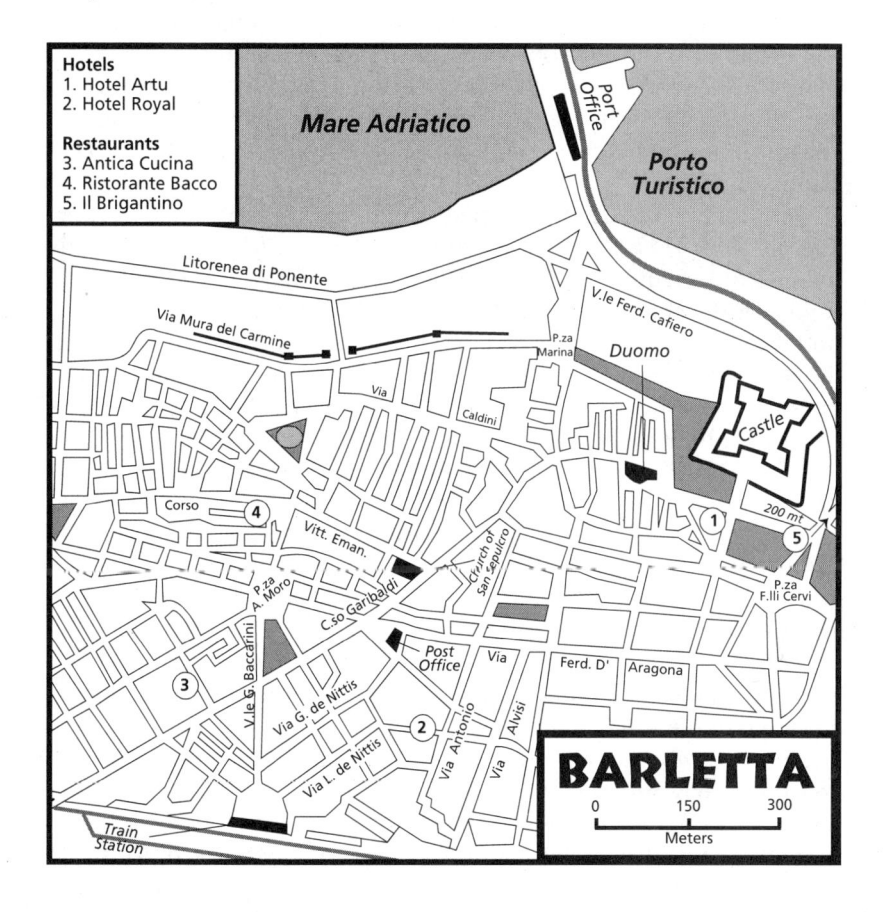

5. IL BRIGANTINO, *Litoranea di Levante, Tel. 0883/533-345. Dinner for two L100,000. Credit cards accepted.*

Located outside of town on the sea this place never closes, ever. It's open every day and year round. This is an institution in Barletta, which is why the place is always crowded. The view of the Adriatic from the terrace is a perfectly romantic spot. The food is all of the local, traditional flavor. A good place to come for an evening's repast. During lunch they offer a "work menu" (*colazione di lavoro*) for L35,000 that includes soup, pasta, and fish.

SEEING THE SIGHTS

From the train station, walk straight ahead down the Viale Giannone to the second street on the right, Corso Garibaldi. Take a right and walk a couple hundred meters to the **Church of San Sepolcro** on the left hand side (*Corso Vittorio Emanuele. Open summer Monday-Saturday 10:00am-Noon and 6:30pm-8:30pm. Open winter 10:00am-noon and 5:30pm-8:00pm*). This is a 12th century Gothic church whose facade is a little worse for wear. You'll know it is the right church by the five meter tall **Colosso** next to the church towers. This is a 4th century bronze statue which represents a Byzantine emperor holding the cross and globe, the symbols of his two realms of power. Inside the church the only ornate item left is the large baptismal font.

Go back to the Corso Garibaldi and follow it to the **Duomo** (*Piazza Duomo. Open 7:00am-noon and 4:00pm-7:00pm daily*). As you walk, the street name changes to the Via Duomo and curves to the right. Also known as the church of **Santa Maria Maggiore**, this is part Romanesque and part Gothic. The west end and *campanile*, built between 1147 and 1193, are Romanesque; the nave and choir inside, built in the 14th century, are Gothic. Some items to admire are the fine pulpit and tabernacle built in the 13th century.

From the Piazza del Duomo you can see the enormous **castle** (*Via del Duomo. Tel. 31114. Open October-April, Tuesday-Sunday 9:30am-1:00pm and 4:00-6:30pm*). This was first a Saracen and Moor outpost, then it was enlarged by the Hohenstaufens (Normans) in the 13th century, and finally the four bastions were added in 1537 by Carl V. The castle is now home to a **museum** and **picture gallery**.

After you've explored the twisting streets of this beautiful medieval town take a walk east of the harbor and go to their **public bathing beach** for a dip in the Adriatic.

If you have a car, take the time to drive 30 km south down **route #170** to **Castel del Monte** (*Route 170. Open Tuesday-Sunday 10:00am-12:30pm and 4:00pm-7:00pm*). This is the most amazing Norman castle in Italy. It was built circa 1241 to be a hunting lodge for Frederick II. This early

Gothic structure is a perfect octagon, ringed by eight towers with eight rooms of the same size on each floor. The rooms on the upper floor, with their particularly fine windows, are believed to have been Frederick II's apartments. The structure was also the final prison for Frederick II's grandsons.

TRANI

Known for its scenic old city and peaceful gardens at the **Villa Comunale**, this is a seaport city seemingly trapped in time. You'll just adore the quaint little harbor with the old city surrounding it. But as in all port cities, no matter how small, especially if they are in the South of Italy, always be aware of your surroundings.

ARRIVALS & DEPARTURES

Trani is between Barletta and Bari. You can take a train from Bari and get here in 30 minutes, or a train from Barletta and get here in 10 minutes. Also if you drive on **highway 16** along the coast between Barletta and Bari, you'll pass through Trani.

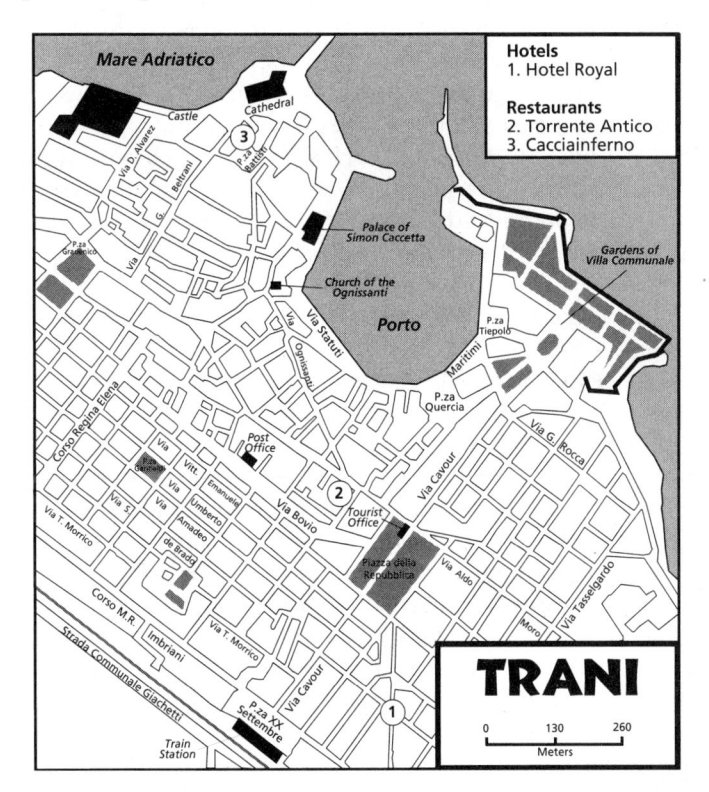

WHERE TO STAY

1. HOTEL ROYAL, *Via de Robertis 29, 70059 Trani. Tel. 0883/588-777. Fax 0883/582-224. 46 rooms all with shower. Single L75,000-115,000; Double L120,000-189,000. Breakfast included. All credit cards accepted.* ****

This was the first Jolly hotel built in the south. Then it converted to a Holiday Inn and now it is a Royal hotel. Located in the center of town near the train station. When you enter through the private tunnel you instantly get the impression that this is a good hotel. There is a quaint gazebo in which you are served your breakfast buffet. The rooms are comfortable and tranquil, and modern since all were renovated in 1990. Even so, the original antique style and charm was saved. Really the only nice place to stay when in Trani. Enjoy.

WHERE TO EAT

Besides trying the food at the hotel listed above, you should sample the food at:

2. TORRENTE ANTICO, *Via E Fusco, Tel. 0883/47911. Closed Sunday nights and Mondays, as well as the second week in January and the last two weeks of July. Credit cards accepted. Dinner for two L140,000.*

The only thing wrong with this place is that it is a little pricey. Other than that, the atmosphere is pleasant, the food is prepared and presented perfectly, and tastes superb. All thanks to the great chef here, Savino Pasquadibisceglie (say that three times fast).

Try their *filetto di spigola con zucchine* (filet of sea bass with zucchini) or the wonderful *salmone gratinato con erba cipollina* (salmon au gratin with herbs and small onions). Also try their *spaghetti alla vongole verace* (with a spicy clam sauce) or their *pennette alla marinara* (small macaroni with a tomato meat sauce) or their *tagliatelli ai porcini* (pasta with a mushroom sauce sautéed in butter). They also serve all varieties of seafood and fish for seconds.

3. OSTERIA CACCIAINFERNO, *Via San Nicola 9, Tel. 0883/585-978. Closed Mondays and the last week in September. No credit cards accepted. Dinner for two L50,000.*

A good little local place in one of the best spots in the city right by the cathedral. There are two rooms and in the summer you can enjoy your meal in the small nearby piazzetta. The clientele are mainly young since the prices here are quite low and the food is good. Try some of their *bruschetta* (garlic bread) to start accompanied by some of their *zuppa di frutta di mare* (seafood soup). Their specialty is grilled meats of all kinds. A real rustic place that I know you will enjoy. The service is informal and relaxed.

SEEING THE SIGHTS

From the train station, take Via Cavour (if you want to, as you walk down Via Cavour, stop at the **tourist office** in the Piazza della Repubblica and pick up a map and some information about other sights) for about half a mile to the **Piazza Plebiscito** and the **Villa Comunale gardens**. Here you can enjoy a relaxing picnic, a scenic view out over the Adriatic, or a panoramic sight of the old city and its cathedral across the harbor.

To get to the cathedral, walk around the harbor. You'll pass the **church of the Ognissanti** (*Via Ognissanti. Open 8:00am-noon and 4:00pm-7:00pm*) with its deep porch and beautiful Romanesque carvings above the door. Keep going around the harbor and take a left into the **Piazza Trieste**. In this piazza is the **Palace of Simone Caccetta** built in the 15th century (*Open 9:00am-1:00pm and 4:00pm-7:00pm.*)

Go through this piazza and into an open area facing the sea. The **cathedral** sits in this area almost on the water's edge (*Piazza Duomo. Open 9:00am-1:00pm and 4:00pm-7:00pm*). Built between 1150 and 1250, this church and bell tower dominate this small town. You'll find beautiful bronze doors made in 1160 and a stone doorway carved in the 13th century. The interior is magnificent with its double columns, the only example of such a construction in Apulia. You'll find the **Crypt of St. Nicholas the Pilgrim** (died 1094) under the transept and the **Crypt of St. Leucius** (died 670) under the nave.

One last sight to see is the **castle** to the west of the cathedral. Built between 1233 and 1249 by Frederick II, it is no longer open to the public since it is now a prison.

LECCE

Situated halfway along the **Salentine peninsula** (the heel of the Italian boot), **Lecce** is the capital of its province and is one of the most interesting towns in Southern Italy. Virtually untouristed, Lecce boasts an array of 17th century Baroque architecture.

The palaces, buildings, churches, and arches are covered with intricate swirls and designs that characterize *barocco leccese*. Even though many different conquerors swept through this area – Greeks, Cretans, Romans, Saracens, Moors, Swabians, and more – as you'll see from the architecture the main influence was the **Spanish Hapsburgs** during the 16th and 17th centuries. It's almost as if everything else was discarded outright and the Spanish remade this town and others in their own image. Some people call the city the *Athens of Apulia* because of its beauty.

Besides viewing Lecce's architecture, the city is the perfect jumping off point to explore the Salentine peninsula, which is dotted with medieval fortresses and castles. You'll also see countless olive tree groves and hill towns. Exploring the base of Italy's heel is like going back in time, but it is an adventure not to be undertaken except by the most experienced travelers.Lecce and this area is only for those travelers who know Italy and have at least a decent command of the language.

ARRIVALS & DEPARTURES

Located about 100 kilometers from Bari, there are three trains a day that go between the two cities. The trip takes about an hour and a half to two hours depending on the number of stops the train makes.

To get into town from the train station, you can either walk for 10-15 minutes straight out of the station down the Viale Oronzo Quarta into the Centro Storico, or you can take bus #1, 2, 3, or 15 from the station. You need to buy a ticket at the newsstand in the station first. The cost is L700 one way.

WHERE TO STAY

1. GRAND HOTEL TIZIANO E DEI CONGRESSI, *Superstrada Brindisi-Lecce, 73100 Lecce. Tel. 0832/4718. Fax the same. 184 rooms 50 with bath, 134 with shower. Single L136,000-139,000; Double L209,000-247,000. Credit cards accepted.* ****

Located a little way outside of town near the Autostrada here you have all the amenities you could want when traveling through the south. There's an indoor pool, a gymnasium, sauna, a good restaurant, a piano bar and more. The hotel and rooms are modern but appear in need of slight upkeep – but that's just Southern Italy taking its toll. The bathrooms are clean and there is air conditioning, which is needed in the deadly summers down here.

2. PRESIDENT, *Via Salandra 6, 73100 Lecce. Tel. 0832/311-881. Fax 0832/372-283. 154 rooms all with bath. Single L100,000-146,000; Double L160,000-203,000. All credit cards accepted. Breakfast included.* ****

One of the finest hotels in the Puglia region, this place offers professional hospitality and comfortable lodgings. Located in the center of the city in a new building with large rooms and functional modern furnishings. The bathrooms are also large and have all necessary four star amenities including courtesy toiletries. The common areas are also large and accommodating and furnished with refinement and comfort in mind. Like the Grand Hotel, a wonderful place to stay when in Lecce.

3. HOTEL RISORGIMENTO, *Via Augusto Imperatore 19, 73100 Lecce, Tel. 0832/242-125. Fax 0832/245-571. 57 rooms one single without a bath. Single without bath L69,000. Single L99,000; Double L171,000. All credit cards accepted. Breakfast L15,000.* ***

This is the first hotel in Lecce situated in an old and historic building. An elegant structure with quiet and comfortable rooms and arranged with antique furnishings. The best rooms are 208 and those between 301 and 306, since they also have private terraces. The entrance hall is elegant, as is the restaurant and party room. The pavement is a wonderfully decorated extravaganza in a style all its own. There is room service, TV and air conditioning and the place is really great, but the breakfast is Italian style, meaning coffee, tea and a roll or two. Not abundant enough for our North American palates. But then there are plenty of places around to grab a more ample bite to eat for L15,000.

WHERE TO EAT

4. BARBABLU, *Via Umberto I #7, Tel. 0832/241183. Closed Mondays, the last week in June, and the first week in September. Credit cards accepted. Dinner for two L100,000.*

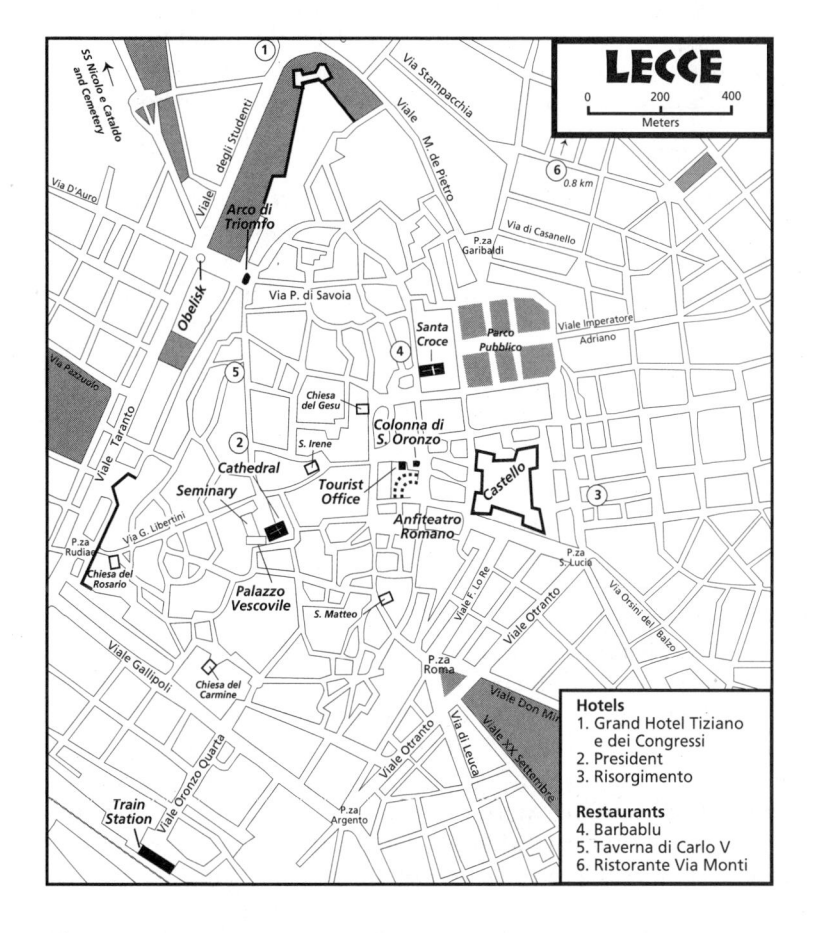

Located in an old building in the Centro Storico, this place has great atmosphere both inside and outside on the terrace and serves wonderful food. The antipasto table is overflowing with goodies like eggplant, pepperoni, local sausage, zucchini, cheeses, and more. For your first course, try the *spaghetti alla vongole verace* (with a spicy clam sauce), it's excellent in these parts. For seconds, they make great fish or meat dishes, so try either. I like the *Saltimbocca alla leccese* (ham shank cooked in tomatoes and spices). It's better than the Roman version. The ingredients are fresher.

    5. TAVERNA DI CARLO V, *Via G Palmieri 46, Tel. 0832/248-818. Closed Sunday nights and Mondays. In the summer also closed Saturdays. In Winter Saturday for lunch. Closed all of August. Visa accepted. Dinner for two L70,000.*

    A classic atmosphere of an old tavern, this place is located on the bottom floor of a building that dates to 500 CE and is located in the Centro Storico of Lecce. You can also sit outside on the terrace and watch Lecce go by as you eat. They make many traditional Lecce dishes here, including *zuppa di farro con ceci o fagioli* (soup made with flour and chickpeas or beans), *zuppa di lenticchie* (lentil soup) and a thick and tasty *stufato di verdure fresche* (fresh vegetable stew). For seconds try some local favorites like the *pezzetti di cavallo alla griglia* (small pieces of grilled horse meat) or *involtini di trippa con patate* (rolled tripe with potatoes). They also have a plentiful supply of fish dishes.

    6. RISTORANTE VIA MONTI, *Via Monti 13, Tel. 0832/390-174. Closed Wednesdays and the last three weeks of August. Credit cards accepted. Dinner for two L120,000.*

    On the outskirts of town, take a cab to and from this restaurant. It is an elegant dining experience, so come appropriately dressed. My favorites are the *linguine ai frutti di mare* (linguine with mounds of seafood) and the *involtini di vitello alla crema di parmigiano* (rolled veal covered with a creamy parmesan sauce). They have plenty of other meat and fish dishes.

SEEING THE SIGHTS

    The old town of Lecce is a maze of small winding streets which are a joy to wander. Start in the center of town at the **Piazza San Oronzo** where the information office is. In the center of the piazza is a the **Colonna di San Oronzo**, with a statue of the saint on top, which once stood, saintless, in Brindisi to mark the end of the Appian Way. Also in the piazza is a partially excavated **Anfiteatro Romano** that dates from the 2nd century.

    North of the piazza in the **Piazza della Profettura** is the best church to see in Lecce, **Church of Santa Croce**, built between 1549 and 1697 (*Open 9:00am-1:00pm and 5:30pm-7:30pm*). It has an ornately decorated facade and a beautiful exterior. The interior is only two simple rows of columns supporting bare white walls. Behind the church are the peaceful **Giardini Publici** where you can relax with a picnic lunch.

East of the Piazza San Oronzo is the imposing trapezoid **Castello**, built from 1539 to 1548 during the reign of Charles V (*not open to public*). To the west of this sight is the **Arco di Trionfo**, erected in 1548 in honor of Charles V. If you're interested in cemeteries, go up the Viale San Nicolo to the church of **SS Nicolo e Cataldo**, founded in 1180, and the cemetery it tends to. The **cemetery** is filled with small mausoleums of every imaginable style and shape all clustered together on tiny paths (*Viale San Nicolo. Open 8:00am-1:00pm and 4:00pm-7:00pm; cemetery is open 9:00am-6:00pm. Sundays 9:00am-1:00pm*).

Back in the center of the city is the **Piazza del Duomo** (*Piazza del Duomo. Open 8:00am-11:00am and 4:30pm-7:30pm*). This is an entire complex of buildings that stand out because of their white facades. First you have the looming **Cathedral of Sant'Oronzo** and *campanile* built from 1658 to 1570 that stands 70 meters high. The interior is mainly from the 18th century. To the right of the cathedral is the **Palazzo Vescovile**, the Bishop's Palace, which was constructed in 1652 (*Piazza del Duomo. Not open to public*). Further right is the **seminary** built in 1709, with its richly decorated facade and courtyard containing a beautiful fountain (*not open to public*).

If you're interested in more churches Lecce has the **Chiesa del Gesu**, **San Irene**, **San Marco**, **Santa Chiara**, **San Matteo**, **Chiesa del Carmine**, and the large **Chiesa Rosario** for your enjoyment. *Chiesa del Gesu (Piazza Gastromediano, Open 8:00am-11:00am and 3:30pm-5:30pm), San Irene (Via Vittorio Emanuele, Open 8:30am-noon and 3:00pm-6:00pm), San Marco , Santa Chiara (Piazza Santa Chiara, Open 8:00am-11:00am and 4:00pm-7:00pm), San Matteo (Via San Matteo, Open 8:00am-noon and 4:00pm-6:00pm), Chiesa del Carmine (Piazza Tancredi, Open 8:00am-11:00am and 4:00pm-7:00pm), and the large Chiesa Rosario (Via G. Libertini, Open 8:00am-11:00am and 3:30pm-5:30pm).*

PRACTICAL INFORMATION
Bank Hours & Changing Money
Banks are open Monday through Friday from 8:30am to 1:30pm and some do reopen from 2:30pm or so to 4:30pm or so. The **Stazione Centrale** has a *cambio* inside that is open from 8:00am to 1:30pm and 2:30pm to 8:00pm Monday through Saturday. The closest **American Express** office is in *Bari (Tel. 080/521-0022)*.

Business Hours
From October to June, most shops are open from 9:00am to 1:00pm and from 3:30pm to 7:30pm, and are closed all day Sundays and on Monday mornings. Then from June to September, when it really starts to get hot in Lecce, the morning hours remain the same, but the mid-day siesta time is slightly extended to 4:00pm and sometimes 4:30pm, which

then pushes closing time back to 7:30pm or 8:00pm. In conjunction with being closed on Sunday and Monday mornings, shops are also closed half-days on Saturday.

Food stores, like *alimentari*, generally are open from 8:30am to 1:30pm (so stock up on your picnic supplies before you need them) and from 5:00pm to 7:30pm, and during the winter months they are closed on Thursdays.

Postal Services

You can buy stamps at local tobacconists (they are marked with a "T" outside) as well as post offices. Mail boxes are colored red. Post offices are open from 8:00am to 2:00pm on weekdays. The one exception to this rule is the **main post office (Palazzo delle Poste)** *located in Piazza Libertini (Tel. 0832/303-000)* which is open Monday through Friday from 8:00am to 7:30pm, and Saturdays from 8:00am to noon. You can't miss it, it's basically in the shadow of the castle.

Tourist Information & Maps

• **EPT tourist office**, *in the center of town in the Piazza San Oronzo between the Duomo and the castle. Tel. 0832/316-461.* Here they can supply you with maps of Lecce as well as Gallipoli (Not the Gallipoli that was immortalized by that Australian World War I movie – that one was in Turkey.)

If you want to charter a bus to take you to the sights, contact the travel office of **CTS** at *Via Palmieri 91, Tel. 0832/301-862.*

ACAIA CASTLE

This is the closest castle to Lecce, making it the most convenient. You can reach it by taking one of the three daily buses that leave from the bus station on Via Adua. Contact the EPT office for more specific schedule information. Located only 10 kilometers from Lecce, and thus only a ten or fifteen minute drive, this castle has long been abandoned and is overgrown with weeds and shrubbery. But you can easily see its former majesty from the mosaic remnants, narrow medieval staircases, huge rooms, and eerily quiet courtyards. This is a good place to start your adventure exploring Southern Italian castles.

WHERE TO EAT

LOCANDO DEL GALLO, *Piazza Castello 1, Tel. 0832/861-102. Closed Mondays, 15 days in September and 15 days in January. Credit cards accepted. Dinner for two L90,000.*

The best place to be in this restaurant is sitting in the shadow of the castle on the terrace. There is a fixed price menu (L40,000 per person) that offers some wonderful local flavor, like the *tubetini con la cernia* (pasta with sea bass or grouper), *meurzi fritte* (pieces of bread and pepperoni fried), and any of their fine game caught in the hills around the castle.

GALLIPOLI

Located on the edge of the Gulf of Taranto and the Ionian Sea, this little port town is situated on a rocky island connected to the more modern city by an ancient bridge, the **Ponte Citta Vecchia**.

The beautiful **old town**, with its narrow winding streets evokes images of centuries past. This is a fun place for a day or two.

ARRIVALS & DEPARTURES

There is a train from Lecce every two hours. The trip takes 45 minutes and costs L5,000. If you go by car, simply take **highway 101** straight to Gallipoli. You'll pass through the country town of **Galapone**. Stop there for a brief visit and enjoy the town's beautiful cathedral and their Baroque **Church of the Crucifixion**.

WHERE TO STAY

1. HOTEL SPINOLA, *Corso Roma 129, 73014 Gallipoli. Tel. 0833/ 261-916. Fax 0833/261-917. 13 rooms all with shower. Single L60,000- 120,000; Double L130,000-190,000. Breakfast L8,000 extra. Credit cards accepted.* ****

Located in the center of the city near the train station, you are within walking distance of all the sights. A quaint little hotel that makes you feel special. The bathrooms are a little tiny, the rooms are clean, and all have air conditioning and TV. A well located place to stay, but nothing truly special.

2. HOTEL JOLI PARK, *Piazza Salento 2, 73014 Gallipoli. Tel. 0833/ 263-321. Fax is the same. 87 rooms all with shower. Single L70,000-80,000; Double L115,000-130,000. Visa accepted. Breakfast included.* ***

Located near the beach and the center of modern Gallipoli, which isn't hard in Gallipoli, since it's surrounded by water, this is an ex-Jolly hotel (hence the play on word with its title: **Joli**). Housed in a renovated old building with a lot of charm, it also has a good restaurant that makes traditional dishes. A quality, clean, comfortable place even though the furniture is a bit eclectic. You have air conditioning and TV in the all the rooms, many of which have great panoramic views. They also have a bus to ferry you back and forth to the old town or the station. And did I mention a swimming pool and a quiet relaxing garden setting.

3. **HOTEL LE SIRENUSE**, *Litoranea Santa Maria di Leuca, 73014 Gallipoli. Tel. 0833/22536. Fax 0833/22539. 120 rooms all with bath. Single L82,000-110,000; Double L136,000-160,000. All credit cards accepted. Breakfast included.* ***

They're located a little ways out from Gallipoli but they have a private beach, snorkeling equipment, horseback riding, tennis, and outdoor pool, a disco, a piano bar – wait, there's more – mini-golf, a bocce course, and a superb restaurant that offers a beautifully romantic view. They also have hairdressers and a nursery for kids as well as a bus to take you back and forth to the city. A perfect location. Private, peaceful and relaxing. And the price is right too.

WHERE TO EAT

4. **IL CAPRICCIO**, *Viale G. Bovio 14, Tel. 0833/261-545. Closed Mondays in the summer and all of October. Credit cards accepted. Dinner for two L120,000.*

The menu here is a combination of traditional dishes and regular Italian fare. A direct result of the many Italian tourists who flock to the beaches in the area during the summer (mainly in August). So if you know your Italian food you can always find something you like. For example: *tagliatelle alla bolognese* (with a tasty meat sauce) *spaghetti all vongole verace* (with a spicy clam sauce), *spaghetti ai frutti di mare* (with mounds of seafood). For seconds, you can't go wrong with the *grigliata mista* (mixed grill of meat and fish) or the *zuppa di pesce* (a thick fish soup). Pleasant atmosphere both inside and out – on their terrace under an awning.

5. **RISTORANTE MARECHIARO**, *Lungomare G Marconi, 0833/266-143. Closed Tuesdays. Credit cards accepted. Dinner for L120,000.*

Located just before the Ponte Citta Vecchia, this place used to be a dump frequented by local fishermen, but it has slowly upgraded its decor. The food is as filling and robust as before. Enjoy their many fish dishes either inside with the rustic decor or outside where you can gaze at the sea. It's a large place, over 200 seats, but reservations would be advised in the high season. For firsts, try the *zuppa di pesce alla gallipolina* (fish soup made Gallipoli style with mounds of seafood) which is so filling it can take the place of a pasta. For seconds try any of the many fish they make roasted over an open flame and you'll come away satisfied.

6. **LA PARANZA**, *Largo Dogana, Tel. 0833/266-639. Closed Wednesdays in Winter. Visa accepted. Dinner for two L100,000.*

Located just over the bridge in the old town, this is a strictly seafood place. The owners also run a seafood wholesale operation so you are sure to get the best seafood here. Sit outside to enjoy the view and enjoy some *gnocchi di patate con gamberi* (potato gnocchi with shrimp) and the scrumptious *fritto misti di mare* (mixed fried seafood).

SOUTHERN ITALY & SICILY 319

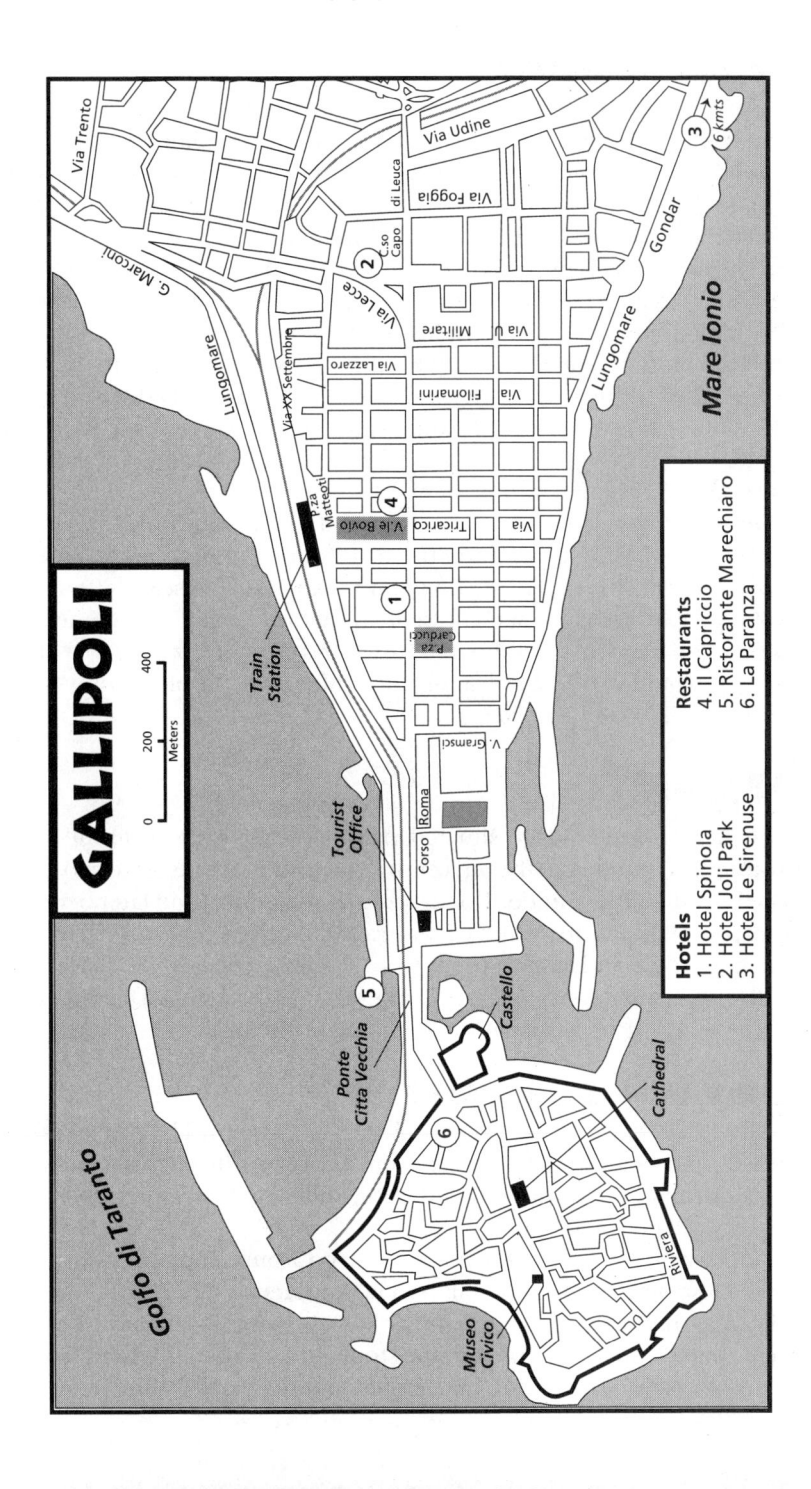

SEEING THE SIGHTS

An old road, the **Riviera**, runs all the way around this small town and offers views of both the **Gulf of Taranto** and the **Ionian Sea**. Visit the **Castello** (*Piazza Imbiani. Open 9:00am-1:00pm and 4:00pm-7:00pm*), built from the 13th century to the 17th century just over the bridge on the left. You can get some great views from the ramparts.

The **cathedral** is located down the Via Antoinette de Pace in front of the castle (*Open 8:00am-11:00am and 3:30pm-5:30pm*). Built between 1629 and 1696, there are some beautiful choir stalls here. Beyond the cathedral on the same road is the **Museo Civico**, (*Via Antoinette de Pace, Open 9:00am-1:30pm and 4:00pm-7:00pm Tuesday-Sunday*) which contains many artifacts, sculptures, and paintings of the region's past. If you arrive in the morning, don't miss the fruit and vegetable **market** in front of the castle in the **Piazza Imbriani**.

After you've visited this scenic, beautiful, and unique little town head up the coast on the Gulf of Taranto side to some wonderful beaches and resorts. During the *Ferragosto* holidays in August, this seaside town of 20,000 people swells to many more than that with Italian vacationers.

For more information about the town and the surrounding area, stop at the **information office** just across the bridge from the old town at *Corso Roma 225, Tel. 0863/476-202*.

OTRANTO

A little fishing village situated panoramically on a beautiful bay, **Otranto** was founded in the 6th century CE by the Greeks (Hydrus). The small port then came under Roman rule (Hydruntum) and later became the capital of Byzantine Apulia. It was razed to the ground in 1480 by the Ottoman Turks and all its citizens were slaughtered.

There are some ancient churches here, and a castle with a terrific view where you can gaze across at the Republic of Albania.

ARRIVALS & DEPARTURES

There are two trains a day from Lecce to Otranto. The trip takes 45 minutes and costs L5,000. By car from Lecce, go through the seaside resort of San Cataldo with its lighthouse, and take the scenic coast road. The trip will take about 45 minutes.

Once you arrive, from the train station go around the right side of the circle and bear left down the hill on **Via Pantaleone**. There will be signs indicating that you should go right. Follow them and you'll have a much longer walk. Instead, go through the stoplight and go to the **Lungomare d'Otranto**, which runs along the beach. Go three blocks to the right and

SOUTHERN ITALY & SICILY

you'll hit the **Piazza de Donno**. Bear to the left down **Via Vittorio Emanuele II** and you'll enter the old town in a few blocks.

Turn right on **Via Basilica** to get to the local tourist office and the cathedral. Pick up a map here and begin your exploration into the byways of this charming seaside escape.

WHERE TO STAY

HOTEL DEGLI HAE-THEY, *Via Sforza 33, 73028 Otranto. Tel. 0836/801548. Fax 0836/801576. 21 rooms all with shower. Single L55,000-99,000; Double L99,000-150,000. Credit cards accepted* ****

Located just away from the center of town, this country four star has impressive amenities. There's a pool, piano bar, great views from the terrace and most importantly a shuttle bus to bring you back and forth to the sights. Clean and comfortable rooms with relatively small bathrooms.

GRAND HOTEL DANIELA, *Litoranea San Cataldo, 73028 Otranto. Tel. 0836/806-648. Fax 0836/806-667. 146 rooms all with shower. Single L90,000-180,000; Double L180,000-360,000. Credit cards accepted.* ****

Ooo-la-la – what luxury! Great views, a private beach, snorkeling equipment, sauna, gymnasium, bocce courts, tennis courts, horseback riding, swimming pool, nursery for the kids, hairdressers, piano bar and much more. This is the place to stay to have all the luxuries of the world at your fingertips when you're in the middle of nowhere. Located outside of town, they also have a shuttle bus to take you to the sights and back.

HOTEL VALLE DELL'IDRO, *Via D. Grasso 4, 73028 Otranto. Tel. 0836/801-224. Fax 0836/802-374. 27 rooms all with shower. Single L75,000-90,000; Double L90,000-130,000. Credit cards accepted.* ****

Another inexpensive four-star. This place doesn't have nearly as many amenities as the Grand Hotel Daniela but they make you feel taken care of. Located outside of town near the beach, this is really only a place to rest your head for a few days and not for a full vacation. They have a passable restaurant and a welcoming bar for an evenings *aperitif*.

HOTEL BELLAVISTA, *Via Vittorio Emanuele 19, 73028 Otranto. Tel. 0836/801-058. 22 rooms, 2 with bath, 20 with shower. Single L50,000-60,000; Double L70,000-80,000. No credit cards accepted.* **

The best budget choice in the area in terms of cost, and you get air conditioning, which is imperative in the summertime down here. They have their own restaurant attached to the hotel which serves great local food. There's a full board option for only L88,000 per person.

WHERE TO EAT

TRATTORIA DA SERGIO, *Corso Garibaldi 9. Tel. 0836/801-408. Closed Wednesday in Winter, February and November. American Express accepted. Dinner for two L120,000.*
    Exclusively a local style seafood restaurant. Some great dishes here are *frutti di mare con linguini or risotto* (linguini or rice with mounds of fresh seafood), *gamberoni alla griglia* (large grilled shrimp) or some great *pesce spada alla griglia* (grilled swordfish). You can enjoy both inside and outside seating.

TRATTORIA VECCHIA OTRANTO, *Corso Garibaldi 96, Tel. 0836/801-575. Closed Mondays in Winter and November. Credit cards accepted. Dinner for two L100,000.*
    Opened in 1981, this rustic restaurant on Otranto's main street is a well respected local place that serves traditional dishes like *tonnarelli alla polpa di ricci e peperoni* (wide strips of pasta with sea urchins and pepperoni) or *zuppa di pesce all'otrantina* (special local seafood soup). They have inside and outside seating. I'd recommend the local flavor inside.

SEEING THE SIGHTS

The **cathedral of Santissima Annunziata**, begun in 1080, is the last home for the remains of those slaughtered by the Ottomans. The church contains ancient columns that have had 12th century capitals placed on them. You'll also find some unique well-preserved 12th century mosaic tile floors that depict the passing of the months and of battles won in the area (*Piazza Duomo. Open 8:00am-noon and 3:00pm-5:00pm*).

A smaller church, **San Pietro**, of 19th century origin sits on a side street in the upper part of town with its Byzantine dome and frescoes. Next visit the **Castello di Aragonese** (*Via Castello. Currently under reconstruction. Open 9:00am-1:00pm and 4:00pm-7:00pm. Admission L5,000*). The castle affords wonderful views, on clear days, across the **Straits of Otranto**. The straits are 75 kilometers wide, and you can see across to the mountains of Albania – a country once ruled by Italy.

For more information about Otranto, and to get a map of the city and surrounding area, contact the local **tourist office**, *Via Basilica 8, Tel. 0836/801-436*, which rests at the foot of the cathedral.

SICILY

Sicily (**Sicilia**) is a mountainous, arid island that is a geological extension of the Apennine Mountains, only separated from the mainland by the **Straits of Messina**. Many powers have occupied this strategically important area over the centuries: Greeks, Romans, Arabs, Phoenicians and today, unofficially of course, the Mafia. The extensive historical sites related to these former powers are part of the island's attraction.

And not just the powers from the past: for probably the strangest tours anywhere, you can actually contact local travel agencies and go on a **Mafia tour** that visits various Family activities and the graves of infamous godfathers and victims.

Among the ancient Greek and Roman ruins on the island are the Greek **Taormina theater** and **San Domenico Monastery** near **Messina**, the Greek theater in **Syracuse**, and the 5th-century BCE **Temple of Concord** in **Agrigento**. It's also a fun adventure to visit the **Isole Eolie**, off the north shore by Messina.

Early Settlements

Before invaders came to Sicily, we know, based on excavations at **Realmonte** near Agrigento, that man's history in Sicily dates back to the early Paleolithic period. There are also early settlements at **Stentinello** and **Lipari** that have been carbon dated to the Neolithic period. During the Copper and Bronze ages, the island's inhabitants traded with many of the other developing Mediterranean settlements. During this time the **Isole Eolie** and its capital Lipari rose in power and began to go off on its own tangent separate from Sicily. They were more influenced by Malta and the western Peloponnesian culture, while Sicily came mainly under the influence of **Greece** and the **Phoenicians**.

Near the end of the Bronze Age, a contingent of people called **Siculi** (thus the island's name) came from the mainland and began to dominate the small settlements of the island, which broke up and headed inland to the mountains for protection. These new people prospered, but were mainly just vassals to the Phoenician and Greek traders. Even though Phoenicia had a great influence in Sicily, especially the port cities, they left the main colonization to the Greeks. They started their settlements on the east coast and gradually pushed the Siculi people westward.

By the fifth century BCE, **Syracuse** on the east coast had become the strongest settlement and had Helenized almost all of Sicily. The Siculi looked to the western Phoenician towns of Marsala and Trapani for assistance; they were holding fast against the Greek colonization. As a result a war was fought between the two Sicilian factions, which had to be settled by Roman intervention with the two **Punic Wars** of 264-212 BCE.

With the Roman domination, the interior of the island began to prosper. Splendid villas and fertile fields sprung up throughout Sicily, providing much of Rome's produce.

Foreign Invasions

After the fall of Rome, Sicily was invaded by the Vandals in the 5th century CE, then by the Goths. Eventually the Byzantine Empire took control and almost three centuries of peace lasted until 826. Then the Moors and Saracens took control of Sicily. Their biggest change was to move the capital from Syracuse to **Palermo**, where it remains today.

In 1061, the Norman conquest began (five years before their successful invasion of another island, England) and the island enjoyed its most successful period in history. In 1302, the era of peace and prosperity ended with the Spanish domination. This period saw the rich get richer and the poor get poorer, creating a division between the people and their governors that still exists today. It may be an exaggeration to say that history passed by the Sicilians for the next five hundred years, but not an awful lot of consequence occurred during this long period.

Then on May 11, 1860, **Garibaldi** landed at Marsala and began to dismantle the Kingdom of Sicily and merge it with the Kingdom of Italy. During this time the people were greatly oppressed, which gave rise to the beginnings of what we know today as the **Mafia**. At the beginning of the twentieth century, a massive emigration began, mainly to America and Australia, spreading the tentacles of the Mafia all over the world.

Sicily Today

Sicily has since to recover economically and remains a poverty stricken island off the coast of Italy, still basically controlled by the Mafia. Everything from the government to industry bends to their will, making it even more difficult for the island to recover. But the Sicilians are fiercely independent people, and most are working hard to combat organized crime and overcome their poor economic situation.

Besides its rich ancient history, there are many other reasons to visit Sicily: water sports, beaches of rock and sand (including black sand), natural beauty, great food and friendly people (for the most part). For touring, the island can be roughly divided into the north shore and south shore areas. The **north shore** has reefs, olive groves, secluded coves and countless seaside resorts, including **Cefalu**, a gorgeous Arab-Norman city with good beaches.

SOUTHERN ITALY & SICILY 325

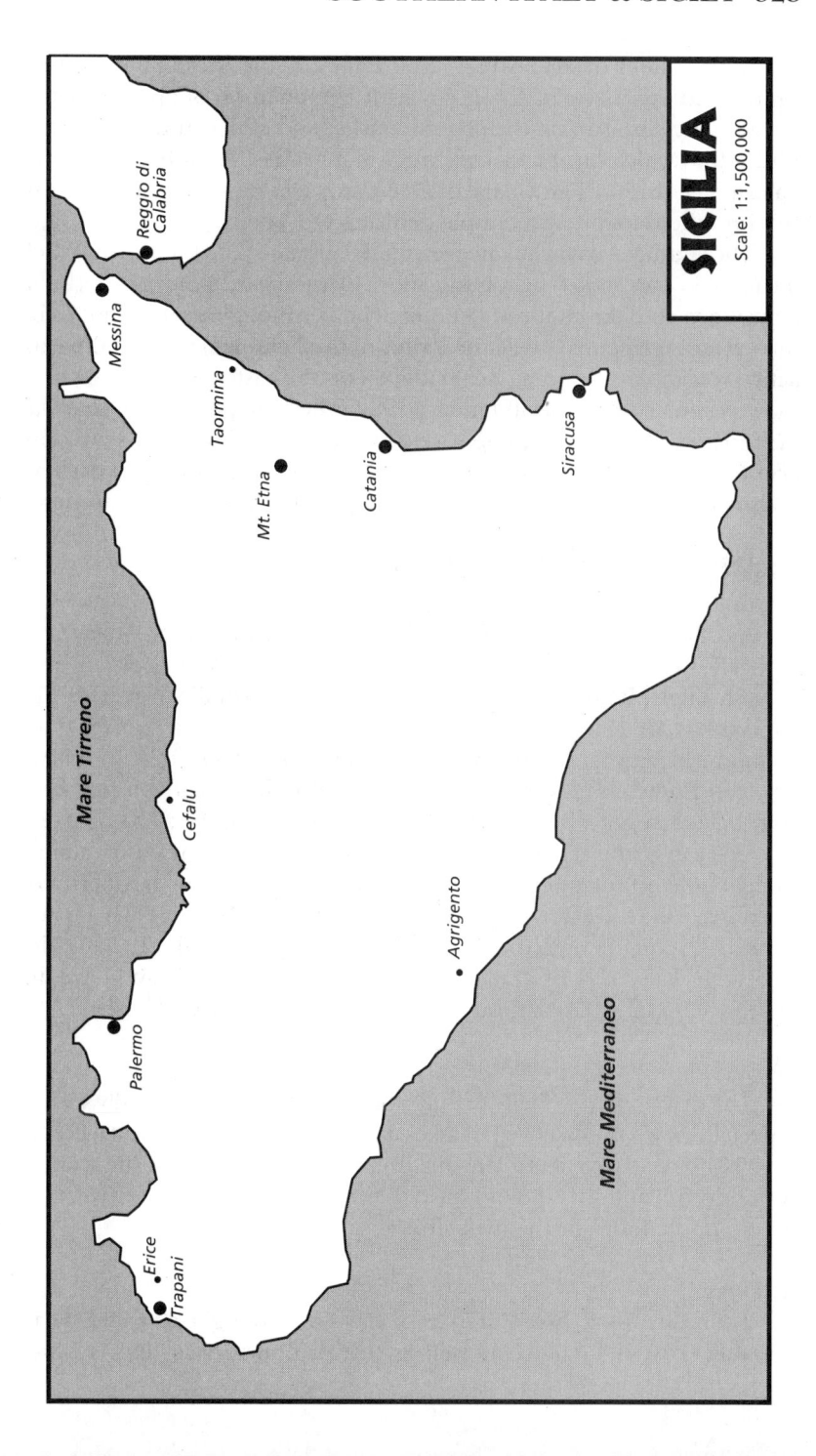

In the center of the north coast is **Palermo**, the ancient and current capital and the island's largest city with a population of approximately 801,000. Be sure to visit the central market and 12th-century **Monreale Cathedral**, which has impressive biblical mosaics. About 80 km west of Palermo lies the ancient village of **Erice**, atop a mountain, where you can still find the remains of a temple dedicated to Venus.

The **southern coast** has an even milder climate than the North, which means you can enjoy swimming most of the year, although between November and March it can get quite chilly. Among the areas not to be missed are **Agrigento** (to see the **Valley of the Temples**) and **Mt. Etna**, an active volcano just topping 3,200 meters on the east coast. The last time the volcano erupted was in January 1992. The time previous to that was in March 1987, when two people were killed. Although scientists say it can erupt at any time, if you play it safe you shouldn't be in any danger. There is also good winter skiing around Mt. Etna that offers great ocean views.

ARRIVALS & DEPARTURES
By Air
As of press time, there were no direct flights from North America or Australia to either Catania in the east or Palermo in the west. You will have to fly through Milan or Rome first, then transfer to **Alitalia** to get to Sicily. Fares today are changing very rapidly, but expect to pay about $300 for a round-trip between Rome and Palermo, and about $302 for a round-trip between Rome and Catania. It may be slightly cheaper if you purchase your tickets in Italy, but it might also be more expensive ... go figure.

You can get direct flights from London to both Palermo and Catania, so this could be an option for you when traveling from North America or Australia. There are also direct flights from Dublin to both Palermo and Catania. In conjunction, you can catch a flight from all major Italian cities directly to Palermo or Catania, so if you're already in Italy and have the urge to see Sicily it is easy, but not inexpensive, to get to the island.

By Car
The drive down to Sicily through Southern Italy is beautifully scenic, especially down the coast, but it takes quite a while. From Rome it will take over 14 hours just to get to Messina. But if you have the time, the scenery is wonderful, and if you don't have the money to fly you can drive, take the train, the ferry, or the hydrofoil.

By Ferry
There are over twenty ferries a day from **Reggio di Calabria** to **Messina** (cost is L5,000), as well as a hydrofoil service that is faster

(L6,000) but doesn't allow cars. You can also catch ferries from the cities listed below as well as others in Italy:
- **Genoa to Palermo**, 23 hours
- **Naples to Palermo**, 11 hours
- **Naples to Catania to Syracuse**, 15 hours/19 hours
- **Naples to the Aeolian Islands to Milazzo**, 7 hours/8 hours
- **Cagliari Sardinia to Palermo**, 14 hours
- **Cagliari to Trapani**, 11 hours
- **Livorno to Palermo**, 19 hours

So if you are in one of these cities, have time to spare, and don't get seasick too easily, try the ferry option.

By Hydrofoil
For a faster alternative to ferries from Naples, try the hydrofoil. It'll cost a little more but the ride will be smoother and it will be over sooner.
- **Naples to Palermo**, 5 hours and 30 minutes
- **Naples to the Aeolian Islands to Milazzo**, 4-6 hours

By Train
If you like long train rides you can enjoy the Southern Italian scenery and take the train from any place in Italy to Sicily. From Rome it will take over 14 hours just to get to Messina. But if you have the time, the scenery is wonderful, and if you don't have the money to fly this is a nice, scenic option.

The train fare from Rome is L50,000. The ferry ride from Reggio di Calabria is included in the train fare.

CLIMATE & WEATHER
The climate of Sicily varies throughout the entire island. To the north, along the coast, you can expect hot summers and wild winters making it perfectly Mediterranean. The temperatures along the southern coast and inland, are much higher and you can have more drastic temperature fluctuations. Rain is rare but it does increase with altitude. This makes Sicily, strangely enough, a great place to ski in the winter, since the mountains above 1,600 meters get well covered with snow.

In the summer expect to experience the hot and humid *Scirocco* that blows in from the Sahara, bringing with it discomfort and clouds of reddish dust.

When to Go
Anytime is a good time to travel to Sicily. The climate doesn't vary

greatly, making Sicily a pleasant trip any time of year – although the summers can get unbearably hot at times. The northern coast's climate is more stable than that of the southern coast and inland. If you want to try the beach from November to March, it's not a good idea, since it will be like autumn back in the US.

So the best time to go to Sicily and enjoy good warm weather is September through the first week in November. To enjoy good skiing, go between December and March.

PUBLIC HOLIDAYS & FESTIVALS

Offices and shops in Sicily are closed on the following dates, so prepare for the eventuality of having virtually everything closed. This is your cue to stock up on picnic snacks, soda, whatever, because in most cities and towns there is no such thing as a 24 hour a day 7-11.

- **January 1**, New Year's Day
- **January 6**, Epiphany
- **April 25**, Liberation Day (1945)
- **Easter Monday**
- **May 1**, Labor Day
- **August 15**, *Ferragosto* and Assumption of the Blessed Virgin (climax of Italian family holiday season. Hardly anything stays open in the big cities through the month of August)
- **November 1**, All Saints Day
- **December 8**, Immaculate Conception
- **December 25/26**, Christmas

Local Events & Festivals
- **Agrigento**, *Sagra del Mandorlo in Fiore*, 1st to 2nd Sunday in February
- **Catania**, *Festa di San Agata*, February 3-5
- **Acireale**, *Carnevale Acese*, Sunday and Shrove Tuesday
- **Sciacca**, *Carnevale*, Sunday and Shrove Tuesday
- **Trapani**, *Processione del misteri*, Good Friday and Easter Sunday
- **Marsala**, *Sacra rappresentazione*, Holy Thursday
- **Acata**, *Festa di San Vincenzo*, 3rd Sunday after Easter
- **Pergusa**, *Sagra del Lago*, 1st Sunday in May
- **Naro**, *Festa di San Calogero*, June 18
- **Palermo**, *Festa di U Fistinu*, July 11-15
- **Marsala**, *Sagra del Vino Marsala*, 3rd Sunday in July
- **Messina**, *Passeggiata dei giganti*, August 14
- **Siracusa**, *Festa di San Lucia*, December 13

SOUTHERN ITALY & SICILY

GETTING AROUND SICILY

Sicily is interconnected by an extensive highway system, a superb train system, and naturally, since Sicily is an island, a complete shipping service involving ferries, hydrofoils, and liners. Your mode of transport will depend on how long you're staying in Sicily and what you want to see.

If you're only visiting coastal towns, it might be fun to take a ferry between them. If you are going to rural, off the beaten path locations, you'll need a car, because even if the train did go to where you're going, the *Locale* would take forever since it stops at every town on its tracks.

By Train

You can get most anywhere in Sicily by train, much the same as on the mainland. There are more extensive rail systems on the east of the island to accommodate the flow of trains from the mainland. Here you should expect delays since the trains may have had trouble getting across on the ferry.

There are some small towns that the trains do not go to, but you should avoid these anyway. You never know when you're going to stumble onto something better left unseen in one of the mountain villages.

By Car

The expressways, called **Autostrada**, are superhighways and toll roads. They connect all major Sicilian cities and have contributed to the tremendous increase in tourist travel. By car is the best way to see Sicily since you don't have to wait for the trains, which are inevitably delayed, something that rarely happens on the mainland.

Driving is the perfect way to see the entire variety of Sicily's towns, villages, seascapes, landscapes, and monuments. The Sicilian drivers may be a little *pazzo* (crazy), but if you drive confidently you'll be fine. A word of caution, again: Sicily is best explored along its coastline and a little inland. Once you start roaming through the mountain towns, unless you know what you're doing, anything could happen.

BASIC INFORMATION

Banking Hours

Banks in Sicily are open Monday through Friday 8:35am to 1:35pm and from 3:00pm to 4:00pm, and are closed Saturdays, Sundays and national holidays. In some cities the afternoon open hour may not even exist. Even if the bank is closed, most travelers checks can be exchanged for Italian lire at most hotels and shops and at the many foreign exchange offices in railway stations and at airports.

CAR RENTAL IN SICILY

You have all the major international and national players in the car rental business here in Sicily. Below please find a list of their addresses and phones numbers separated by city.

IN CATANIA
- **Avis**, Via Federico de Roberto 10, Tel. 095/374-905; Via Giuseppe La Rena 87, Tel. 095/347-975; Aeroporto Fontanarossa, Tel. 095/340-500
- **Hertz**, Via Toselli 45, Tel. 095/322-560
- **Maggiore**, Piazza Gioeni 6, Tel. 095/338-305; Piazza Verga 48, Tel. 095/310-002; Aeroporto Fontanarossa, Tel. 095/340-594

IN MESSINA
- **Avis**, Via Vittorio Emanuele 35, Tel. 090/58404
- **Hertz**, Via Vittorio Emanuele 113, Tel. 090/363-740
- **Maggiore**, Via T. Cannizzaro 46, Tel. 090/775-476

IN PALERMO
- **Avis**, Via Principe di Scordia 12, Tel. 091/586-940; Aeroporto di Punta Raisi, Tel. 091/591-684
- **Hertz**, Viale Michelangelo 200, Tel. 091/204-277; Aeroporto di Punta Raisi, Tel. 091/591-682
- **Maggiore**, Via Agrigento 27, Tel. 091/625-9286; Aeroporto di Punta Raisi, Tel. 091/591-681

IN SYRACUSE
- **Avis**, Piazza dell Repubblica 11, Tel. 0931/69635
- **Maggiore**, Via Tevere 14, Tel. 0931/66548

IN TRAPANI
- **Maggiore**, Via Torre, Tel. 0923/21567

Business Hours

Store hours are usually Monday through Friday 9:00am to 1:00pm, 3:30/4:00pm to 7:30/8:00pm, and Saturdays 9:00am to 1:00pm. Most stores are closed on Sundays and on national holidays. Don't expect to find any 24-hour convenience stores just around the corner. If you want to have some soda in your room after a long day of touring you need to plan ahead.

Also, plan on most stores not being open from 1:00pm to 4:00pm. This is Sicily's siesta time. Don't expect to get a lot done except find a nice restaurant and enjoy the pleasant afternoons.

Consulates
- **United States**, Via GB Vaccarini 1, Palermo. Tel. 091/302-590

Safety & Precautions

Sicilian cities are definitely much safer than any equivalent American city. You can walk most anywhere without fear of harm, but that doesn't mean you shouldn't play it safe. Listed below are some simple rules to follow to ensure that nothing bad occurs:
- At night, make sure the streets you are walking on have plenty of other people. Like I said, most cities are safe, but at night the rules change.
- Always have your knapsack or purse flung over the shoulder that is not directly next to the road. Why? There have been cases of Italians on motorbike snatching purses off old ladies and in some cases dragging them a few blocks.
- Better yet, have your companion walk on the street side, while you walk on the inside of the sidewalk with the knapsack or purse.
- Better still is to buy one of those tummy wallets that goes under your shirt so no one can even be tempted to purse snatch you. That's really all you should need, but always follow basic common sense; if you feel threatened, scared, alone, retrace your steps back to a place where there are other people.
- Be especially on guard against street thieves and pickpockets in Palermo and other large towns.

SPORTS & RECREATION

Sicily is an island, thus the water sports at their beach resorts are prevalent. But they are also a mountainous island, so their skiing is actually quite good too, despite the fact that they are close to Africa. Sicily is a prime vacation spot for both winter and summer sports, so if you're in the mood for either while on the island you can find what you want.

FOOD & WINE

Food

Most Sicilian food is cooked with fresh ingredients raised or caught a short distance from the restaurant, making their dishes healthy, fresh, and satisfying. There are many restaurants in Sicily of international renown, but you shouldn't limit yourself only to the upper echelon. In most cases you can find as good a meal at a fraction the cost at any *trattoria*. Also, many of the upper echelon restaurants you read about are only in business because they cater to the tourist trade. Their food is good, but the atmosphere is a little hokey.

The traditional Sicilian meal has been influenced by the Middle East, Greece, France, and Spain as a result of the island's past conquests. Other influences include the sea (what better place to find a meal) and the fact that the island's climate is perfect for growing all sorts of herbs and spices, and vegetables and fruits.

Suggested Sicilian Cuisine
You don't have to eat all the traditional courses listed below. Our constitution just isn't prepared for such mass consumption.

ANTIPASTO - APPETIZER
- **Arancine di Riso** – Rice balls filled with meat sauce and peas. Very Middle Eastern.
- **Antipasto Di Mare** – Mixed seafood appetizer plate. Differs from restaurant to restaurant.
- **Tomate, Mozzarella ed olio** – Tomato and mozzarella slices covered in olive oil with a hint of basil
- **Minestre di pesce** – Fish soup. Varies by region and restaurant.

PRIMO PIATTO - FIRST COURSE
Pasta
- **Pasta con le sarde** – Made with sardines, raisins, pine nuts, onions, tomatoes, fennel and saffron.
- **Spaghetti alla Norma** – Made with tomato, fried eggplant and ricotta cheese. Typical of Eastern Sicily.
- **Penne alla Paola** – Short ribbed pasta tubes made with broccoli, pine nuts and raisins.
- **CousCous** – Made with fish, chicken, beans or broccoli. Middle Eastern.

Zuppa – *Soup*
- **Minestre di pesce** – Fish soup. Varies by region and restaurant.

SECOND PIATTO - ENTRÉE
Carne – *Meat*
- **Involtini** – Meat stuffed with cheese and onions
- **Salso Magro** – Meat stuffed with salami, hard-boiled eggs and cheese
- **Coniglio alla cacciatore** – Rabbit cooked with red wine, tomatoes and spices.

Pesce – *Fish*
- **Tonno alla cipollata** – Tuna made with onions.
- **Pesce spada alla ghiotta** – Swordfish made with tomatoes, olives and capers.
- **Pesce spada alla griglia** – Grilled swordfish

Contorno – *Vegetable*
- **Caponata** – Eggplant, tomatoes, spices, capers, olives, tuna eggs and shrimps cooked together.

- **Fritella** – tomatoes, onions, artichokes, beans and peas all stewed together.

Formaggio – *Cheese*
- **Pecorino** – Sheep's cheese
- **Piacentino** – Pecorino flavored with peppercorns and saffron.

DOLCE – DESSERT
- **Cassata** – Sponge cakes made with ricotta, almond paste, chocolate and candied fruits
- **Cannoli** – fried pastry with a mixture like the Cassata

Wine

Sicily's best wines are *Etna* (red and white, wide variety) from the Catania area and *Marsala* (white, dry or sweet) from the Trapani province. You should also try some *Casteldaccio*, a dry white from around Palermo, and if you like sweet wine, an *Eloro* from around Syracuse should suffice. If you're on the Eolie Islands, try their unique red and white *Malvasia*.

PALERMO

Palermo started off as a Phoenician city, which the Greeks referred to as Panormos. The city then came under Roman rule during the two **Punic Wars** in 254 BCE. After that they endured Byzantine rule (353–830 CE), then Saracen domination (830-1072). Finally Norman (1072-1194) influence placed its stamp on the city. These conquerors were succeeded by the Hohenstaufens in 1194, then the House of Anjou ruled from 1266 until a popular uprising in 1282.

After that, Palermo came under Argonese and Spanish rule and eventually passed to the Bourbons in the 18th century. It finally became part of Italy on May 27, 1860, when it was liberated by Garibaldi. Today Palermo is Italian but ruled by the Mafia.

Palermo is large, busy, noisy, congested and polluted, the perfect capital for the Mafia. Today there is the beginning of a popular backlash against *La Cosa Nostra's* influence in the city, evidenced by anti-Mafia posters on the walls. But as a tourist you have little to worry about from the Mafia. In Palermo you need to protect yourself against pickpockets and purse snatchers, especially if you roam away from the Centro Storico.

Centuries ago the city was divided into four quarters, which all merged at the square known as the **Quattro Canti** (four corners) in the center of town. This square is at the intersection of **Corso Vittorio Emanuele** and **Via Maqueda**. The **Albergheria** is northwest of the *quattro canti*, **Capo** is southwest, **Vucciria** is northeast and **La Kalsa** is southeast.

Each of these quarters had distinct dialects, cultures, trading practices and markets for their products. There was limited intermingling and intermarriage would result in being ostracized.

Today, the area around the Quattro Canti is where most of the sights are located. Today the area is an eclectic mix of medieval streets and Norman, Oriental, and Baroque architecture, broad modern avenues and large buildings, and bombed-out vacant lots from World War II.

As such it is not nearly as charming as Florence or Venice, and it also has less historical architecture and museums than Rome. But Palermo is still an interesting city to explore. There's a heavy Middle Eastern influence, almost a *souk*-like atmosphere at some markets that differentiates Palermo from other Italian cities. Stay to see Palermo's sights, marvel in its sounds and smells (sometimes only traffic and pollution), and then hop on a train and go explore some other less hectic part of Sicily.

ARRIVALS & DEPARTURES
By Air
You can fly into Palermo from Rome or Milan. The fare is changing all the time, but at last check it was $300 from Rome. It may be even higher by the time you read this, but look for various excursion fares or even package deals with **Alitalia** or **Lufthansa**, the major airlines flying in and out of Sicily. You can also get direct flights from London or Dublin to Palermo, so this could be an option for you if you're crossing the Atlantic.

By Train
Palermo is about one hour away from Cefalu by train.

Other Options
Bus will be your best budget travel option, but you can also get here by ferry or hydrofoil from other parts of Sicily or the mainland. Consult the various schedules from the town you plan to depart from for the most up-to-date information.

GETTING AROUND TOWN
Palermo is a city you can enjoy walking in, but getting from one end of it to another can be tiring. That's why we recommend using the **buses** whenever you can. They cost L1,000 for a ticket that lasts an hour. You buy them at *Tabacchi* (stores marked with a blue **T**) or at AMAT's kiosks. If you know you're going to be taking the bus a lot, buy an all day pass for L3,000. Remember to stamp a single ticket or a day ticket in the machines as you get on the bus. The day pass only needs to be stamped once and kept on your person in case an inspector shows up. If you don't have a ticket you will be immediately fined L50,000.

SOUTHERN ITALY & SICILY 335

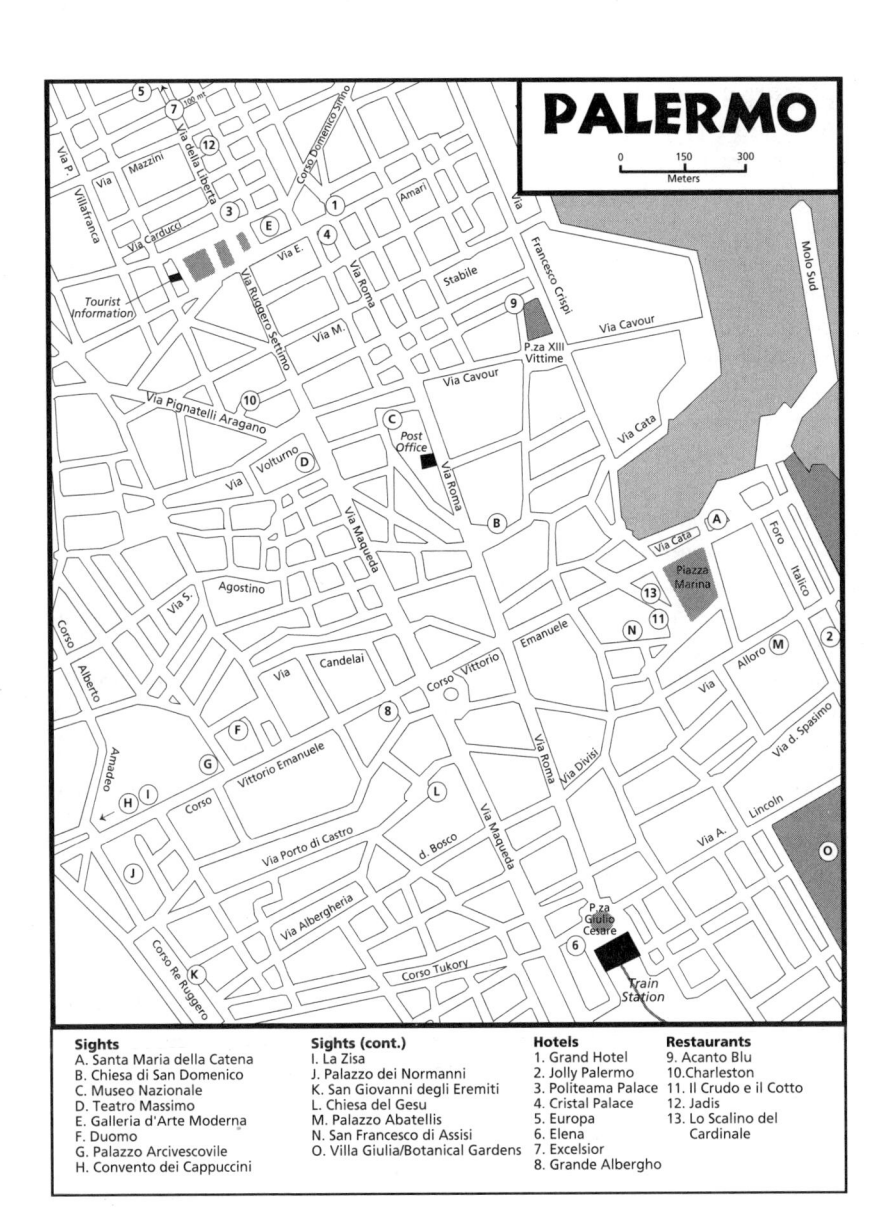

PALERMO

Sights
A. Santa Maria della Catena
B. Chiesa di San Domenico
C. Museo Nazionale
D. Teatro Massimo
E. Galleria d'Arte Moderna
F. Duomo
G. Palazzo Arcivescovile
H. Convento dei Cappuccini

Sights (cont.)
I. La Zisa
J. Palazzo dei Normanni
K. San Giovanni degli Eremiti
L. Chiesa del Gesu
M. Palazzo Abatellis
N. San Francesco di Assisi
O. Villa Giulia/Botanical Gardens

Hotels
1. Grand Hotel
2. Jolly Palermo
3. Politeama Palace
4. Cristal Palace
5. Europa
6. Elena
7. Excelsior
8. Grande Albergho

Restaurants
9. Acanto Blu
10. Charleston
11. Il Crudo e il Cotto
12. Jadis
13. Lo Scalino del Cardinale

If you don't want to deal with the push and pull of public transport, simply flag down a **taxi**, get caught in traffic, and watch your fare skyrocket.

WHERE TO STAY

1. GRANDE HOTEL ET DES PALME, *Via Roma 398, 90139 Palermo. Tel. 091/583-933. Fax 091/331-545. 187 rooms, 103 with bath, 84 with shower. Single L90,000-180,000; Double L120,000-240,000. All credit cards accepted. Breakfast included.* ***

Located on the busy Via Roma, the windows here are double-paned so you are insulated from the traffic noise. This is a huge, clean, and comfortable hotel whose rooms are adequately sized. The ones with bathtubs instead of showers seem to be bigger. Each room also has a separate floor/area for work space. The entrance hall is magnificently elegant with antique furnishings and huge Doric columns. There is an in-house restaurant where your meal will be good but expensive; try one of my suggestions in *Where to Eat* instead. There is also room service and an American style bar downstairs. The bountiful breakfast buffet is served in a 'yellow' room with a beautiful floral arrangement on the center table.

2. JOLLY PALERMO, *Foro Italico 22, 90133 Palermo. Tel. 091/616-5090. Fax 091/616-1441. Toll free in Italy 167-017703. Toll free in US and NYC 1-800/221-2626. Toll free in NY State 1-800/247-1277. 277 rooms, 207 with bath, 70 with shower. Single L90,000-180,000; Double L115,000-225,000. All credit cards accepted. Breakfast included.* ****

Since it is located a ways from the center, the hotel offers shuttle bus service for its guests. Situated on the Foro Italico, the hotel is a little tacky looking, but it's fun to people watch in the evenings. The hotel has a pool, nice restaurant, room service, laundry service, air conditioning and satellite TV in the rooms. The place, like all Jolly hotels, is as modern as they come, but it is mainly a businessman's hotel – meaning the rooms are medium sized. The bathrooms are comfortable and come with a complete courtesy toiletry set and a hairdryer. The buffet breakfast is a rich international spread in a room filled with mirrors and lamps made on the island of Murano near Venice. In summer breakfast is served in the gazebo in the interior garden. A Jolly place to stay.

3. POLITEAMA PALACE HOTEL, *Piazza Ruggero Settimo 15, 90124 Palermo. Tel. 091/322-777. Fax 091/611-1589. 102 rooms, 37 with bath, 65 with shower. Single L150,000; Double L200,000. All credit cards accepted. Breakfast included.* ****

A modern building in one of the best piazzas in Palermo houses this hotel, which is near the Modern Art Gallery and the tourist office. The amenities include air conditioning, TV, and an in-house restaurant that is acceptable. Room furnishings are modern and comfortable and come with sound-proof windows. The best accommodations are on the top floor since they all have splendid panoramic views. The bathrooms, most of which only have a shower, are medium size and come with hairdryer and complete courtesy toiletry set.

4. CRISTAL PALACE HOTEL, *Via Roma 477, 90139 Palermo. Tel. 091/611-2580. Fax 091/611-2589. 90 rooms, 39 with bath, 51 with shower. Single L117,000-137,000; Double L165,000-194,000. All credit cards accepted. Breakfast included.* ***

Located on the busy and noisy Via Roma, this is a completely modern building made almost entirely of glass. Besides super clean and comfortable rooms with air conditioning and satellite TV, the hotel offers a restaurant, a piano bar, a disco, an American Style bar and a gymnasium. Each room has a separate level for work. The bathrooms are smallish with hairdryers and a minimal courtesy toiletry set. This is a good place to stay.

5. HOTEL EUROPA, *Via Agrigento 3, 90141 Palermo. Tel. 091/625-6323. Fax is the same. 73 rooms, 58 with bath, 15 with shower. Single L100,000-110,000; Double L150,000-165,000. All credit cards accepted. Breakfast included.* ***

In a comfortable location near the Viale Liberta and six blocks north of the Modern Art Museum, this is a nice hotel. The rooms are about medium size, all laid out the same with simple furnishings and a separate level/area for work. If you want a mini-bar you need to request the rooms on the first floor. The bathrooms have hair dryers and the minimal courtesy toiletry set. The rooms also have air conditioning and TV.

6. HOTEL ELENA, *PIazza Giulio Cesare 14, 90127 Palermo. Tel. 091/616-2021. Fax 091/616-2984. 56 rooms only 22 with bath. Single without L38,000-45,000; Single L50,000-58,000; Double without L55,000-65,000; Double L70,000-82,000. No credit cards accepted.* **

Located at the train station, this hotel should be used as a quick stopover if you're only going to be in Palermo a day or two and are leaving by train. You don't want to go walking at night around the station, so make sure you get a comfortable room with a bath. The rooms are as clean as can be expected from a two star by a train station. One big minus is that there is no air conditioning, a must for a Palermo summer. Definitely a budget traveler's stop.

7. EXCELSIOR PALACE, *Via Marchese Ugo 3, 90139 Palermo. Tel. 091/625-6176. Fax 091/342-139. 128 rooms all with bath. Single L150,000-185,000; Double L200,000-240,000. All credit cards accepted. Breakfast included.* ****

Centrally located, this hotel's former glory was resurrected in 1987 with a complete renovation of the premises. Near the English gardens for relaxing walks and the Via della Liberta for shopping at their pricey boutiques. In the entrance and other public rooms the lamps are from the island of Murano, off Venice. The rooms are large, and come with soundproof windows to block out the traffic noise, but for some reason only 18 rooms have mini-bars. The best rooms are on the second floor with their beautiful bordeaux bedspreads and wall coverings. The bathrooms are a little small but have everything you need. If you need more room, the 16 suites offer it for about L100,000 more. And to top it off the service is professional and attentive. A great place to stay.

8. GRANDE ALBERGHO SOLE, *Via Vittorio Emanuele 291, 90139 Palermo. Tel. 091/581-811. Fax 091/611-0182. 154 rooms 138 with bath. Single without L40,000-80,000; Single L75,000-150,000; Double without L80,000-125,000; Double L100,000-200,000. All credit cards accepted. Breakfast included.* ******

Located a few paces from the Duomo in a hectic central location. The entrance hall is elegantly adorned with antiques along with a small display of archaeological relics. The rooms are adequately comfortable even though the furnishings are a little dated. The bathrooms are spacious and come with a minimal courtesy toiletry set, but no hair dryer. Breakfast is Italian, which means coffee and a roll. A fine location, but that's about it.

WHERE TO EAT

9. TRATTORIA ACANTO BLU, *Via F Guardinone 19, Tel. 091/326-258. Closed Sundays and September. No credit cards accepted. Dinner for two L50,000.*

A small little place that serves basic rustic cuisine. You can either enjoy the air conditioning inside or the terrace outside. Try some of the extensive antipasto table, especially the fried vegetables with a spicy hot sauce. Next try what they call *riso dei poeti* (rice of the poets), which contains apple, radish and fish. It's quite delectable. Then save the best for last, *funghi infornati cotti nella mollica condita con olio e peperoncini* (fresh mushrooms baked in a mold of bread served up with fresh olive oil and peperoncini).

10. RISTORANTE CHARLESTON, *Piazzale Ungheria 30, tel. 091/321-366. Closed Sundays. All credit cards accepted. Dinner for two L130,000.*

One of "the" places to go in Palermo, but that doesn't mean they're any good. This restaurant is known for their fish dishes, but they can't seem to get them right. Their sauces are too thick or too pungent, the fish is overcooked and the presentation is horrible. Maybe it's one of "the" places to go because it's Mafia owned? I didn't want to ask. What saved the meal was a great wine list and a *Sambuca con mosche* (a sweet liquor with coffee beans) afterwards.

11. IL CRUDO E IL COTTO, *Piazza Marina 45a, Tel. 091/616-9261. Closed Tuesdays and variable holidays. No credit cards accepted. Dinner for two L70,000.*

In the beautiful Piazza Marina you can get a great meal at this tiny family run *trattoria*. You have Laura in the kitchen and Franchino and Giovanni greeting people and working as waiters. Get a seat outside so you can enjoy the view. Try their *riso ai frutti di mare* (rice with mixed seafood) then a succulent *bistecca* (steak) or *pesce spada alla griglia* (grilled swordfish) for seconds. To wash it all down get some of their house wine, which comes from the local mountains.

12. JADIS, *Via Liberta 121, Tel. 091/349-323. Closed Sundays and Mondays and August. Open only at night. No credit cards accepted. Dinner for two L70,000.*

Located a few blocks north of the Museum of Modern Art, this is a very popular place with the arts crowd as well as with people who appreciate good food. You have a choice of outside seating, which is wonderful on cool evenings. Try their *carpaccio di vitello* or their *carpaccio di pesce spada* (steak of veal or swordfish)

13. LO SCALINO DEL CARDINALE, *Via Bottai 18, Tel. 091/3310124. Closed Mondays, for Lunch, and the last half of September. Credit cards accepted. Dinner for two L70,000.*

A great local place that is always packed during the week. With its terrace in use in the summer there seems to be plenty of space, but in the winter it's difficult to find a spot to eat. Try some of their *crocchette al latte* (croquets with milk) or *al primo sale fritto* (fried with a local cheese). For seconds, try their *pesce spada al profumo di Cardinale* (swordfish with a creamy sauce with sliced bell peppers).

SEEING THE SIGHTS
North of Corso Vittorio Emanuele

As you move from the east of Corso Vittorio Emanuele to the west, you may want to catch rides on the frequent bus #27 to quicken your pace.

A. SANTA MARIA DELLA CATENA

Via Vittorio Emanuele. Open 8:00am-11:30am and 3:30pm-7:00pm.

Built in the early 16th century, this church is named after the chain that used to be dragged across the old harbor, **La Cala**, at night to protect the vessels inside. This used to be the main port of Palermo until it started silting up in the late sixteenth century. The main industrial shipping moved north and this little inlet was left to the fishermen. It's a great place to take a short stroll and take in the sights, smells, and sounds of the Sicilian seafarers.

Not far away, located almost at the eastern part of the city, is the **Porta Felice**, which was built in 1582 to compliment the slightly older **Porta Nuova**, which is all the way to the west. Since these two gates were once the ancient boundaries of old Palermo, this is a good place to start your tour, because from here you can get a good feel for the true extent of ancient Palermo.

Past Porta Felice is the popular but relatively tacky promenade, **Foro Italico**, with its own little **amusement park**. On summer nights residents come out here to sit, talk, walk, stare, and share the beautiful evenings with each other.

B. CHIESA DI SAN DOMENICO

Piazza San Domenico. Open 7:30am-noon.

Walk down Via Vittorio Emanuele towards the Porta Nuova and take a right on Via Roma to get to the Piazza San Domenico and the **Church of San Domenico**. This beautiful 17th century church with an 18th century facade is the burial site of many famous Sicilians. At night the facade and the statue-topped marble column are lit up, creating quite a spectacle. The perfect spot to sip an *aperitivo* at one of the outdoor cafes surrounding the piazza.

Just behind the church, on Via dei Bambinai #16, is the **Oratorio del Rosario di San Domenico**, which contains some interesting stucco work created by Giacomo Serpotta as well as a magnificent altar piece by Van Dyke (*open 7:30am-Noon*).

C. MUSEO NAZIONALE

Piazza Olivella. Tel. 662-0220. Open Monday-Saturday 9:00am-1:30pm, Tuesdays and Fridays also open 3:00pm-5:30pm. Sundays and holidays only open 9:00am-12:30pm. Admission L3,000.

Go back to the Via Roma and walk north to the **National Museum**. Also known as the Museo Archeologico Regionale, if you've been out discovering Sicily's archaeological sites or intend to do so, you'll love this museum. Located in a former monastery, their collection of pre-historic relics, Etruscan, Greek, Egyptian and Roman pieces is quite extensive and well presented.

The museum has frescoes from Pompeii, bronze works from Greece, Roman sculptures, and much more. Especially imposing are the 56 lion head water spouts taken from Himera in the 5th century BCE. This is one of the finest museums in all of Italy.

D. TEATRO MASSIMO

Piazza Verdi, 90139 Palermo. Tel 091/605-3111, Fax 091/605-3325 or 605-3324. Hours 9:00am-1:00pm and 4:00pm-7:00pm. Admission L3,000.

The **Teatro Massimo** is down Via Maqueda from the Archaeological Museum. Also known as **Teatro Vittorio Emanuele**, this theater was built from 1875 to 1897 and can seat 3,200 attendees. As such it is the second largest theater in Europe, second only to the Opera house in Paris. Currently under renovation, you probably will not be able to get a tour inside, but it doesn't hurt to ask.

E. GALLERIA D'ARTE MODERNA

Gallery open Tuesday–Sunday 9:00am–1:00pm and 3:00–6:00pm. Admission L6,000.

I know you didn't come to Sicily to look at modern art, but a trip to the **Modern Art Museum** is a breath of fresh air after looking at relics all day long. Italy's art treasures don't all belong to the past, so visit here and see some beautiful and interesting modern works.

Nearby is the main **tourist office**, past the English gardens in front and past the equestrian statue of Garibaldi in the square. Stop here to get ideas about current happenings and what else to see in Palermo and elsewhere in Sicily. Walk back down Via Roma to the **Quattro Canti** (The Four Corners) – Via Roma, Via Vittorio Emanuele and Via Maqueda converge here at what is the imagined center of the old city.

F. DUOMO

Piazza del Cattedrale. Open 7:00am–noon and 4:00pm–7:00pm.

The **Duomo** is three hundred meters past the Quattro Canti on the Via Vittorio Emanuele. The church was begun by the Normans in 1185, and thereafter underwent many architectural transformations from the 13th century to the 18th, though the Norman towers and triple-apsed eastern side remain today. With its many styles, the intricate exterior is a joy to study. The same can't be said for the interior, which was recreated in a bland neoclassic style.

To the left as you enter you'll find six imposing tombs which contain the bodies of past kings of Palermo, including Frederick II and Roger II. In the chapel to the right of the choir is the silver sarcophagus that contains the remains of the city's patron saint, Rosalia. The **treasury**, located to the right of the apse, is infinitely more interesting since it contains some exquisite, jewel encrusted ancient clothing (L1,500 to enter). You also find the remains of some saints preserved here.

G. PALAZZO ARCIVESCOVILE

Via Papireto Bonnello. Open Tuesday–Sunday 9:00am–1:00pm and 3:00pm–6:00pm.

Immediately southwest of the cathedral is the one-time **Archbishop's Palace** that contains the **Dioclesan Museum**. The museum features many works of art that were salvaged from other churches during the Allied bombings of World War II. If this is closed check out the **Mercato delle**

Pulci, just up Via Bonello (next to the Palace) in **Piazza Peranni**. This is a great junk/antique market held everyday from 8:00am to 2:00pm.

A little further down the Via Vittorio Emanuele is the **Porta Nuova**, which was erected in 1535 to commemorate the Tunisian exploits of Charles V.

H. CONVENTO DEI CAPPUCCINI

Open Monday-Saturday 9:00am-Noon and 3:00pm-5:00pm. The visit is free but a donation of about L2,000 per person is expected.

No, this isn't a shrine to that wonderful frothing espresso product. This is a bizarre yet fascinating place, in a morbid kind of way. To get here, walk 1.5 km west past the Porta Nuova or catch bus #27 going west from the Via Vittorio Emanuele to the Via Pindemonte. After you get off, it's a short walk to the convent. Just follow the signs.

This is like something out of a horror movie. Bodies stacked everywhere. Almost 800 of them. For many centuries this convent was the burial place not only for church members but also for rich laymen. You'll find bodies preserved with a variety of methods with differing results. Some bodies still have their hair and skin. Others have decomposed completely. The saddest sight here, though, are the remains of the tiny infants and young children that never made it into adulthood. A gruesome place to visit, yes. But an experience you will never forget.

I. LA ZISA

Open Monday-Saturday 9:00am-2:00pm. Sundays 9:00am-1:00pm. The visit is free.

Since you're already out here, you might as well walk a short way north to **La Zisa**, a huge palace begun by William I in 1160 and finished by his son William II. Take the Via Corradino di Svevia, take a right on Via Eugenio L'Emiro (the first road), then take an immediate left onto Via Edersi, then take the second right onto Viale Luigi Castiglia and you'll turn left after about fifty meters into the piazza that houses La Zisa.

This is a wonderful replica of an Arabian palace (Zisa means *magnificent* in Arabic) and was used as a retreat for the king where he had lush exotic gardens tended and wild animals housed.

South of Corso Vittorio Emanuele
J. PALAZZO DEI NORMANNI

Open Monday-Friday 9:00am-Noon and 3:00pm-5:00pm and Saturdays and Sunday 9:00am-11:00am. The chapel is closed Sundays.

The **Norman** or **Royal Palace**, just past the Porta Nuova going east on Corso Vittorio Emanuele, is a terrific place. Originally built by the Saracens and remodeled and reinforced by the Normans, this is an

SOUTHERN ITALY & SICILY 343

imposing fortress-like building that sits on the high ground overlooking the city below. Since the palazzo is the current seat of the Sicilian Parliament, you must be escorted by a guide through the rooms. Don't playfully attempt to sneak off; security is pretty tight because of the Mafia problems.

One room you can't miss is the **Cappella Palatina**, the Palatine Chapel, which contains some of the best **mosaics** outside of Istanbul and Ravenna. The tile art describes scenes from the Old Testament. Another room adorned with mosaics, with a flora and fauna motif, is the **Sala di Ruggero**, King Roger's Hall.

K. SAN GIOVANNI DEGLI EREMITI

Corso Re Ruggero. Open 9:00am-1:00pm. On Tuesdays, Wednesdays, and Fridays also open 3:00pm-5:00pm.

Founded by Roger II, and built in 1132, the architecture of **St. John of the Hermits** has Arabic influence. Just down the road from the Norman Palace, this church was built over a mosque and is dominated by five Arab-looking domes. To get to the church you must walk up a path lined with citrus trees, behind which are some 13th century cloisters. A beautiful sight to see.

L. CHIESA DEL OF GESU

Via Porto di Castro. Open 7:00am-noon and 5:00pm-6:30pm.

Follow Via Porto di Castro from the Norman Palace to this small church with its green mosaic dome. It has a multicolored marble interior and an almost surreal interpretation of the *Last Judgment*. In the church's small courtyard, you can still see the effect of Allied bombings during World War II. You can see this same bombing effect near the **Palazzo Abatellis** that is home to the **Galleria Nazionale Siciliana** (see below).

M. PALAZZO ABATELLIS

Via Alloro. Open 9:00am-1:30pm and also open on Tuesdays, Thursdays and Fridays 4:00-7:00pm. Sundays and holidays 9:00am-12:30pm. Admission L4,000.

This palace houses the **Galleria Nazionale Siciliana**, one of Sicily's wonderful regional art museums. The gallery gives a comprehensive insight into Sicilian painting and sculpture. Some of the work is quite crude, some is magnificent, but if you've never been exposed to Sicilian art, this is your chance to learn.

N. CHURCH OF SAN FRANCESCO DI ASSISI

Via Paternostro. Open only from 7:00am-11:00am every day.

You have to be an early bird to catch this sight: the church is known for its intricate rose window that looks magnificent from the inside when the early morning sun streams through it. The zig-zag design on its exterior is common to many of the churches in the area. Built in the 13th century, there were two side chapels added in the 14th and 15th centuries.

O. VILLA GIULIA PARK & BOTANICAL GARDENS

Via Lincoln. Park open until dark. Botanical Gardens open Monday-Friday 9:00am-noon and Saturday 9:00am-11:00am. Admission L2,000.

This is Palermo's best centrally-located park, which gives you a respite from the hectic pace of Palermo. Besides wildlife roaming around like deer and ducks, there are gardens, a small kiddy train and a pretty **Botanical Gardens**. The gardens feature tropical plants from all over the world. It's an uplifting spot after a few days touring through Palermo.

NIGHTLIFE & ENTERTAINMENT

There is plenty to do at night in Palermo, but I recommend that you enjoy a nice meal, then retire to your room. Crime is a problem, including violent crime – I don't want you walking down the wrong street. If just having dinner is too boring for you, locate a restaurant near your hotel and stop there for after-dinner drinks before making the short walk back to your hotel.

Opera

If you are in Palermo from December to June, the traditional opera season, have the proper attire (suits for men, dresses for women), and have a taste for something out of the ordinary, try the spectacle of the opera.

• **Teatro Massimo**, *Piazza Verdi, 90139 Palermo. Tel 091/605-3111, Fax 091/605-3325 or 605-3324*

SHOPPING

Food shopping can be done at the markets that are located off Via Roma on the **Via Divisi**, as well as between the **Palazzo dei Normani** and the train station at **Piazza Ballaro**.

For inexpensive clothing, try the **Via Bandiera** near Chiesa San Domenico. For more expensive clothing, try along the main thoroughfares of **Via Roma** and **Via Maqueda**.

PRACTICAL INFORMATION

Banking Hours & Changing Money

Banks are open Monday through Friday from 8:30am to 1:30pm and some do reopen from 2:30pm or so to 3:30pm or so. Besides banks there

SOUTHERN ITALY & SICILY 345

are plenty of exchange bureaus (*casa di cambio*). One that is open until 9:00pm on weekdays, and until 2:00pm on Saturdays is in the Train Station. Another option, if all else is closed is to simply change your money at your hotel. You won't get the best rate but at least you'll have money.

If you need **American Express** service, contact Giovanni Ruggeri e Figli *at Via E Amari 40, Tel 091/587-144. Open regular business hours.*

Business Hours

From October to June, most shops are open from 9:00am to 1:00pm and from 3:30pm to 7:30pm, and are closed all day Sundays and on Monday mornings. Then from June to August, when it really starts to get hot in Sicily, the morning hours remain the same, but the mid-day siesta time is slightly extended to 4:00pm and sometimes 4:30pm, which then pushes closing time back to 7:30pm or 8:00pm. And also, in conjunction with the all day Sunday and Monday morning closings, shops also close half-days on Saturday.

Food stores like *alimentari* generally are open from 8:30am to 1:30pm and from 5:00pm to 7:30pm, and during the winter months they are closed on Thursdays.

Local Festivals & Holidays
- **July 11-15**, Festival of Santa Rosalia with fireworks and insanity
- **September 4**, pilgrimage-like walk to Monte Pelligrino in honor of Santa Rosalia
- **Last week in September**, International Tennis Tournament

Postal Services

The **central post office** in Palermo *is at Via Roma 322.* Open Monday through Friday 8:30am–5:00pm, Saturday 9:00am–Noon. But if you're in a hurry, stamps can be bought at any tobacconist (stores indicated by a **T** sign outside), and mailed at any mailbox, which are red and marked with the word *Poste* or *Lettere*.

Tourist Information & Maps
- **Main Information Office**, *Piazza Castelnuovo 34 (Tel. 091/583-847) across from the Modern Art Museum*
- **Information Office**, *in the train station, open Monday–Friday, 8:00am–8:00pm.* If the office at the station is out of information and/or maps, take bus #101 to the piazza and the main office. They both supply detailed maps and information about Palermo and other places of interest. There is also a tourist office in the Stazione Maritima and at the airport.

TRAPANI

Located on a sickle shaped peninsula on the northwest coast of Sicily, **Trapani** is the island's largest fishing port. The city, called *Drapanon* (which means sickle) by locals, used to be the main port for the ancient Greek city of **Eryx** (Erice – see next section). Trapani flourished as a trading center, mainly with customers in Africa and the Middle East. The town has an ancient elegant **Centro Storico** out on the end of the sickle of a peninsula.

Today the city's lifeblood still depends on the trading of salt, wine, and fish. It's a modern city, developed after most everything else was destroyed during Allied bombing in World War II. Trapani is a friendly city and should definitely be one of your destinations while in Sicily.

ARRIVALS & DEPARTURES

Located 94 kilometers from Palermo as the crow flies, the journey by car is about 110 kilometers; by train you will end up putting in closer to 130 kilometers, since the tracks wind along the coast until Castellammare del Golfo then turn inland to follow the main roads.

By car there are a number of options. The journey along highway 186 out of Palermo, which connects with highway 113, will take about 2 hours. After Alcamo you will be able to get on Autostrada A29 which can shorten the time. The best route but the longest would be to take highway 113 to 187. This runs along the coast until Castellammare del Golfo, then heads inland and passes by Erice along the way.

The train usually stops at every town along the way, which means that your journey will take about 3 hours.

GETTING AROUND TOWN

The **Centro Storico** occupies about a square kilometer on the peninsula, so everything in it is within walking distance. The **train station** lets you off just on the edge of the old town, and the docks along **Via Ammiraglio Staiti** (which runs half the southern length of the old town) are where you can catch ferries to the **Egadi Islands**.

To get to the city's museum in the new section of town, you'll need to catch bus #1 or #10 from the train station.

WHERE TO STAY

Most of the hotels in Trapani are located in the new city. The two below are the best and closest to the town's old city.

1. HOTEL VITTORIA, *Via F. Crispi 4, 91100 Trapani. Tel. 0923/873-0444. Fax 0923/29870. 65 rooms all with bath. Single L80,000; Double L130,000. All credit cards accepted. Breakfast included.* ***

Located about two blocks from the train station. Exit and walk to the right down Via F. Crispi and you'll run right into it. Really the only good hotel in the Centro Storico area, and is perfectly situated for exploring the old town as well as getting to the station quickly to explore points outside of Trapani. The rooms have air conditioning, room and laundry service, great views over the sea and the park, and are clean and comfortable. Also, the bathrooms are immaculately kept and have necessary modern amenities.

2. CRISTAL, *Piazza Umberto 1, 9100 Trapani. Tel. 0923/20000. Fax 0923/25555. 70 rooms all with bath. Single L131,000. Double L190,000. All credit cards accepted. Breakfast included* ****

Located right next to the train station, it is a lovely experience to spend the night here in the heart of Trapani. Strangely peaceful, quiet and calm, this modern hotel offers all necessary amenities and conveniences to make your stay pleasant and relaxing. The common areas are bright and accommodating. The rooms are large and comfortable, and the bathrooms are clean with all necessities, including a telephone.

WHERE TO EAT

3. RISTORANTE P&G, *Via Spalti 1, Tel. 0923/547-701. Closed Sundays and August. Credit cards accepted. Dinner for two L90,000.*

The decorations are not something to write home about, but the food here is excellent. Once you start digging into your antipasto, your mouth will come alive with the flavors of the Mediterranean, not just Italian. Try some of their *cuscus con la cernia* (couscous with stone bass) for primo, then move onto some *tonno al forno* (oven cooked tuna steak) or *alla brace* (grilled tuna steak). You should have at least one meal here while in Trapani, especially if you work for Proctor and Gamble (P&G, get it?). There's only 50 seats so make reservations or come early.

4. RISTORANTE DA PEPE, *Via Spalti 50, Tel. 0923/28246. Closed Mondays. Credit cards accepted. Dinner for two L90,000.*

Just down the road from P&G, they're known for their house pasta dish made with the local pasta, *busiati*, which is actually just *fusilli*, a spiral shaped pasta. The sauce is made with cooked garlic, tomatoes, and basil and is fantastic. And of course for seconds try any of their varieties of *pesce spada* (swordfish) or *tonno* (tuna) steaks.

SEEING THE SIGHTS

The look and feel of this medieval port city, with its European and Arab influences, makes you feel as if you've stepped back in time. The medieval and Renaissance fabric of the streets blends well with the tapestry of the Baroque buildings. It should take one full day to see everything that Trapani has to offer if you want to do it right.

348 ROME & SOUTHERN ITALY GUIDE

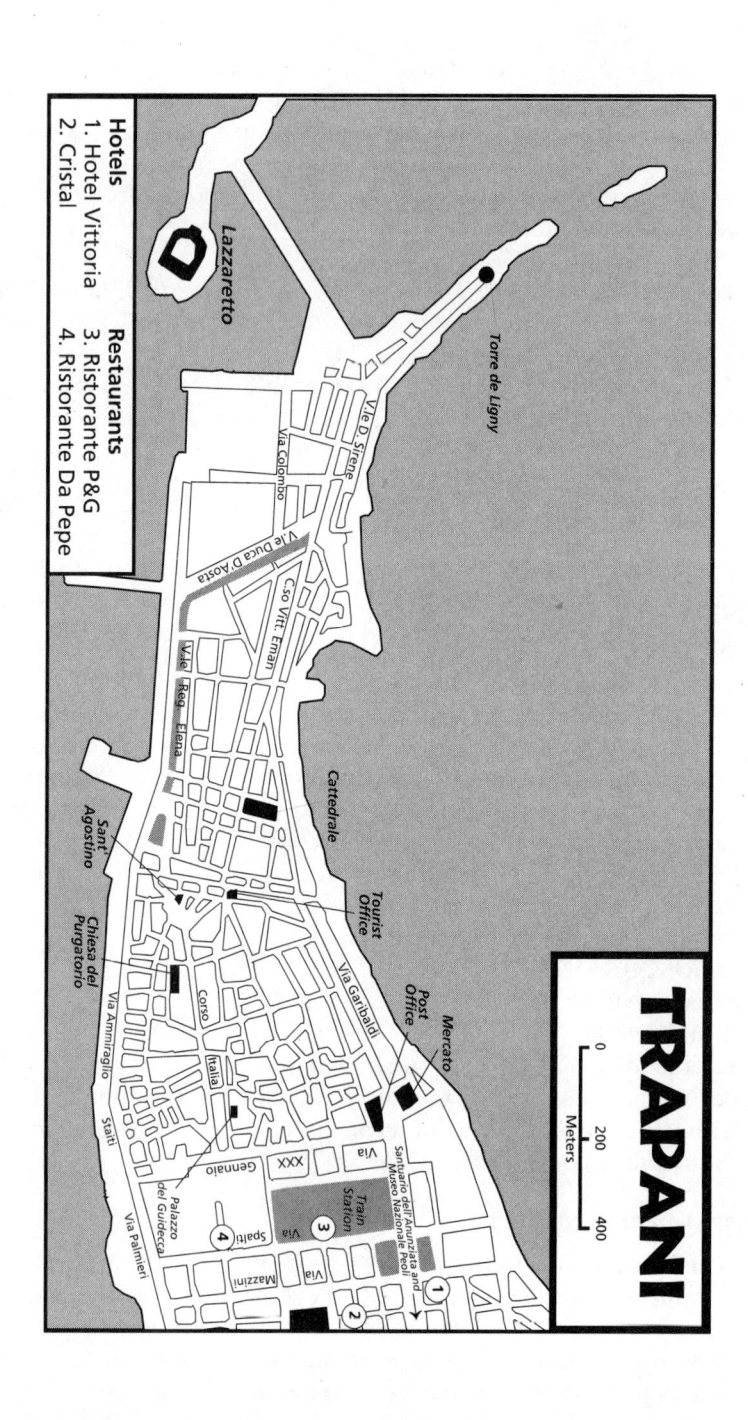

And when you're done here, use the city as a jumping off point to visit **Erice** and other sights in the area.

CATTEDRALE
Corso Vittorio Emanuele. Open 8:00am–noon and 3:00pm–6:00pm.

With its Baroque portico and immense exterior, and with it's colorful dome and stucco walls, the **Cathedral** can be an imposing sight compared to the other tiny churches in the old city. Most of the others have been closed for years for restoration, but you may be in luck and find one of them open. A number of them have an interesting mix of Muslim and Christian influences.

TORRE DE LIGNY
Located at the most eastern point of the city, this is a great spot to watch the sunset, and since the town seems to close down around 9:00pm, you can watch the sunset then retire for a romantic evening at your hotel. The tower also houses the surprisingly interesting **Museo di Preistoria** *(Open Monday–Saturday 9:00am-1:00pm and 4:00pm to 8:00pm; admission L2,500)*, which contains Neanderthal bones, skulls and tools, as well as the remains of prehistoric animals.

MERCATO DI PESCE
Walk up the Via Mura di Tramontana Ovest on the north side of the peninsula from the tower and you'll come to the bustling fish market. Here you can see fishermen selling their catch, and fruit and vegetable vendors clamoring for your attention. But remember to get here in the morning, because it shuts down by 1:30pm.

SANT' AGOSTINO
Piazzetta Saturno. Open 8:00am–noon and 3:00pm–6:00pm.

Near the cathedral and adjacent to the main tourist office is the small church of **Sant'Agostino**. This 14th century church is mainly used as a **concert hall** and its main attraction is its stunning rose colored window.

PALAZZO DELLA GUIDECCA
Via della Guidecca 43. Open 9:00am–1:00pm and 4:00pm–7:00pm.

Located in the heart of Trapani's old **Jewish Ghetto** that was established during the medieval oppression of the Jews, this 16th century building has a plaque-studded facade with some Spanish-style windows. An elaborate and intricate architectural piece.

CHIESA DEL PURGATORIO

Via Cassaretto. Open Monday-Saturday 10:00am-noon and 4:30pm-6:30pm.

The most fascinating church to see in Trapani, not really because of itself but because of what it has inside. The church is home to a large set of life-sized wooden statues called the **Misteri** that have been paraded through town during Good Friday celebrations every year for the past 600 years. Each statue represents a member of one of the trades, such as fishermen, cobblers, etc. It's quite a sight to see.

SANTUARIO DELL'ANUNZIATA

Via Conte Pepoli. Open 8:30am-noon and 4:00pm-6:00pm. No Charge.

Really the only reason to venture into the new city is to come see these last two sights. If you don't want to hike 3 km down a large boulevard, catch either bus #1 or #10 from the station out here. Remember to buy a ticket at a Newsstand or *Tabacchi* first (L800).

This 14th century convent and church contains the town's main treasure, the smiling *Madonna and Child*. This statue has supposedly been responsible for a number of miracles, so it is kept secured here and is usually surrounded by many kneeling worshipers.

MUSEO NAZIONALE PEPOLI

Via Conte Pepoli. Open Monday-Saturday 9:00am-1:30pm. Sunday until 12:30pm. On Tuesdays, Thursdays and Saturdays also open 4:00pm-6:30pm. Admission L3,000.

Fans of numismatics (that's the study of coins to you and me), hang on to your hats! Next to the convent and church is a **museum** with a wide variety of artifacts, including an extensive Roman, Greek, and Arab coin collection. Don't miss the 18th century guillotine, the local coral carvings, or the quaint folk-art figurines. It's a great museum for kids of all ages, but remember to come during the day since the lighting doesn't seem to be adequate in the evening.

NIGHTLIFE & ENTERTAINMENT

Trapani closes down around 9:00pm, but before that people are out, just after dinner, along the **Via Vittorio Emanuele** for a stroll or a sip of Sambuca at a sidewalk café. If you're interested in sampling a local delicacy try a *biscotto coi fichi*, a very tasty fig newton-like cookie.

PRACTICAL INFORMATION

Banking Hours & Changing Money

Banks are open Monday through Friday, 8:30am-1:30pm and some reopen from 2:30pm to 3:30pm. Besides banks there are plenty of exchange bureaus (*casa di cambio*). One that is open until 9:00pm on weekdays, and until 2:00pm on Saturdays is in the Train Station. Another option, if all else is closed is to simply change your money at your hotel. You won't get the best rate but at least you'll have money.

Business Hours

From October to June, most shops are open from 9:00am to 1:00pm and from 3:30pm to 7:30pm, and are closed all day Sundays and on Monday mornings. Then from June to August, when it really starts to get hot in Sicily, the morning hours remain the same, but the mid-day siesta time is slightly extended to 4:00pm and sometimes 4:30pm, which then pushes closing time back to 7:30pm or 8:00pm. And also, in conjunction with the Sunday and Monday morning closings, shops also close half-days on Saturday.

Food stores like *alimentari* generally are open from 8:30am to 1:30pm (so stock up on your picnic supplies before you need them) and from 5:00pm to 7:30pm, and during the winter months they are closed on Thursdays.

Local Festivals & Holidays
- **Good Friday**, Procession of Wooden Statues from 3:00pm to 7:00pm
- **Last Three weeks of July**, Luglio Musicale Trapanese. Musical festival in the Villa Margherita at 9:00pm each night.

Postal Services

The **central post office** in Trapani *is in the Piazza Vittorio Veneto (Tel. 0923/873-038) at the ends of Via Garibaldi.* Open Monday through Friday 8:00am–5:00pm, Saturdays 9:00am–Noon. But if you're in a hurry, stamps can be bought at any tobacconist (stores indicated by a T sign outside), and mailed at any mailbox, which are red and marked with the word *Poste* or *Lettere*.

Tourist Information & Maps
- **Main tourist office**, *Piazza Saturno (Tel. 0923/29000).* They have maps, brochures, and all sorts of information about the town and surrounding area.

ERICE

Only a forty-five minute bus ride from Trapani, don't miss **Erice** when in Sicily. It is a walled mountain town that used to be the biggest in the area (Trapani was just its port), but is still completely medieval with its winding streets, alleys, and ancient buildings. You may actually want to stay here rather than in Trapani and do the reverse commute into the larger city, then escape back to this town's silent charms at the end of the day. It's what I should have done on my last trip here.

The views from Erice's terraces are fantastic. You can see all of Trapani as well as the **Egadi Islands** (Isole Egadi) and on a good day the coast of Africa. Besides the views and the charming streets there is little of importance to see in Erice, but these are types of ancient towns you came to Sicily to see. Don't be upset if there's no Michelangelo's *David* to admire – the town is a masterpiece in itself.

ARRIVALS & DEPARTURES

After a 45 minute bus ride from Trapani, the bus will drop you off at the **Porta Trapani** at the southwest edge of town. From here cross the piazza to the **tourist office** *(open regular business hours, closed Sundays; Tel. 0923/869-388)* and pick up any information you think you might need.

WHERE TO STAY

If you want to stay in Erice during the summer months, make reservations well in advance. Listed below are the three hotels in the town.

1. ELIMO HOTEL, *Via Vittorio Emanuele, 91016 Erice. Tel. 0923/869-377. 21 rooms all with bath. Single L120,000-140,000; Double L190,000-250,000. No credit cards accepted. Full board L180,000.* ***

A quaint little hotel that is the second best in the city. It has a fine restaurant and a relaxing bar for an evening's refreshments, and quaint old surroundings. The rooms have heat since it can get chilly here at night, as well as a TV if you get bored with ambiance and views. They are also smallish but clean and very comfortable.

2. HOTEL MODERNO, *Via Vittorio Emanuele 63, 91016 Erice, Tel. 0923/869-300. Fax 0923/869-139. 40 rooms, 6 with bath, 34 with shower. Single L100,000-130,000; Double L150,000-180,000. American Express and Visa accepted. Full board L140,000-180,000.* **

The best hotel in the city with clean rooms and relatively modern furnishings. They have laundry and room service as well as a good in-house restaurant that is large, elegant, and serves superb food, especially their *cous cous di pesce* (a Middle Eastern rice dish with fish) or their *vitello al forno* (veal cooked perfectly in the oven). Request a room with a view, since the panorama is spectacular. Each room is laid out and furnished differently from the others. But each is filled with local products, from the carpets to the bed frames. The bathrooms have a small courtesy toiletry set and hairdryers.

SOUTHERN ITALY & SICILY

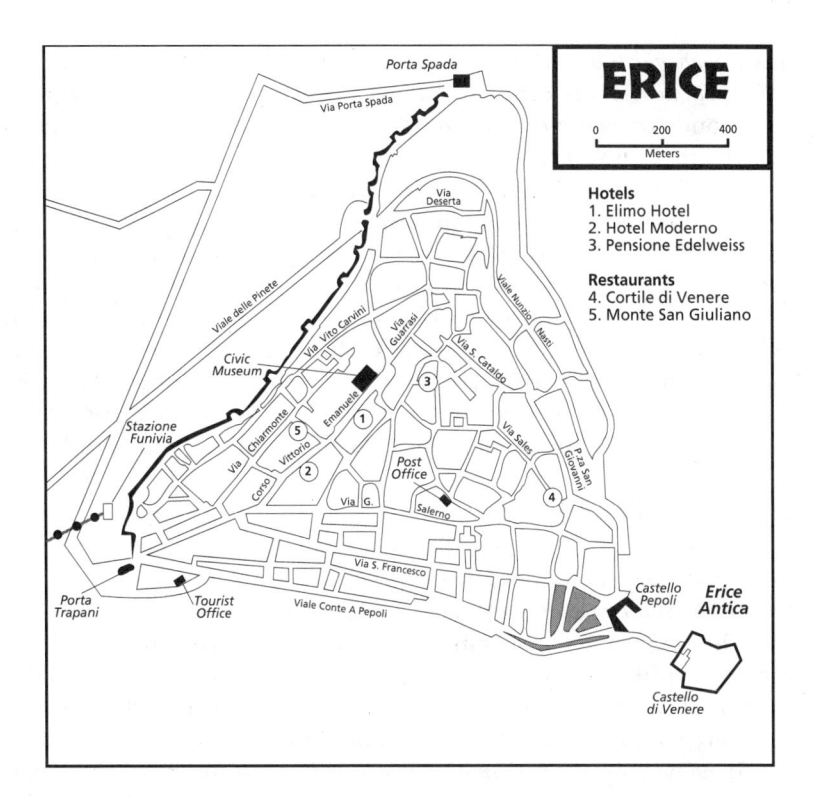

3. PENSIONE EDELWEISS, *Cortile Piazza Vincenzo 5, 91016 Erice. Tel. 0923/869-420. Fax 0923/869-252. 13 rooms, 13 with bath. Single L100,000; Double L130,000. American Express and Visa accepted. Full board L130,000.* **

Since there are only three good hotels in Erice, this makes the Edelweiss the third best hotel in town. In a quiet alley off the Piazzetta San Domenico, this is a simple family-run place that is comfortable and clean, even if the furnishings don't seem to match. If you're a budget traveler this is your only option, even though the accommodations are better than budget.

WHERE TO EAT

You're not going to find an inexpensive meal in Erice unless you grab a sandwich at a sidewalk café, but if you try one of these places, at least you'll be eating well.

4. CORTILE DI VENERE, *Via Sales 31, Tel. 0923/869-362. Closed Wednesdays. All credit cards accepted. Dinner for two L100,000.*

In the summer you can eat in a splendid courtyard surrounded by buildings from the 17th century. The *gamberi marinati* (marinated grilled shrimp), *spaghetti al pesto ericino* (with a pesto sauce Erice-style) and the *tagliolini al uova di tonno* (thin pasta with a sauce of tuna eggs) are all great. For seconds try some of their *involtini di pesce spada* (rolled swordfish steaks stuffed with spices), *calamari ripieni* (stuffed calamari), or a *costata di Angus alla brace* (an Angus steak grilled over an open flame). Definitely the best food and atmosphere in town.

5. **MONTE SAN GIULIANO,** *Via San Rocco 7, Tel. 0923/869-595. Closed Mondays. All credit cards accepted. Dinner for two L100,000.*

If you want to get one of the tables that looks out over the water and the Isole Egadi, you need to get here early or reserve in advance. Their *busiati con pesto ericino* (twisted pasta made with almond paste, garlic, tomatoes, and basil) is exquisite. For seconds, I love their *grigliata di calamari, gamberi e pesce spada* (grilled calamari, shrimp, and swordfish).

SEEING THE SIGHTS

As you enter the town you'll be confronted by the **Chiesa Matrice**, whose tower served as a lookout post, then a prison before getting religion (*Via Vito Carvini, open 8:00am-noon and 3:00pm-6:00pm*). There are five other churches, much smaller in scale, in Erice. When you find them, stick your head inside and take a peek. They are definitely not St. Peter's or the Duomo in Florence, but they help you step back in time to medieval Erice.

There's a small, really insignificant **museum** (*Corso Vittorio Emanuele, open Monday-Saturday 8:30am-1:30pm, Sundays 9:00am-noon*). So if you want a dose of art stop in here; it's free. After wandering through the streets, avoiding the hordes of tourists in the summertime, walk up past the public gardens and the ancient **Torretta Pepoli**, a restored 15th century tower, and go to the **Castello San Venere** (*open Saturday-Thursdays 10:00am-1:00pm and 3:00-5:00pm*). Built on the site of an ancient temple to the Greek god Aphrodite and later the Roman god Venus, from here you can get the great views we spoke of earlier. Don't forget your camera.

AGRIGENTO

Nobody comes to **Agrigento** to visit its quaint medieval streets and buildings, where butchers and bakers share storefronts with Fendi. Even though the city is quaint beyond compare and is exciting to explore, tourists come for another reason. It's also not the more than four kilometers of pristine beaches; the reason people come here is for the most captivating and well-preserved set of Greek remains and Doric temples outside of Greece – the **Valley of Temples**.

These temples were erected during the 5th century BCE, below the Greek town of Akragas, the forerunner to Agrigento, as testament to the

SOUTHERN ITALY & SICILY 355

Hotels
1. Hotel delle Valle
2. Hotel Villa Athena
3. Hotel Belvedere

Where to Eat
4. Kalos

Sights
A. Valley of the Temples
B. Santo Spirito
C. Santa Maria dei Greci
D. Chiesa del Purgatorio

AGRIGENTO

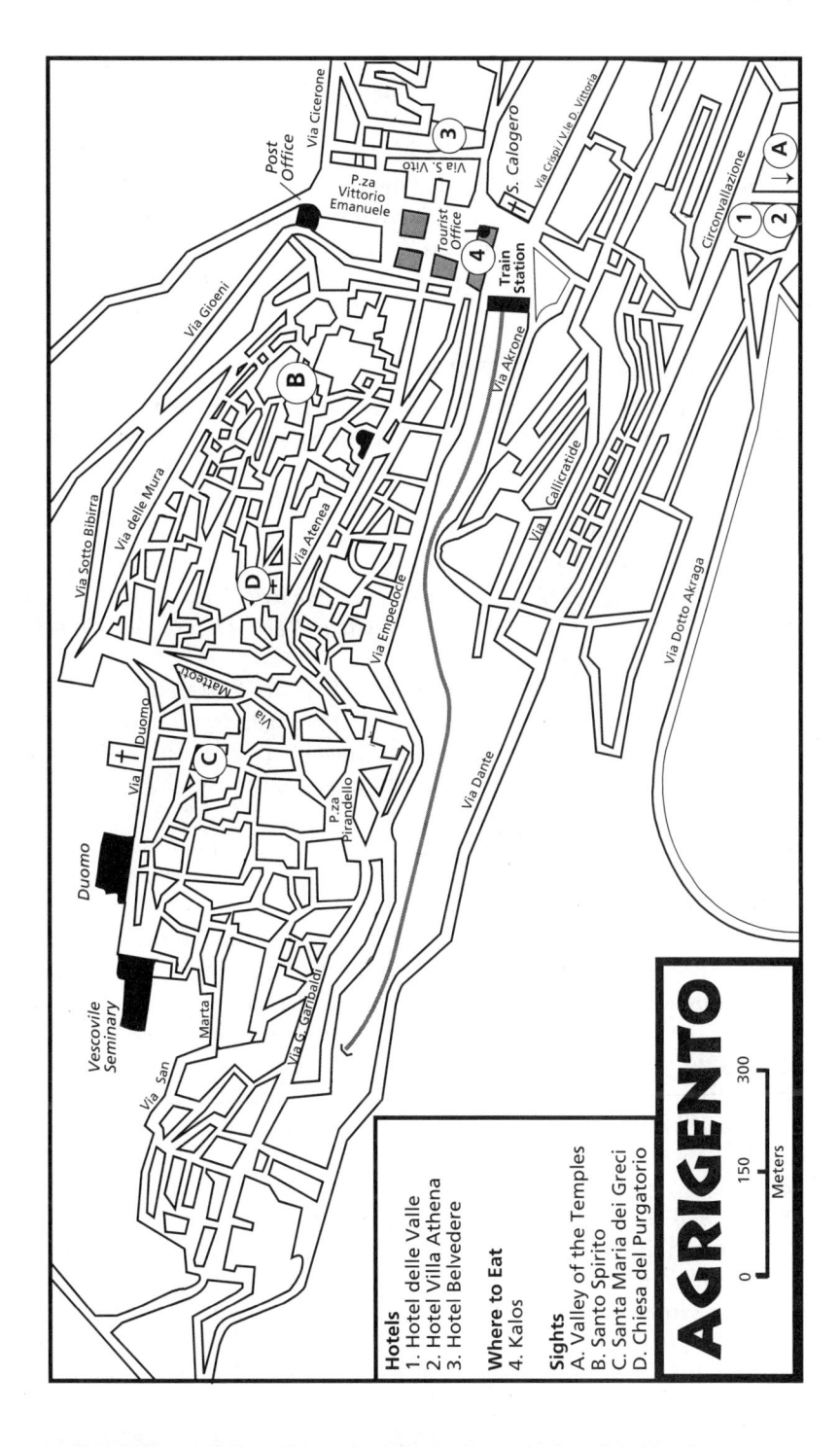

wealth and prosperity of the town. Today Agrigento survives from the tourist trade, and, it is rumored, through Mafia money.

ARRIVALS & DEPARTURES

Since Agrigento is off by itself in the southern part of the island along the coast, with few other towns of tourist interest around, getting here can be quite a haul either by car or by train. By car follow route 115 along the coast, route 640 from Enna (which is on the way from Catanie or Messina), or route 189 from Palermo.

GETTING AROUND TOWN

Walk and explore the tiny medieval streets. To get to the Valley of Temples, catch bus #8, 9 or 10 from the train station. Ask to be let off at the **Museo** (the museum) when you get there.

WHERE TO STAY

1. HOTEL DELLE VALLE, *Via dei Templi 94, 92100 Agrigento, Tel. 0922/26966. Fax 0922/26412. 93 rooms, 89 with bath, 4 with shower. Single L80,000-110,000; Double L110,000-170,000. Full board L200,000. All credit cards accepted. Breakfast included.* ****

On the road to the temples, take bus #8, 9, or 10 from the station to get here. They have a swimming pool, tranquil gardens, a fine restaurant, air conditioning, TV and clean and comfortable rooms. The bathrooms are medium size and come with hairdryer and courtesy toiletry set.

2. HOTEL VILLA ATHENA, *Via dei Templi 33, 92100 Agrigento. Tel. 0922/596-288. Fax 0922/598-770. 40 rooms, 8 with bath, 32 with shower. Single L170,000; Double L250,000. Full board L200,000. All credit cards accepted. Breakfast included.* ****

In the Valley of the Temples, this place has all the amenities you could want, including a pool surrounded by tranquil gardens, a good restaurant, laundry and room service, air conditioning and more. Located in a quaint old romantic building, your rooms are clean as are the bathrooms. The rooms are comfortable and the view from many of the rooms, onto the temples, is exquisite, especially at night, when they are all lit up.

3. HOTEL BELVEDERE, *Via San Vito 20, 92100 Agrigento. Tel. 0922/20051. 35 rooms, 5 with bath, 13 with shower. Single without L15,000-35,000; Single L30,000-60,000; Double without L25,000-50,000; Double L35,000-70,000. American Express and Visa accepted.* **

Located near the train station, I would advise getting a bathroom of your own because there are not many in the halls and they aren't too inviting. Little or no amenities, except a good view from some of the rooms. Try to reserve room #30, which has a large balcony where you can relax in the evenings. A budget traveler's hotel.

SOUTHERN ITALY & SICILY 357

WHERE TO EAT

There are plenty of little bars and cafés at which you can grab a snack, as well as some local restaurants. Below is the one I feel is the best.

4. KALOS, *Piazza San Calogero, Tel. 0922/26389. Closed Sunday Nights. Credit cards accepted. Dinner for two L80,000.*

Located in the small piazza near the station and the church of San Calogero, this is a clean, modern looking place, with professional service. Try their *Macceroncelli al pistacchio* (macaroni with pistachio sauce, gorgonzola and parmesan cheese). For seconds, get any of their succulent fish or meat cooked on the grill.

SEEING THE SIGHTS

There are only a few sights to see in town. The main show is out at The Valley of the Temples.

A. THE VALLEY OF THE TEMPLES

Open Sunday-Friday 8:00am-Dusk.

After being dropped off by the bus #8, 9, or 10 from town, walk down the hill to the **Museo Nazionale Archeologico di San Nicola** *(open Tuesday-Friday 9:00am-1:30pm and 3:00pm-5:00pm, Weekends 9:00am-12:30pm)* to admire the artifacts removed from the ruins for safekeeping. This museum will help give you a feel for the people that used to worship at these temples. You can find vases, candlestick holders, lion's head water spouts, excellent model reconstructions of the site below, coins, sarcophagi and more.

The **church** that the museum is named after is next door and contains many Roman sarcophagi with intricate relief work. The church isn't open too often. Walking down the road in front will lead you to the Valley of the Temples.

Most of these temples were destroyed by earthquakes and human destruction. Despite the state of the temples, it's still awe inspiring to walk among structures that once stood erect in the 5th century BCE.

IT'S A BEAUTIFUL NIGHT IN THE VALLEY OF THE TEMPLES

*At night the monuments are illuminated, so be sure to take a night stroll down the **Viale della Vittoria**, the street that leads to the temples from just in front of the train station. Bring your camera and some high speed film. This is one of my favorite scenes in all of Italy, and I think you'll like it too.*

The **Tempio di Giove (Temple of Zeus)** would have been the largest Doric temple ever built had it been completed. It was to be dedicated to the Olympian god Zeus, as you can guess from its name (Jove in English, or *Giove* in Latin, is Zeus). You can still see the remains of one of the standing *telemones*, human figures that were to be the support columns.

The **Tempio della Concordia (Temple of Concord)** is probably the best preserved most probably because it was converted to a Christian church in the 6th century CE. It has been fenced off to keep scavenging tourists from tearing it apart. But even from a distance it is a joy to behold.

The **Tempio di Giunone (Temple of Juno/Hera)** is not as well preserved but it is still an engaging structure. You may notice some red and black marks in the stone. These could be remnants of fires that were set when the temple was sacked many centuries ago.

B. SANTO SPIRITO

Piazza Santo Spirito. Accessible 9:00am–noon and 3:00pm–6:00pm.

Built by Cisterian nuns in 1290, this complex contains a church, convent, and charterhouse. The church contains some fine stucco work. You'll need to ring the bell on the church to gain admittance. Be patient. It's considered rude to keep ringing the bell.

C. CHURCH OF SANTA MARIA DEI GRECI

Via Santa Maria dei Greci. Open 8:00am–noon and 3:00pm–5pm.

Built on a 5th century BCE Greek temple, you can still see evidence of the columns in the walls, as well as the base of the columns in the foundation below the church. Make time to search out the entrance in the courtyard. Also inside are some interesting Byzantine frescoes.

D. CHIESA DEL PURGATORIO

Via Fodera. Open 8:00am–noon and 4:00pm–7:00pm.

The main draw for this church are the eight statues inside that represent the eight virtues. Next to the church is the entrance to a network of underground avenues and courtyards, built by the Greeks in the 5th century BCE.

NIGHTLIFE & ENTERTAINMENT

The bars and cafés along **Via Atenea** and in the **Piazzale Aldo Moro** is where the town congregates for its evening *passegiatta* (stroll). Come out with the Italians at about 8:00pm, sit at a cafe and sip an *aperitivo*, or stroll among the natives enjoying the relaxing evenings in Agrigento.

PRACTICAL INFORMATION

Banking Hours & Changing Money

Banks are open Monday through Friday from 8:30am to 1:30pm and some do reopen from 2:30pm or so to 3:30pm or so. Besides banks there are plenty of exchange bureaus (*casa di cambio*). One that is open until 9:00pm on weekdays, and until 2:00pm on Saturdays is in the Train Station. Another option, if all else is closed is to simply change your money at your hotel.

Business Hours

From October to June, most shops are open from 9:00am to 1:00pm and from 3:30pm to 7:30pm, and are closed all day Sundays and on Monday mornings. Then from June to August, when it really starts to get hot in Sicily, the morning hours remain the same, but the mid-day siesta time is slightly extended to 4:00pm and sometimes 4:30pm, which then pushes closing time back to 7:30pm or 8:00pm. And also, in conjunction with the Sunday and Monday morning closings, shops also close half-days on Saturday.

Food stores like *alimentari* generally are open from 8:30am to 1:30pm (so stock up on your picnic supplies before you need them) and from 5:00pm to 7:30pm, and during the winter months they are closed on Thursdays.

Local Festivals & Holidays
- **First Sunday of February**, Almond Blossom Festival in the Valley of The Temples
- **Late July/Early August**, *Settimana Pirandelliana*. A week long festival of plays, opera and ballets all performed in the Piazza Kaos.

Postal Services

The **central post office** in Agrigento *is in the circular building in Piazza Vittorio Emanuele*. Open Monday through Friday, 8:30am–5:00pm, Saturdays 9:00am–Noon. But if you're in a hurry, stamps can be bought at any tobacconist (stores indicated by a T sign outside), and mailed at any mailbox, which are red and marked with the word *Poste* or *Lettere*. There is a currency exchange window inside that is open in the mornings.

Tourist Information & Maps
- **Tourist Office**, *Piazza Aldo Moro #123 (Tel. 0922/20391), just to the left as you exit the train station.* Here you can get free maps and information about the town and the Valley of the Temples.

SIRACUSA

Most of the city of **Siracusa** (**Syracuse**) is situated on an island separated by a narrow channel from the east coast of Sicily. Because of the quaint older town, the scenic **Bay of Porto Grande**, its beautiful natural surroundings, and the monuments and relics of a glorious past, Siracusa is one of the most frequented spots in Sicily for tourists.

Founded in 743 BCE on the island by a few colonists from Corinth, **Ortygia** (later to be named Siracusa) grew into a feared and powerful city in the Greek world. In 415 BCE, the city was drawn into the conflict between Athens and Sparta, but when an expedition from Athens in 413 BCE ended in the complete annihilation of the Athenian fleet and army, the Greeks began to leave the locals alone as they concentrated on their internal strife. Siracusa detained over 7,000 Athenians in squalid conditions for over 7 years. From that point until 212 BCE, Siracusa was arguably the greatest and most powerful city in the world. Just after that time, the city expanded from its easily defensible island to the mainland. The ruler at the time, Gelon, built the market area and necropolis which is now the famous **Archaeological Park** with its preserved buildings, temples, and theaters that people from all over the world come to see.

After the first Punic War, in which Siracusa was allied with the Romans, the city changed its alliance in the second Punic War to the Carthaginians. Big mistake. The Romans attacked and conquered the city in 212 BCE, and thus began the city's decline. During this two year assault, the city defended itself with an ingenious variety of devices created by the great scientist and inventor Archimedes. This last great thinker of the Hellenic world was hacked to death in retribution after the Romans finally sacked the city. The city never really recovered its past glory, but it did remain the main port in Sicily. It also briefly became the capital of the Byzantine Empire in 663 CE, when the Emperor Constans moved his court here. After that the city, like much of Sicily, was overrun by waves of Arab, Norman, and other conquerors. In conjunction the area was repeatedly devastated by earthquakes and other natural disasters. But today it is a great city to visit.

ARRIVALS & DEPARTURES

By car the best route is along the coast road, route 115, from Catania. Both by train and by car will take in excess of an hour to traverse the 60 kilometers from Catania.

GETTING AROUND TOWN

If you're staying in a hotel in or around the center city, Siracusa is a perfect city for walking. From the train station, located almost on the edge

SOUTHERN ITALY & SICILY 361

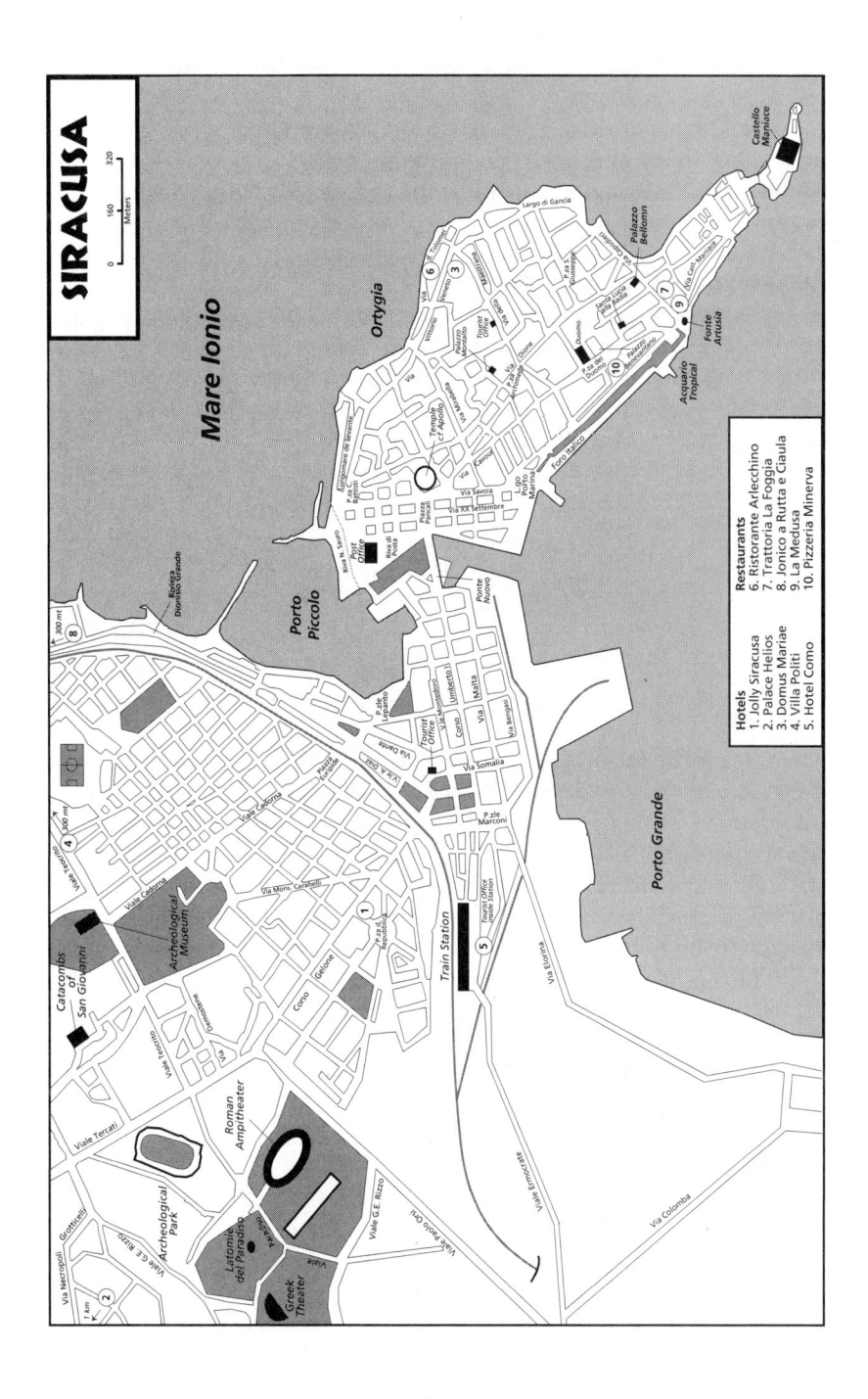

of the island, you are within walking distance of the **Centro Storico** and **Stazione Maritima** on the island, as well as the **Archaeological Park** to the north on the mainland.

The Archaeological Park and Museum are about a fifteen minute walk away, so if you're tired you may want to catch either bus # 4, 5 12, or 15 from the Piazza della Poste or from Largo XXV Luglio, which will pass by both of these stops.

WHERE TO STAY

1. JOLLY SIRACUSA, *Corso Gelone, 96110 Siracusa. Tel. 0931/461-111. Fax 0931/461-126. Toll free in Italy 167-017703. Toll free in US and NYC 1-800/221-2626. Toll free in NY State 1-800/247-1277. 100 rooms, 56 with bath, 44 with shower. Single L110,000-200,000; Double L140,000-230,000. All credit cards accepted. Breakfast included.* ****

Located in the commercial center of Syracuse in a quaint building. The rooms are modern with a separate level designed as a work space, making them quite large. Every window is sound-proof to keep out the traffic noise. The bathrooms are a little small and offer hairdryers as well as a courtesy toiletry set. A clean and comfortable hotel that has a good restaurant (L270,000 for full board if you're interested), a little American-style bar, room service and laundry service, but little else. Located near the train station, you'll find air conditioning and satellite TVs in the rooms.

2. PALACE HELIOS, *Viale Scala Greca 201, 96100 Siracusa. Tel. 0931/491-566. Fax 0931/756-612. 136 rooms, 39 with bath, 97 with shower. Single L110,000-160,000; Double L160,000-220,000. All credit cards accepted. Breakfast included.* ****

Located outside of town and north of the Greek Theater in the Archaeological Park, this place is a little way from everything, so getting the L200,000 full board option at their in-house restaurant would be a good idea. The rooms are old but comfortable and the darker furniture contrasts well with the white floors. The bathrooms come complete with phone and courtesy toiletry kit.

3. DOMUS MARIAE, *Via Veneto 76, 96100 Siracusa. Tel. 0931/24854. Fax 0931/24858. 12 rooms all with bath. Single L90,000; Double without L140,000; Double L78,000-120,000. No credit cards accepted. Breakfast included.* ***

Located in an old building that has been successfully restored to maintain the original architectural charm. Situated in the *centro storico* almost directly on the water, this place offers the service and accommodations of a four star at three star prices. The rooms are extremely spacious and finely appointed with antiques. The bathrooms are elegant with all necessary amenities such as toothbrush, toothpaste, hairdryer and more. A great place to stay in Siracusa.

4. VILLA POLITI, *Via M Politi Laudien 2, 96100 Siracusa. Tel. 0931/ 412-121. Fax 0931/36061. 94 rooms, 85 with bath, 9 with shower. 2 Suites. Single L92,000-127,000; Double L132,000-200,000. All credit cards accepted. Breakfast included.* ***

This is another great place to stay while in Siracusa. The rooms are a little run down, but are clean and comfortable, the restaurant offers great local cuisine (L170,000 full board), and the hotel is located in a quaint historic building. You have air conditioning in the rooms, a disco for dancing at night, a swimming pool surrounded by flowers and vegetation, tennis courts, bocce courts, and great views over the sea. It's located a short distance outside of town, but is about equidistant from the town and the Archaeological Park. For a three star, this place offers many options and is priced well.

5. HOTEL COMO, *Piazza Stazione 10, 96100 Siracusa. Tel. 0931/464-055. Fax 0931/61210. 14 rooms all with shower. Single L72,000-79,000; Double L102,000-113,000. All credit cards accepted. Breakfast L6,000.* **

A good location near the station, air conditioning in the rooms, satellite TV, room service and laundry service, which may seem a bit much for a two star, but they're at the high end of this category. Near everything, this small hotel has spotless bathrooms with phones and courtesy toiletry kits, and comfortable rooms. Everything was renovated about three years ago so it still has a luster about it. Good for budget travelers and above.

WHERE TO EAT

6. RISTORANTE ARLECCHINO, *Via del Tolomei 5, Tel. 0931/ 66386. Closed Mondays. All credit cards accepted. Dinner for two L100,000.*

Located in Ortygia, from the entrance you have a great view of the sea. This modern, well-lit place is huge; over 260 people can be seated at the same time. It caters to tourists, but mainly of the Italian variety so the food is good. Try their antipasto buffet table for starters that is overflowing with seafood. Then for more seafood with the spaghetti *ai ricci di mare* (with the riches of the sea) or the *tortelloni con scampi allo zafferano* (large cheese stuffed pasta with a shrimp and sauce). For seconds try any of their oven roasted fish as well as their many meat dishes.

7. TRATTORIA LA FOGLIA, *Via Capodieci 29, Tel. 0931/66233. Closed Tuesdays. All credit cards accepted. Dinner for two L80,000.*

Located in Ortygia, this is a small local place that changes its menu daily based on whatever ingredients chef Nicoletta was able to get at the market. Usually the antipasto will be vegetables, like *fritelle di finocchietto* (fried small fennel). Try one of their soups for your primo to save yourself for their exquisite fish dishes. Only 25 seats, so make a reservation.

8. JONICO A RUTTA E CIAULU, *Riviera Rionisio il Grande 194, Tel. 0931/65540. Closed Tuesdays, the end of the year and Easter. All credit cards accepted. Dinner for two L110,000.*

Located up the coast near the Grand Hotel Villa Politi, the best place to eat is on the terrace where you have a fine view of the Ionian Sea. Here you can get some good local dishes at somewhat high prices. Try some of their *spaghetti alla siracusano* (with anchovies and scraped toasted bread sauce), which doesn't sound too appetizing but I like it, or some *spaghetti con tonno fresca* (with fresh tuna sauce). For seconds they serve some great tuna and swordfish steaks.

9. LA MEDUSA, *Via San Teresa 21, Tel. 0931/61403. Closed Mondays and August 15 to September 15. American Express accepted. Dinner for two L40,000.*

Another restaurant in the Ortygia district, this place is run by a Tunisian who has been in Siracusa for over 15 years. You can get some great couscous with either *pesce* or *carne* (a rice based dish with either fish or meat) for primo. The antipasto is good too with the *pesce spada marinata* (marinated swordfish), *gamberetti* (small shrimp) and more. For seconds try their *arrosto misto di pesce* (mixed roast fish). Great atmosphere and good food.

10. PIZZERIA MINERVA, *Piazza Duomo 20, Tel. 0931/69404. Closed Mondays and November. No credit cards accepted. Dinner for two L40,000.*

In the summer this is the perfect pace to end a long walk through Ortygia. The place seats over 130 people, but not all outside in the piazza facing the Duomo. Try and get one of these outside seats. You can get any pizza imaginable here, but if you want it American style you have to order *doppio mozzarella* (double cheese).

SEEING THE SIGHTS

The archaeological park and museum is the big draw here, but there are some lovely squares and churches in town that are great for poking around.

ORTYGIA

On the island of **Ortygia**, the ancient nucleus of Siracusa, you can find remains from over 2,500 years of history. A small area, almost half a kilometer across and only one in length, this little parcel of land contains much of the charm and adventure from all of those centuries.

TEMPLE OF APOLLO

Just over the **Ponte Nuovo** from the mainland is the oldest Doric temple in Sicily. Built in the 7th century BCE, little remains of this once glorious temple except for two pillars and parts of some walls. To really get an idea of what it used to look like, go to the Archaeological Museum for a scale model.

PIAZZA ARCHIMEDE

This is Ortygia's **central piazza**. The square has some bars and cafés with outside seating where you can sit and enjoy the sight of the 12th century fountain with a woodland nymph cavorting under a cover of modern moss. Down a small road from the square is the **Via del Montalto** on which you can find the **Palazzo Montalto** (*not open to public*), with its fabulous double and triple arched windows. The building's construction was begun in 1397 and is constantly undergoing renovations.

PIAZZA DEL DUOMO

A piazza surrounded by some beautiful 17th and 18th century palazzos and dominated by the impressive Baroque **Duomo**. The square was built over and encompasses an earlier Greek temple, the 5th century BCE Ionic temple of Athena. You can still see evidence of the previous structure in the walls, where 26 of the original 34 columns remain. Because much of its earlier wealth was stolen and a majority of it was destroyed in the earthquake of 1693, this cathedral contains a wide variety of differing architectural styles, from Greek to Byzantine to Baroque.

The **Palazzo Benevantano** (*at #24 on the piazza, not open to the public*) is worth a look because of its attractive 18th century facade and serpentine balcony. At the far end of the piazza is the small church of **Santa Lucia alla Badia** built from 1695 to 1703 (*open 8:00am-noon and 3:30pm-6:00pm*). The church is significant because it contains the remains of the city's patron saint, Santa Lucia.

GALLERIA DI PALAZZO BELLOMO

Via Capodieci 14. Open Tuesday-Sunday 9am-1pm. Admission L3,000.

Almost behind **Santa Lucia alla Badia** is the **Palazzo Bellomo**, a 15th century palazzo that contains a wonderful gallery of all kinds of artwork, including ancient bibles, medieval carriages, sculptures, tombs, paintings and more. The most famous painting is the *Annunciation* by Antonello da Messina.

Walk down to the Via Capodieci to arrive at the **Foro Italico**, the main promenade for the citizens of Ortygia. On this tree-lined promenade you'll find rows of bars and cafes on the land side, and rows of yachts lining the water. It's where the local citizens come to enjoy the evenings before they retire home. At the beginning of this promenade is the fresh water fountain **Fonte Aretusa**. If you take notice, this fountain is located virtually out to sea so it is considered some kind of miracle that it serves fresh water. Just past the fountain is the **Aquario Tropical** *(open Saturday–Thursdays 9am–1pm, admission L3,000)* that offers 35 different species of tropical fish for your aquarium-viewing pleasure.

CATACOMBS

Via San Giovanni. Open 9:00am–1:00pm and 2:00pm–7:00pm. Closed Wednesdays. Guide tours of catacombs cost L3,000.

The **catacombs of San Giovanni** are located under the basilica of the same name, and contain a quantity of faded frescoes. This is an ominous tour through a labyrinth of passageways, but you won't encounter any bodies. Most of these were destroyed by looters and their riches stolen, so to see a sarcophagus you need to go to the Archaeological Museum.

ARCHAEOLOGICAL MUSEUM

Viale Teocrito. Open Tuesday–Saturday 9:00am–1:00pm and Sundays 9:00am–12:30pm.

To get to the museum, you can take the 15 minute walk or catch bus #4, 5 12, or 15 from the Piazza della Poste or from Largo XXV Luglio. Since this museum is the most extensive antiquities museum in Sicily, you should spend some time browsing through the collection. The museum contains fossils, skeletons, figurines, sarcophagi and more, but the collection's tour de force is the *Venus Anadiomene*, the coy statue of Venus rising from the sea. If you're into antiquities, this is a great place to spend a few hours.

ARCHAEOLOGICAL PARK

Open Tuesday–Sunday 9:00am to an hour before sunset. Admission L3,000.

To get to the park, you can take the 15 minute walk or catch bus #4, 5 12, or 15 from the Piazza della Poste or from Largo XXV Luglio. The structures preserved here were constructed between 475 BCE and the 3rd century CE and many remain somewhat intact. An example of this preservation is the **Greek Theater**, originally made from the side of the hill around 475 BCE. The structure was enlarged in 335 BCE and could seat up to 15,000 people. If you want to see a performance here, come in May and June on the alternate year when Classical Greek plays are staged. They are quite stirring.

Next door to the Greek Theater is the **Latomie del Paradiso**, the **Paradise Quarry**, so named because many of the 7,000 Athenians captured in 413 BCE went to the afterlife from here. In the quarry are two interesting caves: **Grotta dei Cordari**, where rope makers used to work at their craft because the damp cave kept the strands of rope from breaking, and the **Orecchio di Dionisio** (Ear of Dionysis), so called because the entrance resembles an ear, and the cave has amazing acoustic qualities.

Up from the grotto is the **Roman Amphitheater** which was built in the 3rd century CE, by, you guessed it, the Romans. Here they held their vicious gladiatorial games pitting man against man as well as beast. Just one hundred and forty meters long, it's not quite as impressive as the Coliseum in Rome, but knowing that countless people and animals lost their lives here, it has an effect on you.

NIGHTLIFE & ENTERTAINMENT

The only nightlife to speak of is along the **Foro Italico** promenade, where you can sip a drink or have a light meal and watch the citizens of Siracusa walk by.

PRACTICAL INFORMATION

Banking Hours & Changing Money

Banks are open Monday through Friday from 8:30am to 1:30pm and some do reopen from 2:30pm or so to 3:30pm or so. Besides banks there are plenty of exchange bureaus (*casa di cambio*). One that is open until 9:00pm on weekdays, and until 2:00pm on Saturdays is in the Train Station. Another option, if all else is closed is to simply change your money at your hotel.

Business Hours

From October to June, most shops are open from 9:00am to 1:00pm and from 3:30pm to 7:30pm, and are closed all day Sundays and on Monday mornings. Then from June to August, when it really starts to get hot in Sicily, the morning hours remain the same, but the mid-day siesta time is slightly extended to 4:00pm and sometimes 4:30pm, which then pushes closing time back to 7:30pm or 8:00pm. And also, in conjunction with the Sunday and Monday morning closings, shops also close half-days on Saturday.

Food stores like *alimentari* generally are open from 8:30am to 1:30pm and from 5:00pm to 7:30pm, and during the winter months they are closed on Thursdays.

Local Festivals & Holidays

- **May to June**, every even numbered year Classical Greek drama is performed at the Greek theater. Reservations required.

Postal Services

The **central post office** in Siracusa *is in the Piazza delle Poste (Tel. 0931/ 684-16) located in the Centro Storico island just over the bridge from the *mainland.* Open Monday through Friday 8:30am–6:30pm, Saturdays 9:00am–noon. But if you're in a hurry, stamps can be bought at any tobacconist (stores indicated by a **T** sign outside), and mailed at any mailbox, which are red and marked with the words *Poste* or *Lettere.*

Tourist Information & Maps
• **Tourist office**, *just outside the train station*
• **Tourist office**, *on the island at Via Maestranza 33, Tel. 0931/652-01*
• **Tourist office**, *on the mainland near the catacombs at Via San Sebastiano 45, Tel. 093/677-10*

All three can offer you maps of the area and the Archaeological Park, as well as brochures and information about hotels.

MOUNT ETNA

One of the world's largest active volcanoes, **Mount Etna's** presence dominates the skyline of this coastal area. The last two eruptions have, in 1985 and 1992, destroyed local roads and threatened local villagers, who, for some reason, continue to live at the base of this accident waiting to happen. Despite the possibility that the volcano could erupt at any time, Mount Etna is still a great tourist draw.

There are two ways to see the volcano, from the safety of a train that tours the base, or from the volcano itself.

ARRIVALS & DEPARTURES
By Train Around the Volcano

The first option can be achieved by riding the private railway **Ferrovia Circumetnea**, which goes from Catania around Mount Etna to **Riposto**, up north on the coast. This three hour ride is quite scenic, even if you're not going up the side of the volcano. The train passes through small towns and settlements along the way (**Adrano**, **Randazzo**, and **Giarre**) complete with castles and medieval walls. If you wish, you can disembark, walk around for a while then catch the next train for the coast. But remember there are only three trains a day. Ask the conductor if another is coming along behind.

You can catch this private train, that does not accept Eurorail or Italorail passes, in Catania at **Stazione Borgo** *(Via Coraonda 350 just north of the Bellini Gardens; cost is L12,000 one way)*. Once you reach **Riposto**, you'll need to catch a one way regular local train back to Catania which should cost L5,000 and tack another half an hour onto your trip.

SOUTHERN ITALY & SICILY 369

By Bus To the Volcano
  Skirting the base of the volcano will give you perspective on this natural landmark and afford you some nice views, but actually ascending to the top first-hand will give you a better feel for the awesome strength of this volcano. To get to the mountain, catch a bus from Catania's central train station at 8:00am and return at 4:00pm. The round-trip ticket costs L5,000. Buy it inside the train station at the AST window. The bus reaches its destination at the **Rifugio Sapienza**, 1,440 meters below the summit.

SEEING THE SIGHTS
Ascending Mt. Etna
  You have three options to get near the top: walk, cable car, or minivan. The highest you're allowed to go is to the **Torre del Filosofo**, a lava tower built by the Romans to commemorate Hadrian's climb to the top. From this spot you're not far from the top and should be treated to gaseous explosions and molten rocks being spit up from the crater. The whole landscape is otherworldly in appearance.
  The **cable car** option, if working, costs L45,000 per person, takes two hours, and gives you about 45 minutes of walking around. The **minivan option** costs L40,000 and gives you about the same amount of time. **Walking** can be tiring and treacherous, since the footing is not too secure with lava pebbles hindering your traction. You'll also be climbing a little over 1,000 meters in oxygen-thin air, so you must be prepared.

TAORMINA

  Despite being Sicily's main tourist attraction, **Taormina** still retains much of its medieval hill town charm to make it worth a visit. Since it is rather expensive to stay here, and considering how quick and easy it is to get here from Catania, you may want to come early in the morning and leave late in the evening for a full day's enjoyment.
  This town is situated in a place of unsurpassed beauty. Located on a cliff top with two coves below, I am hard pressed to imagine a more beautiful sight. Lately some high rise hotels have sprung up along some of the outlying beaches below, but if you stay in the old town or just visit the old town you'll see none of that. But you will see tourists, in numbers that make Taormina uncomfortable in the summer. So the best time to come here is between October and March, when you'll have the whole place, almost, to yourself.
  The town is tiny and filled with 15th to 19th century buildings along its main street and in its twisting alleys. Besides wandering through the town's medieval beauty, you can also visit the quiet hill town of **Castelmola**,

or frequent the beaches below. There is a cable car that runs between Taormina and its closest beach, **Mazzaro**.

ARRIVALS & DEPARTURES

If you took the train around the base of Mount Etna to Riposto and are not returning to Catania, Taormina is only a short train ride away. If you're leaving from Catania, there are 30 trains a day that take 45 minutes each way and cost L5,000.

The train station is located far below the town of Taormina and you must catch one of the frequent buses up the mountain. They run until 10:30pm.

WHERE TO STAY

Since this is a tourist town there are plenty of places to stay, but if you arrive in the peak months from April through September without a reservation, you may not be able to find a room or you'll have to settle for less than stellar accommodations.

Below are the best options in each category.

1. SAN DOMENICO PALACE, *Piazza San Domenico 5, 98039 Taormina. Tel. 0942/23701. Fax 0942/625-506. Toll free in Italy 167012205. 101 rooms, 100 with bath, 1 with shower. Single L250,000-380,000; Double L400,000-620,000. All credit cards accepted. Breakfast included.* *******

This is the best place to stay in Taormina. An excellent five star deluxe hotel with super professional service and every amenity under the sun. Here you can rub elbows with some of Europe's *glitterati* while enjoying superb dining, a heated swimming pool, tennis courts, a great view, and a private beach. The hotel is located in an old convent for Dominican fathers that was built in 1430. It is filled with character, ambiance and romance. If you have the money, a perfect place to stay. The rooms are all different but each is perfectly comfortable. The abundant breakfast buffet is served in a classic room with terra cotta tiles with a perfect view of the sea.

2. CAPARENA LIDO, *Locanda Spisone, Via Nazionale 189, 98039 Taormina. Tel. 0942/652-033. Fax the same. 88 rooms all with bath. Single L150,000-210,000; Double L200,000-280,000. All credit cards accepted. Breakfast included.* ******

This place has only been open about three years and it is a beauty. Settled in by the water and surrounded by greenery, this place has a private beach, a swimming pool, satellite TV, a good restaurant serving typical Sicilian dishes, and exercise facilities. The rooms are large and comfortable and the bathrooms have every imaginable convenience, including telephone and hairdryer. Breakfast is served in a wonderful room on the top floor with large windows offering a fantastic view of the

SOUTHERN ITALY & SICILY 371

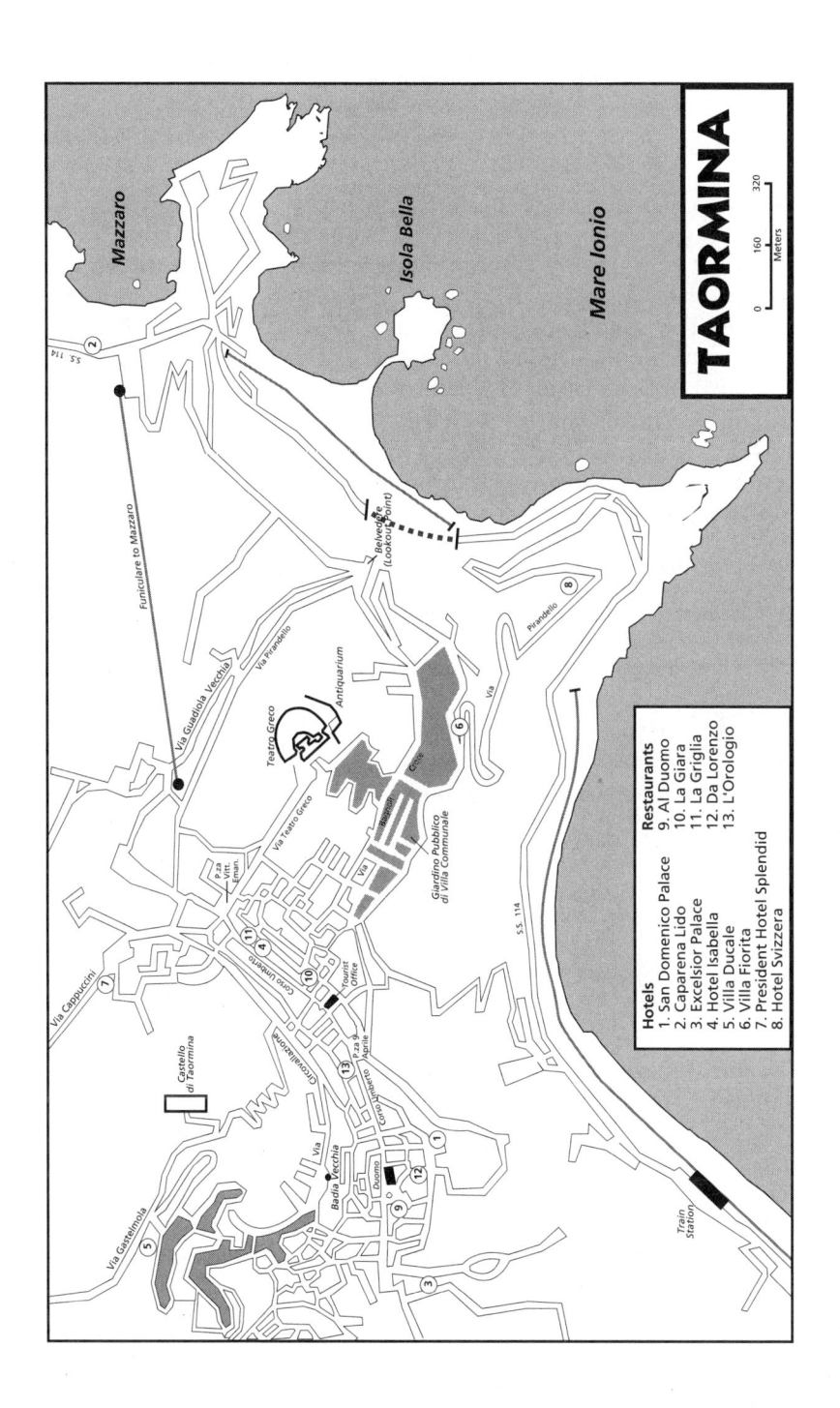

TAORMINA

Hotels
1. San Domenico Palace
2. Caparena Lido
3. Excelsior Palace
4. Hotel Isabella
5. Villa Ducale
6. Villa Fiorita
7. President Hotel Splendid
8. Hotel Svizzera

Restaurants
9. Al Duomo
10. La Giara
11. La Griglia
12. Da Lorenzo
13. L'Orologio

sea. At the beach you have your own gazebo bar, paddle boats, umbrellas for shade, deck chairs, and musical entertainment in the evenings. A wonderful place to stay.

3. EXCELSIOR PALACE, *Via Toselli 8, 98039 Taormina. Tel. 0942/ 23975. Fax 0942/23978. 87 rooms all with bath. Single L110,000-180,000; Double L160,000-260,000. All credit cards accepted. Breakfast included.* ****

Located in the center of town but with great views of both Etna and the sea. A truly tranquil place to stay. Established in 1903 and renovated in the 1980s, this place is filled with antiques and every modern convenience. The rooms are more recently renovated and are filled with modern furnishings and all have a view of either the sea or the gardens that surround the hotel. The bathrooms are small but accommodating, with hairdryer and courtesy toiletry kits. There is also a large pool in the middle of the hotel's park that opens in the beginning of spring. The restaurant is also the breakfast room where you are served an abundant buffet of fresh fruit, juice, croissant, cakes, pies, eggs, yogurt, milk, coffee and tea.

4. HOTEL ISABELLA, *Corso Umberto 58, 98039 Taormina. Tel. 0942/ 23153. Fax 0942/23155. 29 rooms, 10 with bath, 19 with shower. Double L110,000-180,000. All credit cards accepted. Breakfast included.* ***

A modern building on the main drag in Taormina. The rooms are medium sized and comfortable with coordinated wall coverings and bed sheets in sober colors, but the bathrooms are really tiny. The shower is the entire bathroom, so don't leave anything out when you turn on the water since it'll get soaked. In the summer breakfast is out on the sun deck. A simple, basic place to stay.

5. VILLA DUCALE, *Via Leonardo da Vinci 60, 98039 Taormina. Tel. 0942/28153. Fax 0942/28710. 10 rooms all with bath. Single L140,000-190,000; Double L200,000-250,000. All credit cards accepted. Breakfast included.* ***

A lovely, lovely, lovely little hotel that has all the character, charm and amenities to be a five star. So it is beyond me why they only recently have been upgraded from two star status. You have wonderful views of both the sea and Mount Etna. The rooms are all different from one another and are filled with Sicilian ceramics, locally made bed frames and bed covers of damask cloth with the hotel's logo in gold on them. Some have handmade furniture created by Tino Giammona, and all have wonderful terraces with stunning panoramic views. The bathrooms are super-accessorized and tastefully decorated with ceramic tile from Cattagirone. And the breakfast is absolutely excellent. If you get the chance you should try this place.

6. VILLA FIORITA, *Via L. Piarandello 39, 98039 Taormina. Tel. 0942/ 24122. Fax 0942/625-967. 26 rooms all with bath. Double L150,000. All credit cards accepted. Breakfast included.* ***

In the three star category, the Villa Fiorita distinguishes itself because of the charm of its location. Virtually engulfed by lavish gardens, the hotel also has great views. The entrance hall is small and is paved with authentic Sicilian terra cotta tiles. The rooms are large and well decorated with antique furniture and vases, paved with tiles from Cattagirone, and the wall and bed coverings are coordinated white and blue. Some rooms have only small terraces; the rest have balconies and all have deck chairs. The service is professional and courteous. Breakfast is either served out on the terrace or in a lovely and romantic room, an abundant buffet of croissant, jams, and danishes all made in house, with many different types of bread, and eggs made to order. The pool is quite beautiful, surrounded by greenery.

7. PRESIDENT HOTEL SPLENDID, *Via Dietro Cappuccini 10, 98039 Taormina. Tel. 0942/23500. Fax 0942/625-289. 50 rooms all with bath. Single L40,000-55,000; Double L70,000-90,000. American Express, Visa accepted.* **

A fantastic place to stay for any budget. A little run down in places, but the rooms at the front have great panoramic views and most have balconies from which you can sit, enjoy room service, and enjoy the view. The restaurant serves superb local food (the full board for only L80,000 is a steal) and the view from most of the tables is magnificent. They also have an outside pool and a relaxing bar downstairs. Located about 150 meters from the center of town, this place is trying to upgrade its facilities to get three stars. Their next step is to get air conditioning in the rooms.

8. HOTEL SVIZZERA, *Via L Pirandelo 26, 98039 Taormina. Tel. 0942/ 23970. Fax 0942/625-906. 16 rooms, 4 with bath, 12 with shower. Single L40,000-60,000; Double L70,000-100,000. No credit cards accepted.* *

A quaint little place on the outskirts of town near the water. Only 16 rooms though, so remember to reserve well in advance. There is a relaxing garden setting from which you can enjoy an after-dinner drink. They also have a shuttle service to pick you up at the train station. No air conditioning or TV in the rooms, but they are clean and comfortable enough for budget travelers.

WHERE TO EAT

As a tourist town, there are plenty of little places to eat. Listed below are the restaurants I think are best.

9. AL DUOMO, *Vico Erbrei 11, Tel. 0942/625-656. Closed Wednesdays. All credit cards accepted. Dinner for two L80,000.*

In the summer the best place to eat is on their little terrace facing the Piazza Duomo. They have a small antipasto plate of cheese and salad that

I can't recommend. But their pasta dishes are superb, especially the *pennette vecchia Taormina* (little macaronis with a spicy tomato and vegetable sauce). For seconds, try their *polpette arrostite nelle foglie di limone* (roasted meatballs with a touch of lemon sauce).

10. LA GIARA, *Vico La Floresta 1, Tel. 0942/23360. Closed Mondays but not from July to October. Only open on weekends in November, February and March. All credit cards accepted. Dinner for two L120,000.*

Elegant and sophisticated, this large place is located in the heart of the old town, and has a great terrace that is used year round with wonderful views all the way to the beach at Giardini Naxos two kilometers away. The cooks serve the regular local dishes here, as well as creative adaptations of them. Try the *foie gras* for an antipasto or the *insalatina di crostacei* (little salad with crustaceans). For primo try the *raviolini di Crostacei in salsa di scampi* (ravioli stuffed with crustaceans in a shrimp sauce). For seconds try any of their regularly prepared meats or fish, or *mignon di carne al tartufo nero* (filet mignon covered with black truffles). You can prolong the evening after dinner by getting a drink at their piano bar.

11. LA GRIGLIA, *Corso Umberto 54, Tel. 0942/23980. Closed Tuesdays and November 20 - December 20. All credit cards accepted. Dinner for two L110,000.*

On the main street in Taormina, this place is known for their aquarium stuffed with lobsters and fish that you can choose for your meal. This is a rustic but refined place, with professional service preparing you for fine Sicilian food. Try the *vermiccelli incasciati* (fried vermicelli pasta made with a tomato sauce) or the classic *penne con sarde e finicchietto* (tubular pasta with sardines and fennel). For seconds try anything they have on the grill – after all, the name of the place means "The Grill."

12. DA LORENZO, *Via M Amari 4, Tel. 0942/23480. Closed Wednesdays and November 15 to December 15. All credit cards accepted. Dinner for two L90,000.*

Situated a stone's throw away from the Piazza Duomo, during the summer the best place to eat is out on their patio. In this small intimate restaurant that only seats around 45 people, the best antipasto samplings are the *ricci di mare* (a large plate of mixed seafood), *occhie di bue* (oxen eyeballs - go ahead, be adventurous, they're much better than mountain oysters), or *calamaretti fritti* (fried small squid). For primo try their *fusilli al carciofo* (pasta with a tasty artichoke sauce) and for seconds try any of their roasted or grilled meat or fish.

13. L'OROLOGIO, *Via Don Bosco 37a, Tel. 0942/625-572. Closed Mondays and November. All credit cards accepted. Dinner for two L100,000.*

You can sit outside on their enclosed terrace year round. For antipasto try their *gamberetti con rucola* (small shrimp with cheese), or *il prosciutto di porcellino* (ham from a young pig) that comes with *bruschette* (garlic and oil smothered bread covered with tomatoes). Next try their *ravioli di carne di cinghiale al finocchietto* (ravioli stuffed with wild boar meat in a fennel sauce). Then for seconds try their excellent *Fantasia dell'Orologio* (mixed fried seafood, meats and cheeses).

SEEING THE SIGHTS

Taormina's main attractions are really the steep stepped medieval streets, quaint old buildings, and scenic views over the water, but here are a few other sights of interest.

TEATRO GRECO

Via Teatro Greco. Open 9:00am–1 hour before sunset. Admission L3,000.

Founded by the Greeks in the 3rd century BCE, this theater was almost completely redone by the Romans in the 1st century CE for their gladiatorial displays. It's so well-preserved that tourists are still allowed to clamber around on the stone seats still in existence today.

GIARDINO PUBBLICO

Via Bagnoli Croce. Open during daylight hours.

Directly in front of the Greek (Roman) theater are the gardens of the **Villa Comunale**, where you can enjoy a peaceful stroll or relax on a bench sunk into a flower bush. From the walls there are some wonderful views over the water and the beach areas.

TEATRO ROMANO

Via Corso Umberto. Open all the time.

Back in town there is a smaller Roman theater that is partially covered under the **Church of Santa Caterina**. You can peer down from the railings in the street or enter the church to see more of the theater through the floor. Located right next to the tourist office.

CASTELLO

Castle is open to the public 9:00am–1:00pm and 4:00pm–7:00pm.

If you're in the mood to climb small steep steps up a mountainside for about 30 minutes, then you can enjoy the best views of the area. Located above town, this tumble-down medieval castle isn't much in itself, but the panoramic views are superb.

NIGHTLIFE & ENTERTAINMENT

There are plenty of discos to choose from, all of which will cost you between L10,000 and L20,000 just to get in. If you want a more relaxing evening there is nothing better than sipping a good Sicilian wine at one of the outdoor cafés and watching the world go by. That will be a little expensive too, about L6,000 per glass, but your eardrums will still be intact.

PRACTICAL INFORMATION

Banking Hours & Changing Money

Since this is a big tourist town, during the high season banks are open Monday through Saturday, 8:30am-1:30pm and from 4:00pm-7:30pm. Besides banks there are plenty of exchange bureaus (*casa di cambio*) around and **American Express** is represented in the offices of **La Duca Viaggi** at *Via Don Bosco 39, Tel. 0942/625-255*.

Also there is a *cambio* in the train station at the information office that is open Monday-Sunday, 9:00am-9:00pm.

Business Hours

Most shops are open from 9:00am-1:00pm and from 3:30pm-7:30pm Monday-Saturday, and Sundays 9:00am-1:00pm.

English Language Bookstore

- **Libreria Interpress**, *Corso Umberto 37, Tel. 0942/24989*. Open regular business hours. Not exclusively an English-language bookstore, but they do carry a few popular titles in English.

Local Festivals

- **May**, *Sfilato del Carretto*. A dazzling display of colorful Sicilian carts.
- **July to September**, *Taormina Arte*. Theatrical, film and musical productions all over the city.
- **Christmas**, Festive parade

Moped Rental

- **Sicily on Wheels**, *Via Bagnoli Croce 90, Tel. 0942/625-657*. Must be over 16 to rent. Open daily from 9:00am-1:00pm and 4:00pm-7:00pm. You can also rent cars here, but driving a car in crowded Taormina is not advised. A great way to see the countryside or just go for a spin down to the beach is by moped.

Postal Services

The central post office in Taormina is *at Piazza San Antonio (Tel. 0942/23010)*. Open Monday through Saturday 8:30am-5:00pm, and since this is a tourist town, Sundays 9:00am-noon. Stamps can be bought at any tobacconist (stores indicated by a T sign outside), and mailed at any mailbox, which are red and marked with the word *Poste* or *Lettere*.

SOUTHERN ITALY & SICILY

Tourist Information & Maps
• **Tourist Office**, *Piazza Santa Caterina, Tel. 0942/232-43*. Can help you find a place to stay and give out maps and other information. Open Monday–Saturday, 8:30am–2:00pm and 4:00pm–7:00pm.

ISOLE EOLIE

The **Isole Eolie**, named after the Greek God of the Wind, are also known as the **Lipari Islands** in reference to the largest island in the chain. There are seven inhabited islands in total that lie between 30 and 80 km off the north coast of Sicily. The population of the islands today is about 14,000, which is a decrease, since the islands were once used as ancient penal colonies.

Today the islands attract people interested in scuba diving and snorkeling, as well as those wishing to enjoy one of the most unspoiled seashores in Italy. The main island, **Lipari**, is more prepared for dealing with tourists. It also has a beautiful Castle, archaeological ruins, and a variety of churches. **Vulcano** is aptly named since it is basically a bubbling volcano itself. **Stromboli** is also an active volcano and is the most scenic of all the islands.

These three islands are horribly crowded in the summertime with tourists, but you can visit the other four **Panarea**, **Salina**, **Filicudi** and **Alicudi** and enjoy a bit of solitude. These islands really should be enjoyed as a relaxing vacation in and of themselves.

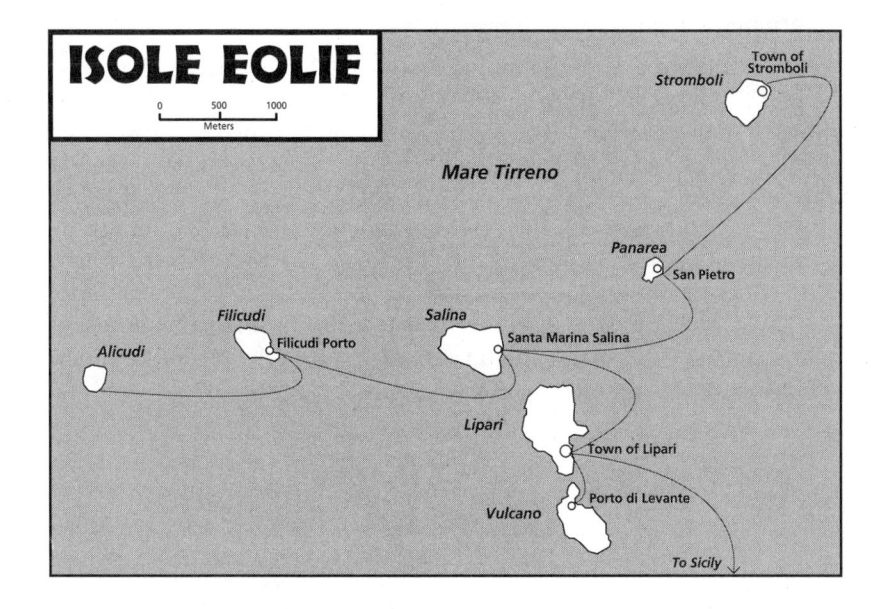

378 ROME & SOUTHERN ITALY GUIDE

ARRIVALS & DEPARTURES

Access to the islands is easiest from **Milazzo** on the north shore of Sicily. There are year round ferries and hydrofoils that leave several times a day. These ferries stop first at Vulcano, then at the main island Lipari. Here you can disembark and catch a smaller local ferry to any of the other islands.

But you can also catch ferries and hydrofoils to the islands from cities in Sicily (**Palermo**, **Cefalu**, and **Messina**) as well as **Naples** and **Reggio di Calabria** on the mainland, and **Calabria** in Sardinia.

Ferries & Hydrofoil Companies in Milazzo
- **SNAV**, *Via L. Rizzo 14, Tel. 090/928-4509*. Hydrofoils (L32,000) only.
- **Siremar**, *Via dei Mille 32, Tel. 090/928-3242*. Ferries (L16,000) and hydrofoils (L32,500).
- **Navigazione Generale Italiano**, *Via dei Mille 26 Tel. 090/928-4091*. Ferries (L16,000) only.

LIPARI

The island of **Lipari** is the most visited since it is the largest and most beautiful. The main town of the same name has quaint little pastel colored houses, and is surrounded by the medieval **Castello** that crowns the small town. Inside the castle walls there are four churches, the town's **Duomo**, and an **archaeological park**, which reveals that there were people in Lipari as far back as 1600 BCE.

GETTING AROUND TOWN

There are buses every 45 minutes or so that leave Lipari and traverse the island. Any of the other villages are no more than half an hour away by bus. If you're feeling adventurous, rent a moped and ride around the island. They can be rented at one of the many rental shops along the **Via Marina Lunga**.

North of the town of Lipari is the village of **Cannetto**. Visitors come to enjoy the **Spiaggia Bianca**, a small walk north of the village, where topless and sometimes bottomless bathing occurs. If you're in for a climb, walk the four kilometers uphill to **Quattroochi**. You get a magnificent view of the town of Lipari, and the island of **Vulcano** in the background. Remember to bring your camera.

WHERE TO STAY

HOTEL VILLA MELIGUNIS, *Via Marte 7, 98055 Lipari. Isole Eolie. Tel. 090/981-2426. Fax 090/988-0149. 32 rooms all with shower. Double L150,000-300,000. Credit cards accepted. Full board L150,000-230,000.* ****
Not far outside of the town of Lipari, this is one of two four star hotels on any of the islands. The other is on Vulcano. This place has a private beach, their own restaurant, a tranquil little park, and first class service. The rooms are luxurious and comfortable with mini-bar, TV, and air conditioning. They also have a shuttle bus that runs guests back and forth all over the island.

HOTEL CARASCO, *Porto delle Genti, 98055 Lipari. Isole Eolie. Tel. 090/981-1605. Fax 090/981-1828. 89 rooms, 20 with bath, 69 with shower. Single L90,000-165,000; Double L160,000-320,000. Visa accepted. Full board 150,000-240,000.* ***
Located out of reach of Lipari and even the smaller villages on the island, this is truly a resort type environment. Set in a romantic old building, this place has a swimming pool, disco, piano bar, a private beach, great views of the water and other islands, a great restaurant and an accommodating bar. The rooms are relatively large, very clean, quite charming, and extremely comfortable. This is the place where Italians come to relax in the Isole Eolie. They have a shuttle bus that can take you all over the island.

HOTEL ORIENTE, *Via G. Marconi 35, 98055 Lipari. Isole Eolie. Tel. 090/981-1493. Fax 090/988-0198. 24 rooms all with shower. Single L40,000-60,000; Double L60,000-120,000. Visa Accepted.* **
A small place in the town of Lipari that is geared to the budget traveler. They have air conditioning, a rarity in two stars, a beautiful little private park/garden, and a comfortable downstairs bar. The rooms are small and clean but are definitely not someplace to hang out in.

HOTEL MACOMBO, *Via C. Battisti 192, 98055 Lipari. Isole Eolie. Tel. 090/981-1442. Fax 090/981-1062. 14 rooms all with shower. Single L68,000-135,000; Double L85,000-170,000. No credit cards accepted.* **
Located in the village of Canneto north of the town of Lipari, this is an expensive little place that has easy access to the area's topless and nude beaches. The hotel's rooms are quaint, comfortable, and clean but are not luxurious. They have their own little restaurant from which you can get full board for L100,000, the price of one meal for two elsewhere. They also have a small bar and importantly, air conditioning in the summertime.

WHERE TO EAT

There are plenty of family-run restaurants all over the island. Most are open only in the high season to fleece the tourists. This restaurant below is the best choice on any of the seven islands:

RISTORANTE FILIPPINO, *Piazza del Municipio, Tel. 090/911-002. Closed Mondays (but not in high season) and all November 15 to December 15. Credit cards accepted. Dinner for two L100,000.*

Great local food, especially the *maccaruna alla Filippino,* a tasty homemade pasta dish with a sauce of tomatoes, eggplant, mozzarella and ham, as well as other culinary delights. You can expect to taste some of the best prepared fish anywhere. I don't know what they do or how they do it but any fish you try, whether it's baked, fried, or grilled will melt in your mouth. They also make their own bread in-house and it is stupendous.

PRACTICAL INFORMATION
Banking Hours & Changing Money

Banks are open Monday through Friday, 8:30am–5:30pm. Most of them are located on the **Via Vittorio Emanuele**. Besides banks there are a few exchange bureaus (*casa di cambio*) around. Another option, if all else is closed is to simply change your money at your hotel.

Business Hours

During high season most shops are open from 9:00am–1:00pm and from 3:30pm–7:30pm, and are closed all day Sundays and on Monday mornings. In the off-season, the shops that cater specifically to the tourists close down entirely.

Food stores, like *alimentari,* generally are open from 8:30am–1:30pm (so stock up on your picnic supplies before you need them) and from 5:00pm–7:30pm, and during the winter months they are closed on Thursdays.

Postal Services

The **central post office** in Lipari *is on the Corso Vittorio Emanuele 207 (Tel. 090/981-1379).* Open Monday through Friday 8:30am–5:00pm, Saturdays 9:00am–noon. Stamps can also be bought at any tobacconist (stores indicated by a T sign outside), and mailed at any mailbox, which are red and marked with the word *Poste* or *Lettere.*

Tourist Information & Maps
• **Tourist Office,** *Via Vittorio Emanuele 202 (Tel. 090/988-0095)* and is open regular business hours. You can get free information on buses, sights, and a not very useful map.

VULCANO

Some geologists think this small volcano of an island (hence the name, **Vulcano**) will explode sometime in the next decade, so beware when you go. Despite the pungent sulfurous smell, you can enjoy a relaxing bath in the heated bubbling water around the island, or coat yourself in the famous **fanghi**, or mud baths. These are located just up the Via Provinciale from the Porto di Levante, where the ferries dock on the east side of the island on the way to the beach. The mud is slightly radioactive, so don't sit in it too long, and pregnant women and small children shouldn't even think of going in.

If caking yourself with mud is not for you, walk down to the beach and immerse yourself in the bubbling **aquacalda** (hot water). You can also go up and peer into the **Gran Crater** (Great Crater) that simmers and boils. You need to be in reasonable shape to get up to the top. Once there you'll have some fabulous photo opportunities of the surrounding islands. You'll need to go in the early morning or late afternoon, since the face of the volcano gets quite hot from the sun and the lava inside at midday.

Almost everything on the island is closed before June and after September, so if you want to stay on the island or grab a bite to eat when it's low season, you may be out of luck.

WHERE TO STAY

LES SABLES NOIRS, *Porto Ponente, 98050 Vulcano. Isole Eolie. Tel. 090/985-2461. Fax 090/985-2454. 33 rooms. 8 with bath. 25 with shower. Single L160,000-290,000; Double L240,000-400,000. Credit cards accepted. Full board L218,000-370,000.* ****

Quite an exclusive establishment located in a truly romantic setting. They have their own private beach where you can rent snorkeling equipment. The hotel also has an outdoor swimming pool, a sun deck, a beautiful view, a piano bar and really good hotel restaurant that serves local cuisine as well as dietetic food. They also have bus service that can take you around the island. The rooms are quaint and comfortable. This place deserves its four star rating.

EOLIAN HOTEL, *Porto Ponente, 98050 Vulcano. Isole Eolie. Tel. 090/985-2151. Fax 090/985-2153. 88 rooms all with bath. Single L83,000-154; Double L129,000-256,000. Credit cards accepted. Full board L126,000-186,000.* ***

Tennis courts, outdoor pool, relaxing garden, a fine restaurant, and more. This place is definitely a good deal. Why the three star rating? The hotel is older than Les Sables Noirs, is well maintained but not quite as polished, and a private beach means much in the rating games on the islands.

HOTEL CONTI, *Porto Ponente, 98050 Vulcano. Isole Eolie. Tel. 090/985-2012. Fax 090/988-0150. 62 rooms, only 61 with shower. Single with or without shower L65,000-130,000; Double L160,000-170,000. Visa accepted.* **

One of the bigger establishments on the island, they have their own private beach, a fine restaurant, a relaxing garden, a shuttle bus service – but no air conditioning. Stay here if you can stand the heat. The rooms are relatively large, with inconsistent furnishings, but they are clean and quite comfortable.

STROMBOLI

Another volcano in this chain of islands, **Stromboli** is the furthest from Sicily. This place is super-crowded in high season and is almost completely shut down in the low season. If you want to stay here you need to make reservations well in advance. The year round population of the island is only about 400, but when the tourists come you can have as many as 3000 more staying the night and many others just for the day.

There are two towns on the island, tiny Ginostra on the southern end, and a combination of Piscita, Fiocogrande, San Vincenzo, and Scari which make up what is popularly called **Villaggio Stromboli (Stromboli Town)**. You'll find most places to eat and stay in Stromboli Town, with only one small no-star pensione in Ginostra. But Stromboli is an island to visit for the day and is not really a destination in itself.

The only real attraction here is the climb up the **volcano**. To legally do this you need to go with an official guide, who can be hired from the **Club Alpino Italiano** at their offices *in Piazza Vincenzo (Tel. 090/986-263)*. The cost will be between L20,000 and 25,000, depending on how well you bargain. You start off in Piscita and the trip should take around three hours up and two hours down, so you have to be in really good shape. You'll also need to wear well-soled boots and bring along at least 1.5 liters of water. Don't drink it all at once. You'll want it later.

About halfway up you'll come across the **Sciara del Fuoco**, the volcanic trail that vents the lava directly into the sea. At the top, be careful not to lean over too far. Once you drop in you'll be hard-boiled forever.

On your descent from the top you may decide to go down the other side to **Ginostra** (follow the red, yellow and orange marked rocks) where you can enjoy a less touristy environment. There are ferries from here back to Stromboli Town, as well as Lipari.

Another fun side trip here is a visit to the **lighthouse** on the small rock island of **Strombolicchio**. From Via Marina and the ferry dock, you can hire a boat to take you out there for between L15,000 and L25,000, depending on how well you bargain.

WHERE TO STAY

LA SCIARA RESIDENCE, *Via Soldato Cincotta, 98050 Stromboli. Isole Eolie. Tel. 090/986-121. Fax 090/986-284. 62 rooms, only 59 with shower. Single without L41,000; Single L80,000; Double without L82,000; Double L200,000. Credit cards accepted. Full board L281,000-340,000.* ***

A truly romantic and relaxing place to stay. They have their own private beach, a swimming pool, tennis courts, magnificent views and a good hotel restaurant. The one thing they do not have is air conditioning, but try to get a sea view room, open your window, and the sea breeze will cool down the place quickly. A quaint, clean, and comfortable place.

LA SIRENETTA PARK HOTEL, *Via Marina 13, 98050 Stromboli. Isole Eolie. Tel. 090/986-025. Fax 090/986-124. 43 rooms all with bath. Single L80,000-135,000; Double L140,000-240,000; Credit cards accepted. Full board L135,000-230,000.* ***

Established in 1952 and renovated in 1983, this place is quaint and comfortable. The relaxing garden and outdoor swimming pool add to the ambiance. Besides all the regular amenities for a three star, they also have a nursery to care for your child while you frolic around the island. One item missing is air conditioning, but the breezes from the water usually alleviate any problems.

SALINA

Salina is an uncrowded alternative to the three main islands, but that may soon change, so come here soon to enjoy the peaceful tranquillity of a place where time stands still. You arrive at **Porto Santa Maria**, the island's main port, where you can rent mopeds or bicycles to traverse the island, or take one of the many buses to any of your destinations.

Just three kilometers south of the port is the little village of **Lingua**, that is really only a small clean beach and a tiny cluster of *pensione* and *trattorie* with great views of Lipari. A nice place to grab a bite to eat. If you head north from the port you'll pass through **Malfa**, a quaint little village that has a backdrop of decaying fishermen's huts. There is also a good beach here. Further along you come to **Pollara**, the site of the last eruption on the island back some 12,500 years ago. The village sits on a crescent-shaped crater from that eruption.

If you arrive on the island on August 15, you will be surrounded by pilgrims celebrating the Assumption of the Virgin festival, enroute to the **Sanctuary of the Madonna del Terziot** in **Valdichiesa**.

WHERE TO STAY

If you really want to get away from it all, here's one of the better little hotels on the island:

LA MARINARA, *Via Alfieri, Lingua. Salina. Isole Eolie. Tel. 090/984-3022. 14 rooms all with bath. Single L40,000; Double L75,000. No credit cards accepted.* *

A small place with a great restaurant. You can get full board for L95,000 a couple. But since there are a few other restaurants in Lingua you may want to sample some of these. The rooms are simple and rustic but if you decided to stay on this island you should be expecting this. They also have a relaxing little garden where you can relax in the evenings.

PANAREA

Located between Lipari and Stromboli, **Panarea** is the smallest of the seven islands as well as the prettiest. That's why it is slowly becoming the hangout for more and more members of the jet set. From this island you can venture to some smaller islets that surround the east side for some great swimming. You should be able to hire a boat at the ferry dock at **San Pietro** for about L25,000 per person.

At **Punta Milazzese**, you can explore an archaeological dig of a Bronze Age settlement. There is little else to do on the island except eat, drink, and relax.

WHERE TO STAY

HOTEL CINCOTTA, *Via San Pietro, 98050 San Pietro. Panarea. Isole Eolie. Tel. 090/993-014. Fax 090/983211. 29 rooms all with showers. Double L200,000-300,000. Credit cards accepted. Full board L180,000-250,000.* ***

A rustic little place that has small, clean, and comfortable rooms. You can get full board at their fine local style restaurant for L210,000 per couple, which is rather expensive. But you won't do any better at any other place on the island. Since everything has to be imported, food prices are sky-high. They also have a swimming pool surrounded by lush gardens.

LA PIAZZA, *Via San Pietro, Panarea. Isole Eolie. Tel. 090/983-176. Fax 090/983-003. 25 rooms all with bath. Double L180,000-260,000. Credit cards accepted. Full board L200,000-240,000.* ***

A small place, established in 1967 and renovated in 1993, with all the necessary amenities including an outdoor pool and a peaceful garden setting. Definitely a fine place to stay. They are also pet friendly, so you can bring Fido along with you if you want.

FILUCIDI

From the **Porto Filucida** where the ferry docks, take a walk north up to the almost abandoned village of **Valdichiesa**. If you keep walking all the way to the west side of the island, you'll be able to see the huge phallic rock formation **La Canna** thrusting out of the sea. You'll see lots of couples

SOUTHERN ITALY & SICILY

here. If you don't want to walk all the way there, you can hire a boat at the ferry pier to take you for about L25,000 per person.

You can also go across the island over the thin peninsula to the other coast to the tiny village of **Pecorino**. If you walk along the peninsula east, you'll come to the archaeological site of **Capo Graziano**, where there is a site of Bronze Age structures that predates those on Panarea.

One last place to see here is the **Grotta del Bue Marino (The Seal Grotto)**, which can only be reached by boat.

WHERE TO STAY

HOTEL PHENICUSA, *Via Porto, 98050 Filicudi. Isole Eolie. Tel. 090/984-4185. fax 090/988-9966. 36 rooms, 2 with bath, 34 with shower. Single L100,000; Double L1800,000. No credit cards accepted.* ***

Located at the ferry port, this place has its own private beach and a really good restaurant. Take the option of the full board for L121,000 per couple since you only have one or two other options on the entire desolate island. The rooms with bathtubs are the best, but there are only two of them, so reserve early. The other bathrooms are tiny but clean. The rooms are all decorated in whatever furniture and bedding the hotel could find, but they are comfortable and clean.

ALICUDI

This is the place to go if you really want to get away from it all. There are only 125 inhabitants, one hotel, electricity only recently installed, and no paved roads. This tiny island used to be a rocky penitentiary maintained by the Italian government, but now the island is all but abandoned. From the island's only town and the ferry dock, **Alicudi Porto**, you can follow a path north to the ruins of a **castle** that used to house the prisoners. Other than that, and swimming along the rocky shore, there's nothing to do here except relax and enjoy the escape from the commercial world.

On your way here you will pass by the large rock phallus, **La Canna**, off the west coast of Filucidi.

WHERE TO STAY

HOTEL ERICUSA, *Via Regina Elena, 98050. Alicudi. Isole Eolie. Tel. 090/988-9902. 12 rooms all with shower. Double L100,000. No credit cards accepted. Full board L110,000.* *

I suggest you take the full board of breakfast, lunch, and dinner for L95,000 extra, since your options will be limited on Alicudi. Besides small but comfortable rooms, and tiny but clean bathrooms, the hotel has little else to offer. Very rustic, but oh-so-peaceful and relaxing.

INDEX

Abruzzi 90
Acaia Castle 316
Adriatic 17
Agrigento 13, 209, 323, 326, 354-359
Air Canada 54
Airlines 54
Aldo Moro 47
Alicudi 377, 385
Alitalia 53, 326
Alps 24
Altar of Augustus 158
Amalfi 287-291
Amalfi Coast 12, 13, 94, 283-194
American Airlines 54
American Embassy 23
American Express 145, 222, 228, 345, 376
Amusement Park 217
Antiques 203
Apartments, Renting 58
Apennines 24
Appartamento Borgia 181
Apulia 90
Arch of Constantine 151
Arch of Septimus Severus 154
Arch of Titus 155
Archimedes 360
AT&T 84
ATM Machines 221
Augustus 37
Aurelian Wall 159
Avis 64

Babbington's Tea Room 21, 188
Babysitters 221
Bank Americard 222
Banks 221, 329
Bargaining 200

Bari 13, 295-306
Barletta 306-309
Basilicata 90
Baths of Caracalla 156, 211
Baths of Diocletian 156, 177
Beaches 242
Beautification Program 187
Bel Canto Opera 212
Bellini, Vincenzo 212
Bernini 161, 164, 166
Best Hotels in Rome 108
Best Places to Stay in Rome & Southern Italy 94-99
Best Restaurants in Rome 133
Best Sights in Rome 146
Bicycling 217
Blue Grotto 268
Boating 217
Bookstores 206
Borghese 210
Borghese Family tombs 174
Borghese Gallery: see Galleria Borghese
Borghese Gardens 167
Borromini 164
Botticelli 209
Bowling 217
Bristish Airways 54
Browning, Robert & Elizabeth 188
Budget Rent a Car 65
Buses 69, 79, 72
Business Hours 222, 330
Byron, Lord 188

Caesar 37
Caffe Greco 188
Calabria 90
Campania 89, 90

INDEX 387

Campidoglio 20, 146, 156
Campo dei Fiori 14, 19, 21, 22, 116,
   139, 165, 184, 189, 203, 204
Canada Direct 84
Capitoline Museum 146, 157, 176
Capri 13, 98, 247, 268-275
Car Rental: see Renting a Car
Carthage 36, 360
Castel Gandolpho 231
Castel Sant'Angelo 20, 146, 160, 166
Catacombs 158, 210
Central Italy 12
Cervetri 239
Changing Money 221
Charlemagne 39, 162
Chiaramonti Museum 180
Church of Bones: see Santa Maria
   della Concezione
Churches in Rome 223
Ciampino Airport 51, 61, 63
Circus Maximus 157
Citibank 222
Climate & Weather 49
Clothing Sizes 199, 200
COIN 196, 202
Colosseum 20, 150
Column of Marcus Aurelius 160
Computers 223
Consulates 56, 224, 330
Convents 125
Courier Flights 54
Crafts 215
Credit Cards 222
Culture & Arts 209-216
Customs 53

Delta Airlines 54
Department Stores 196, 202
Dickens, Charles 188
Diner's Club 222
Doctors & Dentists 224
Donatello 209
Donizetti, Gaetano 212
Driving in Italy 64, 73

Egyptian Museum 180
Electricity 80
Embassies 56, 224

Emergencies 224
Emilia Romagna 89, 90
English Language Movie Theaters:
   see Movies in English
Erice 13, 351-354
Eritrea 43
Etruscan Museum 180
Etruscans 32, 34, 209
Exchange Rate 79, 80
Excursions from Rome 229-246

Fascism 43, 44, 45
Fax 83
Ferries to Greece 297
Ferries to Sicily 326, 327
Festivals 213-215, 224-226, 328, 367
Filicudi 377, 384, 385
Folk Festivals: see Festivals
Fontana del Tritone 170
Fontana delle Alpi 170
Fontana di Trevi: see Trevi Fountain
Food & Wine 16, 87, 331-333
Forum 33, 146, 209
Forum of Augustus 148
Forum of Caesar 148
Forum, Roman 151
Forum, Trajan's 148
Forums, Imperial 146
Frascati 12, 22, 232-238

Galleria Borghese 23, 167, 178
Galleria Nazionale d'Arte Antica 169
Gallipoli 317-320
Garibaldi 42, 324
Gauls 32, 35
Ghiberti 211
Gianicolo 171
Giotto 209
Goethe 188
Golf 218
Greece 297, 323, 360
Greek Art 209
Greek ruins 209
Grotte Vaticano 182
Grotto Azzuro: see Blue Grotto

Hadrian's Villa 229
Herculaneum 12, 13, 209, 247, 265, 267

Hertz 65
History 32, 50, 51, 213-215, 328, 367
Holy Roman Empire 39
Hostels 60
Hotel Reservations 101
Hotels, General 56-58

Insurance, Travel 53
Internet Access 223
Irish Style Pubs: see Pubs
Ischia 13, 247, 278-282
Island of Capri: see Capri
Island of Procida: see Procida
Isola Tiberina 20, 168
Isole Eolie 323, 377-385
Italian Food 126
Italian Phrases 28-31, 197-200
IVA Rebate 197

James, Henry 188
Jewish Ghetto 126, 171

Keats 188
Keats/Shelly Memorial 188

Lago di Bracciano 238
Latin League 35
Laundry 226
Lazio 33, 89, 90
Lecce 13, 311-316
Leonardo da Vinci 209, 210
Leonardo da Vinci Airport 51, 61, 63
Lido di Ostia 240, 242
Liguria 89, 90
Limoncello 129
Lipari 377, 378-380
Lipari Islands: see Isole Eolie
Literary Rome 187
Literature 215
Lombardia 88, 90
Long Distance Phone Calls 84
Lord Byron: see Byron, Lord
Lost Credit Cards 222

Mafia 324
Mail Service: see Postal Service
Marche 90
Mark Twain: see Twain, Mark

Market, Trajan's 148
Markets, Food 207
Markets, Outdoor 204, 205
Mastercard 222
Mausoleum of Augustus 158
Mausoleum of Hadrian 160
McDonalds 27
MCI 84
Medici 39
Mediterranean 17
Menus, Reading Italian 91-93
Metro, Rome 70, 147
Michelangelo 162, 173, 177, 183-187, 209-211
Modem Usage 84
Mona Lisa 210
Money Exchange: see Changing Money
Mount Etna 24, 326, 368, 369
Mount Vesuvius 24
Movies in English 195
Museo della Civilta Romana 182
Museo delle Terme 177
Museum of Roman Civilization: see Museo della Civilta Romana
Museum of Villa Giula 178
Music 211
Mussolini 43, 44, 45

Naples & The Amalfi Coast 247-294
Naples 12, 13, 247, 248; Where to Stay 250-254; Where to Eat 254-257; Seeing the Sights 257-263; Nightlife & Entertainment 263-264
Napoleon 41
National Gallery: see Galleria Nazionle d'Arte Antica
National Museum 177
Newspapers 81, 206
Nightclubs & Bars 193, 194
Northern League 47
Northwest Airlines 54

Obelisk (p.za del Popolo) 170
Opera 211
Ostia 209, 238, 240
Otranto 320-322

INDEX 389

Packing 50
Palatine Hill 151, 156
Palazzo Barberini 169
Palazzo Farnese 169, 184
Palermo 324, 326, 333-345; Where to Stay 336-338; Where to Eat 338, 339; Seeing the Sights 339-344; Nightlife 344; Opera 344; Shopping 344
Panarea 377, 384
Pantheon 20, 120, 140, 145, 166, 185
Papacy 40
Papal Audiences 226
Papal States 40
Pasquino 195
Passports 52
Pets 81
Phoenicians 323
Piazza Barberini 23, 170
Piazza del Popolo 18, 120, 140, 169
Piazza di Spagna (see Spanish Steps)
Piazza Navona 14, 19, 20, 116, 139, 145, 146, 164, 185, 189
Piazza Santa Maria in Trastevere 14, 19
Piemonte 90
Piramide: see Pyramid
Pius Clementine Museum 179
Police 227
Pompeii 12, 13, 209, 247, 265, 266
Ponte dei Quattro Capi 168
Ponte Fabricio 168
Ponte Milvio 159
Porta Portese Market 23, 203, 204
Positano 94, 283-287
Postal Service 82, 227
Procida 13, 247, 276-278
Pubs 189-193
Puccini, Giacomo 212
Punic Wars 36, 324, 333
Pyramid 158

Raphael 109, 161, 210
Raphael, Loggia of 182
Raphael, Rooms of 181
Ravello 291-292
Red Brigades 47
Religious Ceremonies in English 223

Renaissance 39, 40, 210, 211
Renting a Bicycle 68
Renting a Car 64, 74, 330
Renting a Moped 66, 67
Restaurant Listings, Explanation 89
Restrooms, Public 227
Rinascente 196, 202
Risorgimento 41
Roman Cuisine 126, 127
Roman Republic 34
Roman Senate 37
Rome 12, 14, 18, 94; Where to Stay 100-125; Where to Eat 126-144; Seeing the Sights 145-188; Nightlife & Entertainment 189-195; Shopping 196-208; Sports & Recreation 217-220
Romulus 33
Rossini, Gioacchino 212
Rural Retreats 244

Safety 82, 83, 331
Salerno 292-294
Salina 377, 383, 384
Sambuca 129
San Clemente 21, 175
San Giovanni in Laterano 21, 174
San Pietro in Vincoli 21, 173, 186
Sant Maria Sopra Minerva 185
Santa Cecilia in Trastevere 21, 175
Santa Maria della Concezione 170
Santa Maria in Trastevere 21, 176
Santa Maria Maggiore 21, 174
Santa Maria Sopra Minerva 21, 173
Santa Susanna 186, 223
Sculpture 211
Seeing the Pope: see Papal Audiences
Shakespeare 26, 215
Shelley 88
Shopping 196-208
Shopping Streets 203
Shops: see Stores
Sicilia; see Sicily 89
Sicily 13, 89, 90, 99, 323-385; Sports & Recreation in Sicily 331
Siracusa 209, 323, 360-368; Where to Stay 362, 363; Where to Eat 363, 364; Seeing the Sights 364-367

Sistine Chapel 19, 146, 181, 183, 211
South Tyrol 46
Southern Italy 12, 13, 295-322
Spanish Steps 15, 18, 23, 114, 137, 146, 165, 188
Sprint 84
St. John in Lateran: see San Giovanni in Laterano
St. Paul's Outside the Walls 21, 146, 172
St. Peter's 14, 20, 146, 161, 183, 211
STANDA 196, 202
Stores 197-199, 208
Stromboli 377, 382, 383
Supermarkets 228
Swimming 219
Swiss Guards 163
Syracuse: see Siracusa

Taormina 209, 369-377
Taxis 68, 83
Telephones 83
Temple of Hadrian 160
Tennis 220
Termi di Caracalla: see Baths of Caracalla
Termini Train Station 61, 62, 64, 101
Thomas Cook 145
Time 84
Tipping 85
Tivoli 229, 230
Tomb of Umberto I, King 167
Tomb of Victor Emmanuel 167
Toscana 89
Tour Companies 228
Tourist Information 228
Tours by Airplane 151
Train Departure Board 77
Trains 74-78
Trajan's Forum: see Forum, Trajan's
Trajan's Market: see Market, Trajan's
Trani 309-311
Trapani 346-351
Trastevere 14, 19, 131, 171, 189
Travel Agents 54
Travel Insurance: see Insurance, Travel
Trentino Alto Adige 26, 90

Trevi Fountain 15, 19, 20, 109, 134, 146, 165, 203
Trieste 46
Tuscany 33, 90
TWA 54
Twain, Mark 188

Umberto I, King 43, 45, 167
Umbria 90
United Airlines 54
UPIM 196, 202
US Airways 54

Vaccinations 52
Valle d'Aosta 26
Value Added Tax: see VAT
VAT 196
Vatican 183, 210
Vatican City 163
Vatican Library 180
Vatican Museums 14, 19, 146, 179, 184
Veneto 89, 90
Verdi, Giuseppe 212
Via Appia Antica 62, 171
Via dei Condotti 19, 188, 202
Via del Corso 19, 202
Via delle Croce 18, 19, 202
Via Veneto 23, 109, 134, 170, 203
Victor Emmanuel 41, 42, 43, 45, 167
Villa Borghese 23
Villa d'Este 229
Villa Giulia 178
Villa Gregoriana 229
Villas, Renting 58
VISA 222
Vittorio Emanuele II Monument 168
Vulcano 377, 381, 382

Wagons-Lit 145
Weather: see Climate & Weather
Weights & Meaures 86
Wine 90, 129
World War II 44

Yellow Pages, English Language 86

Zoo 167

THINGS CHANGE!

Phone numbers, prices, addresses, quality of food, etc, all change. If you come across any new information, we'd appreciate hearing from you. No item is too small! Drop us an e-mail note at: Jopenroad@aol.com, or write us at:

Rome & Southern Italy Guide
Open Road Publishing, P.O. Box 284
Cold Spring Harbor, NY 11724

OPEN ROAD PUBLISHING

U.S.A.
Hawaii Guide, $17.95
Arizona Guide, $16.95
Texas Guide, $16.95
New Mexico Guide, $14.95
Disneyworld & Orlando Theme Parks, $13.95
Boston Guide, $13.95
Las Vegas Guide, $13.95
San Francisco Guide, $14.95
California Wine Country Guide, $12.95
America's Cheap Sleeps, $16.95
America's Grand Hotels, $14.95
America's Most Charming Towns & Villages, $16.95
Florida Golf Guide, $16.95
Golf Courses of the Southwest, $14.95
Washington DC Ethnic Restaurant Guide, $9.95

MIDDLE EAST/AFRICA
Israel Guide, $17.95
Egypt Guide, $17.95
Kenya Guide, $18.95

UNIQUE TRAVEL
The World's Most Intimate Cruises, $16.95
New Year's Eve 1999!, $16.95
Celebrity Weddings & Honeymoon Getaways, $16.95
CDC's Complete Guide to Healthy Travel, $14.95

SMART HANDBOOKS
The Smart Runner's Handbook, $9.95
The Smart Home Buyer's Handbook, $16.95

CENTRAL AMERICA & CARIBBEAN
Caribbean Guide, $19.95
Caribbean With Kids, $14.95
Central America Guide, $17.95
Costa Rica Guide, $17.95
Belize Guide, $16.95
Honduras & Bay Islands Guide, $15.95
Guatemala Guide, $17.95
Southern Mexico & Yucatan Guide, $14.95
Bermuda Guide, $14.95
Bahamas Guide, $13.95

EUROPE
London Guide, $14.95
Rome & Southern Italy Guide, $14.95
Paris Guide, $13.95
Moscow Guide, $15.95
Prague Guide, $14.95
France Guide, $16.95
Portugal Guide, $16.95
Ireland Guide, $17.95
Spain Guide, $17.95
Italy Guide, $19.95
Holland Guide, $15.95
Austria Guide, $15.95
Czech & Slovak Republics Guide, $16.95
Greek Islands Guide, $16.95
Turkey Guide, $17.95

ASIA
China Guide, $18.95
Hong Kong & Macau Guide, $13.95
Vietnam Guide, $14.95
Thailand Guide, $17.95
Philippines Guide, $16.95
Tahiti & French Polynesia Guide, $17.95

*To order any Open Road book, send us a check or money order for the price of the book(s) plus $3.00 shipping and handling for domestic orders, to: **Open Road Publishing**, PO Box 284, Cold Spring Harbor, NY 11724*